PRAISE FOR
Divinity of Doubt

"I found myself following my wife around the house reading passages of Bugliosi's book to her out loud. I wish I'd written this wonderfully funny deeply moving antidote to the false certainties—both religious and irreligious—that have divided our society into warring camps yammering at each other about things no one understands."

—Frank Schaeffer *New York Times* bestselling author of *Crazy for God: How I Grew Up as One of the Elect, Helped Found the Religious Right, and Lived to Take All (or Almost All) of It Back*

"Always eloquent, this is a fascinating read."

—*Publishers Weekly*

"Bugliosi's arguments, while familiar, are well-reasoned, clearly presented, and provide a good introductory survey of the theist-versus-atheist-versus-agnostic debate."

—Booklist

"Intelligent, thought-provoking and superstition-challenging."

—BookPleasures.com

"No matter what your beliefs, this argument is a compelling addition to any spirituality collection."

—The Midwest Book Review

DIVINITY

——— OF ———

DOUBT

ALSO BY VINCENT BUGLIOSI

Helter Skelter (with Curt Gentry)

Till Death Us Do Part (with Ken Hurwitz)

And the Sea Will Tell (with Bruce Henderson)

The Phoenix Solution:
Getting Serious about Winning America's Drug War

Outrage: The Five Reasons Why O. J. Simpson
Got Away with Murder

No Island of Sanity:
Paula Jones v. Bill Clinton: The Supreme Court on Trial

The Betrayal of America: How the Supreme Court
Undermined the Constitution and Chose Our President
(with forewords by Molly Ivins and Gerry Spence)

Reclaiming History:
The Assassination of President John F. Kennedy

The Prosecution of George W. Bush for Murder

DIVINITY

— OF —

DOUBT

God and Atheism
on Trial

VINCENT

BUGLIOSI

Vanguard Press
A Member of the Perseus Books Group

Copyright © 2011, 2012 by Vincent Bugliosi

Published by Vanguard Press
A Member of the Perseus Books Group

Editorial production by Marrathon Production Services. www.marrathon.net

DESIGN BY JANE RAESE
Set in 12.5-point Bulmer

Cataloging-in-Publication Data for this book is available from the Library of Congress.

LCCN: 2011921790

ISBN 978-1-59315-708-1 (paperback)
ISBN 978-1-59315-666-4 (e-Book)

Vanguard Press books are available at special discounts for bulk purchases in the U.S. by corporations, institutions, and other organizations. For more information, please contact the Special Markets Department at the Perseus Books Group, 2300 Chestnut Street, Suite 200, Philadelphia, PA 19103, or call (800) 810-4145, ext. 5000, or e-mail special.markets@perseusbooks.com.

10 9 8 7 6 5 4 3 2 1

To my wife and children

Contents

Acknowledgments

I feel very fortunate to have been associated once again with two of the top people in the book publishing industry, the inimitable and very perceptive Roger Cooper, who had the courage to publish such a highly controversial book as this one, and his young associate publisher, the extraordinarily gifted Georgina Levitt, for whom I predict the sky is the limit in the world of book publishing.

I also want to thank my secretary, Rosemary Newton, for being of so much assistance to me in the writing of this book. Uncommonly dependable, she not only typed up more than 100,000 words of my handwriting, but in recent years has augmented my research from original sources by providing me, on frequent occasion, with additional, ancillary information from the vastness of the Internet.

Also, my special thanks to Susan Caulfield, Director of Publishing, for the tremendous effort she made in expertly doing whatever was necessary, and then some, to ready this revised edition of the book for publication. This edition owes much to Susan.

Thanks are also in order to my long-time friend and literary representative, Peter Miller.

And of course I want to thank my wonderful wife, Gail, who, as with the writing of all my previous books, sacrificed much time she wanted us to spend together. Always supporting me one hundred percent in my every endeavor, she has unfailingly been my rock of Gibraltar through the years. I'll never be able to repay her for all she's done for me.

Preface

My view is that sometimes it's nice to know a little bit about an author beyond the biography on the inside of the book's jacket—at least insofar as it relates to the book you are about to read.

Other than the fact that I am a very hard worker and am able to draw sensible inferences from simple realities, what qualifies me, if anything, to go outside of my field of the law and weigh in on the biggest mystery of all, the question of God's existence? I do have to say that whatever abilities I may have as a trial lawyer, I fortunately found them easily transferable to my dealing with the arguments for and against the belief in God's existence—mainly, objectively analyzing the various issues, then marshaling the evidence in support of my position and exposing what I perceive to be the weaknesses of the opposing side. But apart from that I have found that at least in my professional life (I go through my private life blindfolded) I seem to naturally—and not as a result, I can assure you, of any special intelligence at all—see what's in front of me completely uninfluenced by the trappings of reputation, hoopla, conventional wisdom, and so on, put on it by others.

"Let me test you, the reader, with a hypothetical question so that you can see where you are on this issue. If you were told that Winston Churchill said something about World War II, and a bum in a Bowery gutter said something quite the opposite, whom would you believe? There's only one answer to that question, and it's not the one that 99 percent of people would reflexively give—Winston Churchill. The only proper answer to the question is "I'd have to hear what they had to say." This is obviously true since we know that just as a wise man can say something foolish, a fool can say something wise. Now, if neither Churchill nor the bum had weighed in on the issue yet and you were asked, "Who is more likely to say something intelligent about the matter?" the obvious answer would be Churchill.

What we're talking about here is the fact that most people see what they expect to see, what they want to see, what conventional wisdom tells them to see, not what is right in front of them in its pristine condition. Put another way, they only hear the music, not the lyrics of human events. The only reason I mention this phenomenon is that in the book you are about to read, I will in many instances be taking a position different from what many people are expecting to read, or would prefer to read, or what conventional wisdom tells them they should believe. And I feel that you, the reader, may be more receptive to the arguments I make and the inferences I draw in this book if you make a conscious effort to avoid this common, intellectual trap.

In learning that I was writing a book about God and religion, more than one person asked me why I was writing the book, questioning what could be said that hasn't already been said. The question has a certain amount of merit to it. After all, I am joining a 2,000-year-old conversation. What can I possibly bring to the table? But let me tell you this about me. I never write anything for public consumption, or appear on any radio or TV show, unless I feel I have something to say that's not being said. For example, several years ago, although I am not a rich man, I turned down an offer of $1 million from a major New York publishing house to write a book about the Jon-Benét Ramsey murder case because, not being involved in the case as a lawyer or an investigator, I didn't feel I was in a position to write with any special insight and authority the kind of true crime book I try to write.

The discussion of God, of course, is the most well-traveled terrain in the history of man, and therefore the majority of this book will necessarily address topics familiar to a well-versed reader. But if at the end of this book, you didn't find many fresh insights that caused you to say to yourself, "Hey, I never thought of this before," not only will I be surprised, but, more importantly, I will feel I had no business letting trees be cut down to print this book.

Another thing you should know about me is that I am an extremely critical person. Indeed, you'd have a difficult time finding someone as critical as I. I told Geraldo Rivera once, "Geraldo, I'd find fault with a beautiful morning sunrise." (However, I'm also a very complimentary person.) Curiously, though, I am not cynical, a trait so often associated with that of being critical. In fact, my late wonderful mother, the most feminine woman I've ever met in my life, and two sisters, one of whom is fortunately still living, thought I was a naïve person. I define cynicism as seeing yourself in other people, and for whatever reason I don't see myself in other people. That said, at the first thing I see wrong, I criticize, rarely keeping my criticism to myself.

Most of what I criticize in this book, in my opinion, flows from stupidity and/or ignorance. (As you know, the words "stupid" and "ignorant" are frequently used interchangeably, although they have quite different meanings. Everyone is ignorant about a great number of things in life. I mean, if Einstein never played or knew anything about the game of chess, he'd be ignorant about chess.) One could say that people can't help it if they are stupid or, to a lesser degree, ignorant. And if they can't help it, why get upset with them? Because stupidity and ignorance are not benign. They are responsible for much, if not most, of the great problems, misery, and injustice in this world. And when I see stupidity or its frequent companion, ignorance, resulting in great suffering and loss of life (such as the ignorance of the American people in being so easily led into a terrible war against a nation, Iraq, that was in no way an imminent threat to the security of this country), I respond with very critical and sometimes harsh rhetoric. That's just the way I am.

Among many other things that anger me are hypocrisy and incompetence, the latter being rampant in our society, from presidents on down. In fact, it's very frequently so bad that the only adjective in the dictionary I've been able to come up with that adequately describes it is "staggering." It's so common that I expect it, and when I find competence, I am pleasantly surprised.

I tell you these things because what follows is an almost unremitting, scathing indictment of God, organized religion, atheism, and theism. And many people, being sensitive of nature, are offended by highly critical discourse. If you are that type, I admire your civility, but this book may not be for you. To tell you a little bit more about myself, for good or for bad in some ways, I'm still in the nineteenth century, working with a yellow pad and pencil, and not having a computer or even a cellphone. It is said that thinking is hard work. I guess that's why so few people engage in it. However, I believe that another reason for the paucity of thinking among us is the continuous wall-to-wall barrage of distractions to thinking in the form of television and radio, cellphones, and the particularly invasive internet world of the computer. But I can assure you that whether you are already so inclined or not, this book is going to force you to think. I know because I've been told this many times by people who have read the book.

I would ask you to join me in this journey of mine to try to make sense of the religious and theological arguments and beliefs that I wrestle with along the way. I say wrestle with because if there is a God, he has chosen to keep those he created in the dark about him. So we are all handicapped, mentally handcuffed, in our desire to understand the mystery of life. If, as you read, I offend your sensibilities in any way, I apologize sincerely to you in advance. If there is something I write that you feel is in error, or I miss an important point you feel I should have made, I would certainly like to hear from you.

Voltaire tells us that common sense is not that common. Though in one way this is true, it is nonetheless linguistically contradictory—that is, if common sense is not common, from whence does the term "common" sense come? May we define common sense, then, as that which, *once stated*, is recognized by all reasonable people as being rational and of sound judgment? I feel I will have succeeded in this book if you, the reader, for the most part don't raise your eyebrows and wonder how I can strongly state on one page an argument that goes in the direction of supporting a belief in God and on the very next page set forth an argument that goes precisely in the opposite direction. In other words, you could say to yourself, "This author is contradicting himself." If you don't reach that point, it probably means that you are being swept along by what I hope is the uniform thread of common sense in my evaluation of the evidence—my only master—on the question of God.

NOTE TO READER: I learned from the hardcover edition of this book that many readers, like typical readers, did not read the endnotes ("Notes") following the main text, believing they probably were, as is common with books, mere odds and ends. However, most of my endnotes are substantive, some going on for several pages. In fact, a comment I got from many readers of the endnotes was, "This endnote was so important. Why didn't you put it in the main text?" The reason is that as relevant and important as the endnote was, I felt that it interrupted the flow of the main text. In any event, I would recommend that you read the "Notes" section of this book.

1

God, Etc.

There ain't no answer. There ain't going to be any answer.
There never has been an answer. That's the answer.
—GERTRUDE STEIN

Can you understand the mysteries surrounding God?
They are higher than the heavens and deeper than the nether world.
So what can you do when you know so little, and these mysteries
outreach the earth and the ocean?
—JOB 11:7–9

SINCE THE DAWN OF RECORDED TIME, human beings throughout the world have looked to the heavens for help in their daily lives, and eternal life after death. These people who sought the intervention of an invisible being with supernatural powers eventually became known as theists, those who believe in "God." Two other much smaller groups emerged: atheists, who believed no such being greater than man exists, and agnostics, who scratched their heads and took no position.

Although, in the vernacular, agnostics are those whose position is "I don't know" whether God exists, neither believing nor disbelieving in a deity, it is thought that the better definition of an agnostic is one who believes that the existence versus nonexistence of God is "unknowable." Of course, if it's unknowable, one can't know. From a historical perspective, the word "agnostic" is of relatively recent origin, but the date of the word's first usage by its creator, British biologist

1

Thomas H. Huxley, is not clear. In his 1889 essay, "Agnosticism," Huxley speaks of the word agnostic coming into his head as the "antithetic to the 'gnostic' of Church history."[1] Huxley goes on to say that he used the term at "the earliest opportunity" he had before the English Metaphysical Society, of which he was a member, but he doesn't say when that was. However, a January 1870 article ("Pope Huxley") published in the British magazine *Spectator* referred to Huxley as a "severe agnostic," so his appearance before the Metaphysical Society had to have been before January of 1870, most historians settling on the year 1869.

Though the word is not old, obviously the notion of agnosticism goes back centuries. Huxley himself, in his 1878 book "Hume, with Helps to the Study of Berkeley," called Socrates "the first agnostic." Perhaps the first known written discussion of agnosticism was by fifth-century BC Greek Sophist and philosopher Protagoras, who wrote in his *Essay on the Gods,* "Concerning the gods, I have no means of knowing whether they exist or not or of what sort they may be. Many things prevent knowledge including the obscurity of the subject and the brevity of human life."

Perhaps no person has been quoted more on his beliefs with respect to the existence or nonexistence of God than Albert Einstein. And whether deliberately or not, the great physicist's many words on the subject throughout the years have given fodder to theists, atheists, and agnostics in claiming Einstein as one of their own, e.g., "God does not play dice with the universe," suggesting he was a theist. But the only time I'm aware of that he chose to actually use one of these appellations to describe himself was in a letter to one M. Berkowitz dated October 25, 1950, just five years before his death, in which he wrote, "My position concerning God is that of an agnostic" (Albert Einstein Archive 59–215, Princeton University, Princeton, New Jersey).

When one writes about God and religion, one deals with millenniums, not years, frequently not even centuries. For instance, the New Testament and Jesus go back 2,000 years. When we get into the

Old Testament* and Genesis, we're dealing with a much greater number of years. With this in mind, and though it is not a parallel, I hope you, the reader, will not mind my briefly going back just fifteen years to what I wrote in a short section on agnosticism in the epilogue of my book *Outrage: The Five Reasons Why O. J. Simpson Got Away with Murder*. I herein present excerpts from it as a prelude to this book on the subject.

"God, Where Are You?"

When tragedies like the murders of Nicole Simpson and Ronald Goldman occur, they get one to thinking about the notion of God. Nicole was only thirty-five, Ron just twenty-five, both outgoing, friendly, well-liked young people who had a zest for life. Their lives were brutally extinguished by a cold-blooded murderer. How does God, if there is a God, permit such a horrendous and terrible act to occur, along with the countless other unspeakable atrocities committed by man against his fellow man throughout history? And how could God—all-good and all-just, according to Christian theology—permit the person who murdered Ron and Nicole to go free, holding up a Bible in his hand at that? When Judge Ito's clerk, Deidre Robertson, read the jury's not guilty verdict, Nicole's mother whispered, "God, where are you?"

I said earlier "if there is a God" because although there are good arguments for the existence of God (e.g., the cosmological one, that is, the first-cause theory; and the teleological, which takes as its starting point the observed order in the universe), in my own little mind, I, for one, can't be sure at all there is a God.

---

*The many references in this book to the Old Testament refer only to the Christian bible. Because the words "Old Testament" suggest there is a New Testament, and Jews don't believe in the New Testament, Jews refer to the Old Testament as the Tanach, or Hebrew bible, not the Old Testament. Actually, the Hebrew bible contains fifteen fewer books than the Christian bible's Old Testament.

To the question of whether I believe in God, if we were in court I'd object on the ground that the question assumes a fact not in evidence. To a follow-up question, "So you don't believe in God," I would respond that I'm not in a position to believe or disbelieve in him. You know, the atheists, who not only believe but know there is no God, are just as silly as those who seem to have no doubt that there is. Over the centuries, thousands of tomes and trillions of words have been written on the subject, yet neither side can come up with one single fact to support its position. But in this realm, where people's minds have been on permanent sabbatical, that fact is apparently immaterial.

Are we getting into metaphysics here with the question of what a fact is? I don't think so. By fact I mean a truth known by actual experience or observation. And something that cannot be logically explained in any other way.

My bottom line is I like Clarence Darrow's observation about the existence vis-à-vis non-existence of God: "I do not pretend to know what ignorant men are sure of." While it is true, then, that I don't believe in God, it has to be added that I don't disbelieve in him either. I'm an agnostic, and have been since the day in my early twenties when I said to myself that if there was a heaven and if I ever went there, I wanted to take my reason with me; that there was no earthly justification to *unthinkingly* buy into the myth of a God and of heaven and hell. In other words, although I'm actually from a little town in northern Minnesota, Hibbing, I'm from Missouri on the God issue.

Not only is there a question in my mind about whether there is a God, but perhaps more important, what type of fellow is he? We certainly know he's shy, keeping his whereabouts and form, if he has one, known only to himself. I realize that there are many people who claim to have actual conversations with God, but the question I've always had for these people is what voices are talking to them when the Lord isn't on the line?

I grew up a Catholic, attending Assumption Hall, a Catholic school with nuns of the Benedictine order as teachers, through the eighth grade. And of course it was inculcated into me that God was all-good, all-powerful, and all-knowing. The conundrum which most of us have heard, that either God can prevent evil but chooses not to, which means he is not all-good, or he wishes to prevent evil but cannot, which means he is not all-powerful, was not something I, as a believer, concerned myself with in those early years. But something similar was troubling to me.

The head of the Blessed Sacrament Church, which was associated with the school I attended, was a gray-haired eminence named Monsignor Limmer. The monsignor appeared ancient to us kids, and with his deep, baritone voice and dour expression, someone not only to look up to but fear. Though he lived in the back of the church, we sensed that he really came from some other place, some place where ordinary humans did not go. The good monsignor would visit our classroom for ten minutes or so once every week or two, and we listened in awed silence to his wisdom about God and Christ. One day when I was in the third or fourth grade, he was explaining that God was all-good, all-powerful, and all-knowing, and I asked him why (I had a yen for the why question even back then), if God was all-good, he would put people on this earth who he knew were going to end up in hell, burning throughout eternity. The monsignor proceeded to tell me it was a good question, but he had the answer. God gives all of us free will, the monsignor assured us, and when we come to the fork in the road where one path will lead us to heaven and one to hell, we have a choice, and God is not responsible for what choice we make. Yes, I said, but if God is also all-knowing, he knows what path we're going to take before we take it. So, I said, I still didn't understand how God would put people on this earth who he already knew were going to end up in hell. The monsignor coughed nervously, noted it was the end of the hour, and said we'd talk about it some other time, a time that never came. No one in Christianity, to my knowledge, can answer that question.

I even have trouble with the whole concept of prayer, in which literally billions of people throughout history have begged God for mercy. But since God is supposed to be all-good and merciful, why would we have to beg him to be what he supposedly already is? Most of those who believe in God also believe in the devil, who they feel is responsible for all the evil in the world. I'm going to sound laughable here, and it's nothing I'm recommending, since I don't believe in the devil, but logically speaking, shouldn't people be praying to the devil? One doesn't have to beg a good being to be good, one only has to ask a bad being to be good. No? Since the devil is the bad guy, isn't he the one we should be begging for mercy? Yet the Jesus prayer, and informal personal ones, says: "Lord Jesus Christ, have mercy on me."

We of course always hear people saying, "God answered my prayers." But I know that those who say this do not realize the import of what they are saying, because if they did, they wouldn't think very much of God, which they do. Saying that "God answered my prayers" *necessarily* means two things: that God has the power to answer prayers, and more important, for the 99 percent of the other humans who pray and beg for God's merciful intervention in time of desperate need, God told them to take a walk, get lost, he couldn't care less. He said no. "God answered my prayers," necessarily and inevitably means he chose to disregard the prayers of others who were begging for mercy or compassion in their lives; in fact, the vast majority of others. We have proof throughout history that if God is sitting up there deciding who gets mercy, he rejects the plea most of the time. Don't you think people pray to be spared when they have terminal cancer? Don't you think the Jews at Auschwitz prayed to God to be spared? Maybe we have been praying to the wrong entity all along. People who believe in prayers could hardly do worse praying to the devil.

I've heard that at Nicole Simpson's funeral, one of the speakers told Nicole's grieving survivors and friends that we can't "question God's will." *So it was God's will* that Simpson slaughtered Nicole? Really? When a Puerto Rican mother of three young children in New York City whom she supported all by herself, holding down three jobs to do so, was murdered out on the street by an addict to get a few dollars for a fix, leaving the three youngsters without any parent, the pastor at her funeral said, "It was God's will." When an eighteen-year-old black youth from San Diego who was an honor student, student body president, and champion wrestler, who dreamed of becoming a doctor, who "did all the right things, and said no to all the wrong things," was gunned down in a drive-by shooting as he left a graduation party, again, a pastor said, "It was God's will." When a young woman had gone to Russia to devote her life to helping some of the most desperate people of an increasingly troubled nation, the orphaned children of Russia, was found slain in her apartment in Moscow, her mother said: "God had always taken care of her. What happened was God's will. I guess he decided he wanted her back." But why would he want her back? To keep him company? She's doing good things for young people in need, and the mother is satisfied that God had better things for her to do in heaven?

When President <u>Kennedy was blasted into eternity by</u> Lee <u>Harvey Oswald on November 22, 1963</u>, again, some preachers said, "It was God's will." The evangelist John R. Rice wrote: "The assassin's bullet which cut down President Kennedy did the will of God."

"God has his reasons," we are told, for permitting all these atrocities. As the Reverend Rice wrote: "It was a matter of his choice. He had reasons for permitting the assassination of President Kennedy." And, of course, the unquestioned assumption is that whatever the reasons, they are good ones, reasons that justify what he did or permitted to happen. So even though he wanted these horrors to occur, he is still all-good. No matter what happens (murder, famine, genocide, deadly plagues, etc.), don't question God. He has his reasons and they're all good.

But my question is: If a good and powerful God doesn't prevent evil, why should we automatically assume that there is a good reason *for* the evil? Who tells us that when it comes to God, we must reject all conventional notions of logic and common sense and assume there is a valid and satisfactory reason for all the horrors and tragedies and misery in the world? It would seem that the only justification we would ever have for taking that position would be if God, appearing in the sky, told us that although what has happened doesn't make sense to us mortals, it is part of a grand scheme he has for life in the universe. Wouldn't that be the only possible sufficient cause for our belief that despite his willing or permitting the horrors of life, he is still all-good? Apart from God's apparition in the sky telling us this, what human being can possibly convince us of this absurdity?

The myth in Christianity that God is all-good, all-knowing, and all-powerful is so ingrained in our history, civilization, and culture that it may persist no matter how much our civilization progresses. Imprinted on all of our coins and all of our currency are the words "In God We Trust." But why? What has God done to earn this trust? Won't someone please tell me? I know it is said that there are always 10 percent who "don't get the word." Maybe I'm in that 10 percent. No one, but no one, even the tyrants of history, ever bad-mouths God, even though he supposedly permits all the evil in the world to exist.

In the Simpson case, God (if there is a God) not only permitted the butchery of Ron and Nicole, but seemed to be working overtime to ensure that the killer, Simpson, would get off, that justice would be thwarted. If anyone was ever in the corner of a murderer, it was God with Simpson. He didn't just permit an atrocity to be committed. He seemed to be conspiring to see that Simpson walked out of court a free man, and with a smile on his face, Simpson getting every conceivable break imaginable, from beginning to end. And apparently Simpson knew. On the night of the not-guilty verdict, Simpson, at his victory party, smiled broadly and held up a Bible in his outstretched hand. This, from the October 4, 1995, edition of the *Los Angeles Times*: "O.J. is free and God deserves the thanks. That was the message—delivered with unbridled cheer and relief—that came pouring forth from the Simpson family Tuesday as his celebrated trial came to a climactic close. 'God is good, see?' said Tracy Baker, O.J.'s niece. 'I know that praying to God is the answer,' Simpson's mother Eunice said. 'Me and my family want to thank God, without whom, I don't know where we'd be,' said Simpson's son, Jason."

Simpson's daughter, Arnelle, said to her brother in the courtroom when the jury returned its verdict, "We did it, Jason. God got us through." And the very first words [defense attorney] Johnnie Cochran used in his post-verdict news conference were: "I want to thank God."

When it comes to theology, I am too confused to be anything but an agnostic. But if there is a God, as there may very well be, the deist philosophy, which holds that after creating the universe, God bailed out, indifferent to that which he created, would seem to do less violence to the accepted principles of logic and common sense. At least the deist philosophy is free of inherent contradictions.

❧

I HAVE TO SAY I WAS SURPRISED by the considerable number of letters I received from readers of my short section on agnosticism in *Outrage*. The book was number one in the country on the *New York Times* hardcover best-seller list, and I received a great number of letters, but more related to this section than to any other part of the book. The letters were usually long letters, some going on as long as twenty-five pages, many even scholarly and with footnotes. They would almost invariably start out saying, in the first paragraph of the letter, how much they agreed with what I had said about Simpson's guilt and the reasons for his getting off. But then they would say words to the effect, "However, there is a part of your book with which I cannot agree" and proceed to tell me why they believed in God, and they would then try, futilely, to answer some or all of the questions I had raised in my agnosticism discussion in the book. I can recall only one letter from a reader who said she stopped reading my book at that point and would never read another book I ever wrote. None of the other hundreds of letters I received from readers on this issue were hostile to me in any way, which they might have been if I had said I was an atheist. Instead, because I was an agnostic, subscribing to the doctrine that nothing can be known about the existence or nature of God, the basic theme of their letters was that my soul, whatever that is, was salvageable, and as good Samaritans they were trying to help me by educating me. I appreciated this, but could only shake my head and smile in amusement at their efforts. Here I was saying we really don't *know* there is a God, and many of the letters, with letterheads indicating the writers were educated and presumably intelligent people, such as doctors, lawyers, and professors, were telling me not only that there very definitely was a God, but that they knew what his plans were. So here were people (I assume at least some among the many) who after twenty or thirty years of marriage may not have really known everything that was on their spouse's mind, but they knew what was on God's mind. Amazing.

Elaborating on something I touched upon in the Preface, one may wonder why I should be so presumptuous as to think I am qualified to write this book about God. That would be an entirely valid question, but only in the abstract, not in reality. It would be valid only if people with more ostensible credentials on the subject than I, such as theologians or religious writers, had written sensibly on the subject. But great numbers of them haven't, uttering terrible absurdities that can be categorized only as downright silly.

Just to give you two examples among a great many. In the book *Toward a New Christianity*, edited by Thomas J. J. Altizer, one Christian theologian writes:

What did the Holy Spirit that spoke through the prophets[2] speak about? The Spirit prophesied the Messiah; that is, it saw God as man and understood that 'God becomes as we are, that we may be as he is.' In Milton, this Messiah is a ratio of the five senses because he created the fallen world with its guinea-sun. Such a creative principle is a Nous, a reason or mathematical order, the automatism by which nature maintains enough permanence to keep from dissolving into nonexistence. This Nous is to be visualized as a father rather than a son, a hoary 'Ancient of Days' such as it stretches out his compasses (notice the mathematical symbol) in the frontispiece to Europe. Jesus is not a Nous but a Logos, a compelling Word who continually recreates an unconscious floundering universe into something with beauty and intelligence. The Son and the Holy Spirit are therefore the same thing. And this Son or Spirit is also the universal Man who is the unified form of our scattered imaginations, in which we visualize as a Father. The three persons of the Trinity are to be connected by or's rather than and's, and the real God is fourfold; power, love and wisdom contained within the unity of civilized human imagination. This God is a God-Man, the Jesus in whose eternal and infinite risen body we find our own being after we have outgrown the imaginative infancy which the orthodox conception of the Fatherhood of God implies for us. The final revelation of Christianity is, therefore, not that Jesus is God, but that 'God is Jesus.'

Unbelievable.

When the late, highly respected religious writer and thinker Joseph Campbell took on the task of describing God in his book *Thou Art*

That, he assured us that "God is no dream. God is no fact. . . . You cannot say God is a 'He.' You cannot say God is a 'She.' You cannot say God is an 'It.' . . . A God should properly be transparent to transcendence. And when God is, so are you. That which is of the transcendent is the *same* in God *as in yourself.** . . . If God opens to transcendence, *you are one with what you call 'God.'* Thus, the God image introduces you to your own transcendence. This may be somewhat hard to grasp." (Well, yes.) Campbell goes on to say, "But when God says, 'I am God,' this says you are just a fact, and so the relationship is between you and the fact that is no fact. . . . When Jesus says 'I am the all,' . . . this does not refer to the one who is talking to you, not to that physical body; it refers instead to that which he indeed, *and you indeed, in fact, are. Thou art that.* . . . Who and what is in Heaven? God is in heaven. Where is God? Within you. . . . *Thou art that.*"

Is Campbell kind of saying that we are all God? I feel so much more powerful. Before I read these words, I had so many questions about God. Now, everything is crystal clear. The only remaining question I have is how can anyone write something like this without being embarrassed? But before we go on, Campbell has another nugget for all of us: "Not seeing the Kingdom of the Father, we live in the world as though it was not the Kingdom. Seeing the Kingdom—that is the End of the World." Say what?

And then we have the abstract and very verbose dissertations on God (with their almost obligatory words such as existential, paradigm, *a priori,* and *a posteriori*) by many of the supposedly fine minds of our time. One can slog through hundreds of pages of their writings without picking up one new, meaningful insight—either because they have nothing original to say, or if they do, are incapable of communicating it in ordinary language that you and I can understand. One sincerely wonders whether their only real and demonstrable ability is to

---

*The many italics in this book are the author's, not the sources being quoted.

speak in riddles (admittedly, not easy), to obfuscate (again, not easy), and to impress people (easy) with their purported intellectualism.

When these "great" religious thinkers finally get around to writing prose that we can understand, it is so very often offensive to any rational person. For instance, St. Augustine was a very important fourth- and fifth-century theologian (AD 354–430) who became a saint of the Catholic church and a major influence on the thought of St. Thomas Aquinas, the thirteenth-century theologian (1225–1274) who was made the official theologian of the church by Pope Leo XIII in 1879. Augustine set forth several religious beliefs that have resonated down through the ages, becoming central tenets of most branches of modern-day Christianity. Here's one of them. If any of us happened to wonder what real love is, Augustine has the answer. "Love is not primarily goodwill for man," he says, "but reverent devotion to God." Can you imagine that? The main passion and object of our love here on earth should not be our mother and father, wife, husband, children, and fellow human beings, but the abstraction God. If you say so, St. Augustine.

Most nonfiction subjects written about in life are amenable to verification. But because verification of God is not possible, most of what is written on the subject is nothing more than sophisticated ignorance. Yet more has been written about God and Jesus throughout history than on any other subject. And a great number of people have made it their job or passion to study all the aforementioned sophisticated ignorance on the subject, many even getting doctorates in theology. Although I am not a theologian, I have read the bible and done much thinking about religion and God through the years.

Perhaps the main strength I bring to this study of God and religion is in simply being able to superimpose on it the very same logic and common sense I have been credited as bringing to all my subjects in the preceding years.

THERE IS SOMETHING OFF THE TOP that I have to say to Christian theologians and believers. And if the principle I am about to state has merit, as I believe it does, and it is applied to what they say, as I feel it must, it would seem, in view of all the things later discussed in this book, to shake the very foundation of many of their most important beliefs. The undeniable truth set forth in this principle is a verity whose binding stricture does not allow religious people and institutions to cavalierly ignore inanities and absurdities by sleight of mouth and proceed merrily on to their next absurdity. Because I perceive this to be important, I want to spend a little time on it.

Although the great masses of humankind who believe in the Christian God and the tenets of their religion do so blindly and without thought, that very definitely is not true of their spiritual leaders, who memorialize their thoughts and the principles of their religion in books, essays, and all other manner of literature that some of the faithful read and, of course, accept. And if you look at any of these books by, for instance, the most widely respected Catholic and Christian thinkers, such as St. Thomas Aquinas, St. Augustine, and C. S. Lewis, all of them, *without exception*, reach the conclusions they reach by resorting to *their* powers of human *reason* and *logic*. They do this for the simple reason that they have no other choice. And these Christian writers, who know God to be, among other things, all-good, all-powerful, all-knowing, all-intelligent, and all-just, never stop with their purported knowledge of God having these qualities that go to the core of their faith. They naturally, and inevitably, go beyond this and tell us they also know *where* this goodness and justice and intelligence in God takes God in his relationship with us mortals. And the Christian writer does this by relying on *his* concept of goodness and justice and intelligence— that is, in a form of anthropomorphism, he imputes *his* concept of these things to God.

For instance, because the religious believer knows that a good human being treats his fellow man with fairness, he imputes *his* concept of fairness to God and therefore has no doubt that God is just and treats the creatures he[*,3] created with fairness. The true believer would never say that God is unjust because if he did, he'd be saying that God is not all-good. And because the believer knows that a truly intelligent human being normally conducts his affairs with logic and common sense, he would never say that God did something stupid or illogical because he would be saying that God is not all-intelligent. Indeed, when we look at Christianity's supposed grasp of God's relationship to man, the believer always imputes to God conventional, *earthly* notions of goodness, justice, and intelligence.

The believers even get nuanced about it—never letting go, of course, of their human logic, common sense, and experience. For example, to the skeptic's question, Jesus only performed miracles (e.g., walking on water, healing the sick, calming the storm, raising Lazarus from the dead) two thousand years ago in front of very few witnesses,[†] why doesn't he perform these deviations from the laws of nature for all of us to see today?[4,5] True believers Norman Geisler and Frank Turek answer that God performs miracles only when he is "trying to confirm a *new* truth. . . . So as not to 'cry wolf,' miracles must be focused on promoting a truth claim and *must be relatively rare if they are to be effective*." In other words, Geisler and Turek stretch logic, but *earthly*, conventional logic, to defend their God.

The very description of God given by Christians shows, then, that he is being described by *our* standards. Indeed, one could ask the question, Inasmuch as none of us has ever seen God, saw him act, or known what was on his mind (In 1 Corinthians 2:16, it is written "Who can know what the Lord is thinking?"), if we didn't describe God in *our* terms, using our sense of reason and logic and morality, *then how in the world would we ever describe God?* Moreover, the words of the God

---

*The male gender is used throughout this book in referring to God. See endnote discussion.

†Likewise, earlier with Jesus' heavenly father appearing to Moses in a burning bush that wasn't being consumed, and using Moses as a conduit to part the Red Sea, etc.

of the New Testament, Jesus, are replete with examples of logic and reason and morality identical to ours. If God's reasoning were, for instance, that giving to the rich, not the poor, is a sign of compassion; that stealing from your fellow man is a virtue, not a crime; and that lying to others is a sign of honesty, even Christians, as irrational as they are about their religion, would say, "That God is crazy. Let's find someone else to worship."

What is the point I am trying to make here? It's that Christians cannot separate, at their convenience, their *human* sense of reason from the way God reasons. They are bound by their own practice and way of thinking. Therefore, if we ask Christians how a good God could have allowed the Holocaust or any of the countless atrocities and tragedies of the past, they are not permitted to say, "I don't know why God permitted these things to happen, but he must have his reasons, and they are all good." They can't achieve the position they claim to possess as the repositors of knowledge of who God is and what his plans are for all of us, which they expropriated to themselves by virtue of imputing to God *their* notions of goodness, logic, and so forth, and then when God does something, or allows something to happen that clearly does violence to, and contradicts, these *very same* notions of goodness and logic, blithely deflect the problem by simply saying, "Though we mortals don't understand it, God has his reasons, and they are always good." To use a modern expression, Christians "can't go there." That door is closed. That option is not open to them. They eliminated it as an option when they imputed to God the virtues of being all-good, all-powerful, all-just, all-knowing, all-intelligent, using *their* reason and understanding of these virtues. They can't bail out when the evidence seems to refute their assertions and premises. That's not the way any game worth its name is played. I believe that the commonsense imperative articulated here is a solar-plexus blow to the body of Christian thought and belief, and I will invoke it off and on in what follows. For those devout Christians who refuse to acknowledge the logic and reality of what I have just said because, well, to accept it would strip them of the only fallback position they have that God could allow all the horror, suffering, and evil in the world to take place and still be good, I hate to inform them that the modern Christian theologian whom they revere the most, C. S. Lewis, in his multimillion bestseller *Mere Christianity* unfortunately says something that knocks their feet right out from under them. He writes: "God is the source from which all our reasoning power comes." To say that God gave us our reasoning power, but this same God-given reasoning is *wrong* when it tells us that a good God would not have allowed the horrors of life, is to say that the Christian notion of God and who he is doesn't make sense.

Let me add on this point that even if we assume for the sake of argument that God, if there is a God, does not think the way we do, which is the position that twelfth-century Jewish rabbi and theologian Maimonides takes in his philosophical treatise *Guide for the Perplexed*, if we can't, in discussing God, hold his actions to conventional notions of morality, logic, and common sense, the *only* source for evaluation of conduct that we inferior mortals have, then under this quasi-nihilistic approach, why don't we just snuff out the candle and not talk or write about God at all?

2

God in Court

MORE THAN ONE PERSON HAS SUGGESTED that I set forth my case for agnosticism (against my opposition, theism and atheism) in a structured way roughly analogous to a trial. But the issues we are dealing with in this book simply do not lend themselves to this approach for several reasons. First, in a trial, the side making the allegation has the burden of proof, and it is this side (the prosecution in a criminal case, the plaintiff in a civil case) that first presents the evidence to prove its allegation or case. The defense presents evidence to poke holes in the other side's case and many times even presents affirmative evidence to prove the opposite, that the allegation is not true. In this context, the theist, making the allegation that God exists, would open the case, and the atheist would try to knock this allegation down by establishing weaknesses in the theist's case and/or by attempting to affirmatively prove that God does not exist. The agnostic would not fit into this theoretical trial because he is not making an allegation one way or another. The only position he is taking is that he doesn't know.

There is a second reason why this theoretical literary trial would not work. At a trial, the parties to the lawsuit have to prove their case by presenting evidence from the witness stand. And you have to know that in this case that witness stand would be as empty as a bird's nest in winter. For example, in a criminal trial for robbery a typical witness would be one who saw the robber hold up, for instance, the bank teller or liquor store proprietor. In a God trial the believers or theists obviously would be unable to call such eyewitnesses to the stand.

But since this is not a real trial, why even talk about eyewitness testimony? At least as to the divinity of Jesus, why can't the case be made through the well-recognized "testimony" of Matthew, Mark, Luke, and John in the gospels of the New Testament? Besides, Matthew and John were among the twelve apostles of Christ and hence were eyewitnesses to everything he said and did throughout his three-year ministry in Galilee and Judea. As John the apostle said, "The one who existed from the beginning is the one we have heard and seen. We saw him with our own eyes and touched him with our own hands. He is Jesus Christ, the Word of life" (1 John 1:1).

However, the gospels would be inadmissible hearsay in a trial. Hearsay is a statement (or writing) made *outside of court*—that is, not from the witness stand at the present proceeding—that is offered into evidence to prove not merely that the statement was made but that it is true. But apart from this technical objection, there are other big problems with the "testimony" of the gospels. One deals with the requirement that a document has to be authenticated; that is, shown to be the writing that the party offering the document claims it to be. Here, no one has established, for sure, when each of the four gospels, which contain Jesus' supposed words and the events of his life, was written, or even whether they were written by the authors whose names they bear. So the source and the authenticity of each gospel is immediately put into question.

Let's take John, the "author" of the last of the four gospels. There is no evidence, nor do biblical scholars believe, that during Jesus' ministry John, or any of the twelve apostles, took notes to record Jesus' words and conduct. After Jesus died, John *preached* his gospel (which means "good news" in Greek, the language in which all four gospels were written)[1] of Jesus' life and teaching far and wide. (Jesus told his disciples, "Go ye into all the world, and preach the gospel" [Mark 16:15].) However, it wasn't until John, living in the ancient city of Ephesus, was believed to have been at least ninety years old, almost sixty to sixty-five years after Jesus died,[2] and with his presumed diminution of memory, that, it is said, he was urged by the bishops of Asia Minor (modern-day Turkey) to put his gospel into writing. But one view that has some currency among biblical scholars is that the actual scribe who penned the gospel of John was not John but a man named John the Elder, who was John's disciple or someone who worked with John.[3]

Similar problems of authorship and memory are found with the remaining gospels, which, all scholars agree, were committed to papyrus only after many years of being passed down orally. The first gospel believed to have been written was by Mark, around AD 70, almost forty years after Jesus died. Mark's identity is not known. What is known is that he was not one of the twelve apostles, and the consensus of scholars is that he wrote what Peter the apostle told him. It is also believed that the gospels of Matthew and Luke (written around AD 85 and 75, respectively) are based, in substantial part, on the gospel of Mark, which as indicated was conveyed by word of mouth—with the almost inevitable distortion in the retelling—from Peter.[4]

And not only hasn't the original writing of any of the four gospels been found—for that matter, no original manuscript of any book of the Old and New Testament, or any part thereof, has ever been found, either being lost or destroyed. Only copies have surfaced. But as author Richard Dawkins notes, the original written gospels "were copied and recopied and went through many different . . . generations by fallible scribes who, in any case, had their own religious agendas."[5]

So the legal requirement that documents—here, the gospels—be authenticated before being received into evidence could never be met.

But even if, since this is not a real trial, we were to relax this requirement, at some point we do have to "get real" if the God trial is to have any value at all. And it would seem that the uncircumventible obstacle to such a trial, at least insofar as testimonial evidence is concerned, is the inability to cross-examine. For example, if Luke's "testimony" in Luke 9:12–17 that Jesus performed the miracle of feeding

5,000 people with five loaves of bread and two fish was offered into evidence by the theists to show Jesus' divinity, the atheists should have the opportunity to cross-examine Luke on this point if this "trial" is to have any credibility at all. John Henry Wigmore, the foremost authority on the law of evidence, called cross-examination "beyond any doubt the greatest legal engine ever invented for the discovery of truth." Because there could not be any cross-examination of Luke or any other "testimonial" witness, it is difficult to see how the gospels could be introduced into evidence at any God trial, even one conducted hypothetically within the pages of a book.

Ah, but some might say, what about circumstantial evidence? As opposed to direct evidence (eyewitness testimony), which, if true, proves a fact in issue without the necessity of drawing any inference, circumstantial evidence is evidence that only *tends* to prove a fact in dispute by proving a secondary fact. From this secondary fact, an inference can then be drawn that the fact in issue exists. For instance, from the secondary fact of a witness seeing a stolen television set in the defendant's home, *one* reasonable inference (there can be others) is that it was he who stole the set, the identity of the thief being the fact in dispute.

The problem for theists is that what makes circumstantial evidence of any kind valid and strong is *prior human experience*, which, with one exception, can never be found in arguments for the existence of God. For instance, we know from our prior human experience that flight from the scene of a crime is circumstantial evidence that the fleeing party was the perpetrator of, or somehow involved in, the crime. Inasmuch as this is circumstantial evidence, there may be other explanations. But normally flight is consistent with guilt, particularly since we know from experience that usually there is other direct or circumstantial evidence in the case, such as finding the party's fingerprints at the scene, compatible with guilt. For the same reasons, we know—again, from our prior human experience—that inconsistent statements during interrogation by the police and silence in the face of an accusatory statement are generally circumstantial evidence of guilt. And so on.

Let's look at an everyday example of circumstantial evidence (proving a secondary fact that tends to prove the fact in issue) and then contrast it with that presented in a God trial. You walk outside in the early morning to pick up the newspaper, and the concrete walkway leading up to your door is completely wet. You know it's not from your neighbor's errant sprinkler because the sidewalk and street in front of your home, for as far as you can see in both directions, are also completely wet. From this secondary fact of water being everywhere, you can naturally infer that it must have rained, even though you were not outside at the time to see it rain and you didn't even hear it because you were asleep. You can make this inference with a 99.99 percent degree of certainty because our human experience has shown us this hundreds upon hundreds of times in the past.

In the God trial, couldn't the believers (the theists) call an astronomer to the witness stand to testify to all the stars and heavenly bodies in the universe as being circumstantial evidence of the existence of God? Yes, but the main reason that this inference won't carry the day is that, unlike the inference of rain from the fact of water being seen everywhere, *we have absolutely no human experience, no framework of reference that tells us that God is responsible for these heavenly bodies in the sky.* We learned from experience very early in our life that water everywhere outdoors meant rain. But when did we learn from experience that the stars in the sky meant God? How could we when the stars we see at night in the sky above are the same ones that our ancestors, and Galileo, and yes, Jesus, saw, none of us ever having one, single human experience of any kind that told us, beyond any reasonable doubt, that the heavens came from God?*

---

*Likewise, the singing birds in the trees and succulent fruit on the vine could arguably be traceable to Charles Darwin's theory of evolution, and we have no human experience that they indisputably came to be because of God.

This does not mean that God is not responsible for the heavens and the stars in the sky. It only means that since there is no past human experience to rely on, Christians are not rationally entitled to assert, with the great confidence they do, that the heavens above prove that a supernatural being, God, is behind it all.

And you have to know that it is no answer to say, as perhaps the majority of deeply religious Christians do, that "God tells us, in Genesis, he created the world," because that assumes the existence of the very fact in issue, that God exists. This is the "I am because I am because I am" type of circular reasoning that gains no admission into the arena of intelligent debate.

So we see that for the most part we are left with things that simply do not lend themselves to proof—a disparate set of beliefs and arguments for and against the existence of God that have come down through the ages, none of them, except for one, rising to the dignity of real evidence. That one exception, to be discussed later, is the principle of cause and effect, which at least arguably leads irresistibly to a first cause, that cause being God.

3

The Christian God
Cannot Exist

IN OUR DISCUSSION OF GOD throughout this book, two related and sobering realities that cannot be disputed should be kept in mind. One is that all religions have been created by man. Certainly not a confidence-inspiring thought. Second, there would seem to be more evidence that man created God than that God created man. (This, however, does not mean that God did not create man.) With respect to man creating God, is it only a coincidence, it has been asked, that God just happens to possess every single trait (all-good, just, merciful, intelligent, etc.) that man could possibly want him to have, and every power (to ensure that there is life after death and that we see our loved ones again) too? Or is it more likely that this is circumstantial evidence that man created God to meet these needs and desires of his?

A 2006 *Newsweek* poll showed that 92 percent of Americans believe in God, 4 percent are atheists, and only 2 percent are agnostic. When I wrote in *Outrage* that I am an agnostic, that needs clarification. I'm an agnostic only on the issue of whether there is a God, a supernatural being who created the universe. I'm not an agnostic on the Christian God, the God of Catholicism and Protestantism. Almost by definition he does not exist, so therefore I have virtually no ambivalence, or lingering agnosticism, on this issue. The *Outrage* piece points out, as many have before me, that while God can be all-powerful or all-good, he cannot be both, since these are irreconcilable virtues in a world

25

rflowing with the bloody crops of evil. Even eliminating all the other
supposed attributes of God, if he is all-powerful, and hence capable of
preventing evil, for him to cause, or do nothing to stop, the unbelievable suffering and horror in this world immediately tells one that God
cannot be all-good, as Christianity believes its God to be (Luke 18:19,
Jeremiah 31:14, Psalm 31:19). As I pointed out in the first chapter,
Christian religions are bound by *their* concept of good and evil, and
they know that a good being would never cause, or, if he had it within
his power, do nothing to stop the suffering, tragedy, and unspeakable
atrocities that embroil the inhabitants of this planet and have throughout history. When these realities refute their belief that God is all-good,
they are not permitted to say, "We can't question God. God has his
reasons for everything he does or does not do, and they are all good."

Lest there be any confusion on this matter, let me reemphasize one
all-important fact: Even if we assume, just for the sake of argument,
that the Christian God does not cause or will the horrors of life, it cannot be denied that at a minimum he at least allows them to happen,
gives them his green light.[1] This is so because all Christians believe
their God is omniscient (all-knowing [John 16:30]) and omnipotent
(all-powerful [Matthew 19:26, Jeremiah 51:15, Revelation 19:6]).
Since he knew (being all-knowing) that, for instance, September 11,
2001, was about to happen, and since his power, in the Christian mind,
is without limitation, he had the power to prevent the horror from happening, yet he allowed 9/11 to take place. This is not in dispute, even by
Christians and their theologians. For example, Billy Graham, the foremost evangelical Protestant in American history, in speaking about another catastrophe, Hurricane Katrina, told *Newsweek* (March 20, 2006),
"I don't know" who caused Katrina, *"but God allowed it."* (Billy Graham
is being kind to God. As we know, things like floods and earthquakes
are commonly referred to as "acts of God.") In Pope John Paul II's
2005 book, *Memory and Identity,* he wrote that "The Lord God allowed Nazism twelve years of existence. Divine Providence *allowed*
that bestial fury to be unleashed for only [only?] those twelve years."

Pope Benedict XVI, at the Nazi death camp Auschwitz during a visit to Poland in 2006, said, "In a place like this, words fail. In the end, there can only be a dread silence—a silence which is itself a heartfelt cry to God: Why, Lord, did you remain silent? How could you tolerate all this?" I should add, particularly when you, God, were right there.

You see, in addition to God being all-good, all-powerful, and all-knowing, Christianity, as well as Judaism, believes God is omnipresent. "God is in every place; and this is everywhere," St. Thomas Aquinas said.[2] As stated in Psalm 139:7–10, "Whither shall I go from your spirit? Or whither shall I flee from your presence? If I ascend to heaven, You are there. If I make my bed, You are there. If I take the wings of the morning and dwell in the uttermost parts of the sea, even there your hand shall hold me." And Psalm 23:4 in the Old Testament, which so many of the Jews Hitler murdered, being Jewish, had undoubtedly read, says that "Even though I walk through the valley of the shadow of death, I will not be afraid, for You are close beside me." How comforting it must have been for these Jews in the gas chamber to know that God was right by their side. Though they screamed out for their lives as the gasses began to burn their eyes and choke their throats, and they cried out for his help, isn't it wonderful that he was right there beside them, even if all he gave them was a deaf ear?

I don't hate God. Why would I when I don't even know he exists? But common sense tells us that the billions who do believe in the Christian God, and believe he is all-powerful, and therefore could prevent evil, should absolutely hate him with a passion and fury reserved for no other person, thing, or entity. Instead, they all proclaim their unlimited love for him, at least allegedly putting him above even their family and country. Why is it that I have never heard any theist, ever, proclaim his unlimited hatred of God? If logic is our guide, how would a theist not have such a hatred? And since atheists and agnostics have no reason to hate God, as I said in my *Outrage* piece, no one but no one ever passionately expresses a hatred for God.

The principal Christian and Judaic defense to the horrors of history happening on God's watch is that God gives all of us free will (see later discussion), and therefore he's not responsible for how we exercise it. But even if, for example, Hitler and Stalin had the free will to do good or bad, and they chose bad, if God is, as Christianity and Judaism say, all-powerful, he had the power to prevent them from carrying out their evil deeds, and he chose not to. So in no way can he escape culpability for what happened.

Let me ask you this question. If there were parents who had a seventeen-year-old son, call him Eddie, who they knew was robbing, raping, and killing people in their part of town, and they had the power to stop him from doing so, what would you think of these parents if they took the position, "Eddie has free will and we're not responsible for how he exercises it. So we're not going to stop him or even try to stop him?" Since you of course would think the parents were absolutely terrible people, *why should you think any differently about God?* To the argument I often hear when I pose this question to Christians, that one can't compare human beings with God because God is transcendent, I would say this. That is a distinction without substance. What difference does it make if the parents are human and God is transcendent? They are both doing the very same, precise thing—allowing horror to take place that they could have stopped. Secondly, the transcendent argument actually goes in the wrong direction, hurting the cause of anyone propounding it. Why? Because if God is transcendent, and also, supposedly, all-good, as they say in the law, *a fortiori* (all the more so) he should intervene. No one is claiming Eddie's parents are all good.

(In Christianity's desperate attempt to explain how its supposedly all-good God could allow the horrors of the world, famed preacher and Christian theologian John MacArthur, paraphrasing Romans 11:32, actually argues that God "allows sin [evil] in order that he might display grace." Translation: In God's [and apparently MacArthur's] eyes, it's better that millions of human beings be brutally murdered so God can display his grace to the murderers if they seek his forgiveness and accept him as their savior, than if the millions of horrible murders had never taken place. What rational person would give an ear to something as outrageously preposterous on its face as this?)

In speaking earlier of Hitler and the Holocaust, perhaps the darkest chapter in human history, 6 million human beings were murdered, and in the most horrible of ways, mostly by slow gassing in a gas-chamber locked shut. Many were shot or buried alive in mass graves. Hans Stark, the registrar of new arrivals at Hitler's main extermination camp, Auschwitz, in Poland, gave a statement concerning his participation in a routine gassing at Auschwitz:

> At another, later gassing—also in autumn 1941—Grabner [head of the political department at Auschwitz] ordered me to pour Zyklon B into the opening because only one medical orderly had shown up. During the gassing, Zyklon B had to be poured through both openings of the gas-chamber room at the same time. The gassing was of 200–250 Jews, once again, men, women and children. As the Zyklon B was in a granular form, it trickled down over the people as it was poured in. They then started to cry out terribly for they now knew what was happening to them. I did not look through the opening because it had to be closed as soon as the Zyklon B had been poured in. After a few minutes there was silence. After some time had passed, it may have been ten to fifteen minutes, the gas chamber was opened. The dead lay higgledy-piggedly all over the place. It was a dreadful sight. (Ernst Klee, Willi Dressen, and Volken Riess, *The Good Old Days: The Holocaust as Seen by Its Perpetrators and Bystanders*, [New York: Free Press, 1988], 255)

And people *still* actually, actually put their hands together . . . and pray to God?? Because he loves them, and is all good, and has the power to stop all of this??

Rutka Laskier, a fourteen-year-old Jewish girl living in Poland under Nazi rule, her mind already "flooded," she said, by the atrocities of war, and having previously assumed that if there was a God, he had to be good, wrote this in her diary on February 5, 1943: "The little faith I used to have has been completely shattered. If God existed, He would have certainly not permitted that human beings be thrown alive into furnaces, and the heads of little toddlers be smashed with butts of guns or be shoved into sacks and gassed to death." And again, according to Christianity, God, being all-powerful, could have easily stopped all of this. But he apparently decided it was just fine with him. "For God so loved the world that he gave his only begotten son to die for our sins," the standard Christian mantra says. But God apparently doesn't love the world enough to prevent or stop all the horror, murder, tragedy, even genocide, *in* the world. Some love.

If God, per the Old Testament, could intervene and inflict the many horrendous plagues on the innocent people of Egypt to get their pharaoh to let Moses lead his people out of Egypt to the promised land of Canaan (Exodus 7–11), why is it that he hasn't lifted his hand to impose his will on the tyrants of history to end their unspeakable crimes against humanity, crimes much worse, and involving much greater numbers of people, than the slavery that the pharaoh was imposing on the Jews?*

---

*Of course, one answer among others (e.g. God doesn't exist or if he does, he isn't all good) is that the story of Moses and his people and the pharaoh is a bad point of comparison because it may never have happened. For instance, although the bible records that en route from Egypt to Israel the Israelites gathered at Kadesh in the Sinai desert "for a long time" (Deuteronomy 1:46; 2:14), "the site at Kadesh was excavated extensively, and to our great surprise there was nothing there earlier than the 10th century [BC]," Ben Gurion University archaeologist Eliezer Oren reported to the media (*Los Angeles Herald Examiner*, March 12, 1988).

Edwin M. Yamauchi, professor of history at Miami University in Oxford, Ohio, writes that "two dates for the Exodus have been proposed: an early date about 1440 BC, and a late date of about 1270. No definitive archaeological evidence confirms the traditional southern route through the Sinai Peninsula" (*The Oxford Companion to the Bible*, edited by Bruce M. Metzger and Michael D. Coogan [New York: Oxford University Press, 1992], 51). In 2007, Dr. Zahi Hawaas, Egypt's chief archaeologist, told a bus-ful of journalists who had gathered at an archaeological site at North Sinai, Egypt, that the story of the Exodus was "really just a myth," and that nothing had ever surfaced to confirm it (*New York Times*, April 3, 2007).

In any event, in our discussion of the Christian God we can take the issue of whether he allows the horrors of life to happen off the table. There is no dispute about this. (And the instances of God not only refraining from helping the victim but also actively helping the evil perpetrator, as one may argue he did with O. J. Simpson, have been countless through the years. Just one example: Richard Allen Davis, the parolee who kidnapped and murdered Polly Klaas in Petaluma, California, in 1993, told the police that the twelve-year-old girl was alive and hidden in the woods nearby while sheriff's deputies freed his car from a ditch shortly after the kidnapping. God was really watching out for the girl's welfare, wasn't he? We see that he was taking care of the kidnapper, not the poor little girl.)

Billy Graham, recognized as "the most famous religious preacher of all time," articulated the classic statement for why God allows the horrors of life to happen: the "God has his reasons" argument. He told a *Good Morning America* national television audience in July of 1999, "God loves you. *He has a plan for your life.* Nothing happens by accident. *Everything is planned by God for a purpose. And that purpose is*

It should be added that Egyptian historical records make no reference to any Jewish settlement in Egypt around the time of the Exodus, nor to the ten plagues, nor to Pharaoh and his entire army being drowned at sea. (Exodus 13:6–10, 14:28). Indeed, the bible itself is weak on this matter in that it doesn't even identify, by name, the pharaoh (king) involved in this biblical story. I mean, the pharaohs did have names, all of which are scrupulously recorded, along with what transpired during their reigns, in Egyptian dynastic history. If the Exodus actually happened somewhere within the period 1440 and 1270 BC, why didn't Moses, or whoever wrote or edited Exodus, specifically name the pharaoh in the all-important Exodus story? (It's not as if pharaohs were never named in the bible— e.g., see Kings 14:25–26 [Shishak], Jeremiah 44:30 [Hophra]). For instance, between 1440–1270 BC, there was Thutmose III (reign from 1479 to 1425 BC) and Amenhotep II (1427–1401), Akhnaton I (1353–1337) and Smenkhkare (1338–1336), to Sety 1 (1294–1279) and Ramesses II (1279–1213). Is it because to name a pharaoh would reveal that the Exodus story was false? One example would be if the bible said that the Exodus pharaoh was Akhnaton, and we know Akhnaton didn't drown with thousands of his troops in the Red Sea, but died a peaceful death, most likely from Marfan Syndrome, a genetic defect. The point has to be stressed that since the Exodus is the central event of the Old Testament, would not the elimination of it in effect destroy the credibility of the entire Old Testament? And the Old Testament is nearly three-fourths of the Christian Bible!

always good. You see, God is a God of love and mercy. And whatever happens to us is in God's plan." But Billy, please. What good purpose of God's was possibly served when a quarter of a million people drowned in the December 26, 2004, tsunami in Indonesia? When more than 200,000 Haitians died in that country's earthquake on January 12, 2010? Don't even try to come up with an answer to this, Billy. Your position is embarrassing enough as it is. And what good purpose of God's was being served when the Third Reich murdered 6 million Jews during the Holocaust? Please don't hurt yourself more by saying that this led to the creation of Israel. And what plan for their lives did God have for the 250,000 Japanese who were bombed to smithereens at Hiroshima and Nagasaki on August 6 and 9, 1945? Was it their purpose in life to test the efficacy of the atomic bomb? So, please, Billy, for your own good in the eyes of rational people, don't go there.

But one shouldn't think that Christian thinkers and their followers have only the feckless "God has his reasons, and they are all good" argument to rely on. That's only the one they employ when the going gets rough and they retreat to it as a last resort. Long before this, however, they have many answers they trot out to justify the horrors of life, none of which are entertainable in the mind of a reasonable person.

❧

WHEN ONE ASKS CHRISTIANS HOW A GOOD GOD could permit all of this evil in the world and why he wouldn't simply eliminate it so that humans could live in peace, harmony, and happiness, one of their principal replies is to tell you, *using their human logic and reasoning*, that if humans were always "happy," it wouldn't mean anything to them because they'd have nothing to compare it with. To really enjoy happiness, they argue, you have to know or experience unhappiness, and God, knowing this, therefore allows all the unhappiness and misery in the world.

In other words, in the childlike thinking of many Christians and their leaders, the lowly experience of man in needing something else to compare something with in order to appreciate it *binds* God (who they nonetheless maintain is all-powerful and can do anything, which would mean he could simply create humans who could be happy without having experienced unhappiness) and prevents him from circumventing this need. But I beg leave to point out that this feeble rationalization is not a valid defense for allowing the horrors of the world to beset man.

Christians also use an argument that is analogous to the happiness-unhappiness one. God knows we could never appreciate good if we didn't also experience evil. My response to this is that I'd rather have an existence where no one robs, rapes, and murders, and we don't know what good and evil are, than a world where men do rob, rape, and murder, but we have the wonderful knowledge of the difference between good and evil. Obviously, this argument is not a valid defense for why God permits bad things to happen to good people. And again, since God is all-powerful, why wouldn't he simply create humans who could appreciate good without having evil to compare it with?

Some theists take the argument further by saying that you cannot even *have* good without also having evil because you can't have anything without having its absence—for example, you can't have water without acknowledging a situation where no water exists. And they say the absence of something is its opposite, as evil is the opposite of good. But this doesn't follow at all. Although, for instance, the opposite of hot is cold, the absence of hot obviously is not cold. It is neither. But even if what the theists say were true, this would in no way dictate that God, if he is omnipotent, would be incapable of creating anything without its opposite. Do theists really want to say that their omnipotent God would not, for instance, have the power to create humans who always told the truth without also making them capable of lying? If they want to say this, they have just destroyed, by their own words, one of the most important pillars (God's omnipotence) of the edifice upon which their entire faith is based.

Theists can't have it both ways. If their God is omnipotent, by definition he has no limitations (other than, of course, he obviously cannot do self-contradictory things, such as draw a square circle or make a whole that is less than its parts.* It would also seem he would not be able to change the past—I can't resist pointing out that only historians can do that). Since they say he had no trouble creating the universe with all its planets and stars, do they really want to hear him say, "But hey, don't ask too much of me. I'm only God. I just can't figure out how to construct a world with good in it without there also being evil. This is something I just can't do." But wait. It seems to me I've heard Christians say so many times through the years that there is absolutely nothing God cannot do except lie (Hebrews 6:18). What I'm saying is that if God could have created our terrible world as easily, why couldn't he have created a wonderful world just as easily?

In struggling to reconcile the inherent contradictions of their faith, Christian thinkers, in the finest traditions of a political spin doctor, convey negative images to their flock, who, without thinking, accept them as, well, the gospel truth. For example, on the matter of our having to have unhappiness and evil to appreciate happiness and good, they say if we did not have this, "What type of world would it be like if everyone was an automaton?" Yeah, right on. No one likes automatons. Translation: Rather than have people always treat others morally and well, we'd rather have the occasional shooting, stabbing, rape, beheading, and defrauding of the aged. It makes life so much more interesting.

---

*Perhaps the most famous paradoxical question that has been asked about God (assuming there is a God) is whether or not he can make a stone so heavy that he cannot lift it. As the thinking goes, if he can, then he is not omnipotent because there is something he cannot do, lift the stone. But if he cannot make such a stone, then he also is not omnipotent. Because omnipotence is believed to be a necessary attribute of the Judeo-Christian God, some atheists believe that the stone example alone is proof of the non-existence of God. But just as God cannot *do* self-contradictory things (see examples above), he obviously cannot *be* self-contradictory things, e.g., he cannot be black and white at the same time. Likewise, he can be powerful enough to make a stone so heavy he cannot lift it. But it cannot be stated that he is not omnipotent because he cannot lift it. He cannot have the power to make a stone he cannot lift, and at the same time have the power to lift it.

The automaton image, of course, is ludicrous beyond belief. Do you want me to prove it to you in just one question? If you knew someone who unfailingly treated you and others in a decent, fair, and ethical way, how would you describe him—in a negative way as an "automaton, a robot," or as "a nice guy, a wonderful person"? And would you be bored by his conduct, hoping that now and then he would cheat you out of your money, kick you in the shins, or try to molest your young daughter?[3]

And it is not a defense to the horrors of the world to argue, as so many Christians do, that, yes, these horrors are terrible and God caused or allowed them to happen, but he will make everything right in a later life by punishing the guilty and rewarding the good. What happens later may bring about a measure of justice, but it does nothing to alleviate the pain and misery and carnage and suffering that have already occurred. All that he has caused or allowed will have already been sustained and experienced by us pathetic mortals, and nothing can take this suffering, pain, and horror away. So no matter what God does in the future, we can never forgive his past.

Moreover, the belief that there will be justice in the afterlife presupposes there is an afterlife, which we do not know; that there is a God, which we do not know; and that he is not a figure of moral neutrality but one who is committed to bringing justice to the conduct of all those he created, which we cannot know. With all these presuppositions, and not one ounce of evidence to support them, how can any rational person feel serene about his position that Party A, who led an extremely honorable life, and died a painful death, will be rewarded in the hereafter over Party B, who brought misery and pain and horror to thousands, even millions, in his life, and died peacefully in his sleep?

As previously indicated, Christianity's most common and, it feels, strongest line of defense to God's allowing the horrors and evil of life is to argue that God gave all of us free will, as the monsignor told me when I was a child, and he's not responsible for how we exercise it. But to begin, one big problem is that there is no scriptural basis for the religious doctrine that God gave us free will except for one short reference in an obscure book in the Old Testament of the Catholic bible (Sirach 15:14). The book is considered apocryphal by Jews and Protestants and therefore does not appear in their bibles. So for Protestants and Jews, apart from a free will argument based on what they perceive to be common sense but is heavily freighted with supposition, the doctrine of free will, without which Protestantism especially could hardly exist, has no more religious weight than that of a vagrant standing atop an orange crate in the town square ranting to passersby about God. Just like Mark Twain's observation that everyone talks about the weather but no one ever does anything about it, Protestants and Jews (as well, of course, as Catholics) talk constantly about free will, and everyone just automatically and unthinkingly accepts it as a given, but when it comes time to pay the piper and offer biblical support for their position, they stay away from the issue the way the devil stays away from holy water.[4]

Notwithstanding Saint Augustine and Thomas Aquinas, it is astonishing that in most major works on religion, even those on Catholicism such as the 803-page official *Catechism of the Catholic Church*, free will *isn't even in the index*. Indeed, in the 4,452 pages of the four-volume *International Standard Bible Encyclopedia,* there are entries for games, instrument, eunuch, atharim, Moab, wind, and wimple among thousands of other entries, but there is no entry for free will! You see, there was a space problem and they couldn't shoehorn free will in. I understand.

Although perhaps no precept in all of Christianity or Judaism is more important than free will inasmuch as God's justice in punishing evildoers could not be explained without it, and although, as indicated, everyone talks about it, remarkably, nearly all religious books have no reference at all to free will, or the author briefly writes about it off the top of his head without citing any biblical sources.

Indeed, not only is there no scriptural support in the Jewish or Protestant bibles for the doctrine of free will, but there is Old and New Testament support in the Jewish, Protestant, *and Catholic* bibles against it. Romans 9:18 explicitly says that "God chooses to *make* some people refuse to listen." For example, Talmudic scholars, not just for years, but for centuries, have been desperately trying to get around (since Judaism believes so strongly in free will) Exodus 4:21 and 7:3 where God tells Moses "I will harden the heart of the Pharaoh and make him stubborn so he will not let the people go," thereby justifying, apparently, his imposition of the ten horrible plagues he visited on the Egyptian people to force the Pharaoh to capitulate and free the Israelites. Elsewhere in the bible, Isaiah 63:17 says: "Why, Lord, dost thou *cause* us (some free will) to stray from thy ways?" Romans 11:32 goes so far as to say that "God *consigns* all men to disobedience." (See also, Ezekiel 11:18–20, 2 Corinthians 4:4, John 6:65, 2 Timothy 2:25, and Ephesians 1:11.)

So contrary to popular belief, the bible does not say there is free will. In fact, it says the precise opposite, that there is no free will.[*] I don't have to tell you the enormous ramifications of this. To repeat, how does one justify God's punishment of evildoers if what they did was preordained? They had no choice. Now mind you, this is not saying there is no free will. (See endnote discussion.) Who is in a position to give a definitive answer to whether there is or is not free will? *We're only talking about the bible here.* A book so important that without it, Christianity and Judaism would cease to exist overnight.

But for the purposes of this discussion, let's overlook the foregoing very serious inconvenient reality that the bible does not support the notion of free will. Even if we assume that the bible is wrong and God does give all of us free will, not only, as I said in *Outrage*, would God, being all-knowing, know who is going to end up in hell before they are born (as it is written in Psalm 139:3, 16, "Lord, you chart the path ahead of me," and "You laid out every moment before a single day had passed"; Saint Augustine said that "to confess that God exists, and at the same time to deny that he has foreknowledge of future things is the most

---

[*]And if we want to go outside the bible, how many Protestants, who constantly preach free will, know that their founder, Martin Luther, wrote in his 1525 classic, *De Servo Arbitrio*, that man has no free will? (See endnote discussion.)

manifest folly"), but also it is implicit in that notion that he knows how we are going to exercise the free will he gave us. Psalm 139:4 adds, "You know what I am going to say before I say it." So the Christian God knows that untold billions of humans whom he supposedly created in his own image are going to exercise the free will he gave them to commit the most evil and inhumane acts against their fellow man.[5] And, although he is all-powerful, he allows all of it to happen.

Do Christians actually believe that it is a preferable state of affairs to have God bestow free will on those he creates, even though it always has and always will result in the atrocities and injustices of life, than for God to not give them free will and simply create humans who always treat their fellow man well? Free will is that great? It's more important than the absence of pain, misery, death, and suffering brought on by the monstrous acts of fellow humans? You know, "Yeah, Stalin killed millions of his people, but it was worth it. At least Stalin had free will, which we want to have *at all costs*." I mean, it's not like God would be doing something new to him to create human beings who would always act in a certain way. In Ezekiel 11:18–20, God, upset with the "detestable" conduct of the Israelites, said, "I will take away their hearts of stone and give them tender hearts instead so they will obey my laws and regulations."

Another problem with Christianity using free will—or, as it is sometimes called, indeterminism—as their explanation for all the horrors of life is that many of these horrors have nothing to do with free will, e.g., natural disasters like earthquakes, the tsunami, and Hurricane Katrina. What about the bubonic plague ("Black Death") of the mid-fourteenth century that in five years killed an estimated 25 million people, over one-third of the population of Western Europe; or people, even children, dying of cancer (certainly, not all resulting from the victim's conduct, such as smoking) or starvation? And what about the innocent victims of murder and war? What do these horrible deaths have to do with the victims' exercise of free will? Do you know what Christians say to this? These horrors are caused by Satan. Or, get this. Some actually say these horrors resulted because God, after creating the universe, somehow became weak and powerless to prevent them. My, my. When does the silliness end when it comes to Christianity? Answer: It doesn't.

Since Christianity defines its God as all-good, all-knowing, all-intelligent, and all-powerful, and we've shown he is not all-good, he cannot therefore exist. Why? Because the God who Christians say exists does not possess all the characteristics Christians say their God has. For instance, if I define a pie as having crust on the top and bottom, and fruit, like apples or cherries, in between, and I have in front of me something that consists only of crust, I cannot say that the thing in front of me is a pie. If Christians define their God as being, in addition to his other characteristics, all-good, and we can easily demonstrate he is not, we are thereby proving that the Christian God does not exist. If Christians insist on having a God, they can do so, but if they have any respect for logic they'll have to redefine who he is. (It should be noted that because the Christian God cannot exist does not mean there is no non-Christian God, essentially a deistic one, who created the universe. See discussion in Chapter 6.)

I'd like to leave my Christian brethren with this question, which has been asked by many others, to ponder: Inasmuch as God, as you say, is all-perfect, and since, you also say, he is all-powerful, meaning *he could have created any world he pleased*, why would he do such a poor job and create such an imperfect world with its deadly earthquakes, floods, hurricanes, tornadoes, droughts, etc.? Your silence is so loud I need earplugs. Wait. Did I hear a faint voice in the back row say that "God had his reasons for what he did, and they're all good"? I'm sorry. You can't go there. That door is closed. And if he is all-perfect, how could he, and why would he, create such extremely imperfect human beings to occupy his world? (Someone once asked whether any plausible defense could be made for the crime of creating the human race.) What gives with God? What's his problem? Is there a psychiatrist in the house? After you chuckle at or denigrate my sarcasm, how about answering my question?

Actually, the true Christian really doesn't even care whether any of his beliefs are logical or not. Religion, the so-called opium of the people, is so much a need of the people I am personally convinced that if God came to earth next week and said, "Jesus was not my son and he did not die on the cross for your sins and there is no such thing as heaven and hell," fanatical Christians would tell him, "Look, we know a lot more about this stuff than you do, so go back to where you came from and leave us alone." In other words, they would simply ignore him and go right on with their beliefs.

4

Atheists: The Nabobs
of Non Sequiturs

B EFORE I RETURN FOR A FULLER DISCUSSION of my main adversary in this book, theism (the belief in a God who created and
rules the universe), I want to discuss theism's opposite, atheism, the
belief in the nonexistence of God. I must say that with all the great
minds who have proclaimed themselves to be atheists (Karl Marx,
Friedrich Nietzsche, Sigmund Freud, Percy Bysshe Shelley, George
Eliot, Albert Camus, Jean-Paul Sartre, and so many others), just as
the theists have identified themselves by their sublime folly, my fine-
feathered friends the atheists, who will concede only that God is the
most fascinating character in all of fiction, have done so by the startling
and embarrassing indigence of their thoughts. Atheists have postulated
several arguments for their denial of God's existence, one of the foremost of which is the moldy non sequitur that if he did exist, we would
not have the horrors of life. But of course if you start out with an erroneous premise, everything that follows makes a heck of a lot of sense.
The only problem is that it's wrong. It's too obvious to state that only
if we assume the correctness of the Christian notion that God is all-
powerful *and all-good* can we find the contradiction of his nature in
what he has wrought. (Moreover, the premise also dismisses without
justification the existence of a deistic God.)

Atheists buttress this non sequitur with a second non sequitur: that
because God's existence cannot be proved, this is proof he does not

exist. (Or, at least, atheism wins by default.) But just as the absence of evidence that something exists is only circumstantial evidence, not proof, of its nonexistence, the failure to prove the existence of something does not necessarily prove it does not exist. For instance, thousands of times each year in American courts, defendants who have actually committed the robbery, burglary, rape, etc., are found not guilty because of the prosecution's failure (for one or more reasons, such as incompetence, intimidation of witnesses, and lost evidence) to prove its case beyond a reasonable doubt.

Setting aside the polemical technicality that theists have the burden of proof since it is they who are starting the argument by affirming the truth of the proposition that God exists, if atheism attacks Christianity, or theism in general, because Christianity believes in God without any proof of his existence, cannot Christianity legitimately attack atheism because it disbelieves in God even though it has no proof of his nonexistence?

Leading atheist Richard Dawkins, in his book *The God Delusion*, after first assuring his readers that one "can never absolutely prove the non-existence of anything"[1] (a popular but erroneous assertion. It's done everyday in courtrooms around the land and elsewhere—see endnote discussion), merrily goes on to assert almost the equivalent of this that "God almost certainly does not exist."

Three sheets to the wind on non sequiturs and unable to find one they don't like, many atheists also argue that evolution, for which they have some evidence, precludes the existence of God, or at a minimum eliminates the need for a God. Again, a non sequitur. Even if we assume that man evolved from a bacteria, flatworm, or what have you, this does not negate the possibility (Darwin thought it to be a probability—see next chapter) that God created these original life forms.

As you may have recently noticed, God is back in vogue today in America. *Time* and *Newsweek* can't do enough feature stories on the subject, including cover stories, and the best-seller lists are full of God books. (Surprisingly, they're all on atheism or theism. Not one is on agnosticism.) As I am writing these words, God's son's mother is on the cover of *Newsweek*, April 12, 2010. Indeed, in speaking about the current popularity of God that has spawned "innumerable books and lecture series," *Newsweek*, in its November 2, 2009, edition, said that three atheists alone, Richard Dawkins, Christopher Hitchens, and Sam Harris, "together have sold more than 3 million copies [of their books] worldwide." That is a staggering number of books where sales of just 50,000 copies usually constitute a best-seller.

Now, if you want a haircut, you go to a barber, right? And you go to a supermarket if you want groceries. So if you want to find out what justification there is for atheism, don't you go to the main books written by the current leading lights of that belief? Particularly since they've had the benefit of their predecessors' thoughts and writings? This is especially true if you're not just a reader but an author like me who is writing a book on agnosticism. I wanted to know what these three leading atheists, so-called New Atheists, had to say.

In my various investigations throughout my career, I have found, and have come to be comforted by, a reality that has never failed me yet. If you start out with a valid premise (not an ultimate conclusion), virtually everything you discover thereafter falls into place, almost an inevitable, coalescent package. The things that don't are distinctly aberrational and do not rock the boat as it sails toward its destination of a correct and inviolate conclusion.

In this case, because the core belief of these three atheistic authors was so intrinsically unsound—not their belief God does not exist, which is a conclusion that is not unsound and may very well be correct, but that they *knew*, or just about knew, that he didn't exist—I likewise just about knew that they could not present any solid evidence or even make any persuasive arguments (my valid premise) for the proposition that there is no God. Although I had a completely open mind, I therefore surmised that I would find their books, as I did the writings of atheists I had read in the past (such as Ludwig Feuerbach, Friedrich "God Is Dead" Nietzsche, Auguste Comte, Albert Camus) to be totally unconvincing. But I did not imagine—and therefore, I have to say, I was actually somewhat shocked—that two of the three books could not even legitimately be called serious books on atheism. Indeed, believe it or not, only one of the three authors, Dawkins, even makes a serious attempt to justify his belief in atheism, but he does it so poorly that not only should it be dismissed out of hand, but, as we shall see, it has placed his very credibility in issue. Let's look at the intellectual poverty and flabbiness of atheism by discussing the main books of these three most prominent purveyors of atheism today, starting with the inimitable Christopher Hitchens.

Hitchens, who passed away this year, has been hailed as "one of the most brilliant journalists of our time" (*London Observer*) and was ranked number five on a list by *Foreign Policy* of the "top 100 public intellectuals." The chain-smoking, hard-drinking British bohemian who charmed the Eastern literary cognoscenti was a very prolific writer of books and essays, had an almost encyclopedic knowledge of historical events, and spoke and wrote in a richly textured way. However, for all his intellectual flourishes, his elevated IQ, his obligatory allusions to Proust and French words and phrases in his conversational English, and for all he's read and written, what Hitchens unfortunately could not purchase, since it cannot be purchased, was common sense, the sine qua non (if Hitchens can resort to French to impress, why can't I to Latin?) to any intelligent writing and oratory. We all know that there is no automatic correlation between intelligence and common sense. IQ doesn't seem to translate that way.

To give you just a few examples of the essential Hitchens, although Saddam Hussein had nothing to do with 9/11 and was as much of an imminent threat to the security of this country as the reader of this book or an aunt of mine who lives up in Minnesota, the cerebral Hitchens felt we had "no alternative" but to invade Iraq. (If any reader disagrees with what I have just said, I would suggest they read a 2008 book of mine on the Iraq war.)

Even though President Bill Clinton had only had consensual sex outside of marriage and tried to cover it up, Hitchens was absolutely outraged at Clinton and fulminated that he should be impeached, convicted, and driven out of office—that is, the will of the American people in the 1992 national election should be nullified. If any reader is, in my mind, so removed from logic, common sense, and reality as to agree with Hitchens on this, there's probably nothing I can say to enlighten him. In an imperfect parallel, it's like what I told a student of mine in a criminal law class I taught one night a week years ago at a Los Angeles law school when he asked me a particularly bad question, "That's a question that requires more than an answer."

Remarkably, Hitchens had nothing good to say about Mother Teresa, even referring to her as "hell's angel" and her supposedly humanitarian work as only "a myth." And he recalls that when he and his friends in London town "heard that JFK had been killed, we drank champagne." One of the latest examples of Hitchens being Hitchens is when he announced two years ago that he (along with fellow atheist Dawkins) was planning to make a citizen's arrest, mind you, of Pope Benedict for crimes against humanity when Benedict came to London.

But enough.

In Hitchens' recent book, *God Is Not Great*, it turns out that the book is primarily not even about God but, as the subtitle of his book declares, about *How Religion Poisons Everything*. Hitchens apparently believes that by slaying the dragon of organized religion, an unworthy opponent, he is therefore slaying God, an obvious non sequitur, since it presupposes that you cannot have God without religion. And Hitchens does a poor job at that of slaying organized religion and the tenets upon which it relies for sustenance.

Hitchens' book is splendid if one wants historical and literary allusions, clever and sometimes eloquent writing by an accomplished wordsmith, stories and tales of interesting people he has met and experiences he has had in his globe-trotting life. But if you want an intelligent, logical, and incisive polemic on why God doesn't exist, I'd have to be magnanimous to give his book a grade of D. He makes only superficial references to first cause, prayer, and free will. Indeed, he doesn't even bother to discuss important subjects like the inherent contradictions in the Christian God's supposed makeup, the holy trinity, the born-again doctrine, and others that are required for any serious book on God and religion. It's nothing short of remarkable that Hitchens' book, though entertaining, can even be considered, as it is by many, to be a serious book on atheism, or even religion.

On those few occasions in his book when Hitchens does address an important issue on the question of God's existence, like intelligent design, I, for one, had a difficult time understanding, from his oblique and abstract prose, how most of what he writes even relates to the issue at hand. He tells one vignette after another that is wide of the mark. But a linguistic archaeologist would be able to discern that Hitchens apparently believes in evolution as the answer to intelligent design. He also barely manages, here and there, to make the point that as an intelligent designer, God could have done a better job—for example, he shouldn't have commanded so many of his creatures to treat hogs as if they were demons or lepers, or created a sun that "is getting ready to explode and devour its dependent planets like some jealous chief or tribal deity."

Hitchens, in his discourse, seems unable to focus clearly on a line of thought for more than two or three paragraphs at the very most, and virtually never strikes a solid blow, only glancing ones at best. His argumentation is so scattered it's almost like that of someone who has just been awakened out of his sleep in the middle of the night by a fire and hasn't gotten his bearings yet.

Even when Hitchens' argumentation is reasonably focused, he often misfires. For instance, he writes, "The best argument I know *for* [For? Not against?] the highly questionable existence of Jesus is this. His illiterate living disciples left us no record [what about the purported gospels of Matthew and John and the epistles of Peter?], and in any event could not have been 'Christians' since they were never to read those later books in which Christians must affirm belief, and in any case had no idea that anyone would ever found a church on their master's announcements." (What conceivable relevance to the issue of the existence of Jesus would the latter two clauses have?) Hitchens goes on to write, "There is scarcely a word in any of the later-assembled gospels to suggest that Jesus wanted to be the founder of a church, either." So what? Isn't that a point of monumental irrelevance? While we're on the New Testament, Hitchens makes the astonishing statement that the four authors of the Gospels "cannot agree on anything of importance." The reality is that they do not disagree on anything of importance, only insignificant details here and there.

As a lawyer before a jury, Hitchens, lacking in the art of persuasion and advocacy, would have a very hard time finding a case he could win. One of his problems is that in his periphrastic fog, he sometimes doesn't even stop to ask himself if the evidence he is offering is helpful or harmful to the argument he is making. Take his chapter on pigs. He is very exercised over Judaism's and Islam's prohibition on the eating of pork (Judaism: Deuteronomy 14:8; Islam: Sura 16:117). But unless Hitchens is a closet proponent of cannibalism, why would he then proceed to argue that "this fine beast [pig] is one of our fairly close cousins. It shares a great deal of our DNA, and . . . if recent advances in cloning [can] create a hybrid, a 'pig-man' is the most probable outcome." But if we humans are that close to a pig, isn't that an argument *against* eating our porcine relatives? As a nice little tag to his argument, we learn from Hitchens "that children, if left unmolested by rabbis and imans, are very drawn to pigs, especially to baby ones."

I'll give this to Hitchens. When, in speaking of the pernicious influence of religion, he says, "Religion kills," I agree. He fails to add, however, that secularism and science don't do too bad a job in this area either.

Actually, Hitchens can't find one good word, one syllable, to say about religion, believing, like Voltaire, that religion is a tree that has borne only the fruits of death and suffering. Though we know religion, as it is said, (believed, by the masses to be true, by most philosophers to be false, and by rulers to be useful) has caused untold misery and tragedy in life, I, for one, have no way of knowing whether or not its deleterious nature outweighs its benefits. A fellow atheist of Hitchens, but one who doesn't write or think with Hitchens' incoherence, is Daniel C. Dennett, distinguished professor of philosophy at Tufts University. Dennett writes in his fine, best-selling book on religion, *Breaking the Spell*, that religion often "makes powerful and talented people more humble and patient, it provides sturdy support for many people who desperately need help staying away from drink or drugs or crime. People who would otherwise be self-absorbed or shallow or crude or simply quitters are often enabled by their religion, given a perspective on life that helps them make the hard decisions that we all would be proud to make."

There are those who say that religion only appeals to people who wish to imbue their lives with meaning in the face of all evidence to the contrary. But whatever the basis for the appeal, religion does indeed give many a sense that we are here for a reason, that life is not an empty, accidental adventure. Indeed, for a great many, religion is their secure anchor in life, without which they would be as lost and bewildered as sheep without a shepherd. And we all know that a religious belief in God gives millions of people an equanimity and strength to overcome fear of the unknown ("It is fear that first brought Gods into the world," Roman satirist Petronius said) and the darkness of death they would not have without it.

But to Hitchens, religion was virtually all bad. If I may be so presumptuous, that's not an intelligent position to take. However, to Hitchens' credit, and admirably, he spoke with disarming candor about himself, had the courage of his convictions, and no one could question his brilliant mind.

Sam Harris writes in a highly coherent and intelligent way in his international best-seller *The End of Faith: Religion, Terror, and the Future of Reason*. The problem for atheists is that the book is only a very indirect attack, if one at all, on the existence of God. Nowhere does Harris expressly say he doesn't believe God exists or even why he is an atheist. Indeed, I don't believe the word "atheism" is even mentioned once in the book. Though he refers to God in many places in his book, and talks up, down, and all around the issue, the closest I could find to any position of his on the existence of God is when he says, in one sentence of his 347-page book, "Biological truths are simply not commensurate with a designer God, or even a good one." That's it?! And if Hitchens notably avoided most of the tough issues that should be discussed in any serious book on atheism, Harris does him one better by not discussing any of them, not even, like Hitchens did, intelligent design.

What he does do is take on the very easy issue of faith (easy, that is, to knock down) and succeeds very well in proving his point that faith is a sworn enemy of reason, and blind faith, which is everywhere among the religious of the world, frequently leads to violence and tragedy, something that all of us already know, though Harris perhaps does as good a job as any before him in making this point. But where does he even attempt to destroy the basic theological principles upon which Christian thinkers, not the unthinking masses, predicate their faith and belief in God, like intelligent design and first cause? He doesn't.

Virtually the only time that Harris even remotely touches upon any substantive issue that you would expect an unbeliever in God to deal with in depth concerns the incompatibility of the virtues of God that religion ascribes to him. And Harris, in a two-sentence allusion to the problem of incompatibility of virtues, could hardly be more wrong and off base. He talks about "the problem" of reconciling "an omnipotent and omniscient God in the face of evil" as being "insurmountable." But not only isn't it insurmountable, it doesn't even rise to the dignity of being easy since the problem is nonexistent. Isn't it so very obvious that an all-powerful and all-knowing God could also be evil? Only being all-powerful and all-good (all-loving, all-benevolent) are incompatible with the horrors of the world. This reality has been discussed for centuries by the scholars of atheism and needs no citation. Even everyday atheists know this and have expressed it countless times. It's one of the main reasons that they became atheists. For instance, an article in the January 25, 2010, edition of *Newsweek* on the earthquake devastation of Haiti quotes a former Christian, now an atheist, as saying, "I just got to a point where I couldn't explain how something like this could happen if there's a powerful and loving God in charge of the world."

It's actually surprising that Harris' book is even perceived as a book on atheism. I suspect it was for two reasons. One, everyone considers Harris to be an atheist. Two, Harris, like Hitchens, seems to believe something that is so wrong it is startling that someone of his intellect wouldn't see it immediately—that gutting religion (as Harris tries to do by his technique of decimating faith that fosters religion) does not, *ipso facto,* topple God. In the 2005 edition of Harris' book, he has a brief Afterword in which he writes about some of the criticism he received on his book—along, I would wager, with many more letters of praise—from readers around the world. He writes these words: "As almost every page of my book is dedicated to exposing the problem of religious faith, it is ironic that some of the harshest criticism has come from atheists who feel that I have betrayed their cause. . . . *If there is a book that takes a harder swing at religion*, I'm not aware of it." In other words, I've destroyed religion, and therefore I've destroyed God. But does Harris actually believe that there can be no God without religion? Indeed, that there can be no belief in a creator, a supreme being, without one being, concomitantly, a member of some organized religion or religious faith? How can anyone believe this? Yet this, apparently, is what at least Harris and his colleague Hitchens believe.

Though what I have said is so obvious it does not require supporting evidence, a February 2010 Pew Research Center national poll found that among eighteen-to twenty-nine-year-olds who are unaffiliated with any religion, 34 percent nevertheless still have an "absolutely certain belief" in God. Among the unaffiliated aged thirty and older, 37 percent do. Unless it is Harris' belief that a mere belief in God, where the believer does not identify himself with any recognized religion, is itself a religion (a highly unorthodox position, religion normally referring to a fundamental set of beliefs agreed upon by a number of people or sects), I just don't understand his and Hitchens' thinking. To believe that one can destroy God or a belief in the existence of God—the objective of all atheists who write on the subject—by simply destroying religion is too obvious a non sequitur and fallacy to be worthy of discussion. The antithesis of God is no God, not no religion. If one wants to prove there is no God, eviscerating religion is only a first step. One is only halfway home.

Although, as it's been said, there are many dawns that have yet to shed their light, it is my belief that the last half of the journey will never be traversed by man, mankind's knowledge never setting foot in this sphere.

When I hear so many theists and atheists pontificating on how they know God does or does not exist, I can only smile at the irrationality and, yes, vanity of the notion. They might not know how much money is in their wallet, or food in their refrigerator, or gasoline in their gas tank, or even what their loved ones would like for Christmas, and they don't know whether it's going to rain or shine tomorrow, or what happened to that important paper they lost or misplaced yesterday, or who is right around the corner, but they damn well know there is or is not a God way up there. My position is capsulized in the earlier quote of Gertrude Stein and in that of a leading Zen master who once said about the ultimate questions of God and the universe, "There's really nothing left to do but have a good laugh." If Freud could exclaim in exasperation on his deathbed, "What do women want?" (this may be apocryphal), I don't think Stein and the Zen master, addressing an even greater mystery, are being too flippant in their words.

The thinking of Harris and many other atheists is that because belief in God is based on faith, if they can demonstrate the invalidity of faith as a basis for belief in God, this *justifies their belief that there is no God*. But I submit that there is a problem with this thinking. If the fulcrum of the debate is faith, since faith can be defined as the belief in something that cannot be proved by evidence, why isn't the belief by atheists that there is no God any less of a faith-based belief than the belief by theists that there is? And if so, isn't that sufficient reason for both atheism and theism to fold their tents and go home? To illustrate the weakness of the atheistic philosophy and putting the shoe on the other foot, what would their reaction be if theists said to them, "Since your belief that there is no God is based solely on faith, not evidence, this is complete justification for our belief that there *is* a God"? They'd think the theists were crazy. Well then . . .

Most atheists only *believe* there is no God. A very vocal and substantial minority, however, say they *know* God does not exist. But wouldn't these atheists have to be *all-knowing* to know there is no God, i.e., wouldn't they have to have as much knowledge as Christianity says God has to *know* there is no God? And because all rational people *know* that their store of knowledge is very limited, oftentimes even about the most mundane things in life, for these atheists to say they know that God, the greatest mystery of all, doesn't exist, is, of course, foolish in the extreme.

Lastly, I want to spend more time on someone who epitomizes supposedly the best that atheism has to offer. And if I can demonstrate that his best can hardly be any worse, it's sad to realize that it's downhill from him in the world of atheism.

At my ripe age, I obviously have seen many people high up in their profession who, under the weakest of microscopes, clearly do not deserve to be. For example, in other writings of mine I have shown that if the average prominent trial lawyer met his reputation out on the street, they wouldn't recognize each other. But I do have to say that it is rare to see someone so painfully devoid of substance (at least on the issue of God) occupy *the* top position in his field as is the case of Richard Dawkins, the evolutionary biologist and Charles Simonyi Professor of the Public Understanding of Science at Oxford University. You see, Dawkins is generally acclaimed to be the world's leading atheist. A *Los Angeles Times* review of his best-seller *The God Delusion* refers to him as the "ayatollah of atheism."

The major magazines of the world seek him out for interviews, and the *New York Times Book Review* made its review of his book *The God Delusion,* which reportedly has sold more than 1.5 million copies, the cover review. He speaks to standing-room-only crowds for hefty fees wherever he goes and has become something close to a rock star in the New Atheist firmament, with his followers flaunting T-shirts, even bumper stickers, with his words and/or likeness on them. I am devoting the time I am to Dawkins here because if he is the world's leading proponent of atheism today, yet he can be so strikingly weak and unsound in his reasoning, this underlines, even italicizes, the intellectual barrenness of atheism.

Actually, Dawkins is so shallow in his arguments on behalf of atheism that there is surprisingly little for me to write about. But there is enough there for us to see that, although Dawkins is a distinguished scholar who writes well in prose that is chock-full, like Hitchens, of historical fact and cultural allusions, when it comes to the basics on the issue of God, he is embarrassingly superficial.

The heart of Dawkins' book *The God Delusion* is, by definition, in his fourth chapter, which he titles "Why There Almost Certainly Is No God."[2] In a writer and thinker the stature of Dawkins, I wasn't expecting to find banal deception, but in my opinion I unfortunately did. Or at least something very close to it. In his book, most importantly Chapter 4, Dawkins relies so heavily on Charles Darwin to support his position of atheism that one could say that without Darwin, Dawkins' hero, there would be no Chapter 4 and hence no book. The problem is that in Darwin's *The Autobiography of Charles Darwin,* which was written in 1876 but published in 1887, five years after his death, he wrote that "when I wrote *The Origin of Species*" (published in 1859 and up to this day the principal text on evolution) the "conclusion was strong in my mind about that time that I deserved to be called a theist." He went on to acknowledge that "very gradually, with many fluctuations," that conclusion had become "weaker," and at the time he wrote his autobiography in 1876, his position was that "the mystery of the beginning of all things is insoluble by us, and I for one must be content to remain an agnostic."

The last known statement by Darwin on his theological belief was in a July 7, 1879, letter from him to his friend the Reverend John Fordyce. In this letter, written just three years before his death, he wrote that it "was absurd to doubt that a man may be an ardent theist *and* an evolutionist." (Charles, you never met Richard Dawkins, who as recently as an October 5, 2009, interview in *Newsweek* declared that his book *The God Delusion* "did make a case against that compatibility.") Darwin went on to write, "In my most extreme fluctuations *I have never been an atheist in the sense of denying the existence of God.* I think generally (and more and more as I grow older) but not always, that an agnostic would be the most correct description of my state of mind."

Inasmuch as Dawkins relies very heavily on Darwin to make his case for atheism, even strongly indicating that a belief in evolution almost inevitably leads any intelligent person to atheism, didn't the thought enter Dawkins' mind that it would have been the right thing for him to inform his readers of Darwin's self-description? You know, wouldn't it have been sporting of the Englishman to have found the space somewhere in his 416-page book to mention this uncomfortable truth? It's not that Dawkins couldn't legitimately still be an atheist after learning that Darwin was not one himself. It's just that it's very clear, at least to me, that this supposed scholar and man of letters had a responsibility not to hide Darwin's agnosticism from his readers.[3] Though Dawkins says that Darwin "made it possible [for him] to be an intellectually fulfilled atheist," what would his readers have felt if they knew that Darwin himself didn't feel that way?

You know, as a trial lawyer, even in a strong case I almost always had something that didn't quite fit into the thrust and mosaic of my argument. That's typically the very nature of a criminal case. But I didn't ignore this thing, such as a piece of evidence, and hope that the jury would fail to detect this weakness in my case. I confronted this weakness head-on and did the best I could to deal with it. Quite apart from the issue of fairness, it also reflects on the all-important issue of a lawyer's credibility in the eyes of the jury. It is my opinion that—consciously, I assume—Dawkins decided to see if he could get away with his glaring omission. I say I assume "consciously" because Darwin's theism and later agnosticism are well known to all Darwinists, as Dawkins is. I mean, I can't exonerate Dawkins of deception without convicting him of having an abysmal lack of knowledge and scholarship.

In *The God Delusion*, Dawkins correctly explains the creationist position of intelligent design. It's the argument of improbability that incredibly complex biological things like the human eye could not have come about by random chance. Hence, there must have been a designer, and that designer is God. Dawkins properly objects that a "deep understanding of Darwinism teaches us to be wary of the easy assumption that design is the only alternative to chance, and teaches us to seek out graded ramps of slowly increasing complexity"—that is, evolution. Fine. So evolution is another possible alternative. Many people would probably agree on this. But how does one leap, in an Olympian way, from Darwinism being "an alternative" to intelligent design, to Dawkins' conclusion "why there *almost certainly* is no God"? Dawkins doesn't say.

Even if we assume, for the sake of argument, that there is evidence of Darwin's theory of evolution (as most but not all biologists agree), whereas there is no evidence of an umbilical cord between God and the animate world of humans, animals, plants, and so on, this fact, per se, doesn't eliminate a sensible belief in God. We only have to look to Darwin's own declared beliefs for this reality; beliefs, as indicated earlier, Dawkins was hell-bent on keeping from his readers.

Intelligent design, aka "the argument from design," is also invoked by creationists (those who believe in the account in Genesis of God creating the universe and mankind) to explain the incredible complexity and order of the universe. Again, they say, the statistical improbability of this happening by chance is far, far too high to warrant consideration. And hence, all of this must be the handiwork of an intelligent designer—namely, God.

Dawkins knows that Darwin's theory of evolution in the animate world of humans, animals, and plants cannot directly help him with the inanimate world; that is, the rest of the universe. However, still desperately clinging to Darwin, he argues that Darwin, in a way, can still be used to help him overcome the argument of intelligent design as to this inanimate world. "By [Darwin] raising our consciousness" of an alternative to design in the *animate* world, he maintains, "we all should feel, deep in our bones, suspicious of the very idea of design" in "the *inanimate* world."

But in this inanimate world, Dawkins takes the superficiality of his thinking to new depths in his attempt to disprove the existence of God. He actually says that "any entity capable of intelligently designing something as improbable as the universe would have to be even *more* improbable" than the universe he created. So? Who is Dawkins to know, or even have a reason to believe, that a creator would be incapable of such complexity? Because Dawkins' answer is no answer at all, I thought that this possibly was just loose writing on his part, and surely elsewhere in his chapter written to demolish the notion of God he would never repeat an articulation so poor and so nonresponsive to the issue. But I was wrong.

It is well known that there are certain immutable components of the laws of physics—usually referred to as "fundamental constants" dealing with things like oxygen, hydrogen, and carbon dioxide levels, and stated in numbers (e.g., 0.007 hydrogen)—the slightest deviation from which would end life as we know it. Dawkins writes:

> The theist says that God, when setting up the universe, tuned the fundamental constants of the universe so that each lay in its Goldilocks [i.e., habitable] zone for the production of life. It is as though God had . . . knobs that he could twiddle, and he carefully tuned each knob

to its Goldilocks value. . . . [But] a God capable of calculating the Goldilocks values for the [many] numbers would have to be at least as improbable as the finely tuned combination of numbers itself. . . . A supremely complex and improbable entity who needs an even bigger explanation than the one he is supposed to provide.

And such an entity, he says, is "very improbable indeed." In other words, Dawkins doesn't believe that such an entity exists because its complexity makes it too improbable.

But as John McEnroe would say, Dawkins "cannot be serious." Dawkins evidently means to prove the nonexistence of God by simply saying he doesn't believe that any being could be that complex and hence have such power. That level of reasoning is so intellectually plebian (actually, almost child-like; you know, "Dad, you say that God created the world, but I don't believe he could be that powerful") that one would think no self-respecting atheist would want to be associated with it. In the first place, if we, including Dawkins, can conceive of the universe being incredibly complex (we don't have to conceive of it, we know it is), why can't we conceive of the entity that created it being even more complex? Isn't it likely he *would* be? Also, why is the complexity of the universe the ceiling of our imagination?

Take computers as just one example. As I have said, I don't have one, but I hear all the time about how complex today's computers are. Yet people have been saying this about computers for years. And with each new system, the computer makers are convinced that their machine is the most advanced that they or anyone else has ever manufactured. But we all know that before the sun goes down, someone, somewhere, is in the process of making an even more advanced and complex computer. There never seems to be a ceiling of complexity beyond which a computer cannot go. And since humans make these computers, we have two options, both of which are inhospitable to Dawkins' argument. Either humans are more complex than the incredibly complex computers they create, which, by analogy, defeats Dawkins' argument, or they are less complex, which also defeats Dawkins' argument that presupposes that something complex (the universe) could only have been created by something as complex or even more so.

In any event, you don't defeat the existence of God by simply saying you find such an entity too improbable to believe. (Your adversary, thank you very much, happens to believe what you disbelieve. As geneticist Francis Collins, director of the National Institutes of Health in Bethesda, Maryland, and a self-identified Christian believer, says, "My God is not improbable to me. He has no need of a creation story for himself or to be fine-tuned by something else. God is the answer to all of those 'How must it have come to be' questions.") It would seem that someone of even rather dull intelligence would know this. Since Dawkins is a man of high intelligence, this gives rise to the possibility that Dawkins, unable to produce common sense to support his position, decided to rely on the hope that his startlingly inferior argument would go over the heads of his readers without their feeling the breeze. (If this is true, based on the sales of his book his gamble apparently paid off.)

You defeat the notion of God's existence in the area of intelligent design by accepting, for the sake of argument, the Christian belief that God is so all-intelligent and all-powerful that he is capable of designing the universe; indeed, being transcendent, he is capable of doing anything. And then, I would think, you point out that if God is that intelligent and powerful, he never would have done what Christians claim he did. (For a fuller discussion of this issue of intelligent design, see Chapter 6 of this book.)

At this point, the reader might be thinking that Dawkins *must* have some *other* more credible argument that hasn't been mentioned for his belief that there is no God. He couldn't be the world's leading atheist with such an anemic argument as his law of probability. But, alas, he does not. In Dawkins' book, he acknowledges that his improbability argument against God's existence (that God is more improbable than the improbability of the universe) is "the central argument" of his book.[4] (What makes this even worse is that as bad as Dawkins' argument is, it's not even his. Though he doesn't inform his readers whose idea it was, it was a fellow Brit of Dawkins, Percy Bysshe Shelley, who set it forth in his 1814 essay, *A Refutation of Deism: In a Dialogue*. See endnote discussion.)

Was there any argument *at all* other than his "central" one that Dawkins used to rebut intelligent design? Yes, a secondary one, his "anthropic principle" (a term coined by British mathematician Brandon Carter more than thirty years earlier) argument. As he explained it to *Time* magazine, "Maybe [*maybe?* So Dawkins is admitting that he is giving wings to his imagination here] the universe we are in is one of a very large number of universes. [I thought the dictionary definition of universe was everything that exists, the totality of all things, known and unknown. Hence, there cannot be multiple universes, although such a notion is popular today in the scientific community.] The vast majority will not contain life because they have the wrong gravitational constant or the wrong this constant or that constant. But as the number of these universes [that Dawkins says *might* exist] climbs, the odds mount that a tiny minority of universes [like the one we know that contains earth] will have the right fine-tuning." Dawkins says in his book that "the anthropic principle kicks in to explain that we have to be in one of those universes." The most acclaimed atheist of today has the effrontery to present a pure fantasy of his (and a virtually impossible one at that, unless one wants to run the zeros of improbability to the end of hundreds of pages) as actual evidence that there's no God, and he does it, I assume, without even blushing.

Elsewhere in Dawkins' book, he completely ignores major issues like free will, the born-again Christian doctrine, and the contradiction of God being all-powerful and all-good (he does talk of a supposed contradiction of his being omniscient and omnipotent—actually, as we have discussed, no contradiction at all), and he dismisses the extremely important cosmological, first-cause argument for God's existence out of hand with just a few brief paragraphs.

Why Dawkins has been elevated onto such a high intellectual pedestal in the debate on God is beyond my comprehension.

⤬

THERE HAVE BEEN A CONSIDERABLE NUMBER of books on atheism down through the years, in none of which have I ever found an irresistible argument for atheism's conclusion that God does not exist. As previously indicated, I have focused here only on the three leading atheists of today and their main books not only because they are the de rigueur authors on the subject today but also because they had access to the best of all books on the subject that came before them. Yet, as I hope you have seen, *they have virtually nothing of value to say*. What does that tell you about the intellectual power and virility of atheism?

What strikes me about these three atheist authors is that each is afflicted with the very same auditory idiopathy that apparently whispers in their ears that they can write a book about atheism without, remarkably, having to deal with most of the issues. I shouldn't have to state the obvious that any author who writes on a subject has to discuss, in depth, the issues central to that subject. In a parallel, if I'm prosecuting a case of first-degree murder, there are five issues I *have* to deal with at a minimum. Did the defendant, or did he not, kill the victim? If so, was there, or was there not, any legal justification, such as self-defense, for his act? At the time of his act, did he have malice aforethought (intent to kill)? Was his intent to kill premeditated? And can I prove my case beyond a reasonable doubt? It would be inconceivable for me, or any prosecutor, to prosecute such a case without directly confronting not one or two or three or four but all five of these issues. It's an automatic. Yet these three leading atheists, out of either considerable hubris or stupidity, think they can write a serious book propounding their belief in atheism without discussing all or even most of the many issues that have to be discussed.

What's perhaps even more astonishing is that they have gotten away with it, and very well indeed. This can only be attributable to the gullibility of their millions of readers. Apparently, all that is required of them is that they be polished writers (all three), entertaining literary raconteurs who have a way with words (Dawkins and particularly Hitchens), intelligent and intellectual (all three), and that they declare (in Harris' case at some prior time) their atheism. The fact they do not confront most of the major issues and present an intellectually sound case for their position is apparently irrelevant.

My God, life has never been that easy for me. Has it been for you folks reading this book? In this book I *will* address and struggle with all the *major* issues dealing with the question of God's existence, and in a fair amount of depth. Whether or not you agree with me is a separate issue.

The invalidation and demythologization of religious beliefs and tenets seem to be the main mission of atheists. And when they think they've succeeded, they proclaim that God doesn't exist. But as indicated earlier, this is terribly illogical. Just because religion makes no sense doesn't mean that God doesn't. It may mean only that religion is a weak adversary. In an imperfect but nevertheless instructive parallel, if A defeats B at tennis, he has the right to proclaim that he is the best player in the world only if B is arguably the second best player. But if B is a proverbial tennis bum, A's defeat of him doesn't establish A's supremacy in the game of tennis at all. Atheists employ this modus operandi because they either know or sense that they can't make a case for God's nonexistence without the help of their favorite whipping boy, religion.

I should add that there are few better examples of the intellectual bankruptcy of atheism than in the case of John W. Loftus' book, *Why I Became An Atheist*. When I said earlier that Hitchens, Harris, and Dawkins were the three leading atheists today, I should have added, "in the public mind." Though Loftus is virtually unknown to the general public, in the small community of atheistic scholars, he is more revered than the aforementioned three. For instance, as David Mills, author of *Atheist Universe*, says: "John W. Loftus is to atheism what Tiger Woods is to golf, or what Babe Ruth is to baseball."

As opposed to Hitchens, Harris, and Dawkins, who, though they give no good reason for being an atheist, at least do not create for themselves, by the very title of their book, the express burden of showing why each became an atheist, the title of Loftus' book suggests he intends to do just that. But his book (a polemically weak but substantive and scholarly tome) does no such thing. In fact, Loftus informs his readers at the beginning of his book not that he is going to explain to them why he became an atheist, the very title of his book, but instead, he says, "why I rejected Christianity." He goes on to say, "I consider this book to be one single argument against Christianity, with each chapter as a subset of that *one* argument." Indeed, one has to wait until page 403 of his 416-page book before he finally gets around to trying to explain why he is an atheist, and the "Babe Ruth of atheism" strikes out, swinging at nothing but air. "I am an atheist. There is no God," he declares. "And there is at least one reason [he gives no other substantive ones] for me not to believe in God, and that is because this universe is absurd when we try to figure it out," i.e., if you can't figure the universe out (what human could?), that must mean the universe had no creator, a simply embarrassing non sequitur.

The reader might be interested to know that between the hardcover edition of this book and the paperback you are now reading, I spoke to two separate groups—one in Los Angeles and the other in Santa Barbara, California—consisting mostly of atheists. I challenged each group to give me a good argument for the nonexistence of God that I could not easily show to be a non sequitur, and they were unable to do so. Now, maybe atheists do have such an argument, but if they do, what is it? And why haven't they been telling us about it in their books?

Although I don't know whether or not there is a God, if there isn't, I do not believe that atheistic dogma leads one rationally to that conclusion.

❧

AS WE LEAVE THE ARISTOCRATS OF ATHEISM BEHIND, what type of analysis do we get from the rank and file of atheist writers? On those

few occasions when they leave home alone without the crutch of religion at their side to bash, and they attempt to prove the illogic of God,
they are usually reduced to syllogistic and metaphysical absurdities
that are so bad they don't even warrant refutation. They all involve setting up their own straw men and then knocking them down. Indeed,
the efforts of these writers are so bad that in giving you some examples
by respected atheists that are published in books and peer-driven jour-
nals, I shall refrain, for their benefit, from mentioning their names. Here
are just a few of the many they come up with:

1. If God exists, then he is transcendent, i.e., outside space and
   time.
2. If God exists, then he is omnipresent.
3. To be transcendent, a being cannot exist anywhere in space.
4. To be omnipotent, a being cannot exist everywhere in space.
5. Hence, it is impossible for a transcendent being to be
   omnipresent.
6. Therefore, it is impossible for God to exist.

Another gem:

1. If God exists, then he is omnipresent.
2. If God exists, then he is a person.
3. Whatever is omnipresent cannot be a person.
4. Hence, it is impossible for God to exist.

Makes a heck of a lot of sense to me.

Listen to this atheist. He finally has the answer as to why the world
is a place too filled with misery, horror, conflict, dysfunction, and madness to be described in words. The answer? If there is a God who created all this mess, *he has no mind to think with*. A mindless entity at
the tiller of the world. And we wonder why there is one disaster after
another? I used to, but no more. Here's how this atheist proves his

point. He starts out by saying that "the combined property of being omnipresent and having higher consciousness" is what he calls "omniconsciousness." He then proceeds to light up the room with the brilliant incandescence of his mind:

1. A being with higher consciousness possesses two abilities: (a) the ability to discern between the object and a representation of the object, and (b) the ability to apply concepts and form judgments about objects.
2. If a being has the ability to discern between the object and a representation of the object, and the ability to apply concepts and form judgments, then that being must be able to grasp the difference between the self and nonself.
3. A being is omnipresent when that being occupies or is present in all places, far or near, in all times, past, present, or future.
4. There is nothing that is nonself for an omnipresent being, by [the] definition of omnipresence.
5. So an omnipresent being cannot grasp a difference between the self and nonself.
6. Therefore, an omnipresent being cannot possess higher consciousness.
7. In short, God cannot have a mind because omniconsciousness is impossible.

It all makes sense to me now.

Before I leave atheism, let me ask this question: Who is more irrational, the theist or the atheist? Although I believe they are both irrational, the theist wins the most irrational honor. I say that because nearly all atheists at least reached their clearly untenable conclusion after some rigorous thought, whereas most theists, Pavlovian to the bitter end, reached theirs without exercising their mind at all, determined to elevate ignorance and vapidity to a virtue.

5

Darwin and Evolution

I BELIEVE I HAVE ALREADY DEMONSTRATED that if our thinking is going to be governed by logic, the Christian God cannot exist. On the separate and much tougher issue of whether a non-Christian God created the universe and mankind, I am irretrievably conflicted, and hence agnostic. Let me begin this discussion by briefly examining English naturalist Charles Darwin's theory of evolution. Although some modern evolutionary biologists attempt to minimize Darwin's contribution to evolutionary science, and although Darwin did not know anything about genetics, DNA, and heredity, all critical to evolution, his theory, as set forth in his 1859 book, *On the Origin of Species*, remains to this day the cornerstone of modern biology.

Origin is difficult reading, and every writer I personally have read on the subject has lacked, in my opinion, the ability to clearly communicate his alleged knowledge of all the complexities of Darwin's theory. In other words, as is so often the case in life, these writers are markedly inept in their ability to impart to others what they claim to know. If they truly understood Darwin's evolution well (not being an evolutionary biologist, I certainly don't, and I didn't intend to get an undergraduate, masters, and doctor's degree in biology before I wrote this brief chapter), they all seem intent on keeping their knowledge a secret to their readers. But my understanding of it is that Darwin believed, as he wrote, that "all organic beings which have ever lived on this earth may be descended from some one primordial form," this form being the root of what he called "The great tree of life." Post-Darwin twenty-first-century biology has discovered the first trace of fossil life on earth around 3.5 billion years ago in the form of bacteria—specifically, per American microbiologist Carl Woese, cyanobacteria, known as blue-green algae.[1]

To digress for a moment, this creates a serious problem for the creationists because the earth has been determined to be around 4.5 billion years old. If they are so positive their God exists, and that he is all-intelligent, why would he have created earth and then left it uninhabited by any form of life for 1 billion years? That is, one thousand million years? Indeed, since it is believed the universe is close to 14 billion years old, why would their God let nine and a half billion years go by before creating the earth in his universe, the only body in the universe, creationists say, on which he created man and woman and sent his only begotten son to die for their salvation? It's no answer for them to say, as they continue to do, that the earth (despite radiometric Carbon-14 testing and dating of fossils making a joke out of their assertion) is only 6,000 years old.

Returning to the blue-green algae discovered around 3.5 billion years ago, this living organism, per Darwin's theory, "evolved" through billions of years into countless species, including, of course, man (Homo sapiens), cats, dogs, birds, fish, and plants, of which there are 500,000 separate species alone. Darwinian evolution holds that the early organisms were locked in a fierce struggle with other organisms for food, water, safety—that is, for life itself. In the struggle, only the most fit survived and avoided extinction, allowing them to reproduce. Concomitantly, the struggle for life caused the organisms to change, to adapt to their demanding environment, the changes making them, as indicated, stronger and more complex.

The term that Darwin applied to this process, "natural selection," seems to me, if clarity is the goal, a rather poor selection of words. This is probably why English philosopher and sociologist Herbert Spencer saw the need to call natural selection the "survival of the fittest" in the first volume (of two) of his book *Principles of Biology* in 1864, just five years after Darwin's *On the Origin of Species*. The new term was so obviously more understandable than natural selection that Darwin himself, in his *Autobiography* written several years later, embraced the term, writing, "Everyone who believes, as I do, that all corporeal and mental organs of all beings have been developed through natural selection, or the survival of the fittest, . . ."

It is well known that Darwin's theory has been accepted by the vast majority of the scientific community as one about which there can no longer be any reasonable doubt. In other words, his theory has been accepted as fact by most scientists on how man evolved, and they therefore reject the notion that God created man. Although they may be right, I can say that viscerally I find it difficult to conceptualize the notion of bacteria evolving into Mozart, or, for that matter, any human. Note that we're not just talking about a species changing within itself by becoming stronger and more complex in order to survive, a type of evolution that few would quarrel about, but even taking into consideration the added stimulus of new environments, actually *changing into a completely different species*, many of such transmutations having had to take place for a bacteria to evolve into a human being. And the acknowledged modifications from the smallish (around four and a half feet tall) *Homo habilis* man (the most ancient ancestral representative of the human genus) more than 4.4 million years ago, through the *Homo erectus* man and *Homo neanderthalensis* man, all bipedal and all a part, as is man, of the hominid family (man and his ancestors), really don't help my conceptualization that much. (The now-extinct Neanderthal man was found in a May 2010 study to have DNA 99.7 percent identical to modern man.)

A *USA Today*/Gallup Poll in June 2007 showed that two-thirds of everyday Americans do not believe in evolution, actually believing that God created humans in their present form within the past 10,000 years.

There has been much angst and resistance in some circles to the notion that one of man's ancestors in the chain of evolution was a monkey;

that, as the expression goes, "man evolved [or descended] from monkeys." (In other words, not just that man and monkeys descended from a common ancestor, but that a monkey was one of man's not too distant—at least in terms of evolution—pre-hominid ancestors.) Darwin, in his 1871 follow-up book to *On the Origin of Species* titled *The Descent of Man and Selection in Relation to Sex*, in which he set forth how his theory of evolution applied to humans, spent much time pointing out all of the anatomical as well as mental and emotional similarities there are between monkeys and man. He even went so far as to say that "many kinds of monkeys have a strong taste for tea, coffee, and spirituous liquors: they will also, as I have myself seen, smoke tobacco with pleasure." Then, in jest, "An American monkey, an Ateles, after getting drunk on brandy, would never touch it again, and thus was wiser than many men." Although Darwin never flat out declared that one of man's ancestors was a monkey, almost as if he somehow felt it was unseemly to do so, he managed to say (as had Thomas Huxley's *Evidence as to Man's Place in Nature* eight years earlier in 1863) the very same thing. Speaking of "Quadrumana" (four-footed primates) he said that "there is no justification for placing man in a distinct order." Elsewhere he wrote, "In a series of forms graduating insensibly from some ape-like creature to man as he now exists, . . ." Apes, of course, are tailless or short-tailed monkeys, but Darwin said "the early progenitors of man must have had" bodies "with a tail," which stung Victorian sensibilities at the time.

What I'm about to say may not be correct, but doesn't the very word "evolution" encompass, in its ultimate expression, the fact that the previous life form no longer exists? That it has evolved into a new and higher form? If so, since monkeys still exist, does that mean, perforce, that they (and chimpanzees, the African ape which most resembles man) were not among the distant early progenitors of man? If they were, why are they still around, in zoos and climbing trees in the jungle? Is the answer that the statement should be that "man evolved from *some* monkeys"? But if so, does that not beg the question, why not from the others?*

Although Darwin himself didn't deal specifically with the issue of the absence of extinction of monkeys, he did say in *On the Origin of Species* that "as natural selection acts solely by the preservation of profitable modifications [in the species], each new form will tend . . . to take the place of, *and finally exterminate,* its own less improved parent. . . . Thus, extinction and natural selection will, as we have seen, go hand in hand." What is it I don't understand here?[2]

Just as I find the leap from a bacteria to Mozart too extreme to envision, there is another, shall I say, jarring (though not altogether in a negative way) thought to me. It is said that evolution is a continuing process. What?! You mean, a billion or so years from now we humans may evolve into some form that is as far removed from who we are today as we are today from monkeys? Although I do not believe today everything I believed yesterday, and do wonder if I will believe tomorrow everything I believe today, this seems rather hard to imagine.

Although the traditional view is that humans are a finished product in the evolutionary scheme, the trend today among evolutionists and anthropologists (though there are many in these two disciplines who are skeptics) is the belief that, as Ohio State University anthropologist Jeffrey McKee says, "every species is a transitional species." Indeed, a research study by anthropologists Gregory Cochran and John Hawks presented to the American Association of Physical Anthropologists in March 2007 found that not only is our evolution continuing, it has actually accelerated since around 200,000 years ago, when humans who were considered "anatomically modern" first appear in the fossil record. Richard Dawkins speaks of "gradual continuity" as

*The evolutionist's answer for the fact that monkeys are still around is that they were never a part of the hominid line that led to modern man, monkeys (apes, chimpanzees) only being "distant cousins" of man. But they offer no evidence of when (just speculation that it was somewhere between 4.5 and 30 million years ago), how, and why the monkey broke off from the pre-hominid line.

an "inescapable feature of biological evolution." The ultimate evolutionist himself, Charles Darwin, wrote in his *Autobiography* that "man in the distant future will be a far more perfect creature than he now is."

My completely uneducated guess is to side with the traditionalists. Why? If I can draw a parallel, I believe certain things in life—irrespective of incredible technological advances—never improve for the simple reason that by their very nature they cannot. For instance, there will never be an improvement, other than cosmetic, to television, which was invented in 1929. Why? Because the next step would be to transport you, and millions of others, to the fifty-yard line at a Super Bowl game instead of watching the game on your TV set at home. For the same reason, radio (apart from innovations such as shortwave, CB, and satellite) is the very same today as it was when it was invented by Guglielmo Marconi in 1895. (One Nikola Tesla, some say, may have invented it a few years earlier.) It's not capable of being improved.

Do humans fall into this category? There is no question that we are an exceedingly imperfect lot in so many ways, mostly moral, and could improve vastly at least in this realm. But other than a surgical operation on human nature itself, how would this ever be possible?

⟋

THERE MAY BE ONE PROBLEM with evolution that requires no knowledge of Darwin's theory to discuss, only a modicum of common sense. One article on evolution will say that the fossil record shows transitional or intermediate forms (a life form that died as it was developing into a more advanced form; that is, an aborted transformation among species, such as the discovery, a short while back, of an ancient fish that reportedly had anatomical features found only in land animals). But the next article, in the minority, by those who reject evolution and often endorse creationism, will aver that the fossil record, as discovered by paleontologists and anthropologists, does not show any transitional forms, that there are "missing links"; as pertains to humans, a missing

link in the fossil record between humans and apes, or lower animals.*
And these anti-evolutionists, several of whom are distinguished biologists, challenge the validity of any and all cases offered by the evolutionists. For example, perhaps the most famous alleged transitional
fossil ever is the so-called "First Bird" (formal name, *Archaeopteryx*)
dating to the late Jurassic period around 150 million years ago and
found in 1861 near present-day Munich, Germany. Having characteristics such as jaws with sharp teeth instead of a beak like a bird, yet
wings with feathers for flight, *Archaeopteryx* is widely accepted among
evolutionists as the clear, evolutionary missing link between two major
classes of vertebrates: reptiles (here, a very small dinosaur known as
Compsognathus—not all dinosaurs, which became extinct around 65
million years ago, were huge) and birds, a link that confirms Darwin's
theory of evolution. But creationists embrace the conclusion of some
biologists that *Archaeopteryx* was not an "intermediate" but simply the
"earliest known member of a totally extinct group of birds," the extinction of a species being a common phenomenon. In other words,
Archaeopteryx had no reptilian ancestors.

I am not in a position to have an informed view on whether or not
there are indisputable transitional fossils, although the majority view
among scientists is that there are, as few as they may be. But it has been
argued that if, indeed, the fossil record is devoid of transitional forms,
this itself would seem to defeat the whole theory of evolution. I mean,
it would have to be the greatest coincidence in history if the only organisms that died for which fossils have been found were those organisms that science knows all about and has already assigned names, be
it a flatworm, dinosaur, monkey, or what have you. We'd have to believe
that no organism in a transitional state (and hence having characteristics that we have not seen before) has ever died. They all survived until

---

*As alluded to earlier, many modern evolutionists say that the ape was not one of man's
pre-hominid ancestors, only that they had a common ancestor. And hence, there is no
need to even look for any missing link.

they became organisms that are known to scientists, dying sometime thereafter. I think we can all reject this hypothesis out of hand.

In a confessional passage in *On the Origin of Species*, Darwin himself wrote that by his own theory of natural selection, "innumerable transitional forms must have existed. Why then do we not find them embedded in countless numbers in the crust of the earth? . . . Why is not every geological formation and every stratum full of such intermediate links? Geology assuredly does not reveal any such finely graduated chain; and this, perhaps, is the most obvious and gravest objection which can be urged against my theory." Note that Darwin anticipated the existence of "innumerable" and "countless" transitional forms— suggesting that the extremely rare (if at all) discovery of these forms might not, per Darwin, prove the correctness of his theory.

Darwin, knowing he was on the ropes, theorized that perhaps the reason for the earth's surface not being rich in transitional fossils is that the remains of organic beings are "embedded and preserved for a future age only in masses of sediment sufficiently thick and extensive to withstand an enormous amount of future degradation; and such fossiliferous masses can be accumulated only where much sediment is deposited on the shallow bed of the sea."

So if these fossils are not where Darwin believes they may be, where does that lead us? Certainly not irrevocably or dispositively, but in the direction of a deity creating man in close to his present form.

It should be obvious to the reader that while I do not reject evolution, I am not comfortable with the notion at all. It's not because I take exception to the methodological naturalism (that everything we experience *in* nature can objectively be scientifically explained *by* nature) that led its followers to their conclusion (although creationist Alvin Plantinga would demur that evolutionists are not religiously neutral). Rather, it's the paucity of supporting evidence that evolutionists bring to the table from the vast museum of the earth's surface. As the *New York Times* observed as recently (in evolutionary terms) as October 4, 1982, "The known fossil remains of man's ancestors would fit on a billiard table. That makes a poor platform from which to peer into the mists of the last few million years." The May 1982 edition of *Science Digest* concurred: "The remarkable fact is that all the physical evidence we have for human evolution can still be placed, with room to spare, inside a single coffin. Modern apes, for instance, seem to have sprung out of nowhere. They have no yesterday, no fossil record. And the true origin of modern humans—of upright, naked, toolmaking, big-brained beings—is, if we are to be honest with ourselves, an equally mysterious matter."

However, it has to be conceded that since then, many hominid fossils, some consisting of a substantial portion of the skeleton (e.g., 45% of the skeleton of "Ardi," 4.4 million years old, discovered in Ethiopia in 1994; a virtually complete skull and partial skeleton of a 10–12 year old boy, 1.8 million years old, in South Africa in 2008) have been discovered around the world, though mostly in Ethiopia, Kenya, Tanzania, and South Africa. But still, the number of discovered fossil remains of man's ancestors remain extremely scanty. Richard Dawkins, in his 2009 book, *The Greatest Show on Earth: The Evidence for Evolution*, argues, however, that not only is the fossil record adequate, but he says a "very telling fact" is that "not a single fossil has ever been found *before* it could have evolved." All discovered fossils have been "in the right temporal sequence," according to Dawkins.

Although I have nothing but respect for the phenomenal achievements of science in so many other areas, nowhere has it even remotely come close to taking the first (or tenth, if you will) life form on the planet and, even allowing for many reasonable extrapolations along the way, shown how this life-form, step by step through identifiable succeeding life-form, evolved into present-day man. The most prominent literature on evolution from Darwin's *On The Origin of Species* on through *Evolution: The First Four Billion Years* (edited by Michael Ruse and Joseph Travis, Harvard University Press, 2009) are, because of the terribly inadequate fossil record, glaringly lacking in this regard. And yet, as indicated, science has the aplomb to treat evolution as being as much of an established fact as its having proved that the earth is not flat and the sun does not revolve around the earth.* Although main-stream biology may indeed be right about evolution, I think it can be said that because of all the blank pages in the presentation of its case it has thus far failed to meet its burden of proof.

I think it also can be fairly asked whether science, accustomed to nailing everything down to the shadow of an atom before reaching a conclusion, would uncharacteristically be so certain about a theory so lacking in empirical evidence were it not for its built-in institutional bias that everything in life can be explained by science. Maybe it can. But then again, maybe it can't.

Darwin's theory of evolution is by definition the theory that *living* organisms change in response to environmental conditions, etc. (In-deed, evolution is a concept of biology, which is the study and science of *living* organisms.) For Darwinian natural selection to do its magic, a *living* organism has to have *first* already been in existence. *How is it possible, then, that most evolutionists and atheists believe that evolution is the answer to how man was created, thus negating the belief by theists that it was God who created man?* How could they have this view when, if we accept the theory of evolution, man could only have evolved from a *living* organism, and evolution doesn't even deal with how life origi-nated? Darwin's book is titled *On the Origin of Species*, not *On the Ori-gin of Life*.

---

*Indeed, one of the few unresolved, serious questions remaining in the minds of most scientists today is whether man evolved, predictably and inevitably, from the evolutionary process through very small, slow but steady changes over millions of years (Darwin's concept of gradualism and "descent with modification,"), or evolved in "fits and starts" by chance (so-called "contingency") from fortuitous circumstances; and if the tape were rewound and replayed, and any of the unpredictable circumstances in the long chain of evolutionary antecedents happened to be even slightly different, most likely we would not be here today (theory first introduced in a 1972 paper, *Punctuated Equilibrium* (*Models in Paleobiology*, Freeman, Cooper & Co., Sam Francisco, 1972, pp. 82–115), by famed Harvard paleontologist Stephen Jay Gould and fellow paleontologist Niles El-dredge of the American Museum of Natural History.

Even if science, someday, proves what they as yet have not; namely, the continuum from the first living microorganisms up to man, where have they shown how this first life form (e.g., bacteria) could have been created out of *non*living, inorganic matter?* Unless it does, the alternative of the first organism or living cell being an act of creation remains attractive. Darwin himself, in the last paragraph of his *Origin of Species*, said that "life" was "originally breathed by the Creator into a few forms or into one, . . . [and] from so simple a beginning endless forms most beautiful and most wonderful have been, and are being, evolved."†

If Darwin was wrong, then how did life on earth began? The evolutionists' most devastatingly blank page—particularly to those evolutionists who are also atheists—is page one. There is no more passionate evolutionist than Richard Dawkins whom *Time* called "evolution's foremost polemist." Yet Dawkins, in *The Greatest Show On Earth*, says this: "This [*Greatest Show*] is a book about evidence, and we have *no evidence* bearing upon the momentous event that was the start of evolution on this planet . . . We have no evidence about what the first step making life was."

In any event, if man's search for his definitive ancestry has so far been in vain, is the reason that he has none?

$\mathcal{C}\!\sim$

---

*Darwinism is biological, not prebiological. But could life have originated from the synthesis of prebiological chemicals that may have been present in the prehistoric earth's surface? No laboratory model (e.g., Miller-Urey) has yet confirmed the viability of this theory. Even if this were to occur, one could legitimately ask, Who put the chemicals there?

†Of course, on the other hand, if we start out with the premise that man is the ultimate expression or product of evolution, and God created the first living organism either with the intent and/or knowledge that it would evolve into man, why, instead, wouldn't an intelligent God simply create man at the beginning? Why, as Darwin believed, would he only breathe life into an original life form that would take billions of years to evolve into man? Does Darwin's belief during his theirstic period make any sense?

AS SUGGESTED EARLIER, Darwin believed that in the struggle of organisms and species for survival, they developed physical characteristics to enable them to survive in the environment in which they found
themselves, their highly refined senses of seeing and hearing often cited
as evidence of evolution. But there is one attribute of higher and lower
forms of life, mainly humans and animals, that has been largely ignored,
even by Darwin himself, and that is memory. In Darwin's two main
books, *On the Origin of Species* and *The Descent of Man*, remarkably,
he doesn't have one single reference to human memory. Indeed, his
lone reference to memory is in *The Descent of Man*, where he notes in
just one sentence that "animals have excellent memories for persons
and places." Although much scholarly work has been done on human
memory, curiously, virtually nothing has been written on the evolution
and development of our memory as it pertains to Darwin's theory of
evolution. For example, Stephen Jay Gould's 1,433-page *The Structure
of Evolutionary Theory*, published by Harvard University Press in
2002, doesn't have one word on memory. How did human memory
develop, if indeed it did, into its present extremely refined state? And
can we glean anything from the faculty of memory to assist us in reaching a conclusion on whether there was a creator?

Let me mention a few examples of human and animal memory that
give me pause when the current scientific orthodoxy of evolution is
mentioned. The human example can be multiplied, for all of us, usually
many times a day, but for some reason I never thought about it until
this particular incident. Since then I've thought about it a lot, as it is a
phenomenon that occurs constantly. My wife and I have been going,
off and on, to a small Italian restaurant for many years and know the
owner well. Neither of us has much imagination when it comes to Italian food, and usually we order either spaghetti or mostaccioli, very infrequently ordering a different type of pasta. A couple years ago while
giving our orders to the owner, George, I became adventurous and
said, "George, how is your ravioli?" Immediately—that is, without a

thousandth of a second pause—George answered, "You liked it the last time you tried it a few years ago," which I had forgotten about.

Now, stop to think about this. George, like all of us, has millions of things in the memory bank of his brain and has taken several thousand orders from a great number of other people since I last ordered ravioli, and yet, instantaneously, he answered my question. This is memory, which we have all routinely experienced, developed to an incredibly fine degree. Although, as I've said, I don't have a computer, I am exposed to computers from time to time, as when I'm at the library and ask someone at the reference desk if she has a particular book. The best technical minds have developed and refined computers, but no computer remotely comes close to answering a question as fast as George answered my question on ravioli, and I have to wait several seconds for the assistant at the library to even get anything for me on the computer screen.

What George did, and all of us do, reminds me of the jukeboxes of the 1940s and 1950s. You'd put a nickel or dime in one, press a song selection, then see an arm behind the glass reach over to the left or right side of the jukebox where the records were, grasp the record selected, and place it on the turntable to be played. But the arm only had to retrieve the record from a small collection of perhaps thirty to forty records. And the arm didn't have to go back into the past to do so.

In view of the fact that George had millions of things stored in his memory bank, how in the world could my question cause his mind to instantaneously retrieve this worthless bit of information from among the deluge of information and images that had flooded his mind through the years and put it instantly (not a tenth of a second, but instantly) on the screen of his mind so that he could answer my question? At least to me, this is nothing short of mind-boggling.

A week or so ago a friend of mine was talking about the many parents of great tennis players who had coached their prodigy children in the early part of their careers. When he said "Jimmy Connors' mother"

I instantly said "Gloria" before he had a chance to do so. In fact, I'm not even sure if he was going to do so. I know absolutely nothing about Jimmy Connors' mother (I've never even seen her), except the fact that at some time thirty or so years ago I heard or read that she had coached him. There would have been no reason for me to have ever thought of her even once in the intervening thirty years. Yet in a nanosecond her name came up on the screen of my mind, something that happens to all of us almost daily.

The question is this. Granted, to have survived under Darwin's theory of evolution, memory, like hearing and sight, was necessary. For instance, if a human had no memory of the last time he burned his hand when he exposed it to fire, he'd keep burning his hand, with all types of adverse physical consequences. But although, as an example, the development and interaction of the lens, retina, and iris of the eye are necessary for the vision humans need to survive, what environment was the human species ever exposed to that required, in adapting to it, that it develop its memory to such an unbelievable degree of perfection that human memories can far surpass the most powerful computers in the world? If there were such an environment (and continues to be), then the examples I've given mean nothing. But if there weren't, then it would seem that this incomprehensible perfection of memory could only be a gift. And if it's a gift, it could only come, it would seem, from a creator.

If you agree with me that human memory of even a meaningless occurrence, sometimes many years earlier, and the immediacy (not quickness) with which we can retrieve it from among a stockpile of millions of other occurrences, is virtually miraculous, an example of memory that follows from the animal kingdom is also somewhat the same. I used to have a very rare Siamese cat (lilac point) whose name was Sherlock, but whom I called "the egg." (The word "egg" is old slang and impossible to define except to say it is favorable and those who use the word know exactly when it is right to do so. "He's a good egg." Suffice it to say that this cat, for whom I had a great love, was an egg.)

The egg was so unusual and exotic in his look (his eyes were virtually human) and his personality was so unlike a cat that people would come to our door asking to look at him. Other people who saw him for the first time, like a guest or mailman, would often ask, "What is it?" The consensus was that no one had ever seen a cat that looked or acted quite like him. Everyone, of course, thinks their pet is completely unusual, and most of these wonderful little creatures are, all having special and different personalities. But when other people say your pet is unusual, then you know you have something special.

My wife and I took the egg to the vet on several occasions (each time upon entering the vet's office, he'd let out a loud, very unusual howl that he wouldn't stop, and when we'd later pick him up to take him home, he'd start that howl from that moment and continue it all the way home in the car to the point where we turned the corner and he saw our home), and at both vet's offices several employees, who see thousands of cats and dogs, told us he was the most unusual cat they had ever had. I recall one day my wife and I were sitting on a sofa with the vet in the anteroom. I was holding the egg, and when I looked up, three employees were standing about ten feet away, side by side in silence, staring at Sherlock. When he died, we got about ten letters from attendants at two vet offices sharing our grief over his passing and speaking in superlative terms about how extremely unusual and wonderful he was.

In any event, the egg and I chummed around for several years even though we didn't see eye to eye on any of the important issues of the day. We also would have fierce fights, usually ending with my pinning the egg down on his back for the count of ten, immediately after which he would burst forward with a very angry growl. (Yes, Sherlock had a growl.) Some of our fights resulted in his drawing a small amount of blood from me. One time, at close range, while he was sitting on my chest facing me and we were duking it out, he threw his right paw at my nose in a movement that looked exactly like a right hand thrown by a boxer. As bright as he was, we had so many fights (sometimes provoked by me, sometimes by him) that at least on one occasion the egg was so confused he was licking my face and growling at me at the same time. I gave the egg his share of rough treatment which he loved, and which he knew he had coming, being the dirty egg he was.

You may wonder why I roughed the egg up. Let me try to explain. You know how sometimes something, whatever it is, is just so rich and so good that it hurts you? You know, "I can't take it." Well, the egg was so incredible that he hurt me. So didn't that give me the right, if you know what I mean, to strike back at him for hurting me? I'd pick the egg up by the nape of his neck, and nose to nose I'd tell him what a dirty egg he was, *so* dirty. The egg would listen but wouldn't change his ways, continuing to hurt me with his being too terrific for words.

About picking Sherlock up, cats are notoriously wiry, and this is why it is so difficult to get most of them into a position you may want them to be in, such as while holding them. But the egg was so loose jointed and relaxed that I would sometimes put him on the bed, head at the bottom, and he'd collapse like a rag doll, his head, tail, and four legs being in such an amorphous lump that it would be hard to discern what leg was which. In this same vein, I could pick him up seated in the palm of my hand and carry him anywhere, his being totally relaxed and apparently confident in me, with his legs resting downward. People said they had never seen anything like this before with a cat.

By the way, I didn't mean to suggest earlier that there were nothing but fights between the egg and me because that would be very inaccurate. He knew I loved him very much, and his favorite place in the house was to lie on the bed, facing me, next to one of my lower legs, his head extended over and on top of one of my ankles. And the egg, like me, would never want any bad blood between the two of us to last more than the time it took us to iron out our differences. For instance, now and then, after I had done something to annoy him—it could be nothing more than a look I gave him he didn't appreciate—I'd see him circling slowly around at a distance, a sure sign he was about to attack. When he did, he'd come racing in my direction and crash into me with an indirect (as opposed to head-on) blow, which he knew would allow him to continue on, in the same direction, as he ran like a bat out of hell down the stairs of our home. But in a minute or so, the egg, tail between his legs, would come back up the stairs, kissing fanny and wanting to make up, nuzzling his head against me. I will never forget this incredible creature. I hope you didn't mind my little riff on Sherlock, but I can never stop talking about him once I start.

℮

Getting to the issue, I may have the smallest strain of a devilish streak in me because a few times when the egg was temporarily in repose, I'd slap my hands loudly to see his startled response. But from the first time I did this (maybe a total of two or three times in the ten years the egg enriched my life—he's buried now in a coffin with a commemorative marker in a pet cemetery), when I would thereafter, perhaps fifteen to twenty seconds later, slap my hands again, the loud noise drew absolutely no response from him. Just think about it. The loud noise from my second clap reached Sherlock's ears instantly, and equally instantly he processed the noise in what had to be some small part of his tiny little brain, and from his memory of the last clap being a false alarm, he knew, from his memory, that the second loud clap was pure bull that he didn't have to deal with, so he ignored it, and along with it, me. All of this (the sound reaching his ears, transferring the sound to his little brain for processing, and his deciding not to react) took place not within a second or even a small fraction of a second but instantly, simultaneously with the clap. What computer could ever be developed, by the best human minds, that could possibly duplicate this speed? And in the evolution of the cat species, why would such an unbelievable refinement and perfection of the faculty I described ever be necessary to survive? If it would, the example I gave of my egg is meaningless. But if it would not, what the egg had was a gift, a gift, it would seem, that could come only from a creator.

Although, as indicated, I am not a biologist, one thing does appear reasonably clear to me. As alluded to earlier, although many believe that God and Darwin can't get along—that they are as incompatible as a mouse and a hungry cat, that a belief in evolution necessarily leads one to atheism—that would not appear to be the case, the notions of God and evolution not being mutually exclusive. Only the notions that God created man and that of evolution are. To repeat, Darwin's book is titled *On the Origin of Species,* not *On the Origin of Life.* So at least theoretically a modus vivendi could be reached wherein God could create the universe and the original microorganisms of life, and evolution could take over from there. As indicated, at one point this was the belief of Charles Darwin himself, who said he "deserved to be called a theist." As Francis Collins, a confirmed theist whose Human Genome research project has revealed all of the 3 billion letters of our DNA, puts it, "If God, who is all-powerful and who is not limited by space and time, chose to use the mechanism of evolution to create you and me, who are we to say that wasn't an absolutely elegant plan?"

Evolutionists, understandably, like to cite the fact that in Pope Pius XII's encyclical *Humani Generis* on August 12, 1950, he grudgingly acknowledged that there might be something to evolution, and if so, the Catholic church might be forced into living with, from a historical perspective, this new kid on the block. Without accepting evolution as a proved fact, he did allow that if indeed it were true, and God did not create man, at least "their souls [were] immediately created by God." And on October 22, 1996, Pope John Paul II issued a statement in which he made reference to his predecessor's prior encyclical and then added that new research in the "almost half a century" since then had increased the "argument in favor of the theory [of evolution]."

However, it should be noted that neither Pius nor John Paul in their pronouncements were speaking *ex cathedra* (that is, with the full authority of their offices they formally declare church doctrine), and therefore their words did not constitute the official position of the Catholic church. That remains in its official catechism, the *Catechism of the Catholic Church,* which resulted from a request to Pope John Paul II in 1985 from the Synod of Catholic Bishops that such a catechism be composed. Starting in 1986, a commission of twelve cardinals and bishops chaired by then Cardinal Joseph Ratzinger, and with an editorial committee of seven diocesan bishops, all theologians, worked on the catechism for six years. That catechism continues to teach that "God created man," "nothing exists that does not owe its existence to God the Creator," and the creation chapters of Genesis were "inspired" by God. (*Catechism of the Catholic Church*, Ignatius Press, San Francisco, 1992, numbers 289, 291, 295, 338, 343, 344, and 355. The latest edition, 2000, with an apostolic letter from Pope John Paul II that said it was "approved and promulgated" by him, is unchanged on these points.)

℘

BEFORE I CONTINUE, I would like to leave the reader with this question: How can it be that of all the earth's creatures, it is believed that man alone can contemplate his own existence and is capable of self-awareness (among other things, the ability to think about our own thoughts, which zoologists do not believe the animal mind can do—do cats and dogs even know that the tail they see in the mirror is theirs?);[3] that he has the ability to reason from the known to the unknown, i.e., to reason his way through situations completely new to him by the help of past experience with situations he has confronted, something that animals, largely limited to instinct and the most rudimentary of reasoning powers, cannot do; and that man alone can teach other members of his species all he has learned, and even store this knowledge for the benefit of future generations and history? How is it that the human mind is so utterly unique and so superior to those of the other 59,811 species of vertebrate animals that it doesn't even lend itself to comparison?

Take dogs (and cats). Have they improved their condition, in any way at all, through the centuries? For instance, Saint Augustine in his treatise *Faith and Works* writes that "a dog returns to his vomit." That was in the early fifth century AD. Going back further, Jesus, in Mark 7:27, refers to "throwing food to the dogs" and in Luke 16:21 to dogs "licking the open sores" of a leper. Matthew, in 15:27, speaks of dogs "permitted to eat crumbs that fall beneath their [owner's] table."

Centuries upon centuries earlier, circa B.C. 1950, a painting depicts a cat who has cornered his prey, a rat, inside the large tomb of the Egyptian provincial governor Baket III.

Dogs leaping up to their masters in excitement when the latter return home, at times barking idiotically; cats, when not checking out nooks and crannies in the house they've already done a sleuth's job on before, content to sleep for hours on end curled in a ball on top of a sofa, both totally dependent for food, care, and shelter on their master, neither of them capable, on their own, of improving the condition of their existence. Is there any reason not to believe that no matter how many millenniums we go back, it was always that way? And always will be?[4]

But let's return to the time of Jesus. Though the human mind, by all indications, was just as good then as it is today (indeed, if I had to guess, there are probably more nitwits walking around today than back then), other than by letter, humans could communicate with each other only through their voices; the range, even when shouting, measured in yards. Today, because of the operation of that same human mind, we can communicate instantaneously by e-mail with people around the world; indeed, by phone, talk to someone in China as if he were in the next room. We fly by jet airplane and have sent rockets and men to the moon. In our living rooms, television shows us events taking place all over the world while they are happening. The hands of man, at the direction of his mind, have constructed buildings so high that they tickle the belly of the clouds, and have built complex factories, computer centers, and other highly sophisticated structures of civilization. Yet after those same 2,000 years, the dog with his tail wagging still leaps to his master and the cat still contentedly sleeps away the day on the sofa. Does anyone believe there is anything these animals can do today that they could not do at the time of Jesus? Or earlier?

Let's look at the Book of Job way back in the Old Testament centuries before Jesus. There is no reason to believe that the manner of existence of the goats, deer, donkeys ("the mountains are its pastureland, where it searches for every blade of grass"), hawks, and eagles ("The eagle hunts its prey, keeping watch with piercing eyes. It feeds on the carcass of the slaughtered") described in Job 39 has changed in the smallest way from then to now.

Why is this so? I would think that the principles of evolution set down by Darwin would be nonselective—yes, nondiscriminatory—in their application. Why have they discriminated against every one of the thousands of species of animals other than man to the point that all of them (the dog, cat, raccoon, elephant, tiger, camel), it appears, will be forever and totally subject, in their pitiable limitations, to the will and caprice of man? Did evolution, or a divine being, select man for this singular preeminence?*

---

*But there is one trait animals have that I, and so many others, would give a pot of gold for, and that's the fact that these very special creatures, who have no airs about them, appear to live only in the moment. I for one have lived mostly in the past and the future, never learning quite how to live in the present.

6

The Intelligence
(or Lack Thereof) of Intelligent
Design, and First Cause

THERE ARE TWO, PRINCIPAL, nonbiblical arguments that are made to support the conclusion that a God created the universe. One, the teleological argument or argument of intelligent design in the universe,[1] is impressive at first sight, and most Christian theologians rely on it as their main argument for the existence of God. But I think we shall see that this argument cannot withstand scrutiny because it falls of its own weight. The other argument is the cosmological, or first cause argument, which *is* strong and seems very difficult to get around.[2]

With respect to the argument of intelligent design,[3] it is maintained that the predictability of spatial occurrences (e.g., eclipses of the sun by the moon many years in advance can be predicted down to the second),* and, most importantly, the operation of the universe in perfect order and synchrony make it obvious that an *intelligent* supernatural being must have created it.[4] And indeed, God's transcendent intelligence is a central, irreplaceable tenet not just of the intelligent design

---

*Bologna, Italy, astronomer Corrado Bartolini, watching Venus pass across the face of the sun in 2004, said, "We can't even tell when a car will reach the Zamboni Gate [in Bologna] in traffic, but we know to a fraction of a second when Venus meets the sun every 122 years."

theory but also of Christianity's entire conception of God. Let me quote to you from the book *I Don't Have Enough Faith to Be an Atheist*, by Christian theologians Norman L. Geisler and Frank Turek, which argues that the Christian God created the universe:

> It was William Paley [English theologian, 1743–1805] who made the argument famous that every watch requires a watchmaker. Imagine you are walking along in the woods and you find a diamond-studded Rolex on the ground. What do you conclude is the cause of that watch: the wind and the rain? erosion? some combination of natural forces? Of course not. There's absolutely no question in your mind that some intelligent being made that watch, and that some unfortunate individual must have accidentally dropped it there. Scientists are now finding that the universe in which we live is like that diamond-studded Rolex, except the universe is even more precisely designed than the watch. In fact, the universe is specifically tweaked to enable life on earth—a planet with scores of improbable and interdependent life-supporting conditions that make it a tiny oasis in a vast hostile universe.

Geisler and Turek proceed to give many examples of how extremely finely tuned the universe is "to support human life here on earth." For the *first and only time* in the faith-versus-science arguments about the existence of God, the creationists, who constantly forswear scientific explanations for what they maintain is God's work, suddenly find that they can't get their fill of science, feeding lustily from its lactating breasts. For instance, Geisler and Turek point out, "On earth, oxygen comprises twenty-one percent of the atmosphere. . . . If oxygen were twenty-five percent, fires would erupt spontaneously. If it were fifteen percent, humans would suffocate." Another example they give is "the gravitational interaction that the earth has with the moon. If the interaction were greater than it currently is, tidal effects on the oceans, atmosphere, and rotational period would be too severe. If it were less, orbital changes would cause climatic instabilities. In either event, life would be impossible."

Yet another example of the "constants" we first met in our earlier discussion of Richard Dawkins: "If the carbon dioxide level were higher than it is now, a runaway greenhouse effect would develop (we'd all burn up). If the level were lower than it is now, plants would not be able to maintain sufficient photosynthesis (we'd all suffocate)." The authors also point out that, although the strength of gravity is "terrifying, it couldn't be any different for life to exist here on earth. If the gravitational force were altered by 0.00000000000000000000000000000000001 percent, our sun would not exist, and therefore, neither would we. Talk about precision."

The authors say there are 122 of these constants (some cosmologists claim as few as 15, even 6) that permit life on this earth, making this incredible fine tuning "the most powerful argument for the existence of God." They assert that these constants could never all have "occurred by chance." Instead, they say, they all "strongly point to an intelligent designer."

In addition to the four constants already mentioned, they then provide ten more:

(1) If the centrifugal force of planetary movements did not precisely balance the gravitational forces, nothing could be held in orbit around the sun. (2) If the universe had expanded at a rate one-millionth more slowly than it did, expansion would have stopped, and the universe would have collapsed on itself before any stars had formed. If it had expanded faster, then no galaxies would have formed. (3) Any of the laws of physics can be described as a function of the velocity of light, now defined to be 299,792,458 meters per second [186,000 miles per second]. Even a slight variation in the speed of light would alter the other constants and preclude the possibility of life on earth. (4) If

water vapors in the atmosphere were greater than they are now, a runaway greenhouse effect would cause temperatures to rise too high for human life; if they were less, an insufficient greenhouse effect would make the earth too cold to support human life. (5) If Jupiter were not in its current orbit, the earth would be bombarded with space material. Jupiter's gravitational field acts as a cosmic vacuum cleaner, attracting asteroids and comets that might otherwise strike earth. (6) If the thickness of the earth's crust were greater, too much oxygen would be transferred to the crust to support life. If it were thinner, volcanic and tectonic activity would make life impossible. (7) If the rotation of the earth took longer than twenty-four hours, temperature differences would be too great between night and day. If the rotation period were shorter, atmospheric wind velocities would be too great. (8) The twenty-three degree axil tilt of the earth is just right. If the tilt were altered slightly, surface temperatures would be too extreme on earth. (9) If the atmospheric discharge (lightning) rate were greater, there would be too much fire destruction; if it were less, there would be too little nitrogen fixing in the soil. (10) If there were more seismic activity, much more life would be lost; if there were less, nutrients on the ocean floors and in river runoff would not be cycled back to the continents through tectonic uplift. Yes, even earthquakes are necessary to sustain life as we know it! (Norman L. Geisler and Frank Turek, *I Don't Have Enough Faith to Be an Atheist* [Wheaton, Illinois: Crossway Books, 2004], 95–96, 105–106)

The authors go on to quote Nobel Laureate Arno Penzias, codiscoverer of the radiation afterglow, as saying, "Astronomy leads us to a unique event, a universe which was created out of nothing and delicately balanced to provide exactly the conditions required to support life. In the absence of an absurdly improbable accident, the observations of modern science seem to suggest an underlying, one might say, supernatural plan."

In other words, theists, using their *own*, not God's, knowledge and understanding of common sense (i.e., these incredibly fine-tuned constants could never have occurred all by chance), are foreclosed from saying, in response to the common sense arguments I'm about to make, "We don't have any answer for what you are saying and the questions you are asking, but God has the answer, and it's a good one." They can't go there.

Let me tell you why, although I haven't the slightest idea why the universe proceeds with such incredible precision (maybe it's due to God, or maybe it's due to laws of nature and physics such as laws of motion, gravitation, thermodynamics, centrifugal and centripetal forces, and other laws most humans know nothing about),* the intelligent design theory, as articulated by Christianity, is self-defeating on its very face. How modern Christianity can hang its supposedly intellectual, logical, and reasoned hat on it is beyond me, and it has nothing to do with the fact that it is not a scientifically testable hypothesis. It has everything to do with common sense.

In the first place, if God, per Christianity, is all-powerful and all-intelligent and can bring about whatever he pleases, why in the world would he create this incredibly complex system of 122 constants to

---

*Some laws we do. The great physicist Sir Isaac Newton discovered that planets revolve around the sun while being controlled by the law of gravitation. Newton even took the miraculous wonder of the rainbow down to earth with his discovery that white light (sunlight) contained all the colors of the rainbow, and the refraction of this light through raindrops produced the startling multicolored arc in the sky.

It is always assumed by the atheistic community that the laws of nature and physics in the universe may be the answer to the precision and harmony in the universe. And if they are, that eliminates the need for a God. But God and nature don't have to be at odds with each other. It's of course a non sequitur to suggest that they are mutually exclusive. If God created the universe, he obviously could have also created the laws by which it operates. Dr. Wernher von Braun, the German rocket scientist who expatriated to America, said, "The natural laws of the universe are so precise that we have no difficulty building a spaceship to fly to the moon, and can time the flight with the precision of a fraction of a second. *These laws* must have been set by somebody."

provide life on earth? You mean that he couldn't create an earth that was self-sustaining and relied on none of these things? That to do so would be beyond his power? That he's not, after all, all-powerful and without limitation? Remember, supposedly he can do anything and nothing is beyond him. ("Nothing is impossible with God" [Luke 1:37].) The fact that there *are* 122 constants out there (any of which, if deviated from in the smallest way, would cause our life on earth to cease) is, to me, very powerful circumstantial evidence *not* that it was God who created all these constants, but of just the opposite, that not one of them has anything to do with the Christian God of people's imagination.

But perhaps an even more important point that negates intelligent design is the watch example itself that Christians give to support their theory, an example they would be wise to never give. Every single component of the watch that the watchmaker puts into the watch *is* necessary to the operation of the watch, whereas 99.99999 (and many more nines) percent of the universe *has nothing to do with life on earth.* There are hundreds of billions of galaxies other than our Milky Way, which collectively contain trillions of stars millions of light years away (a light year is close to 5.9 trillion miles), and the Christian authors Geisler and Turek say that even in the earth's galaxy of the Milky Way alone, "There are one-hundred billion stars" (actually, 200 billion). Obviously, these billions and billions of stars, as well as countless planets, in our Milky Way are not all necessary to life on earth. Even if they were, are we to believe that the trillions of stars in galaxies *outside* our Milky Way are also necessary to life on earth, which is not even a small anthill in the universe?

Phillip E. Johnson, professor of law at the University of California at Berkeley, is one of the nation's leading intelligent design theists. He writes in his book *Darwin on Trial,* "A creationist is simply a person who believes that *the world,* and especially mankind, was designed, and *exists for a purpose.*" Let's stop to think about this for a moment. Although science does not know, it has found no evidence that intelligent life exists anywhere in the universe other than on planet earth. But what they have found over and over again are enormous celestial bodies like Saturn (nearly one hundred times larger than earth—some bodies in the universe are thousands of times larger than earth) that are utterly barren, cold masses of matter floating in space, 99.99999 percent and more of which are completely *outside* (I repeat, *outside*) the earth's galaxy, the Milky Way.

I would ask Johnson and all creationists this question. If God is intelligent, as the Christian God is supposed to be, what conceivable reason could he possibly have had for creating hundreds of billions of stars in the universe that are prodigiously large, dead bodies floating in space throughout eternity? The answer has to be "no reason." An *intelligent* being, by definition, would not create anything, particularly something of incomprehensible size, much less hundreds of billions of them, that are lifeless and serve no purpose (including, obviously, no earthly purpose), their arid surfaces being mere wastelands of rocks and dirt. *If God created these hundreds of billions (trillions if we go beyond our galaxy) of enormous dead bodies in the universe, is there something seriously wrong with him?* He's certainly not the "intelligent" designer whom creationists trumpet as their God. And if he did not create these trillions of dead heavenly bodies, doesn't that necessarily mean that even if there is a God, he did not create the universe? That these bodies resulted from the laws of nature or from some other source presently unknown to man?

And if Christianity wants to get more ludicrous than it already is and say that the trillions of stars and planets in the universe *are* necessary to life on earth, as indicated, *since God is all-powerful and can do whatever he pleases, just as he would not make life on earth dependent on 122 constants, why would he make life on earth dependent on trillions of celestial bodies in the universe?* (By analogy, since we know the earth, at only 8,000 miles in diameter, is but a speck in the universe, bearing the proportion of a tiny drop of water to the ocean, would God create the entire ocean to sustain this drop of water?) Why not just make earth dependent on nothing? If he could create the universe, as Christians believe, by the wave of a hand or the utterance of a command, certainly he would have done this. Surely they don't want us to believe that God could not figure out a way to sustain life on earth without the 122 constants, and without trillions of stars, trillions of miles away to support it. Remember, as I pointed out earlier in this book, Christianity is bound by its *own* concept of intelligence, reason, and common sense in answering this question.

Before we leave our discussion of intelligent design, I think one can say that even more than the argument I've made as to constants, the presence of trillions of dead heavenly bodies in the universe is arguably the strongest argument there is that there is no God, period, and certainly not the all-intelligent, classical God of Christian theology. In my view, though not irresistible, this is a more substantive argument for atheism than any of the blatant non sequiturs that the lords of atheism have ever offered.

And what an irony it is that the principal, nonbiblical argument for the existence of God that Christian scholars usually cite, intelligent design, is, upon deconstruction, the strongest argument there is for the nonexistence of God.

℮∽

FOR ME, THE ARGUMENT that is the strongest for the existence of God, one that for centuries was the principal argument of Christian theologians, but though still firmly embraced, takes a back seat to intelligent design among most Christian thinkers today, is the cosmological, or first cause argument. It was first prominently set forth by the great Dominican teacher and Catholic theologian Thomas Aquinas in four very short (a total of just four pages) "articles" in volume one of his erudite and equally abstruse two-volume classic *Summa Theologica* (1267–1273). (His third and final volume was aborted by his death in 1274.) That argument starts with a premise that can't be disputed—that every effect (i.e., everything in existence, be it a book, a loaf of bread, a chair, a peach on a tree, a car, a human, a teaspoon, a stick on the street) has a cause. A "thing," Aquinas said, "cannot be without being caused." Hence, cause and effect. In other words, we know from our human experience that nothing in existence can give itself existence because if it did, then it would have to have preceded itself, an impossibility.

This book you are reading was printed and bound, as we all know, at a factory on machines that were themselves manufactured elsewhere. The galleys from which the book was published got to the factory by some mode of transportation that itself was manufactured. The galleys resulted from a manuscript I submitted which was typed by my secretary from handwritten pages of mine I gave her. The pencil and paper I used to write the manuscript came from manufacturing companies whose machines, which had their own chain of causation, used the raw material of graphite and wood, which likewise had their own chain of causation, to make the paper and pencil. And so forth.

But although everything has to be caused by something else, and that thing, in turn, by something else, this regression in the chain of causation logically cannot extend backward into infinity. (Although such a "logical" conclusion would not seem to admit of empirical proof.) At some point the chain of causation goes back to something that was not *dependent* for its existence on something else but is *independent*, "a being uncaused," Aquinas said. An uncaused cause, if you will. This independent thing is the uncaused *first* cause, the cause that set everything else in motion.* And Christians as well as great numbers of non-Christians believe this first cause is God ("the first cause of all things," Aquinas says), the only being who could create the first particle or organism and/or the universe because only God, Aquinas says later

---

*Perhaps the first cause argument can be reduced, for purposes of metaphor, to the old question, "Which came first, the chicken or the egg?" Because chickens come *from* eggs, yet eggs are made *by* chickens, it seems we could start the cycle with either a chicken *or* an egg. But since neither could exist without the preexistence of the other, it would seem that only the imposition of a transcendent being could start the cycle by first creating either a chicken or an egg.

in his volume one, "brings things into being from nothing." To atheists who reject the first cause hypothesis, Christian philosopher William Lane Craig responds, "The idea that anything, especially the whole universe, could pop into existence uncaused is repugnant to most thinkers. . . . A proponent of such a theory, if he is an atheist, must believe that the matter of the universe came from nothing and by nothing. Now this is a pretty hard pill to swallow." What cannot be denied is that the first cause theory, which may not automatically dispose of the issue, certainly has logic on its side. How does one get around it?

The easy way, of course, is to say that although the first cause argument necessarily implies a beginning (that is, a first moment in time) which in turn implies a creator, maybe the universe never had a beginning. It just *is*. Therefore, there is no need for a creator. But most find this premise just as difficult to believe as the notion of God creating the universe, and it has few adherents among the scientific and intellectual gentry.[5] One adherent was Aristotle. Another was the English poet and philosopher Percy Bysshe Shelley, who felt it was "easier to suppose that the universe has existed from all eternity, than to conceive an external being capable of creating it."

The way that science attempts to get around the first cause argument is with its "big bang" theory, which has reached the level of accepted science, the vast majority of today's scientists subscribing to it. The theory was first enunciated in 1927 (the term "big bang," and what is believed to be the supporting evidence for it, came years later) by French astronomer Georges Lemaître, who, ironically, was a Roman Catholic priest. It holds that the universe exploded into existence[*] in a flash of energy, mass, and light from a single point in space and time about 13.7 billion years ago, and has been expanding outward ever

---

*Some physicists believe that time goes back even before the big bang. But as physicist Stephen Hawking says, "It would make no sense to create a model that encompasses time before the big bang, because what existed then would have no observable consequences for the present. So we might as well stick with the idea that the big bang was the creation of the universe." (Stephen Hawking and Leonard Mlodinow, *The Grand Design,* [New York: Bantam Books, 2010], 51)

since. In this theory of the origin of the universe, God, if there is a God (many scientists are atheists), had nothing to do with it.

I have little comprehension of things relating to the cosmos, and have to shake my head in bemusement when I try to read articles about the universe in newspapers and magazines, hardly understanding one paragraph of what scientists are saying when they talk about things like "supernovas creating matter-antimatter pairs," "stellar cores collapsing into black holes or neutron stars," "elementary particles vibrating in 10 or 11 dimensional space," etc.

But apart from science, I have problems with the big bang theory. For one thing, I simply cannot even begin to imagine how at some tiny point in time and space, some subatomic particle, trace of energy, or what have you, self-exploded in a zillionth of a second into the universe, though I obviously am in no position to challenge this theory. (Indeed, I find many of the claims of science in the area of evolution and the universe, e.g., bacteria into Mozart, and the claim that the vast universe exploded into existence from something much, much smaller than the point of a needle, just as improbable as the most fanciful of religious beliefs I poke fun at in this book.) It also makes no sense to me that a spontaneous, prodigious explosion of matter into space, which could be expected to produce chaos, could somehow result in a universe of perfect harmony and order. (Eighteenth-century Irish satirist Jonathan Swift, long before the big bang theory, said, "That the universe was formed by a fortuitous concourse of atoms, I will no more believe than that the accidental jumbling of the alphabet would fall into a most ingenious treatise on philosophy.")

But let's give the scientists their due since they know much more about these things than you or I do. However, when we get out of the realm of science and apply the simplest of logic to this same scientific phenomenon, I am in a position to warrant being heard. And my biggest problem by far with the big bang theory, at least insofar as it purportedly invalidates the first cause, God-created-the-universe theory, is the following. When I went to the library to take out some books on the big bang theory, it wasn't to read them cover to cover since, as I indicated, I couldn't understand them, but to search for one thing and one thing only: *What* was it that exploded into the universe?

Remarkably, one 400-page book on the big bang actually managed, in the author's terrible incompetence, to avoid even mentioning this issue. None of them paid more than a very passing reference to it. But from books and articles, here is what a few of the writers say. One said it was "subatomic particles" that exploded in a zillionth of a second into the universe. Another said it was "packets of energy." Another defined the energy as "negative energy in the form of radiation and exotic fields." Another said it was "a primeval atom." Yet another said it was "a swirling dust of mathematical points." I have no idea what any of these things are. But I do know that whatever they are, they are *something*. I repeat. They are something, and that is the big problem. It would seem that no one can actually believe that the big bang exploded out of *nothing*, completely empty space, which would be an impossibility.* It had

*This is notwithstanding anything that the transmundane and highly theoretical quantum mechanics might have to say. Quantum mechanics or physics, which deals with the operation of nature on atomic and subatomic particles down to a size of a billion trillion-trillionth of a centimeter (a centimeter being close to four-tenths of an inch), embraces the notion that "the universe originated, in a certain sense [in a certain sense?], from *nothing*." That is, nothing except "vacuum energy." *Energy?* Last I heard, energy can be measured, quantified. You know, it possesses the properties of mass according to Einstein's 1905 special theory of relativity as expressed in the most famous equation in science, E (*Energy*) = mc². So apparently even the quantum eggheads agree that the universe did not explode into existence from *completely* empty space. (Indeed, in Stephen Hawking's book, *The Grand Design*, he writes: "There is no such thing as empty space. Space is never empty.") If so, have they not dealt themselves out of their competition with God in creating the universe out of nothing? (See Alexander Vilenkin, "Creation of Universes from Nothing," in *Physics Letters,* [Amsterdam: North Holland Publishing, 1982], Vol. 117B, 25–28; and L. P. Grishchuck and Y. B. Zeldovich, "Complete Cosmological Theories," in *The Quantum Structures of Space and Time,* edited by M. J. Duff and C. J. Isham, [London: Cambridge University Press, 1982], 409–422.) Quantum theory giant Richard P. Feynman said, "I think I can safely say that nobody understands quantum mechanics." Perhaps worse, in a supposedly reaffirming offering on QM by Lawrence Krause in his book, *A Universe From Nothing* (New York: Free Press, 2012), the author nonetheless acknowledges, "I have no idea if [the principle of quantum mechanics] can be usefully dispensed with, or at least I don't know of any productive work in this regard." Hmm.

to have exploded out of *something*. And no matter how small or sub-atomic that something is, the question is, *Who put that something there?* If it wasn't the creator, then how did it come into existence? Remember, nothing can create itself because if it did, it would precede itself, an impossibility.*

In any event, let's return to the very powerful theory that God is the first cause. This theory, while accepted by virtually all Christian writers and thinkers, has fallen into disfavor among many of the great intellects of our time because of the rhetorical question—if everything has to have a cause, and God created the universe, then who created God?

Of course, this question presupposes that God would have had to be created. That he wasn't always there, and had a beginning. When people are trying to find out something in dispute, or the origins of something hazy, we all know the old expression, "Let's go to the source" or "the horse's mouth." In the literature I have read in which theologians, over many centuries, have grappled with this issue, I don't personally recall any of them—not even Aquinas in his *Summa Theologica*, in which he quoted Aristotle, Plato, St. Augustine, Gilson, Pegis, and others on the matter—ever specifically doing that on this precise point. And when we *do* that here, we see that Jesus (God, under the doctrine of the holy trinity) said, "I am the one who is, *who always was*, and who is still to come, the Almighty One" (Revelation 1:8). See also John 17:5, where Jesus said, "And now, Father, bring me into the glory we shared *before the world began*." Of course, all of this presupposes that there was a man named Jesus, and that he knew whereof he spoke. But since most scholars believe Jesus did exist (see later discussion), and hundreds of millions of people have believed and still

---

*A problem theists can have if they not only embrace the first cause argument that it was God who created the first particle, but that the universe exploded into existence from this particle, is that they are thereby clearly contradicting traditional Christianity which believes that it was God who created the universe, not just the particle from which the universe exploded into existence.

do that he was, and is, the Son of God, don't you think it only makes sense that the voice of Jesus saying that he wasn't created but "always was" be heard on this issue?

About the question, if God created the universe, then who created God?, I truthfully am somewhat surprised that great minds can so quickly and blithely dismiss the first cause theory by this one question. But many of them have. For instance, British philosopher Bertrand Russell, one of the most celebrated thinkers and logicians of our time, dismissed the first cause argument thusly: "Who made God? That very simple question showed me the fallacy in the argument of the first cause. If everything must have a cause, then God must have a cause." And leading British theoretical physicist Stephen Hawking says that if the universe needs a creator, then "who created Him?" (Richard Dawkins, rejecting the intelligent design theory of the universe, asks, as does fellow atheist John Loftus, "Who designed the designer?" Christopher Hitchens, calling it an "unanswerable question," asks, "Who created the creator?")[6]

Though people like Russell and Hawking have great minds (they did, however, lose altitude in my mind by their far too casual response to this seminal issue), and though they may very well be right in what they say, my response to them is, "Not so fast." Let's let the coffee cool and try to think this thing through for a moment.

Robert Ingersoll (1833–1899), widely considered to be one of the greatest thinkers and logicians of the nineteenth century, did so in seeking to counter the first cause argument for God. Although I don't agree with his premise that every cause must have itself been an earlier effect because this premise, by implication, precludes the existence of God, which Ingersoll was in no position to do, at least he wasn't flippant like those mentioned, and made a yeoman's effort to address himself to this extraordinarily mystifying issue. Ingersoll wrote, "Every cause must produce an effect, because until it does produce an effect, it is not a cause. Every effect must in it turn become a cause. Therefore, in the nature of things, there cannot be a last cause, for the reason that a so-called last cause would necessarily produce an effect, and that effect must necessarily become a cause. The converse of these propositions must be true. Every effect must have had a cause, *and every cause must have been an effect.* Therefore, there could have been no first cause. A first cause is just as impossible as a last effect."

For my own part, somehow I just have the sense, a sense I immediately had the very first time I heard this question being asked years ago, that the question, Who created God? is not necessarily a valid question. Yet remarkably, I'd say astonishingly in view of its great importance, in all of Christian literature down through the many years, I know of no thoroughly persuasive and satisfying response (assuming such a response is even possible) to this question. Instead, what one normally gets are the equally flippant and conclusionary words to the effect that God, being supernatural and all-powerful, didn't need to be created. That he always was, and the law of cause and effect doesn't apply to him.

I have said from time to time that if a person cannot really explain something, it's probably because he doesn't really and truly understand it himself, although I realize some people are simply hopelessly bereft of any communication skills. I'm going to attempt to explain why I feel this question may possibly not be a valid one. I can tell you in advance that my effort definitely falls short. The reason is either that, although I may be right (by chance), I don't have a sufficient grasp of what I'm saying to adequately explain it, or that I'm wrong and I'm trying to make sense of an erroneous thought.

Here's my effort: If we go back and back and back to the point where we have a single particle of matter (or dust or energy) in the otherwise nothingness of space, and if atheists say that we know no God created that particle (and/or the universe) because if he did, who created him, then I ask them who, in their mind, did create the first particle? If they agree, as it would seem everyone must, that everything in existence that can be seen by the human eye or scientifically measured was created or induced by something else, *they cannot exclude from this immutable principle of existence the first particle.* If they want to do so, what is their reasoning? I can't imagine what it would be. And if their position is "Yes, someone or something must have created this first particle," my response is that this acknowledgment of theirs precludes them from asking their follow-up question (then who created God?) because whoever (or whatever) created the particle has demonstrated that we cannot ask a question of him (or it) that could logically be asked of every other human, entity, or thing that ever existed. The reason is that inasmuch as what he (or it) has done in creating the particle out of nothing—something that no person, entity, or thing we know of in history has done or ever will do—is transcendent and otherworldly, *it thereby exempts him (or it)* * *and makes him (or it) immune from the follow-up question,* Then who created God?

To state it in another way: To say that the first cause theory is invalid because of the rhetorical question, Who created God? (i.e., no one; therefore God himself must not exist), is to simultaneously say that even before we get to the last effect (the particle), we have necessarily rejected the law of causation that led back to the last effect. This is so because if we accept the law of causation that regressed to the last effect, how do we conclude that *that* effect had no cause? Because we cannot logically do that, are we not forced to conclude that the first corporeal thing that ever existed (e.g., the particle) was created by God or some other entity? In arguing that God does not exist because no one created him (if someone did, who created that someone, and so on ad infinitum?), are we not thereby rejecting God or some other supernatural first cause by paradoxically also rejecting the very prin-

---

*In an obviously poor parallel, it's like a top tennis player who doesn't have to play and win qualifying matches just to get into the main draw of the tournament because his past record exempts him from this requirement.

ciple that we are forced to admit does exist, the provable law of cause and effect?

Turning to a more nonexplanatory level of analysis, there are *only* two options here—that there was or was not a first cause. And although it is almost impossibly hard for the human mind to imagine an uncaused first cause, it is not too much more so than to imagine that there was no such first cause. That, as alluded to earlier, there is no point where cause and effect ceased, the process extending backward without end. If one rejects this latter possibility, is he not then forced to acknowledge the *only* option remaining—that there was an uncaused first cause? And this can only mean, it would seem, God or some other entity.

Also, if, indeed, there is a God, no one perceives him to be corporeal (physical, measurable), as *all* objects in the chain that regressed back to the first particle were. Therefore, it does not automatically follow that God, being noncorporeal, would have had to come into existence in the same way that all corporeal objects leading backward to the particle were, that same way being the utilization of an antecedent cause. What I am saying is that maybe only things that are corporeal need to be created or caused. God could be an effect without a cause in a non-material world about which man knows nothing.

Yet another way of reaching the same conclusion is that if we *conceive* of a God (not in the ontological sense of the theologian Anselm and French philosopher and physicist René Descartes that if we do so, then he must exist, i.e., since God can be conceived, he must exist—an embarrassing proposition for supposedly great minds), we conceive him to be supernatural, and as such, as the previously mentioned conventional reasoning of theists goes, he is an entity outside the laws of causality,[7] time, and space, and therefore not subject to them. But that begs the question. Meaning what? That he always existed? Or that he created himself? Or that he is not a form of existence that can be defined, and hence no intelligent question can even be asked about "him"? Or is it _____?

Suffice it to say that the first cause theory has good arguments on both sides, but obviously no direct evidence or even persuasive circumstantial evidence on either side. We are all at sea here, clearly dealing with an impenetrable mystery, a mystery that likely will never be solved. And before it is, I think the only intelligent position to take is that of agnosticism.

7

Genesis

THE BOOK OF GENESIS, the first and most important book of the bible, which tells of the origin of the universe and mankind, but not the origin of God, starts out, "In the beginning *God created the heavens and the earth.* The earth was empty, a formless mass cloaked in darkness. And the spirit of God was hovering over its surface. Then God said, 'Let there be light,' and there was light." Now, who wrote these extremely important words? The Jews, needing an author, claim that Moses did—indeed, that he wrote the first five books of the Old Testament (Deuteronomy 4:44), known as the Torah (Hebrew name for the Mosaic "law"). That he authored them in the sense that he "received" the Torah from God at Mount Sinai and thereafter put it into biblical writing for the ancient people of Israel as God instructed him to do (Malachi 4:4).

But other than Judaism's word, what evidence that there is points away from Moses being the author of Genesis. For one thing, as opposed to the four books of the Torah following Genesis (Exodus, Leviticus, Numbers, and Deuteronomy), in which Moses is mentioned, nowhere in Genesis is Moses referred to. Also, as opposed to the four other books of the Torah, the evidence shows that Moses wasn't even born at the time given for Genesis, e.g., the town of Dan in Genesis 14:14 didn't even come into existence by that name until several hundred years after Moses had died. (See Judges 18:27–30; also, Joshua 1:1 and Judges 1:1.)

And the claim of Moses' authorship of Genesis is further weakened by the fact that he doesn't appear to have authored the next three of the four Torah books either. Throughout Exodus, Leviticus, and Numbers are the words "The Lord said to Moses," suggesting that, unless Moses wrote in the third person, which is rather unlikely, some unknown author of these books was writing *about* Moses. In the absence of evidence to the contrary, and the presence of only conjecture that Moses wrote in the third person, the words "The Lord said to Moses" should be given their conventional interpretation: that Moses was not the author. And unless Moses wrote about his own death, which would be no small achievement, we certainly know he at least never wrote the complete last book of the Torah, the Book of Deuteronomy. The unknown author writes an account of Moses' death, even saying, "Since then, no prophet has arisen in Israel like Moses" (Deuteronomy 34:10–11).[1] (See endnote discussion for multiple-author theory for the Torah.)

I think we can conclude that Judaism has failed to meet its burden of proof that Moses wrote Genesis. So who wrote it? Who was the person God supposedly inspired?

Since billions of humans down through the centuries have actually believed the words of Genesis (e.g., that God created the universe and man, and that Adam and Eve caused the fall of man), and they are at the core of Judaism and Christianity, two of the most powerful religions in the world, and because the lives of untold numbers of people have been greatly affected for good and for bad by them, aren't we entitled to know who wrote them? I mean, if in our everyday lives someone presented, let's say, a book to the masses urging them to accept and believe its contents, wouldn't everyone ask, "Who wrote this book? If you want us to believe what's in this book, we want to know who its author is to help us assess its credibility." Of course, the identity of the author of a book, let's say, on ethics, would not truly be relevant if everything contained therein made immense sense and was overflowing with self-evident truth, reason, and common sense.

But the Book of Genesis is not a book of ethics, mathematics, economics, or any subject whose author is theoretically irrelevant to the credibility of the book's contents. It's a book purportedly written by someone who is giving witness to what he claims happened either by his own observation or by what he learned from others. Therefore, his identity and background are relevant to the credibility of what he wrote. Moreover, the Book of Genesis, unlike a book of self-evident verities, is the precise opposite. Yet there are hundreds of millions of people who believe they are born sinners because, according to some completely anonymous author, aeons and aeons ago someone ate some fruit they weren't supposed to.

It is quite remarkable how very poorly put together this short story is, the most important short story in the history of mankind. I mean, Genesis can't get through more than its first four paragraphs without looking foolish. In the fourth paragraph, God creates the sun to "light the earth during the day" and the moon "to preside through the night." Together, they "separate the light from the darkness." But the first paragraph of Genesis already has the "light of day" and "the darkness of night" (Genesis 1:1–5, 14–18).

There is an internal logic even in the world of insanity—that is, one can have a perfectly intelligent conversation with an insane person if you start out from his or her insane premise. Likewise, there should be an internal logic to fairy tales, as Genesis obviously is. Genesis means to tell a logically chronological story ("The basic arrangement of Genesis is chronological," says Dr. Everett Fox in his book *In The Beginning*), but it stumbles very badly right off the bat. Chapter 1 of Genesis says that God created men and women to populate the earth. ("So God created man in his own image. God patterned man after himself. Male and female he created them. God blessed them and told them 'Multiply and fill the earth'" [Genesis 1:27–28].) But when we progress, supposedly chronologically, to Chapter 2, we find God creating Adam and Eve (Genesis 2:7, 22), presumably the first man and woman in human history. But they couldn't be because God had already populated the earth with men and women before this in Chapter 1. As if this isn't bad enough, in Chapter 1 God created man and woman on the sixth day (Genesis 1:26, 31) after every other form of life, such as animals, fish, and birds, had already been created. But in Chapter 2, the first form of life he created on earth was Adam. The other forms of life followed (Genesis 2:7, 19–20). At worst, this alone shows Genesis to be a fairy tale. At best, it's extremely sloppy writing, hardly what one would expect of writing supposedly inspired by God.

As the story goes, God told Adam not to eat any fruit (legend has it, apples) from a particular tree in the Garden of Eden, and warned that he would die (from the context, damnation, not physical death) if he did, an injunction and admonition Adam passed on to Eve. But a serpent (Satan) convinces Eve, who apparently is not taken aback that a snake is talking to her, that no harm will come to her if she eats the fruit, which she eats some of and then gives to Adam, who also partakes (Genesis 2:15–17 and 3:1–6).

One doesn't have to go too much further in Genesis to read this delightful exchange. After Adam and Eve, the biblical parents of mankind, ate the apple in the Garden of Eden that God had told Adam not to do, they felt shame. Genesis says that toward evening "they heard the Lord God walking about in the garden, so they hid themselves among the trees. The Lord God called to Adam, 'Adam, where are you?'" You see, God, who is all-knowing and also omnipresent (everywhere) doesn't know where Adam is hiding. Coming out from his hiding place, Adam replies to God, "I heard you so I hid." God proceeds to ask Adam, "Have you eaten the fruit I commanded you not to eat?" (Genesis 3:8–12). Again, God, all-knowing, didn't know whether Adam had eaten the fruit. In other words, God didn't know any more than you or I or Yogi Berra would if we were in his place. (Is it too far-fetched to speculate that the game of hide and seek may have come from Genesis, the first book to ever be widely circulated? It would be a very fitting place of origin for the most popular children's game ever. What we *do* know for sure is that the biggest game of all, organized religion's God Game, started here.)

Christianity, as well as Judaism, believes that God is all-knowing (omniscient). But if we're to believe God himself, he says he's not. Not only does he say in Genesis that he didn't know for sure where Adam was hiding and didn't know if Adam had eaten the fruit; just pages later in Genesis, he decides to test Abraham's faith and obedience to him by commanding Abraham to sacrifice his son, Isaac, to him "as a burnt offering" on a mountain. When Abraham had the wood and the fire ready to go and was about to kill Isaac with his knife, God said to him, "Lay down the knife. Do not hurt the boy in any way, for *now* I know [Now? He didn't know before?] that you truly fear God. You have not withheld even your beloved son from me" (Genesis 22:1–12). And earlier, he said to Abraham, "I have heard that the people of Sodom and Gomorrah are extremely evil. I am going to see whether or not these reports are true. *Then* I will know" (Genesis 18:20–21).

I don't get it. Is God admitting he's not God? Or did God, at some point *after* Genesis, develop the ability to be all-knowing? Apparently not. After Genesis, he's still pulling into gas stations asking for directions. In Exodus 12:13, he tells the Jews in Egypt to smear blood on their front doors so he'll know not to kill the occupants. And in Zephaniah 1:12, after the stations are closed for the night, he says, "I will search [search?] with lanterns in Jerusalem's darkest corners to find and punish those who are indifferent to the Lord."

Most importantly of all, Genesis 6:5–7 says that God felt the people of the earth he created were wicked and evil and he was sorry he ever made them, and this is why he decided to kill everyone on earth except Noah and his family. But since God is omniscient, which includes having foreknowledge, *why did he create them in the first place*? Further, since Genesis 1–27 explicitly says that "God created man in his own image," if God said that man turned out bad, does this not by definition mean that God is bad? Or at a minimum mean that in some way God was passing judgment on himself? If logic is our guide, is there any way to avoid these conclusions?

Unless one really loves fiction, it is very difficult to continue reading something like Genesis. It doesn't even rise to the dignity of being called insane. Insanity at least has its roots in known realities, and the afflicted person loses contact with these realities somewhere along the way. But the Garden of Eden story isn't even a good fairy tale for children, too ludicrous for refutation, even if, as many modern university courses in theology maintain, we only consider it allegorical, which most true believers do not.

As indicated, we are constantly told that the bible (from the Greek word *biblia*, meaning "books") is "the word of God" (Hebrews 4:12, John 10:35, 2 Timothy 3:16). And if a skeptic challenges a believer on this point, the latter, to prove his point, cites these very same bible passages that say the bible is the word of God. But again, this is circular reasoning. In law school it is referred to as "picking yourself up by your own bootstraps." You can't prove a fact in issue (here, whether or not the bible is the word of God) by the mere assertion that it is. It would be like one saying that "Muhammed Ali is the greatest fighter ever," and when asked why he says this, responds, "Because Muhammed Ali says he is."

Either the bible is or is not the word of God. If it is not, we can all agree it should have no weight, and, much more importantly, the Judeo-Christian religions that are based on it should be treated as a tremendous, devastating hoax or joke. Can we not all agree on that? But if the bible *is* the word of God, and God is supreme and all-intelligent and *all-perfect*, how does one account for all the incredible absurdities and inanities in the bible, so silly they would make the cat smile?

Despite what I have just written and without retracting one word of it, strangely, one could say, I still feel obliged to add that, although one can challenge the alleged divine inspiration of the bible, and fault the bible, as atheists have scaldingly done through the years, for its many absurdities, contradictions, and inconsistencies, it nevertheless has to be acknowledged that the bible is the most important single book, by far, in history, one that tells the greatest story, fictional or otherwise, ever told. And it does so with an unprecedented power and majesty that has resonated down through the centuries. The bible is also a document of enormous wisdom and profundity, and despite the fact that it was written by some forty different authors over a period of around sixteen hundred years, remarkably, on the whole it is cohesive and harmonic on any given subject from beginning to end, e.g., the prophecies of the Old Testament fulfilled in the New Testament.

Since the time Johannes Gutenberg got his six presses going in 1452, the bible's collection of seventy-three books (Catholic bible; the Protestant bible has sixty-six; the Hebrew bible, only twenty-four) has been translated into more than one thousand languages and has sold, like no other book, hundreds of millions of copies all over the world, its bound words found from the icy igloos of the Arctic to the steamy shanties of the tropics. The bible has been studied and scrutinized by scholars far, far more than any other book in history. It has also been quoted thousands of times more than any other book. Moreover, although one can legitimately question the truth of what is on the bible's pages, one cannot reasonably question the book's integrity. To do so would be to imagine one of the biggest undetected conspiracies known to man, a virtual impossibility given the great number of necessary members of the conspiracy, particularly since we know from our own human experience the immense difficulty of keeping a secret, even for the smallest of matters. As I once told a jury in London when my opponent raised the specter of a vast conspiracy whose existence would tend to exonerate his client of murder, but about which not one credible word or syllable had leaked out in close to twenty-five years, "I'll stipulate with you folks that three people can keep a secret. But only if two are dead."

Though, as indicated, the bible has been assaulted and maligned by countless people through the ages, and despite the remonstrances of people like biblical scholar Hector Avalos that the bible has become irrelevant to modern man, it remains today undiminished, as popular and important to the world's culture and thought as ever.

In a word, the bible is not to be ignored.

8

Born-Again Christians and Their Remarkable Beliefs

THE STORY OF CHRISTIANITY, to me, is merely an extension, and in many cases a replication, as others have pointed out, of Greek (as well as some Roman and Sumero-Babylonian) mythologies. But within Christianity ("the one immortal blemish on mankind," per German philosopher Friedrich Nietzsche) is also found the wholly nonsensical "born-again" doctrine, a doctrine believed passionately by the majority of Protestants, mainly Evangelicals, of which Southern Baptists are the largest denomination. A Protestant movement that started in England in 1738, Evangelicals view the bible, particularly the New Testament, as their principal religious and moral authority and compass and stress the importance of the New Testament in bringing them closer to Jesus. The mission of Evangelicals, with their megachurches (think Rick Warren's Saddleback Church in Lake Forest, California, and the biggest of all, Joel Osteen's Lakewood Church in Houston, Texas, which draws upward of an incredible 30,000 people to its Sunday services), music, TV preachers, and missionaries, is to "evangelize," spread the gospel of Jesus Christ to gain converts.

Fundamentalists, your more conservative Evangelicals, whose roots are in the tent revival traditions of the early twentieth century, believe in the inerrancy of the bible, that every single word of it is true. As Christian authors and theologians Norman Geisler and Thomas Howe proclaim in their handbook *When Critics Ask*, "God cannot err. The bible is the word of God. Therefore, the bible cannot err. It does not contain any untruth in it." Geisler and Howe, like all Christian fundamentalists, are apparently not troubled in the least by errors in the bible that science has revealed (e.g., Psalm 104:5 says the earth is stationary in the universe, i.e., that the sun revolves around it, not vice versa as we know the case to be), but by errors that the bible itself reveals. For example, in Genesis 22:2, God reforms to Abraham's "only son, Isaac." But Abraham already had another son, Ishmael (Genesis 16:15).

Perhaps the most prominent Christian fundamentalist ever was Williams Jennings Bryan, the famed orator, lawyer, and political leader who in 1925 prosecuted the high school teacher who taught evolution in violation of Tennessee law, John Scopes. Scopes was convicted in the "monkey trial" and fined $100, but in the world of public opinion, Scopes' lawyer, the celebrated criminal defense attorney Clarence Darrow, humiliated Bryan on cross-examination as Bryan unsuccessfully tried to defend the absurdities of the Old Testament, such as Jonah and the whale. Bryan, a broken man, died in his sleep two days later, and fundamentalism suffered a setback in America, but only temporarily.

Because Fundamentalists are so impassioned, even crazed, about their biblical beliefs, and most are very conservative politically, the calculus of most liberal Americans tells them that Fundamentalists are right-wing zanies who are almost scary people. Some of them definitely are. But my personal sense, from meeting many of them, is that for the most part they're the type of people who walk on stage when the magician asks for volunteers. What they really are, more than anything else, is a frightfully ignorant segment of our population who have been ruthlessly and cynically exploited by the Karl Roves of the world.

As far out as the Fundamentalists are in their religious beliefs, they have to go some to beat the Pentecostals, an increasingly popular offshoot of the Evangelicals that has become the fastest-growing Christian denomination in the world. Pentecostalism started in a small black church in Los Angeles in 1906. It's most famous preacher—indeed more famous than any other female preacher of any religion ever in

America—was the very flamboyant and controversial Aimee Semple McPherson, "Sister Aimee" to thousands of her followers in the 1920s and 1930s in Los Angeles. The Pentecostals, who believe in faith healing, are big on the Holy Spirit, and when they become saved by being born again, they believe that the Holy Spirit enters their body and enlightens them to the truth of Jesus, directing their lives toward a oneness with God. They also believe the Holy Spirit enables them to speak in tongues (glossolalia), a completely incomprehensible speech that becomes part of their ecstatic worship. ("The Holy Spirit prays for us with groanings that cannot be expressed in words," Romans 8:26 says. See also Acts 2:4.) I don't know if the Pentecostals still do this, but in my day they were called Holy Rollers because during their religious ecstasy, during which fainting was not uncommon, they'd roll down the aisle of their house of worship, frequently a revival tent. I think America has a wonderful Constitution, but I'm being only halfway facetious when I wonder if these people should be allowed to vote.

The Pentecostals naturally are the group that is the most fertile soil for the Charismatic movement that has been sweeping Christianity worldwide since its beginnings in the early 1960s. And although most Charismatics are Pentecostal, practicing Charismatics are also found among Roman Catholics, Eastern Orthodox, Lutherans, Episcopalians, even Presbyterians and Seventh-Day Adventists. Charismatics believe that by invoking the spirit of the Holy Spirit into their body, he will manifest himself through them in the very same way he was believed to have done in the first-century Christian church (1 Corinthians 12:6–11). The manifestations come in the form of "spiritual gifts," called "charisms," to the Charismatic person, such as the special ability to give wise advice, have special knowledge, speak in unknown languages (xenoglossy), even heal the sick, perform miracles, and prophesize. Amazingly, there are more than 600 million Pentecostals and Charismatics in the world today.

Along these lines, on the rather substantial margins of born-again evangelism, are those Fundamentalists and Pentecostals, as well as some mainstream Evangelicals, who believe in the "rapture," a word, not found in the bible, that refers to the time which they believe is coming soon within their lives when Jesus will suddenly and without notice return and sweep up all born-agains from their homes or cars or wherever they are at the moment into his embrace and whisk them away in the air to heaven (1 Thessalonians 4:16–17; Matthew 25:13; Mark 13:15–16, 26–27; Revelation 3:3). The Antichrist will then rule the world for three and a half (some rapturologists say seven) years—the so-called Tribulation Period—a time when there will be unimaginable suffering, destruction, and catastrophe, and one-fourth of the population of the earth will be killed (Revelation 6:8, 12–14, 13:5–8, 18:2; 2 Thessalonians 2:3–4; Daniel 9:26–27). This will end with the second coming of Christ, which will be followed by the final battle (Armageddon) here on earth between the forces of Christ and those of the Antichrist—in other words, between the forces of good and evil. Christ will prevail, and this will usher in his kingdom on earth for one thousand years (2 Thessalonians 2:8, Revelation 19:19–21 and 20:1–6). This in turn will be followed by Judgment Day (or "Day of the Lord") at the end of the world when God will pass judgment on (i.e., decide who goes to heaven or hell) every human who ever lived—the living and those raised from the dead to receive their judgment (Matthew 12:36–37; John 12:48; 1 Thessalonians 4:15–17; 1 Corinthians 4:5; 2 Peter 3:10; Revelation 20:11–15), the Christians being taken to heaven "to meet the Lord" (1 Thessalonians 4:16–17). Then the heavens and the earth and ungodly people will be "consumed by fire" (2 Peter 3:7, Malachi 4:1). After the "old heaven and earth disappear," God will then create a new earth and heaven for those saved souls to live in perfect happiness forevermore (Revelation 21:1 and 22:1–5; Mark 13:29–31).

Remarkably, the biggest-selling books in America for the past several years, with sales of close to an incredible 70 million copies, are the sixteen novels in Christian authors Tim LaHaye and Jerry Jenkins' Left Behind series, in which fictional characters live out the Apocalypse and End Times theme of the rapture.[1] It is nothing less than scary that many millions of Americans actually believe such things. Indeed, an

August 2010 national Pew poll showed that four out of every ten Americans, many of whom do not believe in the rapture, nonetheless fully expect the second coming of Jesus to occur by the year 2050.

Since the end of the Second World War, although membership in the Catholic church and mainline Protestant churches hasn't changed that much, there has been a dramatic increase in the number of Evangelical Christians in America. The U.S. government's 2007 *Statistical Abstract of the United States* showed 28.6 percent of the population as being Evangelical, 13.9 percent as mainline Protestants, and 24.5 percent as Catholics.

Returning to the born-again doctrine, its millions of adherents passionately believe that the *only* way anyone can get to heaven is to be born again—that is, repent of your sins, accept Christ as your savior who died on the cross for your sins, and surrender your life to him. What they mean by this—and this is where the utter insanity comes in—is that you can lead the most moral life imaginable throughout your life, but unless you're born again, you can't get to heaven. And if you don't end up there, most believe you end up in hell burning forevermore. Indeed, most born-agains—although they would never say this publicly—believe that all Jews, Muslims, Buddhists, and even Christians who are not born-agains, are going to end up in hell. Can you imagine that? The most elemental invocation of common sense and reason would tell someone how wildly irrational this is. But, of course, reason only visits those who welcome it.

What the born-again doctrine necessarily means is that accepting Jesus as your savior is much more important than helping the needy and always treating your fellow man with fairness and decency.[2]

For those of you who don't already know, I'm not making this up. You can't make up stuff up like this. It's too far out. If you think I'm making it up, let's listen to Billy Graham, the most famous and influential Christian preacher ever and the foremost proponent of the born-again doctrine. In his 1977 book *How to Be Born Again*, Billy says, "While morality or 'do-goodness' may win the approval of men, it is *not* acceptable to God, nor does it reflect His full moral demands." Billy tells the story about "a brilliant surgeon who came to a Crusade of mine and heard me say that *if gaining heaven depended upon good deeds, one wouldn't expect to get there.* He had devoted his life to helping humanity, but at that moment he realized that his sleepless nights with patients wouldn't earn him a place with God." Billy told the man he could only get to heaven "by being born-again."

In all fairness to the born-agains, they did not fabricate the notion that one has to be born again to achieve heaven. They got it from the zaniness of the bible. In John 3:3, Jesus says, "I say to you, unless you are born again, you can never enter the Kingdom of God." Also, in John 3:16 it is written, "For God so loved the world that he gave his only begotten Son, that whoever believes in Him should not perish, but have eternal life."

Billy Graham's statement that leading a good moral life won't get you very far with God, as unbelievable as it sounds, also has a foundation in the New Testament. For instance, Romans 4:2–5 says, "People are declared righteous [and hence worthy of eternal salvation] because of their faith, *not because of their work . . . and good deeds.*" But one of my favorite expressions is that "your conduct speaks so loudly I can't hear a word you are saying." Doesn't it make sense that the one true road to anything worthwhile—assuming there is anything at the end of the road—is our conduct, not our beliefs?

The whole notion of being born again is based on faith. Faith that there is a God. Faith that his son died for our sins. Faith that if we believe in him and accept him as our savior, we'll share eternity with him. But when I hear the words "I have faith that there is a God" or "You have to have faith that there is a God" or "I don't know, but I have faith," these words are alien to me because my natural instincts as well as my trial lawyer orientation is resolving matters by evidence and/or logic. Moreover, it occurs to me, why can't one have faith that there is no God? Can one only have faith in the presence or existence of something, never its absence or nonexistence?

Catholicism puts its own twist on this madness. It starts by being crazy, but not quite as crazy as the born-agains. The Catholic church believes that faith alone won't get you to heaven; you also need "good works" (James 2:17–24). This is a little better than the born-agains. At least we get some credit from God for leading a good life. But the church still requires, as a sine qua non for salvation, that Catholics believe in Jesus and that God sent him to die for our sins (*Catechism of the Catholic Church*, number 161). If any Catholic does not believe this, no matter how good and moral a life he has led, he's going to hell when he dies. Isn't that, as Ella Fitzgerald would sing, just de-love-ely?

As indicated, this is a basic tenet of Christianity. But as Charles Darwin wrote in his *Autobiography*, "I can hardly see how anyone ought to wish Christianity to be true; for if so, the plain language of the text seems to show that the men who do not believe, and this would include my father, brother and almost all my friends, will be everlastingly punished. And this is a damnable doctrine."

Both Protestantism and Catholicism, in believing that you have to believe in Jesus as your savior before St. Peter will let you into heaven, are forced to defend a position that is indefensible. How could an all-just and all-intelligent God, as Christians believe God to be, keep out of heaven those who, for instance, are prevented from knowing him because they are mentally retarded? Or those who in good faith simply do not believe he exists? Or those who believe in Jesus' existence, like Jews and Muslims, but in good conscience reject Jesus as the Son of God? (I have omitted reference to those who lived before Jesus' time because Romans 3:25 says, "God was being entirely fair and just when he did not punish those who sinned in former times.") There is no valid, satisfactory answer to that question, one that has been asked many times throughout the years. And since there isn't, shouldn't that fact alone be enough to cause thinking Christians to realize that there is something terribly, terribly wrong with their faith?

God, if there is a God, could reach *all* of mankind if he chose to, and in such a way (e.g., apparition in the sky) that all of mankind would be convinced of his divinity. *But he has chosen to hide out and remain silent.* And there is an enormous problem with this. One of the most powerfully succinct theological observations I have ever come across was in a September 23, 1931, letter from Sir Arnold Lunn to his religion-debating friend, Ronald Knox. Lunn wrote, "*God has no right to maintain his silence if he imposes the appalling penalty of eternal torture on those who have failed to discover him and consequently obey his laws.*"

Not only has God chosen to remain silent, but it gets even worse. He has also decided to deliberately deceive man. Yes, you heard me right. Listen to this. Even though God, per Christianity, created man, if man's wisdom only sees absurdity in Christianity, the reason is that *this is the way God wants it.* Say again? Though it is impossible to see how God could have seen any benefit in intentionally keeping the truth about himself from man, in 1 Corinthians 1:21 it is written: "God in his wisdom *saw to it* that the world would never find him through human wisdom." Indeed, his desire that man not find him as a result of human logic and intelligence is so great that he resorted to blatant duplicity. "God deliberately chose things the world considers foolish to shame those who think they are wise . . . The wisdom we speak of is the *secret* wisdom of God" (1 Corinthians 1:27, 2:7; see also Isaiah 29:14 and 2 Thessalonians 2:11). Can you imagine that? God has devised this monumentally monstrous game of not only silence, but deception. And on the other side of the table playing the game with him are humans, many of whom need help crossing the street on a green light. When a rational person is confronted with such frightful insanity, does he flee, crying out in horror, or did Voltaire have it right when he said "God is a comedian playing to an audience too afraid to laugh"? So not just from a non-believer's standpoint, but *from the very language of the bible itself*, the religion of Christianity, which has consumed the lives of billions of people for an incredible two thousand years at bottom, is nothing more than one continuous, grand game—starting with Adam and Eve playing hide and seek with God in the Garden of Eden, to God hiding and man seeking him during our lifetime, God tossing in tricks along the way to deceive man. Isn't this just absolutely wonderful?

Many Christians accept the notion that one can never reach God through logic and reason. We can only "experience" God, they quote scripture, by reaching him "through God's Spirit that he gives us" and our "understanding of what the Spirit means" (1 Corinthians 2:12–15). If there is one person out of one hundred million who can explain and make sense out of these words to me, I want to meet him and get his autograph. Till then, this incredible gibberish should be buried halfway between the earth's surface and China. When Christian peddlers of these forever incomprehensible words are asked to try to speak more understandable English, they say we can only reach God spiritually through our emotions and feelings, repeating their mantra that one can't reach God through logic and reason. And they sometimes attempt to shore up their position by pointing out that we attain our deepest romantic love through our emotions. But even under weak scrutiny, this analogy won't prosper. In the first place, we don't use our emotions to help us learn of the existence of the object of our love. We already know that he or she exists. But we do not know that God exists. We're trying to see if he does, and to jettison reason and logic as a means, or at least one of the means, of doing so seems greatly irrational. Moreover, pure emotions so often produce, as we know, the bitterest of fruit when we are imprisoned by them. Cole Porter's great 1930s standard "Smoke Gets In Your Eyes" is not a paean to things glorious, but a requiem for a rain of tears and a broken heart. The expression "love is blind" came from centuries of human experience.

Jesus said, "I am the way, the truth and the life. No one can come to the father except through me" (John 14:6). So if one doesn't find Jesus, there is no salvation. But Billy Graham tells the story about the governor of a state who entertained him at his home, and after dinner said to Graham, "I'm at the end of my rope. I need God. Can you tell me how to find him?" Shouldn't Evangelicals be troubled by the fact that if an intelligent, educated governor of a state, who had been exposed to the bible and organized religion, hadn't found Jesus before having the world's leading Evangelist over for dinner, how in the world can primitives in the jungle and people in remote regions of the world whose kingdom is a small patch of barren earth, a few cows, and a mud hut—as well as millions of other poor and completely illiterate humans elsewhere—become born again by accepting Jesus as their savior when they haven't even heard of Jesus, know nothing about his teaching and divinity, have never even seen a bible, and even if they did, wouldn't understand it because they can't read? Do born-again Christians really believe that their God isn't big enough to accept these people into heaven?[3] That he feels these pathetic creatures who don't know of him (their god may be a tree, a brass monkey, or a goat) should burn forevermore in hell? Really?

The reason I cite Graham so much is not only because he is, by far, the most famous and influential Christian preacher in history (far outdistancing his early-twentieth-century predecessor Billy Sunday), and has spoken to more people in person (believed to be in excess of 100 hundred million) than any other human ever, but also because he is highly respected by believers and nonbelievers alike. Even though he is in physical decline and no longer active in his ministry, in the 2010 Gallup Poll of the most admired men in the world, Graham tied for sixth with Pope Benedict XVI. Amazingly, it was the fifty-fifth consecutive year that Graham had ranked in the top ten. One reason for his immense popularity is that, despite his closeness to the seductive temptation of power, he has led an honorable and exemplary life, unlike so many of his corrupt Evangelical colleagues.

Indeed, and remarkably, his one known glitch seems to be the February 1, 1972, White House tape where, swept up in President Richard Nixon's anti-Semitism and Nixon's further assertion of Jewish domination of the national media, Graham loosely chimed in about their "stranglehold" on the media and then said his many Jewish friends "don't know how I really feel about what they're doing to this country." He apologized profusely with the tape's release in 2002, adding that the words he used "do not reflect my views," and virtually no one believes Graham is truly anti-Semitic. Most importantly, he has always preached solid morality, believes, I'm confident, in everything he preaches, and undoubtedly, through his ministry, has helped give millions of people the world over peace of mind and a new and better direction in their lives. And prior to President Barack Obama and with the exception of President Harry Truman, who called Graham "counterfeit" and told his people to keep Graham away from the White House, Graham has been a religious confidant of all American presidents since Eisenhower. Indeed, on the eve of the Gulf War in 1991, President George H. W. Bush had him spend the night at the White House with him, and they prayed together to God. Richard Nixon even offered him the ambassadorship to Israel, which, to Prime Minister Golda Meir's understandable relief, he declined. George W. Bush says it was Graham, during a walk with him on the beach before he became president, who changed his life completely around and made him a born-again Christian.

But I also cite Billy Graham because as ludicrous as some of his views are, he does not represent aberrational branches of Evangelical Christianity. He represents the orthodox mainstream thinking. So when I tell you that at least 25 to 30 percent of all Americans are Evangelical born-again Christians, I'm telling you that millions upon millions of Americans today believe the same things that Billy Graham does. Indeed, he's been their chief spokesperson for decades.

The problem with Billy, of course, is that Billy is silly, as all people who believe in this Christian nonsense *have* to be. And no one will ever accuse Billy Graham of being a deep thinker. Yet Graham is proud of his superficiality. As reported in the November 15, 1993, edition of *Time*, when a fellow Evangelist once asked him to come to the Princeton Theological Seminary to lay a deeper academic foundation for his preaching, Billy balked. "I don't have the time, the inclination, or the set of mind to pursue [these deeper questions]," he said. "I found that if I say 'the bible says' and 'God says,' I get results." I'm kinda like you, Billy, result oriented.

The whole concept of having to be born again in order to enter the kingdom of heaven is offensive to all sensible people, and no truly rational mind can come to grips with its revolting and artificial essence.

Let me give you proof of what I mean. Thousands of Christian ministers through the years and millions of their followers have preached this born-again doctrine to others, seeking to proselytize them into becoming fellow born-agains. But *everyone* would agree, including *all* born-agains, that the best teacher-proselytizer for the born-again doctrine would be Jesus Christ himself, in the flesh, the one who first stated the doctrine by saying, "I say to you, unless you are born-again you can never enter the Kingdom of God" (John 3:3). Yet when Jesus himself tried to explain to Nicodemus, a learned Jewish elder, the whole concept of being born again and how being born again was necessary for salvation, Nicodemus, totally perplexed by the obvious craziness of it all, asked Jesus, "What do you mean?" causing Jesus to respond, in exasperation, "You are a respected Jewish teacher and yet you don't understand these things?" (John 3:10).

This dialogue between Jesus and Nicodemus is well known. But why doesn't any religious writer go on to point out that if a respected Jewish teacher couldn't understand this metaphysical absurdity, *with Jesus Christ himself as his teacher*, how can God expect the average human being to be able to? Yet Jesus and Evangelical Christians say that if anyone doesn't understand it and, further, doesn't decide to become born again, he's going to burn forevermore in hell. If this is not the most severe blasphemy of reason that one can imagine, then I respectfully ask, What is?

I wish that words like "unbelievable" and "incredible" weren't such tired, overused adjectives so that when, as here, they deserve to be used, they could convey the true nature and depth of the Christian madness. That one should have to devote even one sentence to this is regrettable. The reason I do is that this certifiable and committable insanity is at the heart of Evangelical Christianity and has hundreds of millions of adherents the world over.

9

Jesus Died for Whom?
And for What?

WHAT IN THE WORLD is this business of Jesus dying on the cross as atonement for our sins, one of the very most important and central beliefs in Christianity, all about? The New Testament is replete with this notion. Here are a few examples: "For all have sinned. But God sent Jesus to take the punishment for our sins and *satisfy* God's anger against us. [What?! Under the holy trinity, Jesus *is* God. So God had to kill God to satisfy God?] Jesus shed his blood, sacrificing his life for us" (Romans 3:23–25). "God put into effect a plan to save us. He destroyed sin's control over us by giving his Son as a sacrifice for our sins" (Romans 8:3). "Christ died for our sins that he might bring us safely to God" (1 Peter 3:18). Jesus "tasted death for every man" (Hebrews 2:9). "God so loved the world that he gave his only begotten Son" (John 3:16).

Right off the top it has to be pointed out that the fantastical notion that God had his son, Jesus, die for our sins is, on its own and without the need for any assault on it by nonbelievers, demonstrably false. Indeed, Christians apparently haven't stopped to realize that they themselves don't really believe that Jesus died for our sins. To die means to cease to exist forever. But wasn't Jesus, per Christianity, up and about after three days? (Yes, in his same, physical body, with visible wounds [Luke 24:39–43].) So what definition of death not presently in the

English dictionary can Christianity come up with to justify its saying that Jesus *died* for our sins? Maybe they should say that God showed his love for man by stopping his son's pulse and heartbeat for three days, or that he showed his love by having his son endure terrible pain and suffering on the cross for our sins. But "die" for our sins? Either we're going to use the English language in this discussion or we're not. Okay? Death is not a brief timeout from life.*

For any obstinately rabid Christian who refuses to concede the above, and who argues that Jesus being up and about after three days does not mean he did not die, I respond, okay, so why don't we just say that "Jesus died on the cross for our sins for three days"? If you can live with this compromise, so can I.

In any event, let's set aside, as if it did not exist, the aforementioned uncomfortable truth and address ourselves to the question of whether Jesus died for our sins. Before we explore this issue, we should note that the very question presupposes that Jesus existed. Though not unanimous, particularly among some prominent German and Dutch theologians of the nineteenth century, the vast majority of theologians and religious scholars today believe he did. Moreover, the historicity of Jesus of Nazareth is arguably confirmed by non-Christian writers within a century of the time of Jesus.

The earliest and, it appears, the clearest non-Christian reference to Jesus (though its provenance has been seriously questioned—see endnote discussion) appears in the AD 93 work *Antiquities of the Jews* by the first-century Jewish general and historian Josephus. Born in AD 37, four years after Jesus died, Josephus wrote:

---

*Oh, by the way, as to the Christian belief that God "sacrificed" his son for our sins, just forty days after Jesus' crucifixion God had his son back in heaven with him (Acts 1:3, 9) and sitting at his "right hand" (Mark 14:62 and 16:19), his son apparently none the worse for wear from his earthly experience. Catholic dogma is that Jesus ascended into heaven "with the flesh in which he had risen and with his soul" (Second Council of Lyons, Session 4, July 6, 1274).

Now there was about this time Jesus, a wise man, if it be lawful to call him a man, for he was a doer of wonderful works, a teacher of such men as receive the truth with pleasure. He drew over to him both many of the Jews and many of the Gentiles. He was the Christ, and when Pilate, at the suggestion of the principal men amongst us, had condemned him to the cross, those that loved him at the first did not forsake him; for he appeared to them alive again the third day; as the divine prophets had foretold these and ten thousand other wonderful things concerning him. And the tribe of Christians, so named from him, are not extinct at this day.

Josephus, of course, was writing only what he had heard about Jesus, most probably the oral history passed down by Jesus' disciples. It obviously cannot be said that whatever disciples of a leader—up to and including today's cult leaders and New Age gurus—say about him is true. Nonetheless, even the most far-out believers don't normally rhapsodize about a leader who they know never even existed.[2]

In AD 115, a Roman historian, Tacitus, wrote in his history of Rome, *The Annals*, "He from whom the name Christianus was derived, Christus, was put to death by the procurator Pontius Pilate in the reign of Tiberius." And Suetonius, another Roman historian (AD 69–140), wrote around AD 120 in his book *The Twelve Caesars* that "because the Jews at Rome [a reference to disciples of Jesus who, after Jesus' death, left Palestine to preach the gospel of Jesus to the people of the ancient world] caused continuous disturbances at the instigation of Chrestus" (obviously Christus, Christ in Greek; also, the word "instigation" would not be the best word to use to refer to Jesus since Jesus had already died), Roman emperor Tiberius Claudius (10 BC–AD 54) "expelled them from the city." They returned and were executed under the new emperor, Nero, around AD 64.[3]

Historian Will Durant, in his *The Story of Civilization*, makes this perceptive observation: "That a few simple men [the disciples of Jesus] should in one generation have invented so powerful and appealing a personality, so lofty an ethic and so inspiring a vision of human brotherhood, would be a miracle far more incredible than any recorded in the Gospels." Albert Einstein added an almost equally perceptive observation when he was asked by German poet George Sylvester Viereck whether he believed in the historical existence of Jesus. "Unquestionably! No one can read the Gospels without feeling the actual presence of Jesus. His personality pulsates in every word. *No myth is filled with such life.*"

I believe we can reasonably assume that a man named Jesus lived around the time that Christianity claims he did, but it is quite another thing to say he was the Son of God who died for our sins.

℮⁓

MANY CHRISTIANS ACTUALLY BELIEVE the palpable irrationality that because, they say, all humans are the descendants of Adam, when he and Eve ate the forbidden fruit in the Garden of Eden, Adam's sin entered the human race.* Thus, we are all born with a sinful nature,[4] and this "original sin" is on our souls.

The incontestable implausibility of original sin forbids, in polite society, any serious consideration of the notion. But I do believe in the secular counterpart of original sin—that beneath the veneer and superficiality of everyday social intercourse, mankind is fatally flawed, most humans, when given the opportunity, being disposed to cruelty, avarice, and immorality.

I know that when many of you readers see these words, you will instinctively reject what I have said, believing in the essential goodness of human beings. This, in fact, is the generally accepted view of

---

*Christianity teaches that it was only Adam's sin, not Eve's, that was passed down to all humans forever after in the form of original sin. (See Romans 5:12, 17–19; Corinthians 15:21–22.) His sin was passed on, per St. Augustine, by man's semen from "sinful sexual excitement which accompanies procreation," putting an hereditary stain on the rest of humanity till the end of time.

mankind, even of most philosophers. "Deep down," one always hears, "most people are good." But my view is that people are just fine; that is, until their own interest is involved. When that happens, watch out because most people do not have sufficient character to rise above their own self-interest. Not only do they become bad, but, and this is remarkable, many times perversely so.

I would offer much evidence in support of what I have just said if this book were the proper place for such a presentation, but it is not. But you might think about this little story. A while back when a young woman was remarking to me about the intrinsic goodness of people, I told her that in no more than fifteen seconds I could demonstrate to her not only that she was wrong but that she herself never truly believed what she was telling me. She found this virtually impossible to believe and challenged me to do so. I told her to imagine coming out of her home one morning and seeing her car, parked out on the street, having been dented on the driver's side by a passing car, presumably during the night. On the windshield is a note from the driver with his name and phone number on it, asking her to call him so that he could take care of the damages. "Would you be surprised?" I asked her. After a thoughtful pause, she smiled knowingly to me and said in resignation, "Yes." I didn't have to ask her the obvious question: If most people, as she said, are good, why would she be surprised?

Before we move on, let me just pick one real-life example among hundreds of others I could give you. What about multibillion-dollar pharmaceutical companies like Guidant, Eli Lilly, Bayer, etc., continuing to sell medicines and products that were big moneymakers for them even *after* their own internal studies connected them to consequences like strokes, heart attacks, and deaths, not releasing this information to consumers or prescribing doctors until the Food and Drug Administration, after its own studies, forced them to do so? This is so common that the *New York Times* recently reported it was "routinely" done by the companies.

I know, I know. You're saying it's too hard to believe. The only problem is that it's true. A few among many captions of front-page articles in the past several years: "Drug Makers Sought to Keep Regular Cold Remedies on Store Shelves After Their Own Study Linked Them to Strokes"; "Guidant Corporation Admits That It Hid Problems of Artery Tool" that caused deaths. After an October 27, 2010, *New York Times* headline that "GlaxoSmithKline, the British drug giant, has agreed to pay $750 million to settle criminal and civil complaints that the company for years knowingly sold contaminated baby ointment," a January 18, 2011, *Times* update on Glaxo reported that the company was setting aside $3.4 billion to defend itself from investigations and lawsuits resulting from over 50,000 heart attacks caused by the use of its big-selling diabetes medicine, Avandia. A study revealed that Glaxo's "own research" showed the drug was hazardous, but Glaxo did not warn "physicians or patients."

Corporate executives, drowning in literally tens of millions of dollars from salaries, bonuses, and stock options, find it's just not quite enough. They want that fifth Monet, second yacht, third vacation home. Let me leave the subject with this April 12, 2006, *New York Times* article captioned "Jurors Add Nine Million Dollars in Damages." The article said that "A jury in Atlantic City yesterday found that Merck had misled the Food and Drug Administration about the dangers of its painkiller Vioxx and acted with wanton disregard for patients taking the drug. Epidemiologists estimate that Vioxx may have caused 100,000 heart attacks."

I believe that although there are millions upon millions of very wonderful people in the world who do have sufficient character to rise above their own self-interest, they are in the distinct minority. And I say this not because of my intimate exposure to the darkest side of humanity in my years as a criminal prosecutor, but by being an observer of the human condition.

If you think this assessment of mine is too harsh, for those of you who believe that the bible is the word of God, in Genesis 8:20 God says, "People's thoughts and actions are bent toward evil from child-hood." Worse yet, Ephesians 2:3 says, "All of us are born with an evil nature." Although, as indicated, I don't agree with the all-inclusive nature of that statement, if the bible is correct, and if, as Christianity believes, God created all of us humans, what type of monstrous mal-eficence would cause him to give every human an evil nature?

In any event, getting back to original sin, Christianity believes that we start our life not being in God's grace, having original sin on our soul, and because of this, he cannot accept us into his home in heaven to spend eternity with him. But God wanted to find a way to get us back into his good graces. The only way he could figure out how to do this—listen to this—was to have a virgin (Mary) conceive his son (God had a son? Really?) through the power of the Holy Spirit (God, but only one of the three persons of the holy trinity), without impreg-nation,[5] and then, out of his infinite love for man, have his son die for our sins. Why would his son, Jesus, have to die for our sins? Because of God's sense of justice, meaning that we have to *pay* for the sinful nature we inherited from Adam, a sinful nature that God decided we had to inherit. But knowing that the debt of Adam's sin, which was now mankind's, was so great and the offense to God of Adam's eating the apple was so prodigious that mankind could never find a way to pay for it, instead of *our* trying to pay for our sinful nature, God took upon himself the debt we owed him by sacrificing his son on the cross as payment for our sins (Romans 5:12–21). Jesus, per Christianity, re-deemed us in God's eyes by giving his life "as a ransom" for our salva-tion (Matthew 20:28, 1 Peter 18–19).

As humorist Will Rogers once said in a different context, "That's the most unheard of thing I ever heard of." If anyone *actually believes* this incredible fairy tale after *actually thinking* about it, my view is that there is something seriously defective about his or her mental faculties—namely, a very severe intellectual hernia.[6]

Before I get further into the inherent nonsensicality of it, let me see if I have this right. Adam and Eve disobey God and eat the apple (probably not because they were bad—as Christianity, in its religion, needs them to be—and wanted to eat the apple more than they wanted to obey God, but because they were human and wanted what was forbidden), and God gets so teed-off that he decides to punish billions of people throughout the rest of time for it by giving them a sinful nature. (Talk about Italians having long memories.) And then he has his son die on the cross as atonement for our sins and for the sinful nature he, yes he, gave us.* My, my. If, as Sophocles said, a lie never lives to be old, this cannot be said of a false belief.

In addressing ourselves to Romans 5:12—"When Adam sinned, sin entered the entire human race, for everyone sinned"—we must ask, If God is all-just, how can he possibly punish you and me for what Adam did? No court in the land, no court of public opinion, would ever impute to a man the sins of his father, and we're talking about his immediate father, not Adam, his alleged ancestor of, per the bible, thousands of years before he was born.† I mean, there are verses in the bible itself that speak out against this. Ezekiel 18:20 explicitly says, "The one who sins is the one who dies. The child will not be punished for the parent's sins." (See also Deuteronomy 24:16 and 2 Chronicles 25:4.)

So how can God do something like this? Apparently because, if we're to believe holy scripture, this perverse, wrongful, topsy-turvy,

---

*Let me further see if I have this right. This whole story started only because man (Adam and Eve) at the apple, a completely harmless act of disobedience that incurred God's great wrath. Then God allowed man to be redeemed in God's eyes for this act when man *murdered* God's son? Ding-a-ling-a-ling.

†Not that it has to be added to prove the irrationality of this notion, but even if we accept, for the sake of argument, its viability, what reason did God have for creating a world in which billions upon billions of innocent animals throughout history have been subjected, in the food chain, to the most horrible deaths imaginable, literally being eaten alive? Adam wasn't *their* father, was he? So what sin did they commit or have imputed to them to warrant their terrible fate? In God's omnipotence and omniscience, couldn't he have provided for their food (as well as man's food by making us vegetarians), and circumscribed their undue proliferation, in some other way?

repugnant type of injustice, where the completely innocent are punished for the sins and crimes of the guilty, is God's MO. For example, in Exodus 20:5, he tells the Israelites, "I punish the children for the sins of their parents to the third and fourth generations." In 2 Samuel 24:1–15, because David, the king of the Jews, took a census of the people of Israel and Judea, God sent a pestilence on the people of Israel for three days, killing 70,000 people in anger over David's sin (the implication was that because all the people belonged to the Lord, only he should know their exact number). And, of course, he punished thousands of the poor innocent people of Egypt, including their firstborn male babies, because he didn't like the obstinacy of their pharaoh. And Christianity believes that God is all-just? *What figure in history has had a more warped and twisted sense of justice than the Christian and Jewish God?*

But ah, born-agains would say if you tell them that we shouldn't be punished for Adam's sin, "You don't understand. Adam *represented* mankind." But I didn't choose him to be my representative. God did. To punish mankind forevermore for the sins of the first man on this planet is, on its face, grotesquely unjust. If God not only created a defective human in Adam, as Christians insist he did, but also decided to make him representative of mankind, isn't it very clear that God was doing *everything* here (creating Adam and also deciding to make him represent mankind)? As such, how can he make us responsible for things only he, not us, had anything to do with?

It must be noted that if Jesus died for our sins, we know *he achieved absolutely nothing by his sacrifice.* Why do we know this? As indicated, Romans 8:3 says that *God* "destroyed sin's control over us" by giving his son as a sacrifice for our sins. *Yet we know that his death on the cross didn't stop humans from sinning at all.* A thousand trillion sins, many extremely grievous, have been committed by mankind since Jesus died on the cross. So isn't Christianity forced to concede that Jesus' mission was a terrible failure? And if Jesus was God, how could he fail to achieve what he intended? Isn't this a question that deserves an answer?

Additionally, we also know by the New Testament's own language that no one is saved by the mere act of Jesus dying for our sins. Per Evangelical Protestantism, this can only be done if we are "born again"—confessing our sins, believing that Jesus is our savior, and turning our lives over to him. And per Catholicism, if we don't have faith in Christ *plus* good works (James 2:20), or we die with a mortal sin on our soul, we're going to hell.

Also, we have to be baptized to be saved. (By the way, why was Jesus baptized? [Mark 1:9].) Jesus himself said, "No one can enter the Kingdom of God without being born of water" (John 3:5; see also Acts 2:38). Jesus also said, "Anyone who believes *and* is baptized will be saved" (Mark 16:16). "If anyone shall say that baptism is optional; that is, not necessary for salvation, let him be anathema" (Council of Trent, 1547; Denzinger-Schonmetzer, 1618).

Even the argument that Jesus' death on the cross erased the original sin we inherited from Adam from our souls is rejected, at least by Catholicism. The *Catechism of the Catholic Church*, number 405, says that it is "baptism" that "erases original sin."

So we know that Jesus' death on the cross, by itself, was a *totally useless act*. Except it supposedly gave God some perverse, incomprehensible type of personal satisfaction that he was paid back for man's offending him by having his son die for man's sins. Can you imagine that?

In an eight-page cover story in *Time* magazine on April 12, 2004, on the question, Why Did Jesus Have To Die?, the six contributing writers, acknowledging that they didn't have the answer, and looking for anything at all that made sense, even mentioned this theory advanced by some early theologians:

The payee [in Christ's death] was not God but the devil, who some felt had a legitimate claim on humanity because of Adam's fall. . . . The Crucifixion and Jesus' subsequent descent into what they called Hades[7] [was] a kind of divine bait-and-switch scheme whereby the devil thought he had claimed a particularly virtuous human victim

[Jesus] only to discover he had allowed into his sanctum the power that would eventually wrest humanity back from his grasp. Saint Augustine likened the devil to a mouse, the Cross to a mousetrap, and Christ to the bait.

My God, is there any end to this madness? Answer: No.

As outrageously unhinged as what you have just read is, it's not too much more foolish and far-out than the more mainstream explanations for Jesus' dying on the cross. Swirling, as we are, in a maelstrom of craziness, let's examine further the seminal Christian tenet that God had Jesus die for our sins. Isn't this a non sequitur of exquisite proportions? How would God having *his son* die on the cross expiate *our* sins? It makes no sense at all, and no Christian thinker has ever begun to adequately answer this question. As I've indicated, the Christian writer and thinker modern Christians respect the most, someone whom Billy Graham cites frequently, is the late C. S. Lewis, and no less than five copies of his best-selling book *Mere Christianity* were sent to me by readers of my *Outrage* piece on agnosticism, assuring me that the answer to all my questions would be found in his book. But I found that Lewis, in trying to defend things absurd on their face, was almost invariably very sappy himself. Lewis' attempted answer to this question was to say, "It is a matter of common experience that when one person has gotten himself into a hole [here, mankind], the trouble of getting him out usually falls on a kind friend [here, God through Jesus]." Swell, but here, the kind friend who gets us out of the hole is the very same person, God, who put us in the hole in the first place by holding us to be guilty of Adam's sin.[8]

Many Christian theologians argue that God's sacrificing his son for our sins shows the great love that God has for man. But why did God feel the need to show us his love? Were people out on the road in ancient Palestine demonstrating with signs beseeching God to show them his love? In other words, other than Mel Gibson, who *needed* this? No one, apparently, but silly God.

Further, why would it be *necessary* for Jesus to die on the cross for our sins to be forgiven? You mean, Jesus' dying on the cross *allowed* God to absolve man of his sins? He could *only* do it by having his son die on the cross? No other way? Pardon the expression, but for chrissake, the act of Jesus dying on the cross for our sins is so devoid of any sense that even Jesus himself, the one who supposedly died for our sins, had no idea what it was all about, crying out from the cross, "*Eli, Eli, lema sabachthani?*" (Aramaic for "My God, my God, *why* hast thou forsaken me?" [Matthew 27:46]). I mean, if even Jesus Christ, the Son of God, never had a clue what this was all about, how can you and I be expected to?

And it is no defense to allege, as Christianity does, that this was the human side of Jesus talking. Even if we take this to be true, this human side, through the gospels, is the only side of Jesus the world has ever known. And two points cannot be disputed. Per the New Testament, this human side was a million times closer to God the heavenly father than any other human ever was or ever will be. And therefore, if Jesus didn't know what was going on, I repeat, how can we be expected to? So whether we emphasize the humanity or divinity of Jesus, there is no way to get around the profound implications of his cry from the cross on Golgotha.

Also, assuming for the sake of argument that God had his son die on the cross to pay for the sinful nature imputed to us by the sin of Adam, *why did he see fit to give us this sinful nature?* What did he hope to gain by this? Indeed, why did he create Adam and Eve with a sinful nature in the first place, knowing (remember, he's all-knowing) that they would eat the fruit of the forbidden tree, that this fall of man in the Garden of Eden would require him to sacrifice his son to atone for it, and that even this atonement would not be sufficient to prevent billions of humans from suffering eternal damnation throughout time? Is this some type of treacherous game he is playing that makes him guilty of the worst villainy that can be imagined?

Christianity embraces beliefs and concepts that run completely counter to common sense. They can be defended only if we make assumptions and adopt rules of logic that are never used or even heard of in any other area of human thinking. I'd like to buy some of the things that Christianity preaches, but my intellect, as limited as it is, keeps getting in the way.

If God was willing to have his son die for our sins, why can't he do the *infinitely less* serious thing of forgiving us weak mortals for our sins on earth and letting us spend life in heaven with him? I mean, the bible says it is God's nature to be forgiving (Psalm 86:5, Colossians 3:23). Since he is also supposed to be all-merciful (James 5:11), forgiving us would have to be easier for him than having his own son crucified on the cross. And if the Christian answer is that he is also all-just (Deuteronomy 32:4), I say his *forgiving* nature should trump his *just* nature, particularly when the justice he wants to bring about is against people he himself made, with all their defects, in *his* image, and it wasn't even they who ate the forbidden fruit, but their long-ago ancestors.

In the very same vein, Jesus, on the cross, said, "Father, forgive them for they do not know what they are doing" (Luke 23:34). If Jesus could forgive those who *murdered* him, how can he not forgive those who commit the infinitely lesser sin of not believing he is the Son of God and their savior, instead condemning them to hell (Mark 16:16)?

Billy Graham gives us another reason that God had Jesus die on the cross. "He was not only dying for our sins but he was dying to destroy the power and the works of the devil." (See also 1 John 3:8.) But Graham forgot to tell us how in the world Christ's dying on the cross could destroy the devil. What's the connection? It's just another silly non sequitur in the long litany that litters the Christian landscape. Also, even if we assume, for the sake of argument, that Graham is correct, since God is all-powerful, why wouldn't he just wave his hand and destroy the devil? Why would he permit his son to be nailed to the cross to do so? God is supposed to be all-intelligent, is he not? This sounds really stupid to me, Billy.

But let's go on. Since Billy says that God had Jesus die on the cross to destroy the devil, did it work? Billy acknowledges that "we don't see that destruction *yet.*" *Yet*, Billy? This is 2,000 years later! Billy Graham doesn't stop to realize that, as alluded to earlier, God failed here, and this means that he's not all-perfect and all-powerful.

Graham says he believes that the miseries of life will finally end and peace on earth will come "when Jesus comes back as the Messiah," but says he does not know when that will be. But whenever it is, Billy, it will be too late by then. Say he comes 1,000 years from now. Billy, we've already had 2,000 years of suffering and carnage. We're going to have to endure another 1,000 years of wars and murder and pain before it all ends by Jesus' second coming? Again, Billy, we need an end to all this horror *now*, not 1 or 2 or 3,000 years from now. It's already 2,000 years too late. Jesus, after his resurrection, said to his followers about his second coming, "Behold, I am coming *soon*" (Revelation 22:12). Right.[9]

One further observation before we move on. Christian theology asserts not just that God had his son die on the cross to expunge the stain of Adam's sin from man's soul. Christianity goes way beyond this. It maintains that Jesus "died for our sins *for all time*" (1 Peter 3:18, Hebrews 10:12), that Jesus' sacrifice on the cross "obtained eternal redemption" for mankind (Hebrews 9:12). Billy Graham says, "Christ paid the penalty for our sins, past, present, and future. That is why he died on the cross." Christian author Dave Hunt writes that Jesus "suffered the demands of his own justice in payment for every sin ever committed or that will ever be committed by any person." So he died on the cross not just to eliminate the lone sin of original sin, which we inherited, but also to atone for *all* our "sins." If we take these words to mean what they say, then why should billions upon billions of sinners have to pay for their sins by burning forevermore in hell? If we're to believe the bible, haven't their sins already been paid for by Jesus?

But, of course, no one believes that Jesus' death on the cross accomplished this, not even Christianity, the religion that continues to trumpet the absurdity that Jesus died for our sins. So if Jesus' death didn't accomplish this, and God his father, being omniscient, already knew this, and also knew that man's sins and horrendous crimes would continue, after Jesus died on the cross, to saturate the earth until the end of time, then why did Jesus have to die on the cross? There cannot be a valid answer to this question. And because there cannot, that tells all rational men that the fall and redemption of man, which is really the entire story of Christianity, is the biggest myth in the history of man.

10

If Jesus
Wasn't the Son of God,
Then Who Was He?

ALTHOUGH ATHEISTS CONTENT THEMSELVES with the belief,
a belief I myself embrace, that the notion of Jesus Christ being
the Son of God is too fantastic a thought to visit a rational mind, such
a rejection of Jesus as the Son of God necessarily begs the question. If
he wasn't the Son of God, then, as many Christian authors such as
Josh McDowell in his good book *Evidence That Demands a Verdict*
scoff at unbelievers, who was he? And, admittedly, that question does
not lend itself to an easy answer. Some say he was like a modern cult
leader, his apostles and disciples being his followers. But he certainly
wasn't the ancient counterpart of today's typical cult leader since
there's no indication that he exploited his followers for money, sex,
or any other type of personal gain. Indeed, he lived a life of asceticism. He also led a highly moral life. Jesus "knew no sin," Paul wrote
(2 Corinthians 5:21).

Some say Jesus was insane. But there's no indication of this. I say
that for two reasons. Although some people will follow a person with
morally twisted values, even evil people, there is little precedent, if any,
that they will follow someone they believe to be insane. "We can't
follow that guy. He's crazy," they'll say.* Moreover, other than his
indicating that he was the son of the creator, Jesus spoke exceptionally

141

well, even conveying his messages by way of parables, which is difficult to do. The clarity and power of his moral teachings all bespeak a rational person, one with a penetrating insight into human nature.

Some say he was simply a very intelligent man and a great moral teacher. But if he was an intelligent person and he wasn't insane, why would he claim to be the Son of God (John 10:30)? And how could a moral person who is not insane deliberately mislead his followers into thinking he was the Son of God? "He never deceived anyone" (1 Peter 2:22).

Was he a fraud in any way we are not considering? If he was, then, to quote from the classic comic strip *Little Orphan Annie*, when the "jig was up" and the Roman governor Pontius Pilate gave him every opportunity to save his life by renouncing the very reason he was in front of Pilate—Jesus' claim by unmistakable implication that he was the messiah, the king of the Jews, a sacrilege and heresy to the Jews of the time—instead of saying, "No, of course I'm not the king of the Jews. I was just having fun," or words to that effect, he refused to give up his claim of who he was. Pilate asked Jesus, "Are you the King of the Jews?" and Jesus replied, "It is as you say" (Mark 15:2).

❧

BEFORE WE CONTINUE ON THIS ISSUE OF WHO JESUS WAS, let's briefly go beyond from the Son of God allegation to his alleged resurrection. If true, it is by far the strongest argument there is that Jesus was divine. (Not the Son of God. As we shall see in Chapter 12, that's been eliminated by Isaiah 7:14. But *divine*, God-like.) Indeed, one could say that Christianity rises or falls on the resurrection. That is, if Jesus did not

---

*By insanity, I mean here someone who has totally or substantially lost contact with reality, the type of people who are routinely committed to institutions for the clinically insane. I am not referring to those who, like the Reverend Jim Jones and David Koresh in recent times, lost contact with reality on a single matter, such as their irrational paranoia about the establishment, and their followers buy into the paranoia completely.

rise up from his grave, then he was not divine. And as Paul said in 1 Corinthians 15:14, 19, "If Christ has not been raised, our preaching is void of content and our faith is empty too, and we are the most pitiable of men."

To me, the most persuasive argument supporting the position that Jesus did rise from the dead and met with his disciples is that if he didn't, why would these disciples, his followers, knowing he was not divine, have been willing to continue to preach his gospel throughout the Mediterranean world all the way to Rome, gladly accepting persecution, even death and martyrdom? Would they be willing to do this for something they knew to be a lie?[1]

On the other hand, there are two things, among others, that militate somewhat against the resurrection. According to the gospels of Mark and Luke, after Jesus rose from his grave, he walked around in apparent disguise (Mark 16:12, Luke 24:13–16), choosing to show himself only to his disciples (1 Corinthians 15:6–8). Why didn't he show himself to his hostile unbelievers, such as the members of the Sanhedrin who found him guilty of blasphemy and said he must die (Matthew 26:65–66)?[2] Wouldn't that have been proof of his divinity and done more to further his ministry than anything else?

But the thing that most diminishes the resurrection story is this. The importance of the resurrection, of course, is the belief that no other human, ever, rose from the dead. So if Jesus was the only one, he must be divine. However, we are told in the gospel of Matthew, the same Matthew that attested to Jesus' resurrection, that at the moment Jesus died on the cross, the earth shook, rocks split apart, and tombs opened. "The bodies of many holy men and women who had died were *raised from the dead* . . . They left the cemetery, went into the city of Jerusalem, and appeared to many people." (Matthew 27:51–53). This tends to dramatically reduce the specialness, the uniqueness of Jesus' alleged resurrection, and with it, whether the resurrection even took place. It tends to put the resurrection into the possible realm of mythology, which was so prevalent at the time.

DESPITE THE FACT THAT NOTHING SEEMS TO FIT for Jesus if he was not the Son of God, let's not forget the corresponding reality that Christianity has failed to offer convincing proof that he *was* the Son of God. As understandable as this failure is, it remains important on the issue of whether Jesus was the Son of God or not.

Also, the Jews at the time of Jesus who actually saw Jesus, were present at the time of his alleged miracles, listened to him say he was the Son of man and the Son of God, and later heard of his alleged resurrection, did not believe a word of it. And let's not forget that the Jews of Jesus' time believed completely in the Old Testament, the Old Testament contained many prophecies of the Jewish messiah coming, Jesus was a Jew, and his life fulfilled many of these prophesies. *Yet, as indicated, Jesus himself, in the flesh, could not convince the Jews of his time* that he was the messiah and the Son of God, and they rejected him. And it's not as if they didn't *want* there to be a messiah. Their holy scripture told them there would be one (e.g., Genesis 49:10), and they've been waiting for his arrival ever since.

Even more tellingly, Jesus' own family didn't believe in him. After Jesus chose his twelve apostles and started his ministry in Galilee by reportedly healing the sick, and crowds of people began to gather wherever he went, "when his family heard what was happening, they tried to take him home with them. 'He's out of his mind,' they said" (Mark 3:20–21).* At another point in time, "Jesus' brothers scoffed" at him

---

*If we're to believe Luke 1:31, 35, Mary, a virgin, was told she would have a son whom she was to name Jesus, and that he would be conceived by the Holy Ghost, and people would call him the Son of God. Why, then, when her son, Jesus, started acting exactly as someone conceived as he was would be expected to act, such as by healing the sick, and the people of Galilee called him the Son of God (Mark 3:10–11), would Mary (and her family) have any reason to believe that Jesus was "out of his mind"? Is the answer that the purported virgin birth of Jesus in Luke is all nonsense?

and his "miracles." "Even his brothers didn't believe in him" (John 7:3–5).[3]

If the circumstances surrounding Jesus' birth in Bethlehem were as miraculous as Christianity teaches (the angel Gabriel appearing and speaking to Mary; an angel speaking to Joseph in a dream; the virgin birth; the star in the sky directing the visit of the three wise men bearing gifts of gold, frankincense, and myrrh to the manger where Jesus lay [Matthew 1:18–24, 2:1–2, 9–11; Luke 1:26–38 and 2:6])—no one would be aware of these occurrences more than Jesus' own family, and therefore no one could be expected to accept his divinity more. And yet his family's conduct speaks volumes for the proposition that the very heart of Christianity, from which all else issues, is just bunk. All of this outweighs our inability to say who Jesus was if he wasn't the Son of God, particularly when our ability to do so is almost mortally wounded by the fact that we are making our effort at a distance of some 2,000 years. Truth is oftentimes an elusive fugitive even in our everyday lives. With respect to the identity of Jesus, it seems unobtainable.

But again, if Jesus wasn't the Son of God, then who was he? Nothing seems to make sense. If I may be so presumptuous, let me speculate on the matter. I want to preface this discussion by saying I don't offer what I'm about to say as the truth or even as a belief of mine. I offer it because as opposed to the suppositions I've just mentioned as to who Jesus was if he was not the Son of God, I believe that what I say here at least isn't self-contradictory and doesn't violate sense and reason.

I've said that I don't believe Jesus was insane. But it would not be too far-fetched to suggest that he may have been suffering from a delusion—in this case, a delusion of grandeur, a belief that he was the messiah and the Son of God. Medically, a delusion, of course, is a false, unshakable belief. And those who have them (there are many types) are only "insane" to the extent that they have lost contact with reality *as to the subject matter of the delusion.* But they certainly are not considered insane overall. Indeed, in the treatment of delusions, antipsychotic drugs are rarely prescribed.

There are, of course, many different gradations of delusions, some (like deep paranoia) being so severe that they dominate or incapacitate a person in his daily life. Obviously, Jesus' delusion, if he had one, was a very severe one. Certainly, his own family's observation that he was "out of his mind" when they heard what he was preaching, and their trying to take him home with them (Mark 3:21) goes in that direction.

Since most of the important books of the Old Testament (Hebrew bible) were in circulation among the learned at the time of Jesus—indeed, there is every indication that no other writings at the time came close to them in being read—and because we know that Jesus, by his own statements, read these books of the Hebrew bible (e.g., Luke 24:44; 4:14–20), he most likely was aware of the prophecy of a coming messiah from its pages (e.g., Genesis 49:10, Daniel 7:13–14, Isaiah 9:6–7, and Psalm 119:26). And perhaps no other thing during this period of time captured the imagination and attention of the Jews of Palestine as much as the prospect of the coming messiah.

Moreover, although atheists such as Richard Dawkins and Sam Harris are fond of suggesting that the authors of the four gospels improperly sought, by distortion and in some cases flat-out fabrication, to make Jesus' ministry conform to the many Old Testament prophecies of a messiah so that they could argue he "fulfilled" the prophecies, thereby making him the messiah, the evidence is much stronger that they were simply writing about what they saw (Matthew and John) or heard (Mark and Luke), and that it wasn't they but Jesus, believing he was the messiah and trying to convince everyone of his divinity, who was the one consciously seeking to fulfill the prophecies. Indeed, it seemed that the apostles were actually aware of this. For instance, in Matthew 21:2–3, Matthew quotes Jesus, in the town of Bethphage near Jerusalem, telling two of his disciples, "Go into the village over there and you will see a donkey tied there, with its colt beside it. Untie them and bring them here. If anyone asks what you are doing, just say, 'The Lord needs them.'" Matthew then says, in his own voice, "This was done to fulfill the prophecy" of Jesus entering Jerusalem astride a donkey, which Jesus did (Matthew 21:4–11). The Old Testament prophecy is in Zechariah 9:9. Likewise, in John 19:28 John says about Jesus on the cross: "Jesus knew that everything was now finished, and to fulfill the Scriptures, he said, 'I am thirsty.'" (See Psalm 22:15 and 69:21.)[4]

Indeed, Jesus made it clear that his mission was to fulfill Old Testament prophecies. In Matthew 5:17 he expressly said, "Don't misunderstand why I have come. I did not come to abolish the law of Moses or the writings of the prophets. No, I came to fulfill them." In Matthew 26:53–54 he tells a threatening mob, "Don't you realize that I could ask my Father for thousands of angels to protect me, and he would send them instantly? But if I did, how would the Scriptures be fulfilled that describe what must happen now?" (See also Matthew 13:13–14.) In Luke 24:44, Jesus said to his apostles after his resurrection, "When I was with you before, I told you that everything written about me by Moses and the prophets and in the Psalms must all come true." Jesus frequently quoted from the Old Testament, sometimes word for word. For example, in Matthew 22:32 he quotes exactly from Exodus 3:6. (See also Luke 4:4, 8, 12.)

But, of course, many people throughout history have claimed to be the Son of God (one of whom I prosecuted and convicted of mass murder), and they were all summarily dismissed as being kooks or frauds. What was it about Jesus that made him stand out from those others who were taken to be pretenders? In addition to his moral purity and majestic asceticism, he also just happened to be extraordinarily intelligent, charismatic, and gifted with phenomenal oratorical powers. If we're to believe the gospels, who else could speak with one very powerful parable, with its insightful moral lesson, after another?

In vastly different ways, there are, we know, virtual freaks of human nature (good and bad)—not only, if you will, idiot savants, but also the likes of Socrates, da Vinci, Shakespeare, Hitler, Einstein, and others. Who is to say Jesus was not one of them? If he was, and he also happened to labor under the grand delusion he was the messiah, much of what happened, such as his not backing down before Pilate and his cry to God from the cross, are more understandable. And it was this fateful and coincidental combination of delusion and singular luminosity that produced the most important person, occurrence, and consequence in human history.

For those who maintain that under any circumstance Jesus was a great man, one should be reminded of the French proverb that it belongs to great men to have great defects.[5]

11

The Many Absurdities of Christianity, and Its Monstrous God

B EFORE I GET INTO A DISCUSSION of the many absurdities of the Christian God and the Christian religion based thereon, I want to say that as opposed to truth, which is compatible with its environment and innately uniform in its very nature, falsehoods, as Daniel Webster observed, not only disagree with truths but usually quarrel among themselves. If something is full of falsehoods, absurdities, contradictions, and inconsistencies, as we know the story of Christianity to be, at least as a general proposition we can just about know that its message is not the truth.

As to falsehoods, an entire volume could be written to support the position that much of the bible is false. I mean, for starters, how can one believe that the first few chapters of Genesis are true? And at least one side to a contradiction, of which the bible has hundreds, has to be false.

But let's take absurdities. The bible is lousy with them. Consider these, just as examples: Jonah spending three days and three nights inside the belly of a whale (Jonah 1:17); Samson killing a thousand Philistine soldiers with the jawbone of a donkey (Judges 15:15); locusts with the faces of men but the hair of women, whose wings roared like an army of chariots (Revelation 9:7–9); Jesus telling his disciples that if they had faith as small as a mustard seed, they could say to a mountain, "May God lift you up and throw you into the sea," and it would happen (Matthew 17:20 and 21:21); Jacob having an all-night wrestling match with God and winning (Genesis 32:24–30); a donkey having a conversation with the prophet Balaam (Numbers 22:28–30), etc. Indeed, they are too numerous to mention.

Absurdities can be laughed off. But what about contradictions?

It is an article of faith in Christianity that God is all-perfect (Matthew 5:48, Psalm 18:30) and the bible is the "word of God." Meaning that the words in the Old and New Testament are supposed to be those of God himself, or inspired by God (First Vatican Council, 1868–1870: "Holy Scripture has God as its author"; 2 Timothy 3:16: "All scripture is inspired by God"; and 2 Peter 1:20–21). But if this is so, how could an all-perfect God contradict himself? Isn't that itself a contradiction? In other words, why would God inspire a passage in the bible that contradicts another passage he also supposedly inspired? Yet both the Old Testament and the New Testament contradict themselves over and over again.

Here is just a very small sampling of the great number of contradictions that appear in the bible, contradictions that cannot be harmonized: In Genesis 1:31, God says he is very pleased with what he created in man. In Genesis 6:6, God recognizes he made a mistake and now is sorry he made the human race the way he did. But in Malachi 3:6, God says, "I am the Lord, and I do not change." And in James 1:17, God "never changes." In Exodus 33:11, God speaks to Moses "face to face." (See also Genesis 32:30.) But in John 1:18, "No one has ever seen God." In Jeremiah 17:4, God's anger lasts "forever." But in Psalm 30:5, his anger lasts "but a moment." In Psalm 25:8, we are told the Lord is all-good. But in Isaiah 45:7, the Lord says, "I create woe." In James 5:11, we are told the Lord is merciful. But in Deuteronomy 7:16, he instructs Moses to "show no mercy" to the enemies of the Israelites. In Proverbs 8:17, the Lord says, "Everyone who seeks me finds me" (see also Matthew 7:8). But in the very same book, Proverbs 1:38, the Lord says that for those who had rejected him, they will thereafter "seek me but not find me." In Exodus 15:3, the Lord is described as "a warrior." But in 1 Corinthians 14:33, the Lord is a "God of peace." In John 3:13, it is written, "No man hath ascended up to heaven but he that came down from heaven, the Son of Man." But in 2 Kings 2:11, "Elijah went up to heaven in a whirlwind." Proverbs 3:13 says, "Happy is the man who finds wisdom." But Ecclesiastes 1:18 says, "The greater one's wisdom, the greater the grief. To increase knowledge only increases sorrow." And on and on. It's one thing for humans, being human, to sometimes be contradictory. But God?[1]

Christianity, we know, is the religion of those who believe that Jesus of Nazareth is the Son of God and savior of mankind. Indeed, the very first words of the gospel of Mark are "Here begins the Good News about Jesus the Messiah, the Son of God." The gospels of Matthew, Mark, Luke, and John purport to record the life of Jesus—his words and the significant events of his life from his birth in Bethlehem through his crucifixion at Calvary, just outside Jerusalem, and his believed resurrection three days later. The four gospels are complemented in the New Testament by the epistles, twenty-three letters from several of Jesus' disciples, mostly Paul. Christianity came into being, not by name but, in effect, after Jesus' death* and resurrection when his apostles and disciples began to preach the teachings of Jesus, later memorialized in the four gospels.

---

*Jesus'[2] age at the time of his death is unknown, although it is generally stated by religious scholars that he commenced his public ministry at the age of thirty (Luke 3:23) and died at thirty-three, written AD 33 (Anno Domini—Latin for "in the year of the Lord"; hence, AD 33 being thirty-three years after the birth of Jesus). Other than the circumstances surrounding Jesus' birth in Bethlehem, and his being circumcised on the eighth day following his birth (Luke 2:21), a Jewish tradition, virtually nothing is known of his years in Nazareth before his ministry, except he grew up "healthy and strong" (Luke 2:40), at the age of only twelve he amazed religious teachers in the Jerusalem temple with his understanding and answers to deep questions (Luke 2:46–47), and he became a carpenter (Mark 6:3), the trade of his foster father Joseph (Matthew 13:55).

Jesus' impact on civilization is so great that the entire world tells time by his life, BC meaning before Christ and, as indicated, AD meaning after his birth. Although other major religions of the world that do not believe in the divinity of Jesus (e.g., Islam and Judaism) have attempted to separate themselves from Jesus by coming up, after the advent of Christianity, with the letters BCE (Before Common Era) as a substitute for BC, and CE (Common Era) as a substitute for AD (understandable since they don't recognize the lord in "the year of the Lord" as God), they really haven't succeeded because the years are the same. For instance, BCE 228 refers to the same year as BC 228. So it all starts, going backward or forward, with the birth of Jesus.[3]

The inevitable question is how, pray, can millions of people the world over believe with all their heart not only in the Jesus of the New Testament but also in his father, Yahweh, the God of the Old Testament, the creator of the universe, when the essence of the story of Christianity is fanciful in the greatest degree possible? Remarkably, Christian apologists actually argue that the fact that more than 2 billion people the world over believe in Christianity is itself powerful evidence that the whole story is true. But the number of people who believe in something is not, by itself, an argument for its validity. If 50 million people believe a foolish thing, it's still a foolish thing. And everyone knows there are far more horses' asses at a race track than horses.

What makes the belief by billions in Christianity even more difficult to comprehend is that the forty or so authors of the books of the Old and New Testament lived thousands of years ago, and we don't even know for sure who, precisely, they were. As Sam Harris puts it, "People who demand evidence for everything else in their lives are somehow all too happy to accept the word of long-dead biblical authors in a corner of a long-dead empire." (This is an example of the irony noted by Montaigne that nothing is so firmly believed by people as that which is least known by them.) Of course, these people also believe that the words of these authors were inspired by God.

But there is no way to get around the irrationality that Christianity, as all religions, asks even the most shallow of mind to be certain about the deepest of mysteries.

Let's look at some of the absurdities of Christianity in its beliefs and practices.

Christians cannot even agree on who their God is. Christianity, like most other major religions, such as Judaism and Islam, is monotheistic— that is, it believes there is only one true God. But though Christians don't like to talk about it, as is well known there are really two very distinct, contradictory—vengeful as opposed to forgiving—Gods in the three main branches of Christianity (Catholicism, Protestantism, and Eastern Orthodox): the God of the Old Testament, who is a monster of the first order (Mark Twain said the Old Testament "is perhaps the most damnatory biography that exists in print anywhere"), and the God of the New Testament, who is mostly (more on this later) an exemplar of compassion and morality. Whereas the Old Testament God couldn't possibly have been more vindictive[4] and cruel to those who incurred his wrath, Jesus couldn't possibly have been less so, actually teaching, "love your enemies" (Matthew 5:41).

Indeed, Jesus, the God of the New Testament, is so different from the God of the Old Testament that he actually preached in express defiance of what his father had instructed the Israelites through Moses. "You have heard the commandment, 'an eye for an eye, a tooth for a tooth' [Exodus 21:24]. But what I say to you is: when a person strikes you on the right cheek, turn and offer him the other" (Matthew 5:38–39). So much for the famous dictum of St. Augustine, who to this day is considered a doctrinal authority by Catholics and Protestants alike, in his treatise *The Creed*, that "there is only one will of the Father and Son because there is only one nature. The will of the Son cannot, in any degree whatsoever, be separated from the will of the Father. God and God, both one God."

How is it possible for Christians to believe that Jesus Christ and God are one when they are so totally different? What previously recognized form of logic would one employ to reach this conclusion? The problem that Christianity has in this regard is that it has never said that there are two completely different Gods and that the one in the Old Testament has little to do with the God in the New Testament. They believe it's the same God, and that Jesus, the God of the New Testament, is the Son of the God of the Old Testament. But though he is the son, he is not separate. As Jesus said, "Anyone who has seen me has seen the Father. I am in the Father and the Father is in me" (John 14:9). And, "the Father and I are one" (John 10:30). "When you see me," Jesus said, "you are seeing the one who sent me" (John 12:45). Christianity believes that God is one but at the same time three persons, the Father, the Son (Jesus), and the Holy Ghost or Spirit. Tolstoy said it well: "One may say with one's lips, 'I believe that god is one, and also three,' but no one can believe it because the words make no sense."

So how does the modern Christian deal with the cruel God of the Old Testament? He doesn't. He cherry-picks things in the scriptural vineyard that the God of the Old Testament said or did that he likes, and simply strolls past all the horrendously bad things.

Here are some, but certainly not all, of the monstrous acts the God of the Old Testament committed at the very same time, by the way, that he was demanding high morality of the Israelites.* Though one or more are well known to many people, in the context of the point I am making it is very advisable to mention many of them together. As I set them forth, I would ask the reader to keep in mind that in the eyes of Christianity and Judaism, this God is all-perfect and all-good.

The Book of Genesis tells us that in God's eyes the humans populating the earth had become corrupt and depraved. Instead of God saying, "I made them in my image. I have only myself to blame," he told Noah he was going to solve the problem by destroying all living creatures. How is he going to do this? By flooding the earth. What about Noah? God told Noah he was the only "righteous" person on earth, so he intended to spare Noah and his family. Instructing Noah to make himself a boat (Noah's Ark) to survive the flood and to put his wife and sons and their wives on it (God apparently wanted to try his luck

---

*Actually, the Ten Commandments, which Christianity and Judaism believe God gave to Moses on Mount Sinai to instruct his people on the moral laws they had to live by (Exodus 20:1–17, Deuteronomy 5:1–22), are one of the most truncated versions of morality that there is. Remarkably, the first four, almost half of them, are all about God's own amour propre (e.g., do not worship any other Gods but me, do not take my name in vain). And nowhere could he find the space in the other six (e.g., do not commit adultery, do not covet thy neighbor's wife) to mention the most important moral commandment of all, one that would have necessarily included all he engraved on the two stone tablets he gave to Moses (Deuteronomy 5:22) and then some—to treat your fellow man the way you would want him to treat you. God did include an extremely important commandment—thou shalt not kill—a commandment he himself violated many thousands of times over. You know, don't do as I do, do as I say.

again with a new civilization of people starting with Noah and his family), in addition to every kind of animal, male and female, he tells Noah, "I am about to cover the earth with a flood that will destroy every living thing. Everything on earth will die. . . . I will begin forty days and forty nights of rain. And I will wipe from the earth all the living things I created" (Genesis 6:5–8, 13–19; 7:1, 3–4).

Now it seems to me that if God wanted to murder all humans on earth, he could have just waved his hand, or whatever he did to create the universe, and all their hearts would have ceased to beat. But God, being a nice guy, decided to dust everyone off by one of the most horrific ways of dying that there is—drowning. And to make sure that no one kept enough air in his lungs to stay alive until the raindrops stopped falling, God, according to Genesis, made sure he got everyone by covering the earth with water "for 150 days" (Genesis 7:17–24). That'll fix those no good louses I made in my image.

I don't know how many folks were on the earth before the flood, but one gets the sense from bible verses that there were hundreds of thousands of people whom God drowned. Now obviously, to any sensible person, this is all a fairy tale, and I don't believe one word of it. But that's not the point. Millions of devout Christians believe that the entire bible, of which Genesis is the first and most important book, is the word of God, and they actually believe all of this. And it's their irrational belief, not reality, that I'm talking about here. Why talk about such irrationality? If millions throughout the world believe it; if *Time* and *Newsweek* routinely have cover stories on the bible and God and Jesus; if former president George W. Bush, during his years in office the most powerful man on earth, believes it; if a May 2007 national Gallup Poll found that an astonishing 94 percent of Americans believe or tend to believe in God, 89 percent in heaven, 86 percent in angels, 78 percent in the devil, and 77 percent in hell, can one afford to ignore this madness?

Do Christians and Jews call God indescribably evil for what he did? No, as indicated, he's all-good and all-perfect. (What does it say about humanity that the one thing people think is important enough to talk about is not that, aside from Noah and his family, God murdered the entire human race, but "I wonder if they'll ever find Noah's ark?") So Christians and Jews call God all-good and all-perfect, but when they get around to printing their bibles that describe his conduct, they describe someone who would make history's greatest villains look like very pale imitations by comparison. Would even Adolf Hitler, Josef Stalin, Mao Zedong, Pol Pot, Osama bin Laden, or Tomás de Torquemada do the things the God of Jewish and Christian scripture did?

Another example of the good Lord at work: When many of the Israelites started sleeping with the women of the Midianites (a nomadic Arabian tribe that opposed the Israelites), and the women got them to worship their gods, God, to end his "fierce anger," ordered Moses, the leader of the Israelites, to execute 24,000 of his people, which Moses did (Numbers 25:1–9).

Later, he commanded Moses to slaughter all the Midianite men, women, and boys in the tribe, which Moses, being the devoted and obedient follower of God that he was, proceeded to do. God permitted Moses' army to spare and use the 32,000 young female virgins among the Midianites for their sexual pleasure and to keep, as plunder, all the wealth of the men they had killed (Numbers 31: 2–3, 7, 9–10, 15–18, and 35). Again, nice guy, this God.

In the Book of Joshua, we're told of God commanding Joshua (Moses' successor, most known for his destruction of the city of Jericho) to kill, as he did, all the people in thirty-one kingdoms hostile to the Israelites in a type of ethnic cleansing that included the slaughter of all men, women, and children (Joshua 10:1–43, 11:1–23, and 12:1–24).

The wanton murder goes on and on. In 1 Samuel 15:2–3 and 7, the precious Lord told Saul, the king of Israel, "I have decided to settle accounts with the nation of Amalek for opposing Israel when they came from Egypt. Now go and completely destroy the entire Amalekite nation—men, women, children, babies, cattle, sheep, camels, and donkeys," which Saul did.

In this indictment of unfathomable horror, we should note Thomas Paine, in his *Age of Reason*, observing that "the bible tells us" that all the murders in the Old Testament "were done by the express command of God. To believe, therefore, the bible to be true, we must unbelieve all our belief in the moral justice of God; for wherein could crying or smiling infants offend?"

When young boys mocked the prophet Elisha by calling him a "bald head," God unleashed two bears from the nearby woods to tear forty-two boys to pieces (2 Kings 2:23–24).

The God of the Old Testament is so monstrous that, as French novelist Stendahl put it, "the only excuse that one can make for God is that he doesn't exist." Christianity embraces the "divine command theory" that whatever the God of the Old Testament commanded or did was justified and right. But to paraphrase, I am obliged to say that if murder is not wrong, then nothing is wrong. It is said that no man can outrun his sins. Indeed, Robert Ingersoll observed that "for every bad act, there will be laid upon your shoulders the arresting hand of the consequences. You have got to pay for all of your mistakes, and you have got to pay to the uttermost farthing. That is the only forgiveness known to nature. Nature never settles unless she can give a receipt in full." But God, in the eyes of most on this planet, is infinitely superior to man, and his monumental crimes haven't laid a glove on him. He's still worshipped the world over.

Another argument that Christian theologians remarkably often make in defense of God's commanding the wholesale massacre of tens of thousands of human beings is that in addition to God being good, the bible, they tell you, also says that when man offended God, "he is a God of great wrath" (e.g., Zechariah 7:12, Numbers 32:10–13, 1 Samuel 28:18, Exodus 15:6–7, John 3:36). Translation: The issue is not what God did, but whether he was up front about who he is, i.e., as long as God admits in the bible, his inspired word, that he is also a God of wrath and anger, then all of his murders, including those of innocents, were just fine. You know, if Hitler would have only admitted he was evil, the Holocaust would have been okay.

There are other examples of the benevolent Lord being, in fact, a monster the likes of which the world has never seen, but I'll just mention one more: the famous ten plagues he visited on the people of Egypt as recorded in the Book of Exodus. It seems that the pharaoh was holding the Jewish people in bondage as slaves in Egypt, so God sent Moses to demand the release of the Hebrews. When the pharaoh refused, our loving God, the monarch of vindictiveness, instead of just punishing the pharaoh, decided to take it out on his poor people. He proceeded to hit the people of Egypt with one plague after another, including turning their water into blood, swarming them with locusts and hoards of frogs, and blanketing Egypt with darkness. The pharaoh didn't yell uncle until God started getting more serious by having his angel of death kill every firstborn male Egyptian child, including pharaoh's son, at which time pharaoh capitulated and freed the Israelites (Exodus 7–12).

All of these are instances of God ordering mass murder. But let's briefly look at just a few (there are many more) examples of how God instructed his people to treat their fellow man on an individual basis. He told Moses that "all who curse their father or mother must be put to death" (Leviticus 20:9). A woman who does not bleed on her wedding night must be stoned to death (Deuteronomy 22:13–14, 20–21). "If a man commits adultery with another man's wife, both the man and the woman must be put to death" (Leviticus 20:10). "The penalty for homosexual acts is death to both parties" (Leviticus 20:13).

To pause for a moment, unless God is part homosexual, which I have yet to hear anyone suggest, since the bible says that "God created man in his own image" (Genesis 1:27), how could it come to pass that there are homosexuals in the world? In any event, it's nice to know that we've elevated ourselves considerably since the days of the horrific God of the Old Testament. In *Lawrence v. Texas*, 539 U.S. 558 (2003), the U.S. Supreme Court struck down as unconstitutional a Texas statute, one of several in America, making it a felony punishable by years in the state prison for adult homosexuals to have consensual sex with each other. In his dissent, Justice Antonin Scalia, a darling of this nation's right wing, bitterly criticized the Court for having "largely signed on to the homosexual agenda . . . of eliminating the moral opprobrium of homosexual conduct." The highly enlightened and progressive Scalia allowed that "I have nothing against homosexuals," but added that they had "no fundamental right" to engage in conduct that the state of Texas deemed "immoral and unacceptable." Pushing for a new category of humans, solosexuals, here's Scalia's bottom line: If you're homosexual, fine, but keep your immoral homosexuality to yourself. So under God, we kill homosexuals. Under Scalia and the view of many who agree with him, we lock them up behind bars with robbers, rapists, and murderers. I don't know about you, but I call that progress. (I hope you know I'm being sarcastic here.)

Continuing on, God said that those who "blaspheme the Lord's name" should be "stoned to death" by "the entire community" (Leviticus 24:11, 13–14). My God. And God felt that slavery was just fine (Exodus 21:2, Leviticus 25:44). Indeed, God, being big on family values, said it was perfectly okay if a man sold his daughter into slavery (Exodus 21:7). God even got downright soft over slaves, saying that, although it was alright to beat them, if they died from the beating, the owner of the slave "must be punished," though no punishment was specified. However, "if the slave recovers after a couple of days, then the owner should not be punished, since the slave is the owner's property" (Exodus 21:20–21).*

These are just some of the examples, on the very pages of the word of God, of what most devout Christians and Jews believe their all-perfect, all-good God to be. Though, as we have seen, it would be difficult to conjure up a more monstrous and murderous figure, the official *Catechism of the Catholic Church* promulgated by the late Pope John Paul II says, "God is infinitely good and all his works are good"

---

*By the way, I wonder how many modern Christian women realize that the bible commands them to be totally submissive to their husbands (e.g., Genesis 3:16, 1 Peter 3:1, Ephesians 5:22).

(number 385). Christian theologian Richard Swinburne, in his book *The Coherence of Theism*, writes, "In our sense of 'moral,' all theists hold that God is perfectly good, and this is a central claim of theism." Theologian Stephen T. Davis says that "God is good. God never does what is morally wrong. All his intentions and actions are morally right." But by whose standards, Satan's? With the full knowledge of what the Old Testament, God's own word, says, how are these positions humanly possible?

I know that many Christians do not take every word of the bible literally, accepting that some language is allegorical or metaphorical, which is compatible with the parables in which Jesus spoke so often. But truly devout Christians do not question the authenticity of any language in the bible. Clearly, Christianity's worship of the extraordinarily wicked God of the Old Testament has to be considered demented. Yet this perverse worship is so ingrained on the soul of Christianity that Christians don't even talk about it, much less throw their beliefs out with the daily trash.

❧

LET ME INTERJECT THE CONCERN I have that by my discussing this exquisite lunacy called Christianity, often in the ridiculing, satirical way I do, the only way the folly of Christianity deserves to be discussed, some may say I begin to sound foolish myself. But in discussing an insanity that has existed for 2,000 years and shows little sign of abating, I ask the reader not to permit any of this lunacy to rub off on me. It's the Christian's crazy playpen, and I'm just paying it a visit. I hope you, the reader, will kindly remember this fact as you continue to read this biting polemic against Christianity.

❧

I WAS SAYING EARLIER THAT JESUS, the God of the New Testament, is the antithesis of the monster known as his father. And he was in most ways, all of which were good. But in another sense, he wasn't any cup of tea either. In fact, in this one sense he may have made the Old Testament God look quite lenient by comparison. If we're to believe that the bible is the word of God, it is replete with Jesus' saying, expressly or by implication, that those who do not accept him as God's son and their savior will be condemned to eternal damnation (e.g., Mark 16:16; Matthew 10:7, 14–15, 33; John 3:16, 18; 8:24, and 11:25–26. See also, Revelation 1:1, 21:8, 22:20–21), which is described in the bible as a place where unbelievers will be "tormented with fire and burning sulphur forever and ever and they will have no relief day or night" (Revelation 14:10), a place of "eternal punishment" (Matthew 25:46). Evangelicals tell us, over and over again, that "Jesus loves us with an infinite love." But how "infinite" can this love be if for those who reject him as being their savior, he condemns them to an everlasting hell? As the famous nineteenth-century agnostic and freethinker Robert Ingersoll observed, "In the New Testament [of Jesus], death is not the end, but the beginning of punishment that has no end. In the Old Testament, when God had a man dead, he let him alone."

Although Jesus, unlike his father, was a being of great virtue, particularly shown in his love for the poor ("If you want to be perfect," he told a rich young man, "go and sell all you have and give the money to the poor . . . Then come follow me" [Matthew 19:21]), it is hard to ascribe total moral excellence to someone who commands that if others do not accept him as the Son of God, they should burn forevermore in hell. The notions of moral perfection and that of condemning humans to everlasting punishment seem incompatible, indeed mutually exclusive. And because of it, though Jesus was otherwise (other than that, Mrs. Lincoln, how was the play?) highly virtuous and a great moral teacher, in terms of moral purity he might not quite rank in history with, say, the likes of Socrates, Gandhi, Francis of Assisi Diogenes, Mother Teresa, Buddha, and some others.

12

The Catholic Church:
Great, Grand, and Silly

WHEN IT COMES TO THE ABSURDITIES of Christianity, of which there are many, how can one avoid talking about the Roman Catholic Church, a church that takes absurdity to symphonic and operatic levels? The Catholic church is not only the largest Christian church, with more than 1.2 billion members, it is easily the most powerful. When a new pope is selected, it is front-page news around the world. Catholic or not, most informed people know who the pope is, how he looks, even what his personality is. By comparison, not more than one out of one thousand non-Baptists, non-Lutherans, non-Methodists, or non-Episcopalians would know who, at any given time, the heads of these churches are or anything about them. And since 1929, by way of an agreement between Italy and the papacy (Lateran Treaty), Vatican City, though only 108.7 acres (0.2 square miles), and having fewer than one thousand residents, is actually recognized as a sovereign state. Hence, among many other things, the Catholic church, like no other religion, can send diplomatic representatives, called *nuncios*, to the many governments of the world.

I want to say at the outset of my writing about the Catholic church that it should not be inferred from what follows that I have any hostility toward the church, though from what I say about it that may not seem to be the case. You see, apart from the villainy of many Catholic popes, bishops, and priests through the years that may challenge the sacred connection the church claims it has with Jesus, I feel that the main objection to the church, at least in modern times, is that its irrational dogma and doctrines have undoubtedly caused feelings of deep guilt in millions of Catholics that have hurt them throughout their lives. (On the other hand, my unscientific opinion is that the majority of Catholics, myself included, were raised Catholic with no ill effects at all. I certainly don't share the belief, reflected in an admittedly "off-the-cuff" remark made "in the heat of the moment" by atheist Richard Dawkins, that as "horrible as sexual abuse [by Catholic priests] no doubt [is], the damage [is] arguably less than the long-term psychological damage inflicted by bringing the child up Catholic in the first place.") But this harm by the church surely is not intentional. In other words, at least its heart is in the right place, and the church, in its misguided wisdom, is only trying to help its flock. Lacking, in a criminal sense, mens rea, I therefore have no actual malice toward the Catholic church of modern times.

But before we get into the absurdities of Catholicism, Catholicism may have, at its very core, a defect that nullifies it as a Christian religion before it even leaves the starting gate. The Protestant religions uniformly believe that the bible and its words (the word of God) are the only source (*Sola Scriptura*) of guidance for salvation. (And Proverbs 30:6 explicitly says, "Do not add to God's words.") The Catholic church for centuries has disagreed, holding that in addition to the bible, its sacraments and its dogma have to be followed for salvation.[1] For instance, the Catholic church holds that if you don't attend mass on Sunday, it's a mortal sin (*Catechism*, number 2181), and if you die with a mortal sin on your soul, you go to hell (*Catechism*, number 1861). But neither the requirement that one attend mass for salvation nor mortal sin are in the bible. It is also Catholic dogma that if you've ever committed a mortal sin in your life, you have to spend time in purgatory before you go to heaven (*Catechism*, numbers 1030–1031). But there's no reference to purgatory in the bible. And so on.

But what's the problem? All religions disagree with each other in one way or another. The problem is that Paul, by virtually all accounts the most important apostle of all and, after Jesus, the second most important Christian, says in Galatians 1:8–9 about the word of God in the bible, "If anyone preaches any other gospel than the one we told you about, let him be forever cursed." Since the Catholic church, in several ways, preaches in direct contravention of the bible, does the bible itself negate Catholicism and curse it?

On the problem for Catholicism posed by Galatians 1:8–9, perhaps the most important way that Catholicism differs from Protestantism is in just how we get to heaven. As mentioned earlier, Protestantism makes absolutely no sense whatsoever in its position that if you are a born-again Christian who believes in Jesus, nothing else is required for salvation. Catholicism makes immense sense when it says that good works are also required for salvation.* But when one is dealing with Christianity, sense is not always the coin of the realm.

So who is correct on this seminal issue? If the bible is our main source, it clearly appears Protestantism is. As indicated earlier, the New Testament is overflowing with references to the proposition that faith in Jesus is all that is required. For example, Paul says in Acts 16:30–31, "Believe in the Lord Jesus Christ, and thou shalt be saved." Jesus said, "I assure you, anyone who believes in me already has eternal life"

---

*In 1547, the Catholic church's Council of Trent, Session 6, Chapter 7, Canon 12, harshly condemned Martin Luther's teaching that faith alone was enough for salvation, a seismic departure from fifteen centuries of Catholic dogma that has had an enormous and profound influence in the West since the Reformation. Coupled with his unshakable conviction that because of original sin man was congenitally and irretrievable bad and sinful, Luther extended his "faith alone is necessary for justification" doctrine to the following ridiculous extreme to illustrate his point. In an October 1, 1521, letter to Philipp Melanchthon, a fellow reformer, he wrote: "Be a sinner, and sin boldly, but believe in Jesus more boldly still . . . We must sin, as we are what we are . . . Sin shall not drag us away from Him, even should we commit fornication or murder, thousands and thousands of times a day." (*Briefwechsel*, Vol. 3, 208)

(John 6:47). On the other hand, the support for good works in addition to faith being necessary for salvation is extremely weak, if it has any support at all.[2] (See endnote discussion on good works alone being sufficient for salvation.)

The main New Testament reference that Catholicism relies on, by far, on this issue is James 2:20, 26, and though it's the strongest the church has in its scriptural arsenal, it is, upon reflection, somewhat ambiguous. Apart from the fact that it's virtually the lone soldier facing a battalion in opposition, it's not clear to me that James 2:20, 26 says what Catholicism says it does. When James says, "Faith without good works is dead," it isn't indisputable that he is talking about salvation here. He's not necessarily saying that good works in addition to faith are necessary to get to heaven. I can easily read this language in James to mean that even if you have faith in Jesus Christ, what good is it here on earth if you don't do good deeds? Christian author Dave Hunt, who is not Catholic, has a slightly different take on James 2:20, 26. He writes that James is only saying "that a mere profession of faith, from the lips but not from the heart, can be empty, and that if we are not willing to live what we profess, then it is likely that our faith is not genuine. James is [only] critiquing false faith."

So there is not one single bible verse that clearly says good works, in addition to faith, are necessary for salvation, and a considerable number that say only faith is. Indeed, as alluded to earlier in this text, there are several bible references that specifically say that good works will not help you get to heaven. Romans 3:27 says that whether we are "accepted by God . . . is not based on our good deeds. It is based on our faith." Titus 3:5 says we are saved "not because of the good things we did."

Where does that take us? If one takes the position that the bible is the word of God, which all of Christianity, including the Catholic church (Council of Trent, Session 4, April 8, 1546), subscribes to, then based on the language of Galatians 1:8–9, a strong argument could be made that the bible itself has sounded the death knell for Catholicism, and it shall be cursed, which I certainly do not recommend. Particularly when its position, especially on good works, is a thousand times more sensible than that of Protestantism, despite the vigorous theological defense of "justification by faith" by the Paul Tillichs of the world.

℮⌁

THERE IS ANOTHER, more fundamental problem that goes to the very heart and essence of Catholicism: the purported virgin birth of Jesus by his mother, Mary. Although the virgin birth is a tenet of Christianity, nowhere does it have the preeminence that it has in the Catholic church, where, as an article of faith and dogma, it arguably ranks on Catholicism's chalkboard with the belief in the resurrection of Jesus. The first reference in the bible to the virgin birth is in Matthew 1:18. In Matthew 1:22, Matthew says this virgin birth was a fulfillment of a prophecy by the Hebrew prophet Isaiah in Isaiah 7:14.

Anti-Christian scholars attacking the virgin birth of Jesus point out that such a birth is not even mentioned in the gospels of Mark and John. (But see an indirect allusion to it in John 1:13.) Some also point out the more important fact that in Isaiah 7:14, the word Isaiah used to describe the mother of a child Christianity says was the Son of God was *almah*, a Hebrew word that means "young woman," not virgin. But strangely every biblical scholar and anti-Christian author I am aware of fails to go on and fully develop the absolutely enormous implications of the matter.*

---

*What could possibly be a better example of this failure (one that is also an example of the phenomenon of so many humans, when working on a problem, being unable to put the pieces together in their mind) than that on March 9, 2011, American publishers, after a long consultation with a committee of American bishops and theologians, released a revised Catholic bible (New American) and Protestant one (New International Version) in which the Hebrew word *almah* in Isaiah 7:14 is translated for the first time ever to mean young woman, not virgin. But does anyone think for one single moment that the Catholic and Protestant churches in America are now going to go on and conclude that Jesus was not born of a virgin? That will never happen, of course, the *almah* piece of information being treated as just an isolated piece.

In the third-century BC Greek translation of the Hebrew bible, the Septuagint, the editors translated the Hebrew word *almah* into the Greek word *parthenos*. A professor of New Testament Greek at a Los Angeles university, who is from Greece, told me that in ancient times, including the time of the Greek translation of the bible and the time of Jesus and the New Testament, *parthenos* meant either "young woman or virgin." (In modern Greek, she said, "it has come to mean only virgin.") Matthew and Luke, using the Greek translation of the Old Testament and writing their gospel in Greek, and with a choice between young woman and virgin, described Mary in their gospels as being a virgin (Matthew 1:18, Luke 1:27).

So the essential doctrine of Christianity that Mary was a virgin and became pregnant with Jesus through the Holy Ghost (Matthew 1:18, 20) may actually be predicated on a mistranslation of the word *almah* (or at least a loose one) in the Hebrew bible by the seventy-two editors commissioned by Ptolemy II, the king of Egypt, to translate the bible into Greek for the library in Alexandria, and a self-serving translation of the Septuagint by Matthew and Luke. Since they believed Jesus was the messiah and the Son of God, we can assume this is why they chose the word "virgin" over the term "young woman."

But focusing in on the Septuagint and the possibly self-serving motivations of Matthew and Luke allows us to be too easily deflected from what is really the all-important and only issue here: namely, Isaiah's state of mind. Having to know that a miraculous virgin birth of a child would be of great importance, why would he choose a word, almah (frequently spelled *alma* because of the silent h), that did not mean virgin? When I called Zvi Dershowitz, a prominent Los Angeles rabbi, I had several questions for him, the last of which was the most important. I wanted to confirm whether the word *almah* meant young woman in Hebrew. "Yes," he said. "Can the word *almah* be construed in any way to mean virgin?" "Absolutely not," he replied. "What about in the sense that most young women, particularly back then, were virgins?" "Actually," he said, "it's the reverse. More young people married back then, as early as twelve, than today." Temporarily forgetting what I already knew about Jewish culture, I asked, "Is there a reason why you singled out the age twelve?" He responded that in Judaism, "a female is no longer a child at age twelve, the age of puberty." He reminded me of bar mitzvah for Jewish boys at age thirteen, puberty for males, and the corresponding bat mitzvah for Jewish girls at age twelve.

Most importantly, I asked, "Rabbi, is there a specific word in Hebrew that means virgin?" "Yes, *betulah*. It's a common word that's used all the time." "So if Isaiah meant to use the word virgin in 7:14 he would have used the word *betulah*?" "Of course. Why would he use another word that didn't mean virgin?"

"Rabbi," I said, "you indicated that the word *betulah* was used all the time in Hebrew. Does that include in the Hebrew bible when the context is clearly talking about a virgin?" "Yes, definitely," he said, and proceeded to give me the following chapters and verses where there is a specific discussion of a virgin woman, and the Hebrew bible uses the word *betulah*: Deuteronomy 22:13–15, 17, 19–20; Leviticus 21:3, 14; and Exodus 22:16.

So to suggest that Isaiah, an elite Jewish elder, would try to convey the thought of a virgin birth by using a word, *almah*, that did not mean this at all, and knowingly ignore the word *betulah*, which would be 100 percent accurate and leave no ambiguity about his intent, seems ludicrous.

Remarkably, the official *Catechism of the Catholic Church* quotes Isaiah 7:14 without even mentioning the problem. Nor does *The Companion to the Catechism of the Catholic Church*, which gives theological support for the statements of doctrine in the Catechism. In other words, the position of the church hierarchy apparently is that if we ignore the problem, maybe it will go away.

But perhaps most remarkable is that when I finally found the issue addressed in a 1929 edition of the *Question Box*, a popular Catholic catechism published by the Paulist Press that sold more than 3 million copies, the author, Reverend Bertrand L. Conway, after citing 7:14, wrote, in a blatant falsehood, "The word that Isaiah uses for virgin, *almah*, is always equivalent to virgin in the Old Testament." The author then brazenly cites the following chapters and verses that he claims supports what he just said: Genesis 24:43; Exodus 2:4; Canticles (Song of Songs) 1:2 and 6:7; and Proverbs 30:19. The problem is that Exodus 2:4 doesn't refer to a young woman or a virgin, but to one's "sister," Proverbs 30:19 refers only to a "woman," and the remaining two references specifically use the term "young woman," not virgin, directly contradicting the author and fortifying the case against the Catholic church's improper translation of the word *almah*.

If any reader has any remaining doubt that Isaiah 7:14 does not support Matthew's virgin birth of Jesus, what I am about to point out should eliminate that doubt like shadows before sunlight. In Isaiah 7:14–16, Isaiah did make a prophecy, but it had nothing to do with a virgin birth. Based on a "sign" that "the Lord" chose to give Ahaz, the king of Judea, a sign that Isaiah presumably learned of in a vision or through God's speaking to him, Isaiah prophesied that before the child of the young woman, a boy, was old enough to know right from wrong, the kings of Israel and Syria (Pekah and Rezin), whom Ahaz feared, would be dead. Pekah and Rezin died around 730 BC, which was close to 800 years before Jesus was even born. So this conclusively proves that contrary to what is written in Mattew 1:22, Isaiah's prophecy had absolutely nothing at all to do with the birth of Jesus 800 years later. As indicated, at the time of Jesus' birth, the fulfillment of Isaiah's prophecy had already taken place almost 800 years earlier. (See endnote for further discussion)

Unless there is more to this matter than I know, it clearly appears that the whole notion of the virgin birth of Jesus, so central to the divinity of Jesus in Christianity, has no scriptural basis for it, and hence, being hollow at its core, is nonsense. Indeed, the story of the celestially begotten birth of Jesus, all by itself, should be considered a fable by all reasonable men. But with the imposition upon it of the truth behind Isaiah 7:14, the conclusion of a fable seems unavoidable.

What's the fallout from this? It couldn't possibly be more devastating to Christianity. Matthew, who created Christianity's belief in the virgin birth of Jesus in 1:18–21, expressly quotes Isaiah 7:14[3] to support his assertion that Jesus was born of a "virgin" (Matthew 1:22–23). In other words, Matthew is stipulating that his averment that Jesus was born of a virgin was based on the prophecy of Isaiah in Isaiah 7:14. Therefore, when Isaiah 7:14, whose words in Hebrew started it all, falls, so does Matthew's virgin birth of Jesus.

Does that mean that Jesus couldn't nonetheless be the messiah? No, since the term messiah in Judaism simply means a savior sent by God to deliver his people, the Jews, from suffering and injustice. But it does mean that if his birth was not a virgin birth, then he was the son of a mortal man and woman (here, presumably, Joseph and Mary), and by definition not the Son of God. And if he was not the Son of God, then the Christian doctrine that God had his son die on the cross for our sins necessarily goes out the window, too, in effect ravaging much of Christianity. I would love to hear what the Vatican's response to this is. My guess is that they would rather stare into the noonday sun than address themselves to this matter.[*]

ABOUT THE ABSURDITIES of the Catholic church, it has gone far beyond the bible in its religious buncombe, for the most part inventing out of whole cloth most of what it calls the sacraments, seven rituals intended to lend dignity and authority to an institution sorely in need of both. Only two (Baptism, and Holy Communion from the Last Supper) can

---

[*]For those who feel that the Christian answer to surviving the devastating impact of Isaiah 7:14 is to fall back on the virgin birth in Luke 1:26–35, the latter would be unavailing. Even if Luke contradicted Matthew on this point, since Christianity believes that every word of the bible was inspired by God (2 Timothy 3–16), Mattew could not be ignored. But there is no contradiction. Matthew simply goes beyond and expands upon Luke, asserting that the virgin birth in Luke (and Matthew) was the fulfillment of a prophecy by Isaiah in 7:14.

be inferred from the bible, and they are the only ones that nearly all Protestant denominations recognize. The rest—Confirmation, Penance (only supported in part in the bible), Extreme Unction, Matrimony, and Holy Orders—were created by the church's Council of Trent, which met in sessions between 1545 and 1563 in worried response to the rise of Martin Luther's Protestantism.

The church and its flock take these sacraments very seriously. In the sacrament of Penance, a Catholic confesses to a priest all the sins he has committed since his last confession (usually the previous week if he's a devout Catholic), expresses his contrition, and promises to do the penance assigned to him by the priest. At this point, the priest, according to the church, actually has the power to forgive the sinner, wipe his soul clean, by saying, "I absolve thee from thy sins in the name of the Father, and of the Son, and of the Holy Ghost." Can you imagine that? Your soul is black with mortal sin, and with these few words, a priest, God's representative, makes the soul clean. If any person is gullible enough to believe such unbelievable nonsense, he'd probably believe someone who told him he saw a man jump away from his own shadow, someone walking in procession at his own funeral.

And it gets much more unbelievable. After his soul is clean, and before he sullies it again, the penitent Catholic can receive the body of Christ in the sacrament of Holy Communion (or Holy Eucharist). How does this happen? The parishioner kneels in front of the priest who has a chalice of wine in one hand and a wafer in the other, and when the priest intones the words, as Jesus supposedly did at the Last Supper, "This is my body" and "This is my blood" (Mark 14:22–24), the bottle of cheap wine and the wheat wafer the nuns baked or bought at the local supermarket actually change into the body and blood of Christ. Again, can you imagine that? If you non-Catholics think I'm joking, I'm not. Catholics don't leave their pews and walk solemnly down the aisle and kneel at the rail and stick their tongues out for the priest to put that wafer on it (he drinks the wine and the parishioner gets the wafer,[4] which, being the body of Christ, is believed to also contain his blood) thinking this is all just a game. As crazy as it sounds, they actually believe this,[5] and all books written by Catholic theologians affirm what they call the doctrine of transubstantiation, that the wine and wafer "really and truly become the body and blood of Christ." In other words, it's not merely symbolic, allegorical, metaphorical, or spiritual. As the Catholic Reverends John Tregilio Jr. and Kenneth Brighenti write: "Of all seven sacraments, the Holy Eucharist is the most central and important to Catholicism, because of the staunch belief that the consecrated bread and wine are actually, really, truly, and substantially the body and blood, soul and divinity of Christ." When irrationality is taken to such extreme extremes, isn't there any way for society to protect itself from it; shield itself from the toxic radiation it emits?

The preceding madness doesn't need anything more to make it incredible, but to take it to previously unimaginable heights, the priest who has performed the miracle of all miracles in converting wine and a wafer into the actual body and blood of Christ and who lays the wafer upon the tongue of the parishioner, in thousands of cases throughout the years had just come from sexually molesting a young altar boy in the rectory or intended to go to some youngster just as fast as he could discard his robe after the service. Can anything be more of a grotesque obscenity? Answer, no.

The great irony is that the Christian leaders of organized religion build multimillion-dollar edifices—like the recent $200 million Catholic church hard by downtown Los Angeles—for the faithful to receive Holy Communion and to pray and worship Jesus and God. (These ornate religious palaces cost enormous fortunes to build, fortunes Jesus would instead want to be spent feeding and clothing the poor.) But Jesus expressly told these patriarchs of pomposity, who, arguably for self-serving reasons, have decided to ignore Jesus on this point, that these costly and grandiose houses of worship (think, among hundreds of others, of the Basilica of Santa Maria Maggiore near Milan and the Baroque Frauenkirche cathedral in Dresden even before its recent

$300 million restoration) are the precise places where he does not want his followers to pray to him and his father. He explicitly says in Matthew 6:5 that "when you pray, don't be like the hypocrites who love to pray publicly on street corners and in the synagogues where everyone can see them. I assure you, that is all the reward they will ever get. When you pray, go away by yourself, shut the door behind you, and pray to your Father secretly. Then your Father, who knows all secrets, will reward you." (See also Acts 7:48–49.)

ANOTHER TENET OF CATHOLICISM that it invented out of thin air is its doctrine of mortal and venial sins (the former being the more serious) and whether they have been forgiven by a priest before you die. If you have a venial sin on your soul at the time of your death, or you committed a mortal sin that was forgiven, you can't go straight to heaven, but you don't have to worry. You simply go to a halfway house called purgatory[6] on the suburbs of heaven, where you spend some indeterminate time being punished for your venial and mortal sins, and then you go to heaven after these sins are "purged" in purgatory.[7] But, as indicated earlier, if you die with a mortal sin on your soul that has not been forgiven, you've had it. You're going straight to hell.

So no matter how moral and exemplary a life a man has led, if shortly before a bomb exploded killing him in a terrorist attack, or a robber mugged and killed him, he coveted another man's wife (a mortal sin), since he obviously never had time to schlep his way over to a priest and confess, this person will burn forevermore in hell—eternity in heaven or hell being dependent not on his overall moral conduct throughout his life but on the vicissitudes of life. I see. Even if we were to accept this high-water mark in illogic and unfairness, what type of fiend above is it who creates weak and very flawed mortals, permits (remember, he's all-powerful) the devil to set traps for us by tempting us into sin, and when we bite condemns us with vindictive relish to the everlasting fires of hell?

How is it possible that very intelligent and distinguished Catholic men and women (e.g., the late ferociously religious William Buckley Jr. and Gary Wills, one of the foremost intellectuals of our time) embrace the notions of purgatory, Holy Communion, and all the other absurdities of Catholicism and Christianity like the fairy tales of the Garden of Eden and heaven and hell and the devil and angels? I've given a little thought to this, and the only answer that makes any sense to me is that they first learned of these things not only when they were young and very impressionable, but, just as importantly, this blather was inculcated into them by elders in a formal setting at church, elementary school, or Sunday school. If they had heard, for instance, the Garden of Eden fable in a sandbox, the only place, if at all, it belongs, even though they were children they would probably smile at the silliness of the story. Hearing it from a priest, nun, minister, or respected elder in a formal setting, however, they naturally accept it without question. So they are conditioned, from their youth, to believe and stammer these inanities, and from that point on turn their thinking caps very tightly to the off position, never changing their deeply ingrained thoughts on these matters. I wonder just how many fewer people would believe in God and Jesus and heaven and hell and angels if they had never been exposed to these things as children and were first exposed to all of this as adults?

I should say that although the Catholic church has caused great psychological harm to millions, as I mentioned earlier with regard to Billy Graham, it has also given emotional comfort to vulnerable and frightened millions through the centuries. As I have indicated, I am not a sufficient student of history to weigh in on whether or not, on balance, the church, or other major religions of the world, has been a net force for good or evil through the centuries. But Thomas Huxley, in his essay *Agnosticism* (1889), wrote:

> I verily believe that the great good which has been effected in the
> world by Christianity has been largely counteracted by the pestilent
> doctrine on which all the churches have insisted, that honest disbelief

in their more or less astonishing creeds is a moral offense, indeed a sin of the deepest dye, deserving and involving the same future retribution as murder. If we could only see, in one view, the torrents of cruelty, the lies, the slaughter, the violations of every obligation of humanity which have flowed from this source along the course of the history of Christian nations, our worst imagination of Hell would pale beside the vision.

THERE IS ONE THING ABOUT WHICH there can be no dispute: the arrogance and hypocrisy of the Catholic church. I mean, here's a church that actually holds that things like missing mass on Sunday and fornication between consenting adults are both mortal sins (*Catechism of the Catholic Church*, numbers 2181 and 2353), which, unless confessed to a priest before death, will cause one to forfeit heaven and be consigned to hell, but that has the face to fiercely protect many of these same priests who sexually molest young boys from any type of punishment by refusing to report them to the civil authorities, instead transferring them to different parishes where they can prey on, and destroy the lives of other, young boys. (Just one example among thousands: In June of 2003, Thomas J. O'Brien, the Roman Catholic bishop of Phoenix, signed an agreement with Phoenix prosecutors, enabling him to avoid prosecution, in which he admitted that he knew of accusations of sexual abuse by priests against children in his diocese but had transferred these priests to other dioceses without telling their new supervisors or parishioners.)

But hey, I finally figured it out. There's a certain ethical symmetry here that in all fairness I have to give the church credit for. In the Catholic church, if you're an adult male who has consensual sex with an adult female outside of marriage, the church sends both of you terrible reprobates straight to hell. And if you're a Catholic priest who molests an eight-year-old boy, the church sends you to another parish where you can molest boys in that parish. So in both cases, the church is going to send you away. Who can complain about such evenhanded treatment?

It should be noted that because the church had no legal duty to report instances of child molestation, or any crime, by its priests to the authorities,* for many years the overwhelming majority of dioceses never did so, even though they had to know that it was the right and the moral thing to do.

And in Los Angeles, after the archdiocese paid an incredible $660 million in July of 2007 to 508 child molestation victims, when the district attorney wanted to look at the church's records on the priests, the Los Angeles cardinal, Roger M. Mahony, refused to cooperate and hired high-priced lawyers to resist the inquiry all the way, fighting the release of the records.

By the way, the Los Angeles archdiocese, as with archdioceses in other parts of the country, has argued falsely that the widespread problem of priests molesting children came to its attention only recently. But a 375-page 2004 report, based on the Roman Catholic Church's own documents and written by a Catholic priest and two former monks, "Canonical History of Clerical Sexual Abuse," reveals that the sexual abuse of children by priests goes back at least seventeen hundred years, and the church, fully aware of it, has never taken adequate steps to end it. The report also says that for centuries many priests

---

*In the old British common law, there was a crime called misprision of a felony, which was committed when one, knowing of the commission of a felony, failed to report it to the authorities. A leading book on the criminal law states, "The offense was given a less than warm reception in America, it being wholly unsuited to American criminal law, and has become obsolete" (Charles E. Torcia, *Wharton's Criminal Law*, [New York: Clark Boardman and Callaghan, 1996], Vol. 4, 15th ed., 285). However, in recent years several states have enacted statutes making it a misdemeanor not to report one's knowledge of the single crime of a sexual assault on a child. The crime of accessory after the fact (to murder, robbery, burglary, etc.) occurs when one, with knowledge that a felony (not a misdemeanor) has been committed, in some way intentionally aids the perpetrator in avoiding arrest, trial, conviction, or punishment.

have actually solicited sex in the confessional—that is, during the sacrament of Penance! The church's Council of Treves in 1227 found the problem sufficiently common to decree that confessional solicitation of sex should result in excommunication from the church. Although we Americans naturally read mostly about sexual abuse of children by priests here in the United States, the problem is worldwide. For instance, a nine-year investigation by the Irish government reported in 2009 that for decades, abuse was "endemic" in church-run schools and orphanages, the *New York Times* (January 19, 2011) saying that "thousands of children were victims."

Very few crimes are as heinous and despicable as child molestation, a crime with lifelong consequences, and when done by a priest, of all people, someone in whom the greatest of trust is reposed, it is even worse. Yet the Catholic church, all the way up to the Vatican in Rome, has, throughout the years, been uniformly protective of these pedophile priests. There's only one interpretation to put on this. Just one. Though what the church has done is a form of self-defense, and the instinct for self-preservation is the strongest of all human instincts, the reality still remains that the church was more concerned priest child molestation cases coming to the attention of the public and harming its image, that it wanted to protect, than it was in punishing the offending priests and preventing them from continuing their terrible crimes. In other words, although we can assume that child molestation, mostly of innocent young altar boys, offended the Catholic hierarchy greatly, it nonetheless was something church leaders felt they could live with. Is that what Jesus, per Catholic dogma the founder of the church, would have wanted for those who molest children? In Mark 9:42, Jesus said, "Whoever shall offend one of these little ones that believe in me, it is better for him that a millstone were hung around his neck and he were cast into the sea."

In May of 2001, Pope John Paul II, after consultation with Cardinal Joseph Ratzinger—at the time the head of the Vatican's Congregation for the Doctrine of the Faith, and now the current pope, Benedict XVI

— sent out an apostolic letter (titled *Sacramentorum Sanctitatis Tutela*, or "Safeguarding the Sanctity of the Sacraments") to all bishops in the church instructing them to deal with sexual abuse cases in private; that is, not report the charges of child molestation to the civil authorities. The cases, he decreed, would be adjudicated "subject to pontifical secret." Cardinal Ratzinger noted in a cover letter that actually this instruction had already been "in force" in the church since 1922.

In December of 2002, Cardinal Ratzinger responded to all the headlines in the United States about the rampant pedophilia by Catholic priests by saying, in a lowbrow type of mendacity one wouldn't expect of a high church theologian, that he was "personally convinced" that all the media coverage of pedophilia by Catholic priests in America was a "planned campaign" by the media to make the church look bad. Remarkably, he added that "the percentage of these offenses among priests" was no higher than in other professions, "perhaps even lower." Unbelievable. Ratzinger wanted us to believe that there are just as many or more accountants, engineers, doctors, and lawyers molesting young boys as there are priests. Right. I remember saying to my wife, "It seems that you can't pick up the daily newspaper anymore without reading about some damn accountant who has molested thirty young boys within the past few years." And a February 2, 2003, Associated Press story out of Boston (one of hundreds of such stories) captioned "24 More Priests Accused of Sex Abuse" was just a typographical error. It should have read "24 More Engineers Accused of Sex Abuse."

And now Benedict is the pope, the head of the Catholic church. Not only is Benedict, who is recognized as the top theologian in the Catholic church today and is fluent in ten languages, wrong when he says that other professions have just as many or more pedophiles as the priesthood, but even if what Benedict says were true, is there not any difference between a lawyer or an engineer molesting a child and a Catholic priest doing so? How incredibly unknowing or insensitive can he be about the special obligations of the priesthood, and the special trust that parents and the children themselves place in priests, supposed men of God, something that does not obtain in professions and fields such as law, engineering, or accounting?

It wasn't until April 12, 2010—after Benedict himself was swept up in the exploding scandal by revelations that as archbishop of the Munich, Germany, archdiocese in 1980 he had authorized the transfer of a known pedophile priest to another diocese, where he continued to molest children, and in 1985 was elephantine (taking years) in his ordering of a church hearing to defrock a Wisconsin priest who had molested two hundred boys—that the Vatican finally issued a directive requiring that church officials report priest abuse cases to the civil authorities. So it was only when the church was being strongly buffeted by mounting criticism from around the world, Benedict's approval ratings had plummeted to a new low of 40 percent, vandals were writing obscenities on the home in which he had been born, and the *National Catholic Reporter* observed in its lead editorial, "We now face the largest institutional crisis in centuries, possibly in church history" that the church was dragged, kicking and screaming, onto the morality train.

Before we go on, and in all fairness to the Catholic church and the priesthood, the consensus is that the vast majority of priests, even those of homosexual orientation (estimated to be 30 percent or higher), do not sexually molest minors. However, studies suggest that approximately 50 percent of all priests are not celibate and lead active sexual lives (e.g., see A. W. Richard Sipe, *Celibacy in Crisis: A Secret World Revisited*, [New York: Brunner-Routledge, 2003], 49–51, 301–302).

⟋

THE CATHOLIC CHURCH is an institution whose position on sexual expression is so terribly out of kilter it believes that sex, a normal function of all humans, even animals, should never be engaged in only for pleasure. The only time that sex is not a mortal sin, according to the church, is when engaged in by a husband and wife for the sole purpose of procreation. Though almost impossible to believe, the official position of the Catholic church is that if a married couple engages in sex solely for pleasure, they are committing a mortal sin and an "intrinsically evil" act (*Catechism of the Catholic Church*, number 2370). Hence, the use of all methods of artificial contraception, such as condoms, is a mortal sin because that would reduce sex between men and women to a recreational act, which is prohibited by the church (*Catechism*, number 2370). Therefore, even when millions, yes, millions of poor Catholic Africans are dying of AIDS, the unbelievable (is there any other word?) Catholic church has forbidden Africans, as it forbids all Catholics, from using condoms, even within a marriage where the husband has the disease, and has forbidden its clergy in Africa, where three-quarters of all AIDS deaths worldwide occur, from participating in any program to provide condoms for the people. Why? As indicated, because condoms will prevent procreation, the only authorized purpose for sex. Translation: In the Catholic church, it is better that great numbers of Africans have more destitute children and, even worse, die horrible deaths from AIDS than that they have sex for pleasure. If you know of a different interpretation other than the one I have just stated, what is it?[8] (See endnote discussion for possible male prostitute exception to church doctrine in the future.)

I'll never forget the sight of Pope John Paul II riding through destitute areas of Mexico in his pope-mobile in 1979, raising his arms to bless the poor of Mexico alongside the road, while at the same time forcing them, through fear of burning in hell throughout eternity, not to use contraceptives, the one thing, perhaps more than anything else, that might have lessened their poverty.

I have a suggestion for the Catholic church that will allow it to save face in allowing contraception in very high-incidence AIDS parts of the world like Africa. Why not view contraception as a form of self-defense to save one's life, as the church has always accepted the use of deadly force in self-defense? I mean, even if the pope killed someone in self-defense, would any rational person criticize him? The church, of course, would argue that self-defense is not necessary here, that abstinence will do. But abstinence is virtually impossible. For crying out loud, if the church's own priests can't abstain, how can the Catholic church expect the poor people of Africa to do so?

℃

HERE'S A CHURCH THAT OPENLY SPEAKS out against contraception, sex outside of marriage, abortion, and a host of other conduct it deems immoral, presenting itself to the world as the institutional paragon of morality. But when the moral monster of the twentieth century and beyond had his SS rounding up millions of European Jews for transport to the gas chambers of Auschwitz, Treblinka, and Chelmno, the Catholic church was, pardon the pun, as quiet as a church mouse, refusing to speak out against Hitler. You know, murdering Jews is one thing, but using condoms is something else. Arthur Hertzberg, a professor of humanities at New York University, writes that "in 1930s and 1940s Europe, the Roman Catholic Church was the only institution that possessed the moral stature and strength to denounce and forbid the murder of the Jews. It did not do so."

And apparently, refusing to speak out against Hitler was not enough for Pope Pius XII and his church. In his 1964 book, *The Catholic Church and Nazi Germany*, Guenther Lewy wrote that when the Nazi Party came to power in 1934, it requested of the Catholic church that it help the party "in determining who was or was not fully Aryan, for under Nazi law this depended on the racial (in this case, religious) status of parents and grandparents," and prior to 1876, births had been registered only by the church. Lewy went on to say that the church, which had always cooperated with the German government on other matters, complied with this new request, too. "The very question of whether the church should lend her help to the Nazi state in sorting out people of Jewish descent," he wrote, "was never debated." He quoted a Catholic priest in 1934, writing in the *Klerusblatt*, the organ of Bavarian Diocesan priests, "We shall . . . do our best to help in this service to the people."

Of course, this was 1934, before Hitler's "Final Solution." But all informed people already knew, from Hitler's two-volume autobiography, *Mein Kampf,* in 1925 and 1927, of Hitler's pathological hatred of the Jewish people. (Remarkably, as a harbinger of the future, Hitler even wrote in volume 2 that if "twelve or fifteen thousand of these Hebraic corrupters of the nation had been subjected to poison gas at the beginning" of the First World War, "the sacrifices of millions at the front would not have been in vain.") Much more tellingly, the German-born Lewy wrote that "the cooperation of the Church in this matter continued right through the war years [1939–1945] . . . All of the diocesan archives preserved contain voluminous files of correspondence in connection with the certification of non-Aryan descent." So while millions of Jews were screaming their last breaths in Hitler's gas chambers, the Catholic church was dutifully serving up more Jews to the Nazis for their death chambers.

However, and again in all fairness to the Catholic church, as John Toland writes in his 1976 book *Adolf Hitler,* "the Church, under the Pope's guidance, saved the lives of more Jews than all other churches, religious institutions and rescue organizations combined, hiding thousands of Jews in monasteries, convents and Vatican City itself." In this regard, as bad as the church was in not speaking out against Hitler, the

---

*Remarkably, this brutal indifference ostensibly continued to exist three decades later, at least in the mind of President Nixon's Secretary of State Henry Kissinger, himself a Jew who escaped Hitler's gas chambers by fleeing Germany as a teenager with his family in 1938. After a March 1, 1973, meeting in the oval office between Israeli Prime Minister Golda Meir and Nixon during which she asked Nixon to make a diplomatic effort to get the Soviet Union to allow Soviet Jews to emigrate so they could avoid persecution, the Nixon White House tapes of that date record Kissinger telling Nixon: "The emigration of Jews from the Soviet Union is not an objective of American foreign policy. *And if they put Jews into gas chambers in the Soviet Union, it is not an American concern.* Maybe a humanitarian concern." Maybe? We can probably assume that Kissinger did not truly mean what he said. But on the other hand, how do words like this even come out of one's mouth?

church was much better than the governments of the United States and Great Britain, whose shameful and inexcusable failure to make any effort to stop or even mitigate the Holocaust has left an indelible stain on the moral tapestry of their history.*

⚬⁓

HERE'S YET ANOTHER WELL-KNOWN EXAMPLE of how the church takes absurdity and audacity to vertiginous heights. In his 1632 book during the period of the Roman Inquisition, *Dialogue by Galileo Galilei on the two Chief World Systems, Ptolemaic and Copernican*, Italian astronomer and scientist Galileo declared he agreed with Polish astronomer Copernicus (1473–1543) that the earth was not the center of the universe, that it revolved around the sun. The next year, 1633, the church's "Holy Tribunal" (Inquisition court) proceeded to charge and convict Galileo of heresy since it taught that the earth remained still and the sun revolved around it.[9] This was the geocentric model of the universe first propounded by Aristotle close to four centuries before Jesus, which the church found completely compatible with holy scripture: "God fixed the earth upon its foundation, not to be moved forever" (Psalm 104:5; see also Ecclesiastes 1:5 for movement of sun, and Joshua 10:12–14). Aristotle's ill-advised foray into astronomy is believed to have influenced second-century AD Greek astronomer Ptolemy, whose conclusion of a fixed earth around which the sun revolved became the accepted wisdom before being challenged by Copernicus fourteen hundred years later. The Inquisition court forced Galileo to kneel and renounce his scientific finding, and he was sentenced to life imprisonment. The sentence was later commuted to house arrest (Galileo got off cheap—many heretics were burned at the stake at the time), where he remained until his death in 1642.

The church didn't know any better in 1633. But although the Galileo affair was an embarrassment to the Catholic church for centuries, and despite many calls for it to exonerate Galileo, and the conclusion of a panel of scientists and historians appointed by Pope John

Paul II in 1980 that the judges who condemned Galileo had committed an error, unbelievably, the congenitally arrogant Catholic church absolutely refused to exonerate or pardon Galileo for something that the world's schoolchildren all had down pat. It wasn't until October 31, 1992, more than three and a half centuries after the fact, that John Paul finally agreed to exonerate Galileo, issuing a declaration acknowledging the error of the Inquisition court. As an aside, St. Augustine, the original bible literalist, who remains to this day among the top two theologians in Catholic history, said that "if any error were discovered in Holy Writ, the authority of Holy Writ would perish." Well then?

ONE OF MY MAIN OBJECTIONS to the Catholic church is that it is silly. I mean, isn't it rather difficult to take it seriously? But there's no question that we do. When Pope John Paul II died in April 2005, millions the world over wondered whom the 117-member College of Cardinals would choose as his successor. Television throughout the world treated the pope's death and the election of his successor as the major story of the year. Newspaper headlines and cover stories in *Time* and *Newsweek* dealt in depth with the event. And what all of the media, a group (with notable exceptions) that can always be counted upon to do a minimum of thinking, wanted to know was in what "new direction" the next pope would take the more than 1 billion members of the church.

What new direction? Any person with the most rudimentary knowledge of Catholicism would know that whoever John's successor was, he wasn't going to change one comma. That is so, as I see it, for two reasons. One is that for centuries the Catholic church, with its heaven and hell, purgatory, sacraments, mortal and venial sins, has been absurd to its very marrow, and it is not about to change, for anything, honoring its past as a testament to its future. Besides, once church doctrine or dogma has been formulated by an ecumenical council of bishops of the church, as is well known, that doctrine is "unalterable."

Amid the Catholic church's many unvarying points of dogma, here is the only type of change that one could expect of the Catholic church. And it took the church *eight centuries* to do it! For infants who die before they've had a chance to be baptized, which would cleanse their soul of "original sin," the Catholic Bishop Augustine of Hippo (later, St. Augustine) wrote in the fifth century that unfortunately the church's teaching on original sin dictated that the infants could not be admitted into heaven, creating the specter of hell. And that was the position of the Catholic church for centuries. But the church knew it had a real problem. Yes, the bible told the church that no one could go to heaven unless they were "born-again of water" (John 3:5), but how in the heck did it look for the church to say that these infants were going to hell? No problem. Though it never rose to that of a doctrine of the church, in the thirteenth century the church simply invented a place called limbo for unbaptized infants. In limbo, the infants couldn't see the Lord, but Thomas Aquinas assured concerned Catholics that the infants would be well taken care of and have a substantial degree of peace and happiness in these new quarters of theirs.

In recent years there had been rumblings in the Vatican about limbo. The church has millions of infants who have died since the thirteenth century without being baptized who are quartered there (the church has never told anyone where limbo is located), and the problem is not just that one imagines the quarters in limbo were becoming overcrowded, but some felt that maybe, just maybe, the fair thing to do would be to move these millions of infants to heaven.

Remarkably, in 2005, thirty Catholic theologians from around the world, members of the International Theological Commission, a Vatican advisory panel, met at the Vatican to decide on what recommendation they should make to Pope Benedict XVI whether to abolish (how do you abolish something that doesn't exist?) limbo and give the infants some type of a special papal dispensation pass into heaven, or keep the doors open on the place that the church had been landlording for centuries. Can you imagine that? Thirty grown men with all types of doctorate degrees, wearing suits and ties and boarding planes with their briefcases to fly to Rome and sit around a conference table and actually conduct a serious discussion about limbo. It's mindboggling.

After close to two years of continuing thought and consultation, on April 20, 2007, the distinguished panel of theologians, in a forty-one-page report titled "The Hope of Salvation for Infants Who Die Without Being Baptized," recommended to Pope Benedict that the Catholic church permit unbaptized infants to go to heaven. Two days later, on April 22, 2007, Benedict accepted the recommendation of the panel. However, nothing has been heard from the Vatican since, so there is no way to know for sure if the dormitory was shuttered and all the infants were immediately transported to heaven, or if, perhaps because of overcrowding in heaven, the infants are being transferred as space is available.

In any event, this type of change, if at all, is the only type of "new direction" that one could ever expect to see in today's, and yesterday's, Catholic church. But maybe I'm not being fair. In 1962, Pope John XXIII's Second Vatican Council did say that nuns could wear blue jeans. In 1966, the United States Conference of Catholic Bishops ruled that Catholics, for the first time in centuries, could now eat meat on Fridays. And in 2007, Benedict ruled that priests no longer had to get their bishop's permission to celebrate mass in old-school Latin. Wow.

The second reason that I believe there cannot be any new direction in the Catholic church is what I call "the crisp factor." You see, the church has a problem. If for centuries it has held that, just for instance, sex outside of marriage, masturbation, and homosexual acts are "mortal sins, sins which exclude one from the kingdom of heaven," and hence those dying with these sins on their souls have been burning to a crisp in hell for centuries, how in the world can the church ever later decide that any of these acts is no longer a mortal sin? Wouldn't it have to send an emissary down to hell, saying, "Guys, we were wrong. We made a little mistake." "A little mistake?" a crisp would be likely to pipe up. "Do you have eyes in your head, man? We've all been burned down to the size of a termite, and you say you made a little mistake?" "Yeah, you don't look too good. But what can I say? The pope's the pope. He changed his mind. Hop aboard; we're shipping you to heaven." Of course, I'm being sarcastic and facetious (but as I indicated earlier, is the Catholic church worthy of any other type of treatment?), but the point I'm making is a very real problem for the church, one it avoids by simply not changing a comma.

❧

HOW DOES CATHOLICISM RECONCILE its claim to greatness and sanctity with its pedophilia by priests or the serious corruption, even evil, of some former popes, the most notorious of which belonged to the Borgia family (referred to by some observers as "the first crime family") of Italy and Spain extending from the fourteenth through the sixteenth centuries? Eleven cardinals and three popes came from the family that was noted for its insatiable greed and corruption, even murder. Pope Alexander VI (1492–1503), who became extremely wealthy and made no attempt to conceal his promiscuous life, fathered eight children, some by mistresses, the most well known of whom were the political and military leader Cesare Borgia, the personification of Renaissance profligacy, and Alexander's beautiful daughter, Lucrezia Borgia, who came to symbolize through the ages the evil treachery of a woman. It is not surprising that the duplicitous Niccolò Machiavelli found a welcome home in Cesare Borgia's court, Machiavelli memorializing Borgia in his masterpiece on power, *The Prince*.

It wasn't just the Catholic church's sale of indulgences (certificates guaranteeing their purchasers a speedier passage out of purgatory to heaven after they died) that angered the Catholic priest and reformer Martin Luther to the point that he ignited the Protestant Reformation in Germany in the sixteenth century. In an open letter to Pope Leo X in 1520, he had these kind words to say about the wayward church: "The Roman Church, once the holiest of all, has become the most licentious den of thieves, the most shameless of brothels, the kingdom of sin, death, and hell." Today, many, including some Catholic scholars, consider Luther, who forever fractured Christianity and changed the history of the Western world, to actually have been a lifesaver for Catholicism. And despite his anti-Semitic rants that were quoted by the Nazis in their rise to power, Luther remains a towering figure in Christianity.

The Catholic church maintains that it is the only religion founded by Jesus Christ, all the others being founded by mere men, such as Muhammed, Buddha, Luther, Calvin, Zoroaster, etc. This position of Catholicism that it is the one, true church of Christ is based on its so-called apostolic origin, its raison d'être. That Jesus told Peter, one of the twelve apostles, "You are Peter [Petros, the Greek name for "rock"], and on this rock I will build my church, and the powers of death shall not prevail against it. I will give you the keys of the Kingdom of Heaven, and whatever you bind on earth shall be bound in Heaven, and whatever you loose on earth shall be loosed in Heaven" (Matthew 16:17–20). The belief is that the mission Jesus gave Peter was to be carried out by Peter and his successors until the end of time. And the church claims it can trace an unbroken line of succession from Peter to the present pope, Pope Benedict XVI being the 265th successor to St. Peter.

In a July 22, 1930, letter from Sir Arnold Lunn to his ecclesiastical friend Ronald Knox, the first of an exchange of letters on the church that were published in the 1934 book *Difficulties*, he wrote, "The a priori case for the Roman Catholic Church [having supremacy over all other religions] has always seemed to me quite plausible. It is reasonable to suppose that Christ would not have left the world without some institution to preserve His teaching from corruption. And clearly, the claims of the Roman Catholic Church to be the institution in question are very strong. . . . Christ would take at least as much trouble as John Wesley [founder of Methodism], for instance, took, to provide an effective institution to perpetuate his teaching."

This would seem to be a sensible inference. But if the apostolic origin of the Catholic church means anything, wouldn't one almost expect a long line of saintly men to ascend to the throne of Peter? And yet we know that many of the popes have been corrupt. Doesn't this do violence to this sacred inference, particularly if we assume that Peter's successors in the Holy See would be mindful of the monumental theological responsibilities they had? Again, no problem. Do you know how Catholicism handles this, as well as the aforementioned pedophilia and other crimes of the church down through the ages? The only way it can. Let's hear again from the Reverend John Trigilio, president of the Confraternity of Catholic Clergy and holder of a doctorate in theology. He makes the identical argument that all the leaders of the Catholic church make:

> Often someone will name a corrupt pope, bishop, or priest from history or more recent vintage as an argument against the holiness of the church. Just as you see individual examples of a bad husband or a bad wife here and there, the institution of marriage isn't bad just because some married people can't fulfill their vows and maintain a permanent, faithful, fruitful and loving relationship. Likewise, you've heard of abusive fathers or mothers who abandon their children, yet the institution of family isn't tainted or tarnished by the minority who don't live up to the family values and commitments they ought to. So, why should the church be any different?

If a school of theology can actually teach a priest like Trigilio to utter such absurdities, what does that say about the school? It says that the school should put a lock on its door and not just during evening hours. Such an argument by Trigilio, comparing apples and oranges, should be offensive to all thinking people. People getting married, for instance, have no responsibility in the overall scheme of things to anyone other than to each other. But by Catholicism's own doctrine, popes are "the representatives of Jesus Christ on this earth," and because of it are considered to be "infallible" when they speak ex cathedra on matters of "faith or morals."[10] The Catholic church calls its pope "the vicar of Christ," and he is the spiritual leader today of more than 1 billion Catholics! And as previously indicated, under Catholic doctrine, even priests, through the sacrament of Holy Orders, are given the miraculous power by virtue of their ordination to change bread and wine into the body and blood of Christ, and the incredible power to forgive all of the sins, in the name of Jesus Christ, of any Catholic who confesses to them. For the Catholic church to compare a pope, even a priest, with someone getting married, or an abusive father or mother, is outrageous.

Moreover, I think that the church is playing with fire on this issue. The ultimate question to be asked and answered is this: By the church maintaining that its popes are Christ's representatives on this earth, to the point, as indicated, that when speaking ex cathedra on matters of faith or morals, the pope, by "divine intervention," is infallible (i.e., incapable of error), and to the point where even a lowly priest is invested by Christ with miraculous powers, is the church constructing a spiritual umbilical cord to Christ himself of such closeness that if, indeed, its claims are true, *none of its representatives would be capable* of sins like corruption, murder, or child molestation since Christ would not be capable of such things? What I am saying is that when the church says that an errant priest, bishop, or pope is no different than an errant husband or father, my response is, "Wait a while." Let's examine, in a little more depth, the possible enormous issue involved here.

Normally, an agent who commits a *crime* (say an insurance agent defrauded a purchaser by misrepresenting the coverage of the policy) is deemed to be separate from his employer, and the civil doctrine of *respondeat superior* (the master or principal is responsible for the conduct of his servant or employee) does not apply, meaning that the insurance company is not *criminally* responsible for the agent's crime, although it, of course, would be bound civilly by the agent's representation. Note that the insurance agent only has the power to sell the policy. His insurance company has not invested him with the power, for instance, to change a provision in the company's policy or change the premiums on the policy; these are things that only the company can do. Nor can he satisfy the claim of any policyholder by paying the latter's claim.

Priests, on the other hand, during their ordination by the sacrament of Holy Orders, are invested with powers that only Jesus Christ has, but that Christ, per the Catholic church, reposed in popes and priests. In other words, priests, as indicated, do things that, without Christ's investiture, only Christ could do, such as changing bread and wine during the sacrament of the Holy Eucharist into the body and blood of Christ. Likewise, Jesus had the power to forgive sin (1 John 1:8–9). And this power was given by him to his apostles. "Receive the Holy Spirit. If you forgive the sins of any, they are forgiven. If you retain the sins of any, they are retained" (John 20:22–23). During the Catholic church's Council of Trent, this power was recognized as also residing in priests (Session 23, July 15, 1563, Doctrine on the Sacrament of Holy Orders). During Holy Orders, with the person to be ordained priest on his knees before him, the bishop lays his hand upon the head of the candidate for priesthood in silence. The Catholic church believes that by the imposition of the hands, the Holy Spirit enters the body of the person, thereby investing him with all the Christ-like powers of priesthood.

In an authoritative book on the Catholic church, *The Teachings of Christ: A Catholic Catechism for Adults*, the editors, reflecting Catholic tradition and dogma, write:

> When a person is ordained a priest, he is united to Christ by his ordination, and his priesthood is in some way a permanent part of his being. . . . In explaining how the priest can function as Christ, the Church speaks of the priesthood as an identification with Christ on the most fundamental level. In their reception of Holy Orders, priests are consecrated to God in a new way, and they become "living instruments of Christ." . . . When you behold the priest offering the consecrated bread, see in his hand the hand of Christ himself. (Ronald

Lawler, Thomas Lawler, and Donald Wuerl, *The Teachings of Christ: A Catholic Catechism for Adults*, Huntington, VA: Our Sunday Visitor, 1975, 439–440)

Indeed, Jesus told his followers, "Here is a list of some of the members that God has placed in *the body of Christ.*" The list includes "apostles" (which we've seen includes priests), "teachers," and "those who can help others" (1 Corinthians 12:28). So we have, if we're to believe holy scripture, priests being "in the body of Christ." Jesus Christ and Catholic priests can't get too much closer than that, can they?

In his *Catechism on the Priesthood*, St. John Vianney, a nineteenth-century French priest who is considered the patron saint of all priests, wrote, "What is a priest? A man who holds the place of God—a man who is invested with the powers of God. When the priest remits sins, he does not say, 'God pardons you.' He says 'I absolve you.' If I were to meet a priest and an angel, I should salute the priest before I saluted the angel. The latter is the friend of God, but the priest holds His place."

The official statement of church belief, the *Catechism of the Catholic Church*, says, "In the ecclesial service of the ordained priest, it is Christ himself who is present to his Church. . . . By virtue of the sacrament of Holy Orders [a priest] acts in persona Christi Capitis . . . possess[ing] the authority to act in the power and place of Christ himself" (*Catechism*, number 1548).

The Council of Trent said, "Justly, priests are called not only angels, but even gods, because of the fact that they exercise in our midst the power of the immortal God. . . . The power has nothing equal or like it on earth. It even surpasses human reason and understanding."

It could not be more obvious from the above that on so many levels the relationship of an agent for an insurance company (or car dealership or stock brokerage firm, etc.) to his company cannot be compared to that of the relationship between a priest and Jesus Christ in the Catholic church.

I would ask theologians to give this matter some time and thought. The question is whether it is reasonable to conclude that if popes and priests have the power and intimate identification with Jesus Christ and God that the church claims they do, they would no more be *capable* of being corrupt or immoral than Jesus would. (1 John 3:9 asserts that "those who have been born into God's family do not sin because God's life is in them. So they *cannot* sin." Again, see "in the body of Christ" in 1 Corinthians 12:28, and recall the Council of Trent's holding regarding priests.) If this is their conclusion, it may be that the church, by overreaching, has ironically defined itself out of its own existence. By that I mean the very immoral conduct of many priests, bishops, and popes through the centuries may invalidate the very premise of the Catholic church's legitimacy—that it is the only true church of Christ because Christ chose it to be his representative here on earth.

Pope John Paul II's "Day of Pardon" homily on March 12, 2000, which was meant to acknowledge, confess, and "implore Jesus' forgiveness" for 2,000 years of church sins, corruption, and immorality, went only to the issue of remission, not to the seminal question of how, if the Catholic church is the church of Jesus Christ, it could have done these things in the first place.

13

If God Is All-Good, Why Does He Put All of Us to Death?

THERE IS SOMETHING THAT has always surprised me about human beings in their relationship with their God. I've already mentioned that no one ever seriously bad-mouths God, calling him profane names and saying they hate him. But many people *have* wondered how, if he is a good God, he could allow the atrocities and the horrors of life to happen, and some have gotten angry with him, particularly when the horror strikes them personally, such as in the loss of a child. But even then, they usually reconsider and accept what happened as "God's will." Surprisingly, however, *I do not recall reading or hearing people talk about how a good God could allow all of us to die an ordinary death.* I'm not concerning myself here with things like murder, suicide, or accidental death, just the mere act of death that we, as humans, all have to experience. Something we all accept as a completely natural and inevitable consequence of life. In fact, in a sense we begin to die from the moment we are born, with each passing second in life being a step toward death. While all men strive for a place in the sun, only eternal darkness awaits. Perhaps ninety-nine out of a hundred of us merely experience death, mankind's greatest enemy, in its nonviolent form. Putting things like homicides and war out of our minds for the moment, death is the ultimate atrocity, one whose only virtue is being democratic, its dreadful hand as impartial as sunlight. If it is undeniably false to say we are all born equal, at least we all have a common destiny. Indeed cemeteries are full of people the world could not be without.

Except for those for whom death is a refuge from life, virtually all of us cling desperately to life, either because of our love of life and/or our fear of death.[1] As I said in a double-murder case I prosecuted where I was seeking the death penalty against a defendant named Alan Palliko, "People who are ninety years of age hang on desperately to life with a youthful passion. The world's most wealthy men, on their deathbeds, would give everything they own for the gift of life. Animals fight desperately for life. Henry Stockton and Judy Palliko, if they had had it, would have given Alan Palliko the world *if he would have just let them live.*"

Most of us know, from firsthand experience, how much of a struggle life is with its constant trials and tribulations. No matter. I'm told there is a passage in a novel by Fyodor Dostoevsky in which a character in the story exclaims, "If I were condemned to live on a rock, chained to a rock in the lashing sea, and all around me were ice and gales and storm, I would still want to live. Oh God, just to live, live, *live!*"

We know that animals, in the face of death, fight ferociously for life. Even mice, if they could, would propose that a bell be hung around a cat's neck.

Death is so bad it seems immune from lightening, although American Revolutionary War hero Ethan Allen tried when his physician told him, "I fear the angels are waiting for you." "Waiting are they? Waiting are they?" Allen said. "Well goddam 'em, let 'em wait."

My view is that life, as bad and horrible as it so frequently is, is nonetheless too gloriously rich, exciting, fascinating, and forever promising for any ordinary hand to describe what makes it so.[2] Indeed, I don't believe that Shakespeare or whoever possessed the greatest literary hand in history could do anything but fall short in endeavoring to capture, in mere words, its wonder. One can only describe moments, not the essence of the whole, which cannot be grasped by words, only felt. But the moments themselves are terribly wonderful: a summer afternoon, soaring and thrilling music, a great hamburger when one is famished, sitting center court at a Wimbledon final, first love, physical intimacy, April in Paris, autumn in New York, parents' passion and excitement over their newborn child, starting out traveling in the morning on the open road and stopping at a roadside café for breakfast, the warm sun on one's back on a crisp fall day, a cold drink when you're thirsty, the sight of a bustling city market of fresh fruits and vegetables, laughing from the stomach and rich humor, a great book to read. All are only parts of the whole. The whole—what makes life so wondrous—doesn't lend itself to words. Dostoevsky never even tried, though he proved his point, and well, of how precious life is.[3]

One of the great tragedies of life is that by the time we learn how to live, it's time to die. And when we die, as my son Vince, an eminent doctor, puts it, "we are gone forever and ever and ever and ever." "The undiscovered country," Shakespeare says in *Hamlet,* "from which no traveler returns."

Death is so horrible and so feared that some people, as we know, as early as their fortieth birthday (some even earlier) begin thinking about their mortality, and it gives them increasing anxiety and depression for the rest of their lives. And as the shadow lengthens on their lives, the anxiety and depression only increase. The only thing that makes life reasonably tolerable is that the date when the curtain will fall is usually unknown. For a great many of us, death is so terrible that at one level of consciousness we find our death impossible to imagine. Besides, in the moment we're in, isn't life pulsating with energy, motion, and color—undying? Death would be an imposter for whom there simply is no room. And how can anything be good if it's not permanent? Only when we're at death's portals do we awaken enough to die. Till then, we cannot really and truly accept the transience of life and, to one degree or another, everything in it. "You cannot cross the same river twice," observes an old Hindu saying.

Not only is our death too horrible for most of us to even contemplate for more than a few moments, but the loss of our loved ones, if possible, is even worse. How do you say the final good-bye to the love of your life? How can you do it when you have become a part of each other's life, and in the process a part of each other, for forty, fifty, sixty years? You're losing your lifetime partner, with whom you've gone through everything together, the highs, the lows, the happiness, the tears, the memories (oh, those old photographs). And now one has to leave the other behind. How do you, how can you, say the last good-bye? And how are you going to be able to go on without him or her? There are no words.

Your parents, your father young and virile and your mother young and beautiful in their wedding photographs. As a child, you always knew your father was the strongest and greatest man in the world and your mother the sweetest and most wonderful woman. The strong legs and back of your father that carried you piggyback in the backyard when you were a child cannot even bear the weight of his own body any longer, brought low and weakened by the ravages of life. You talk to him at his bedside and tell him how much you love him, but, his eyes closed, and breathing heavily, he does not answer, though he somehow lets you know he can hear you. You and your family can't bear the thought of losing "Papa" or "Dad," a father you knew would have given his life for you, and you are helpless to stop what is taking place before your eyes. When he breathes his last breath at the hospital, some members of the family scream or cry out in anguish. Usually, all moan uncontrollably. We know that life can't ever be the same. And Mama, or Mom, whose breasts gave you your first nourishment, who cleaned your fanny, and who worried about your welfare throughout her life. When she took her last breath, the family again wailed and cried, and you all knew that nothing in life could be worse than losing her forevermore. How can it possibly be that we will never see Ma and Pa again, except in old photographs, which cut deep into our insides with longing. Even the loss of our sisters and brothers brings great pain and sorrow.*

The death of our loved ones is, of course, greater than any pain we are forced to endure. But we know that the stilling of the heart is just a part of the story. In addition to our being forced to witness the physical withering away of our loved ones, death is often preceded by weeks, sometimes months, even years, of severe pain, suffering, nausea, vomiting, incontinence, delusional utterances. And at the end, there is the bluish swelling of the arms and legs, the cold hands and feet, the gradual but clear "shutting down" of the digestive and urinary systems, the dreaded sound of the so-called death rattle, and dying with tubes inserted into their stomach through their nose and wires protruding from their bodies. With dread, all of these things take place before our own eyes as our parents, sisters, brothers, and spouses struggle to hold on to life. That is, we watch them die, down to the gradual loosening of their grips on the bedside rail they sometimes clutch.

Death is dirty and rotten, horrifying, monstrous, vile, disgusting, grotesque, despicable, indescribably ugly, and if there is a God, the most *evil*. When our loved ones die before our eyes, when we die before our loved ones' eyes, who is responsible for this horrible, ghastly event? If people believe in the Christian (or Jewish) God, why don't I ever hear them talk or write about the fact that it is God, the Good Lord,

---

*Even the loss of our pets is devastating to us. Through the years, in addition to Sherlock, my wife and I have had several pets, and the death of each one, as millions have said about their pets, was like "a death in the family." These four-legged critters with tails and whiskers are so unbelievably cute and lovable that many times I've said, "They almost make you believe in God." Who else could create these little people with hearts so loyal they will kiss the hand that no longer has food to offer? And who, unlike babies, remain innocent all their lives? If they never existed and you asked one hundred of the most imaginative minds in the world to envision something as incredible as we know they are, I don't believe they would come up with anything as wonderful as these creatures.

who decided, yes, decided, to put us to death? Why am I playing games with words here? The question is, why does God kill all of us? God makes no bones about the fact that he kills us. After I had already concluded this about the Christian God a long time ago, I came across Deuteronomy 32:39 in which God says, "I am the one who kills and gives life." Why do we have to die? Why can't we live forever?

If one believes in the Christian God, there can be only one answer—that God doesn't want us to. If he did, Christians must concede that a God who they believe created the universe surely would have the much lesser power of enabling humans to live forever. Indeed, in Genesis 3:22, God said that if Adam and Eve had eaten from the right tree in the Garden of Eden, the tree of life, "man would live forever." In other words, the only reason God does not permit us to live without ever dying is his vindictive and perverse nature in punishing innocent humans for the sins of Adam and Eve.

So God does not deny that we live only as long as he wants us to. There are several unambiguous references to this in the bible. For instance, when Hezekiah, the King of Judah who was deathly ill, begged God for more time, God said "I will add fifteen years to your life" (Kings 20:1–6; see also 1 Kings 3:14, Psalm 91:16).

Before God he wiped out all the earth's people with the flood, according to the bible, people routinely lived to be many hundreds of years old. Adam himself lived to be 930 years old. One of his sons, Seth, lived to be 912. We all know that Methuselah lived to be 969 years old. And many more lived to be 700, 800, and 900 years old. Noah lived to be 950 (Genesis 5:3–8, 25, 27 and 9:28–29).

At some point in time around then, God decided people were living too long and said, "My Spirit will not put up with humans for such a long time, for they are only mortal flesh. In the future they will live no more than 120 years" (Genesis 6:3).[4] (See endnote discussion for French woman who defied God.)

So when we lose our loved ones and cry out in unbearable anguish, one being and one being only is responsible, and that's God. (For purposes of this discussion only, I am presupposing the existence of the Christian God, whom I do not believe exists.) Yet I never, ever hear anyone blame God for their deaths. They automatically take it for granted that the ravages of life, such as old age and disease, not God, caused their death. But that is not so. God, and God alone, deliberately causes death, using the ravages of life as the agent. The Grim Reaper with his scythe, cutting down people's lives as if he were cutting grain, is only doing the work of God, no one else.

Shakespeare said that "every person owes God a death." But Shakespeare didn't stop to ask himself why death was a debt we all had to pay. If he had, the answer could not have been a good one. No one should say, at the end, as you often hear, "It's *my time* to go," or "We all have *our time* to go." Because if you truly believe in the Christian God who is all-powerful and can do anything, it is never our time to go. It is always *his* time that we go.

You frequently hear people say things like this: "We have to make room for others," or "for the young ones." (Even nonbelievers can be heard to say this. Atheist Christopher Hitchens writes that atheists "are reconciled to living only once, except through our children, for whom we are perfectly happy to notice that *we must make way, and room.*") If you are a Christian, you should realize how ridiculous this statement is. Since Christians believe that their God created the universe, including all the prodigious bodies in space, many a thousand times larger than earth, do they really want to further believe that when it came to the earth, God lost all his power and just couldn't make it any larger? Actually, even with the present size of the earth, what you hear people saying all the time about being overcrowded is laughable. Some cities may be, but certainly not the earth. Look down from an airplane window some day. Humanity in the form of cities, towns, and villages is just an occasional small area or speck below. If God could solve the problem of irrigation—for someone who created the universe, this shouldn't be too difficult for him, should it?—we have an incredible amount of space that could be used for habitation here on earth, even with its present size.

Excluding the oceans, probably 95 percent of the earth's surface or more is uninhabited.

Note that Christians cannot even use their favorite scapegoat, the devil (whom they blame when man commits inhumanity toward man in the form of murder and atrocities), for the death all humans have to face. The devil isn't involved here. Even without the baleful intervention of the devil, all of us, little by little, just waste away and die. And again, we die only because God, if there is a God, wants us to die. So when your mother or father, sister or brother dies, wouldn't simple logic dictate that you curse God, calling him evil for taking them away from you? And shouldn't you curse God when you yourself are on your deathbed and want desperately to stay alive, not die, yet you know that you are very close to making the terrifying leap into everlasting darkness, pondering the incredibly horrific thought that shortly you will no longer exist, never to experience life and see your loved ones again?

Yet, as indicated, and strangely, I never hear or read about this. All one ever hears or reads is how could God cause or allow catastrophes or horrible murders and carnage. But isn't the sight of your mother and father on their deathbeds, their faces and bodies devastated by time and disease to the point of no longer resembling who they once were, and gasping their last breaths, bad enough to inflame your passions against God, particularly when, unlike the murder or atrocity, which God may not have caused, only allowed, we absolutely know (God admits it) he caused your parents' deaths?

Apparently not. Where do we take our loved ones after they die and before burial? To the home (church, synagogue) of the being who caused their deaths, and, unbelievably, we praise and glorify him. But praise him for what? Taking our loved ones from us and transforming what was once a healthy vibrant human being into a person of skin and bones who is immobile in bed, whose face is drawn and lips are dry, whose eyes are open but seemingly unseeing, whose mouth is agape, who often moans from excruciating pain? And after death, after we have thrown dirt on top of their coffins, having them serve as food for worms and ants? And we should actually praise the Lord for this? Under what conceivable rationale? I repeat. Under what conceivable rationale or theory?

In a typical Christian funeral, the congregation is told at the beginning that "we are here in celebration of [the decedent's] life." But virtually the entire ceremony that follows, other than the eulogy, is a full-throated praise and celebration of God and Jesus. At a recent Christian funeral I attended, the pastor told those present no less than seventeen times that "God (or Jesus) loves us." Right. That's why he killed the decedent. Some love.

The following is a list of some of the hymns currently available for a church service at a major mortuary in Los Angeles, all, apparently, thanking God for placing in the casket, cold to the touch, the body of your loved one: "Now Thank We All Our God," "How Great Thou Art," "Praise You Father," "Father, I Adore You," "Glorify Thy Name," "The Love of God," and "O How I Love Jesus." The following are passages from some of the prayers available during the funeral service: "God broke our hearts to prove to us that He only takes the best." (On every level imaginable, these words should be offered only by a lifetime resident of a mental institution.) "God wanted me now. He set me free." "God looked around His garden and He found an empty place. He then looked down upon the earth and saw your tired face. He put His arms around you and lifted you to rest."

You can write or say all you want about these passages being recited only to ease the pain of losing your loved one, and not everyone takes these words literally, although many, of course, do. But there are three realities your literary and mental skills will never, if you believe in the Christian God, permit you to get around. First, God killed your loved one. Second, no one ever blames him for it and curses him. And third, by the mere fact alone that Christians then proceed to take the body of their loved one to God's home and say the final good-bye to him or her there, they are by definition honoring the Lord for his handiwork. Don't even waste your valuable time attempting to circumvent these three realities.

Before we move on, I should perhaps mention that no explanation by Christians for God causing death, including causing or permitting the tragedies and horrors of the world, is more preposterous than the following one, which I hear not infrequently, here by a woman who lost her husband in one of the Twin Towers on September 11, 2001: "God uses these things like 9/11 to teach us how to cope [with other horrors he has in store for us] and to bring us closer to him." So God murders or allows the murder of members of our families so that *we* can have a closer and better relationship with him? I'm not even going to comment on the psychotic nature of this notion. But I will mention something implicit in it. If killing members of one's family is worth it to some of the survivors of tragedy because it brings them closer to God, what about those (husband, wife, son, daughter) who were killed in the tragedy? What do they get out of the tragedy and loss of their lives other than apparently making life better for their loved ones in bringing them closer to God? But wait. I have the answer. At the victims' funerals the priest or minister often says, "God *needed*" the victim in heaven. So the victims get to be closer to God, too. But wait again. Under this reasoning, where *everyone* gains from tragedy, murder, and horror, why doesn't God just kill all of us? I guess that's what he does do.

14

What's So Great
Up There in Heaven?

S O MANY PEOPLE PUT GOD FIRST on their list of whom they are
devoted to (You know, "God, family, and country"), and heaven is
where God supposedly is. This is why I have always found it interesting that while everyone wants to go to heaven, no one wants to die to
get there. (Not even Billy Graham, who confesses to having had white
knuckles when told his plane might have to crash land.)

Why is the main objective of the Christian scheme of life and death
to be with God in heaven after we die?* Because, Christians say, God
is all-perfect, and eternity with him will be beyond the greatest happiness imaginable. But how many people stop to ask *why* this will be so.
Okay, so God is the greatest thing since sliced bread. Even greater. *So
what?* What will this do for us humans? As they used to say years ago
in my hometown of Italian, Slavic, and Nordic immigrants in northern
Minnesota to measure the value of what one was doing, "Will it put a
chicken on the table [to eat]?" How does God's being so great and
wonderful translate into our happiness being far greater than we could
ever imagine if we are there *with* him? I don't get it. So he's incredible
and magnificent and perfect and everything else, and I, along with

---

*Mark Twain had it all figured out. "Go to heaven for the climate, hell for the company,"
he said.

millions of others, am by his side. Now what? Where do we go from there? I mean, what will we do in heaven besides worshipping the Lord?

All manner of pleasurable things have been envisioned by people through the years about heaven, the Disneyland of the Christian imagination. Originally, Billy Graham, who at one point said he knew the precise dimensions of heaven—"sixteen hundred square miles" (No. Seriously. *Time*, November 15, 1993, 74)—thought heaven was just going to be about fun. "We are going to sit around the fireplace and have parties, and the angels will wait on us, and we'll drive down the golden streets in a yellow Cadillac convertible," he said. (Billy didn't say if our body or our soul would be in the driver's seat.) But Billy, with age, particularly when he found a passage in the Book of Revelation that says we will *serve* God in heaven, realized that, although life in heaven would all be just glorious, it wasn't going to be all play. He told *Good Morning America* in April of 1997 that "when we get to heaven, I don't think we're going to just sit down. I think God will have other work for us to do. There are billions and billions and trillions of other planets and other stars, and I believe there's life on many of those and God may have a job for us to do on some of those places."

But Billy, none of what you say sounds like a place I want to go to. I never sit around fireplaces, and even if I did, what's so special about sitting around a fireplace in heaven as opposed to one on earth? Also, I'm not a partygoer. And I don't want anyone waiting on me. It makes me uncomfortable. And I have no desire at all to drive a yellow Cadillac convertible down golden streets. And why would I want to work on distant planets till the end of time? I'm not being silly, Billy. You and Christianity are.

Even if what happens in the Christian heaven is the greatest thing ever, such as being in God's presence—like the transfiguration of Jesus at the top of the mountain where his clothing became dazzling white, far whiter than any earthly process could ever make it (Mark 9:2–3)—after a few twenty-four-hour days of this, won't it get awfully tiresome? Or at least humdrum? If not, what about 365 days a year? Or 1,000 years?

What I'm trying to find out, Billy, is after we get to heaven, what's going to happen that's going to be so great that it will make me, and others, so indescribably happy? Given that billions of people throughout recorded history have believed in heaven and everyone wants to end up there, am I being unreasonable to ask?*

Billy, as you know, there is only one person who has ever been in heaven and come down to tell us about it, and that's Jesus. But Billy, I couldn't possibly be more unimpressed with what Jesus says about heaven. He said we'll all "eat and drink at my table" in the kingdom of heaven (Luke 22:30). But I already knew we were going to be with Jesus in heaven, Billy. That's nothing new. Jesus also said we will all "sit on thrones" (Luke 22:30). Billy, you couldn't pay me to sit on a throne. If there's one thing I don't like, it's pretension. Jesus also says that "in my father's house are many mansions" and he will prepare a room for us in them (John 14:2). But Billy, I don't like mansions. They depress me. In fact, I even feel sorry for a rich husband and wife living in a twenty-room mansion. They're obviously searching for something they don't have, such as happiness or the respect of others. And as far as getting me a room in the mansion, Billy, I already have a room down here. Why would I want to hole myself up in a mansion up there? Besides, I don't like anything fancy. For instance, when I travel and my hosts want to put me up at an expensive hotel, I tell them to save their money. Luxury hotels have rooms with features and gadgets I don't want and give me nothing but trouble. I tell them all I want is a small room with a bed, a desk with a light that's bright enough for me to work at, and a thermostat on the wall I don't have to take a course in college to learn how to operate. If the truth be told, Billy, and this is not for you to repeat, as bad as life can be here on earth, from what you and Jesus tell me about heaven, I'd rather be here on earth.

---

*Apparently, we can't even ask Dante. In his canticle *Paradiso*, the last in the trilogy (*Inferno* and *Purgatorio* being the first two) of his *Divine Comedy*, he says he has been "in the heaven which takes most of [God's] light, and I have seen things which cannot be told, possibly, by anyone who comes down from there." Thanks for nothing, Dante.

You know, Billy, even before you and Jesus told me what was up in heaven, I should have known it couldn't have been too much. I mean, if under born-again Christianity a lifetime of hard work to better the lives of one's fellow man doesn't get you a cup of coffee with God, but simply believing in Jesus gets you to heaven, how much can heaven be worth if it can be obtained so cheaply?

And then there's the fact that wanting to be with God in heaven through eternity necessarily presupposes that he is the type of being one would naturally want to be with. But is he? As alluded to earlier, the God of the Old Testament is extremely vindictive and cruel, to the point of surpassing the greatest villains in history. We've all heard of genocide and ethnic cleansing and the human tyrants, like Adolf Hitler and Slobodan Milosevic, who commanded them. But who has ever heard of deciding to kill everyone on the face of the earth, and by drowning, no less? *Why would anyone want to spend one moment in "heaven" with a monster like that?* It's no defense to say, "Well, that was the God of the Old Testament." What in the world does that mean? That the God of the Old Testament is dead? When did he die? And why would we want to spend eternity with someone who caused, or allowed to happen, the millions of atrocities that have occurred throughout history and continue to happen throughout the world to this very day?

Forgetting about the horrors and murders and genocide for a moment, let's expand our analysis into another essence of God, and this includes Jesus. This trait of God and Jesus belongs to one of very small, not large, character. I'm talking about their monumental vanity. For instance, in the gospel of Matthew, Jesus says, "I have come to set a man against his father and a daughter against her mother. If you love your father or mother more than you love me, you are not worthy of being mine. Or if you love your son or daughter more than me, you are not worthy of being mine." He also says in an ancient rendition of "my way or the highway" that "if you refuse to take up your cross and follow me, you are not worthy of being mine. If you cling to your life, you will lose it, but if you give it up for me, you will find it" (Mathew 10:35–39). Indeed, he told his disciples, "You must love me . . . more than your own life" (Luke 14:26).

Though Jesus says in Matthew that you should "love your neighbor as yourself" and gives great importance to this commandment, which is good, he also says, "You must love the Lord your God with all your heart, all your soul, and all your mind. *This is the first and greatest commandment*" (Matthew 22:37–39). In other words, the most important thing in all of our lives, per Jesus, is to love him and his father more than anything else. (And as earlier indicated, we in fact constantly hear people, including our political leaders, saying their priorities are "God, family, and country," in that order.) This is also what God told Moses (Deuteronomy 6:5).

Dear reader, I hope you are truly grasping the meaning of this. *God cares more about our worshipping him than he does about how we treat our fellow man.* Under what form of logic is it possible for us to worship, much less want to spend eternity with, someone as prodigiously vainglorious as this? Does the Christian God have the virtue of humility, which all humans admire, or is he an insufferable egomaniac?

Not only is God incredibly vain to demand our idolatry, but since he has everything that a human mind could ever imagine, why would he want or need our love? What does it do for him? Why is it necessary? Just as the fact that he wants our idolatry shows us a vanity that makes him imperfect, does his *need* for the idolatry show him to be less than complete? *Doesn't need imply absence?* But how can the God Christianity believes to be all-everything have an absence of anything? If the Christian God is infinite, if he can do or be or have anything, then by definition, how can he *need* anything? And of all beings to secure it from—the lowly, wretched, impotent beings he created. Moreover, because he's all-intelligent, why doesn't he know something that all of us mere humans know—that a love procured by way of coercion (if we don't love God, we go to hell) is not much of a real love at all and can never be as good as love that is voluntary and freely given?

We also learn from the bible that God has another highly unfavorable trait, that of jealousy, which the bible itself denounces in Proverbs 27:4 and 14:30. "I am the Lord," God says in the Book of Isaiah. "I will not share my glory with anyone else" (42:8). The Book of Deuteronomy says, "The Lord your God . . . is a jealous God" (4:24). God is actually jealous? Jealous of whom? You? Me? Danny DeVito? Another god? He's all powerful and all-knowing, and as the song goes, he's got the world on a string, and he's jealous? Again, is there a psychiatrist in the house?

Remarkably, Christians find no problem at all with ascribing traits to God, whom they worship as being all-perfect, that they would vigorously denounce as very bad in their fellow man, such as being vindictive, cruel, vain, jealous, deliberately mysterious, and unwilling to lift a hand to prevent harm to another being. I have a question for all Christians and true believers: If you would not look up to any fellow human who had these absolutely deplorable characteristics, why do you look up to and revere someone with these very same characteristics simply because you believe he created the universe and is all-powerful? Unless you can give me an intelligent answer to this question, this should tell you that there is something fatally and irreversibly defective about your entire religious conviction.

I have another question: Since we have all the evidence that even the world's leading skeptic would need to conclude that God made a terrible, terrible mess out of the world he created, what reason would anyone have for believing he has created a perfect existence in heaven? His track record could hardly be any worse.

Still talking about heaven, we all know how much we love our children and our parents. We also know that if there is a heaven, one or more members of a family may end up there, with the other members not making it. So under the Christian scheme of things, a mother and father might be born-again Christians and go to heaven, but, let's say, the daughter is an atheist, and the son has led a criminal life, and they would both end up in hell. We also know that most parents, despite the problems, even crimes of their children, never stop loving them and being concerned for their welfare. The question I have for Christianity is that even if the parents in heaven love God more than their children (isn't this terribly, terribly ludicrous?), unless a lobotomy is a part of one's initiation into heaven, *they still love their children*. And as my late brother, Tony, pointed out, how can they possibly be happy in heaven when they know their two children, whom they loved so much they would have given their lives for them, aren't with them, and they know they will never see them again?

Or how can a woman in heaven be happy when her husband of sixty years, the love of her life, is not up there with her? Indeed, how can the parents in one case and the women in the other have *perfect* happiness, as Billy Graham and Christianity assure us awaits those who get to heaven, if their loved ones not only are not with them but may be burning in hell at the very moment they're supposed to be enjoying a heavenly bliss with the Lord? Billy, this is not an easy question for you or anyone else to answer. In fact, I would say that it's impossible for you to answer. If you find out that you can't answer it satisfactorily, don't you agree that you and your fellow Christians better go back to the drawing board on the matter of heaven, the ultimate reward for complying with all the rules of your Christianity?

We hear all the time from very devout Christians that they love God above all else, which is at the heart of the born-again ethos. But inasmuch as no one is capable of measuring anything beyond our human experience, how can a human being love an imponderable, dreamlike abstraction such as God more than his own wife and children? Yet a 2004 national poll showed, incredibly, that 71 percent of Americans "would die for their God." What in the world are these Christians talking about? Though they probably haven't even stopped to think about it, I believe they must be only mouthing empty words when they talk about a love of God this great. Is it possible that, at bottom, and at a level they are not even consciously aware of, devout born-again Christians really don't have any genuine love for God at all, which would be normal since it's unnatural to love someone you've never met or even seen? And maybe that's why Christians unwittingly betray their true feelings by frequently referring to themselves, not as God-loving people but as "God-fearing" people (fearing that if they don't love him, they will be denied salvation). Can you really love a total abstraction, and one you fear greatly, more than you love your own parents, wife, husband, son, or daughter?

How is that humanly possible?

15

A Brief
Descent into Hell

CHRISTIANS BELIEVE, as the reader knows, that hell is a place for those damned by God for eternity. Most Christians apparently have no problem with the notion that their God created a world with the foreknowledge (being all-knowing), and therefore the intention, that the vast majority of its people would spend eternity in never-ending torture. Hard to believe, but true. Jesus said, "The highway to hell is broad, and its gate is wide for the many who choose the easy way. But the gateway to God's Kingdom is small, and the road is narrow, and only a few ever find it" (Matthew 7:13–14). Indeed, if we're to believe the bible, Revelation 14:3 seems to suggest that perhaps only 144,000 people will ever reach heaven. The rest, presumably, will end up in hell.

Most traditional Christians, following the word of Jesus himself, believe hell is a place of fire and brimstone where the condemned burn forevermore in the possession of the devil, Satan. The gospel of Matthew quotes Jesus as saying that when he returns to judge man at the end of the world, he will say to the condemned, "Depart from me, accursed ones, into the eternal fire which has been prepared for the devil and his demons" (Matthew 25:41). Elsewhere in the bible, Jesus speaks of hell as being a place of "unquenchable fire" (Matthew 18:8) and "eternal punishment" (Matthew 25:46), where there will be "weeping and gnashing of teeth" (Matthew 8:12). Many Christians to-day, incongruously backing away from the words of the one (Jesus) to whom they have consecrated their lives, believe the fire is a mere metaphor for those denied the presence of God, though the context of Jesus' words do not suggest he was speaking metaphorically in any way. All Christians believe that hell is one bad place, not a destination that even the world's leading masochist would put on his travel itinerary. It is a place of punishment beyond the grave that has been part of Christian belief and theology since the time of Jesus.

Apart from the self-evident absurdity of the notion, isn't the idea of the Christian hell of everlasting punishment completely incompatible with a God whom Christians believe to be "full of mercy" (James 5:11)? Doesn't the punishment seem the type that one would expect to be inflicted by Satan rather than by God? I mean, knowing that humans are so weak they stumble over threads, wouldn't one expect a merciful, benevolent God to be more tolerant of most of man's transgressions? As alluded to earlier, the Christians' stock answer is that, yes, God is merciful, but he "loves justice" (Psalm 11:7), and the wicked have to be punished. But if God is just and loves justice, justice connotes proportion—an eye for an eye, say, not a head for a slap on the face—since the very definition of justice is to give one his due. Nothing more, nothing less. What type of God could condemn to hell, *forevermore*, someone who has offended him by not accepting him as their savior? Isn't this punishment, on its face, greatly disproportionate and hence unjust?

Yes, our criminal justice system punishes a petty thief as well as a murderer. But the punishment, everyone knows, cannot be the same. The petty thief might get probation or a fine or a few days in the county jail. But the murderer can get life imprisonment or even death. As the expression goes, "The punishment has to fit the crime." That's just common sense, right? As far back as the very harsh and retributive Old Testament, it is written in referring to "two people who take a dispute to court" that the judge will sentence "the person in the wrong to be flogged," but "with the number of lashes appropriate to the crime" (Deuteronomy 25:1–2). So punishment has to be proportionate. But when we get away from temporal punishment to punishment after death, all we hear from Christianity is hell and fire and everlasting punishment. Where do we hear about the indispensable element of justice—that our time and suffering in hell should be commensurate with our sins on earth? Is God a lunatic? Someone who punishes a common thief or burglar or forger in the same way he punishes a John Gacy, Ted Bundy, or even a Stalin? But if there is going to be proportionality in punishment in hell, why doesn't it say this anywhere in the bible? Does the pope talk about it? Or televangelists? Or itinerant preachers? Can we infer by their silence that this extreme disproportionality in punishment, which could not possibly be more unjust, is just fine with them?[1] (See endnote for further discussion)

The whole notion of hell speaks of sensory pain, even to the extent of the "gnashing of teeth." The inference, despite the fact we know one's remains stay in the grave, is that the body will go to hell and will burn. For instance, in Matthew 13:50, Jesus speaks of "throwing the wicked into the fires" of hell. In Matthew 18:8, he speaks of the damned being thrown into hell "with both their hands and feet." But if the body is to be burned *forever*, it would have to, by definition, be indestructible, which we know is not true. Furthermore, since the pain is meant to be without end, and since a dead person cannot feel pain, apparently the condemned person, if he is to suffer, never *truly* dies (in Mark 9:47–48, Jesus speaks of sinners in hell "where the worm never dies and the fire never goes out"), and burns in hell, as indicated, without being consumed. A lovely ending for pathetic mortals for whom, Christians assure us, God has "a love that endures forever" (1 Chronicles 16:34).

Despite the aforementioned biblical references of the physical *body* burning in hell, mainstream Christianity believes that only the *soul* is immortal, and knowing that the body of man remains in the grave, has interpreted all of the verses in scripture that speak of salvation and damnation in heaven and hell as referring to the soul of man, which it believes separates from the body at death. "As soon as the soul is set free from the body," Aquinas said, "it is either plunged into hell or soars to heaven" (*Summa Theologica*, 887).

Two critical points have to be made in this regard. First, the alleged immortality of the soul (e.g., First Vatican Council, 1870) is by far the most valuable asset that Christianity has. Why? Because Christianity could not survive without it. In view of the physical mortality of the human body, if the soul weren't immortal, what else would the Christian religion have to *offer* the masses (life without end with God in heaven)? And what else would it have to *hold over their heads* as a threat (suffering without end in hell)? Nothing. Because we know the body is mortal, if the soul isn't immortal, then there is no life after death. And people, since the beginning of time, don't want to believe that once they die, that's the end of it for them.

Secondly, I could find no solid support in the bible for the notion of the immortality of the soul in heaven with God and in hell with Satan. It appears that it simply does not exist.[2] (See endnote for further discussion.) Indeed, the bible says that "God alone has immortality" (1 Timothy 6:16).

And because of this biblical absence, when the early Christian church realized that to survive it had no choice but to proclaim the immortality of the soul as one of its central tenets (*Catechism,* number 366), it embraced the much earlier Judaic belief in the immortality of the soul. But if it's not in the bible, where did Judaism come up with it? The *Encyclopedia Judaica* says, "It was probably under Greek influences that the doctrine of the immortality of the soul came into Judaism." If this is true, the Greeks (Homer passingly alluded to the notion earlier in his poetry, but Plato was by far the principal proponent) invented the doctrine of the immortality of the soul out of whole cloth, and Judaism, then Catholicism, followed by Protestantism, accepted without question this doctrine that has greatly affected the lives of billions of people. How nice.

So what did Plato (428–348 BC) have to say about the subject? In his dialogue *Phaedrus,* Plato, speaking through Socrates, his departed mentor, says:

> Our soul is immortal, for that which is ever in motion is immortal. That which while imparting motion is itself moved by something else can cease to be in motion, and therefore can cease to live. It is only that which moves itself that never intermits its motion, inasmuch as it cannot abandon its own nature. . . . Any body that has an external source of motion is soulless, but a body deriving its motion from a source within itself is animate or besouled. And if this last assertion is correct, namely that "that which moves itself" is precisely identifiable with [one's] soul, it must follow that the soul is not born and does not die.

Though Plato purports to know quite a bit about a "soul's immortality," he does allow that "a god [Plato, as was true of virtually all Greeks at the time, believed in many gods, each of whom dwelled on Mount Olympus] alone could tell what manner of thing the soul is." (In his dialogues, e.g., *The Republic, Gorgias,* Plato speaks of heaven and hades [hell].)

Note that in Plato's disquisition, he presupposes the existence of a god, presupposes the existence of the soul, and presupposes the soul is immortal because he presupposes that it was never born. But you see, if we presuppose that I had wings, maybe I could fly. Plato was a great philosopher whose influence on Western thought is considerable. But like everyone else, he had no pipeline to God, heaven, hell, or the soul, assuming any of these entities even exist. None whatsoever. So his belief in the immortality of the soul, which apparently gave birth to Judaism's and Christianity's belief in the notion, and hence life after death, was just sheer, bald supposition on his part.

Christianity attempts to justify its belief in the immortality of the soul by what it calls the "universal belief" and reasoning that a just

God would not impose his moral laws on mankind without the promise of eternal life with him in the hereafter for those who met his demands on earth, and eternal punishment in hell for those who did not.

Similarly, German philosopher Immanuel Kant tried to attack the mystery of whether there is an afterlife from the perspective of ethics. He noted that people everywhere have a sense of right and wrong, the essence of ethics. He then reasoned that for ethics and life to be of any meaning or value, there must be justice. In other words, he asked, why should one be ethical in one's life if there is no payoff, one way or the other, of justice? By definition, he continued his analysis, there cannot be justice unless one survived, in some form, the grave. Also, justice requires a judge, one who is all-intelligent, just, and powerful, i.e., God.

The basic defect of Kant's and Christianity's argument, of course, is that it assumes the existence not only of a God, but a God who is just. Christianity and Kant then further assume, as another premise, that life has to be, and is, meaningful, which is the very point to be proved. And with that assumption, everything flows logically from that. Though Christianity and Kant may be right (not in their clearly faulty reasoning process) that life is meaningful, we don't know this. Perhaps the only point of life is that it is pointless. Shakespeare's *Macbeth* says, "Life's but a walking shadow, a poor player that struts and frets his hour upon the stage and then is heard no more. It is a tale told by an idiot, full of sound and fury, signifying nothing." One thing we *do* know is that even if we accept as true what thinkers like Kierkegaard and Dostoevsky (as well as Christianity itself) say, that life without a just God would be a meaningless existence, this itself is obviously is no evidence itself of the existence of God. I mean, it's not quite that easy to prove there is a God.

In any event, the notion of the soul being immortal has no scriptural basis, and hence what Christianity, Judaism, and many other religions preach about it is nothing but naked speculation. Since we know the death of the body is final, if the soul lives on only in foundationless speculation, what intelligent reason does one have to believe there is life after death?

Getting back to the soul and hell, the word "soul" is used by almost everyone. I have no idea what the soul is, so therefore I cannot have much confidence it exists. I *can* say that what Christians say it is (e.g., the spiritual part of man; the essence of being; the first principle of life in man; the seat of man's emotions) is not comprehensible to whatever kernel of perception my mind can summon. Indeed, 5,000 volumes of theology, philosophy, and metaphysics couldn't explain what the human soul is, much less prove its existence. So I never consciously use the word unless in the most abstract and literary of senses.

But with respect to hell, even if there is a soul, we know it is not something you can see or hold in your hands, meaning it has no corporeal essence. So how, then, can this soul have a sensory ability to feel pain in hell?[3] Not important, except insofar as it is just further evidence that what we're talking about here is pure claptrap, all of this soul business being a monument to mummery.

℘

ONE CANNOT HELP TALKING to an Evangelical Christian without coming away with the feeling he believes the world is a battleground between God and Satan, the divine and the diabolical. The great problem I have with this Manichaean view is that in Christian theology Satan is merely an angel (Lucifer) created by God (Genesis 3:1, Ezekiel 28:12–15) who fell from grace (Isaiah 14:12, Revelation 12:7–9, Luke 10:18). Where in the world did Satan, the devil, *thereafter* get the unbelievable power to even compete on the same playing field with God? And where did he get the power to tempt us into all of our sins? (Or is the devil, as some believe, not a tempter but a perfect gentleman who never goes where he is not welcome? And let's not forget that we never hear the devil's side of the story.)

It is indeed interesting that, although Christianity claims the devil causes all evil, they really have no solid scriptural support for this and are forced to rely on the indirect attribution of evil to him by his tempting us to do evil. And even then, with the exception of Adam and Eve in Genesis 3:1–5 and Jesus in Matthew 4:8–9, the "tempting" is only by implication. But in terms of directly creating evil (e.g., causing someone to do evil, not merely tempting him to do so), the bible, believe it or not, seems to blame God. Amos 3:6 says, "If evil befalls a city, has not the Lord caused it?" In Isaiah 45:7, God says, "I make well-being and create woe. I, the Lord, do all these things." Lamentations 3:38 says, "Is it not from the mouth of the Most High that good and evil come?"

In any event, how would a simple angel who, we are told, went bad, have powers one would think only God has; for example, omnipresence? Not only is Satan everywhere, but Christians also refer to the "struggle" against Satan. Struggle? God and Satan have been around, per Christianity, since time immemorial. Yet Satan, after these thousands of years of fighting with God, who is supposed to be all-powerful, still hasn't been vanquished? He's still in the ring with God throwing punches, and in the struggle between good and evil, evil wins just as much or more than good does? What gives? I don't get it.

Where, in the bible or anywhere else, does it say or even suggest how some former angel ended up having such incredible power? To the point where Paul, in 2 Corinthians 4:4, called Satan "the god of this evil world." And John, in 1 John 5:19, actually says, "We are children of God, and the world around us is under the power and control of the evil one." If Christianity, the proponent of this notion, cannot tell us how Satan acquired this unbelievable power, then why should we believe this nonsense?

Since, Christianity says, God created everyone, even the devil, and since God, we are told, only wants goodness in the world, and since he is all-powerful, why doesn't he just whack the devil? You know, *why doesn't he get rid of the devil altogether*? Psalm 75:10 says, "For God says, 'I will cut off the strength of the wicked.'" But that's the Old Testament, well over 2,000 years ago. If God intends to whack the devil, when does he intend to do it? After the cows come home?

If God doesn't want to destroy the devil, what other reason can there be than that he *wants* the devil to tempt us into sin wherever we turn so that if we yield to the temptation and sin, we end up in hell? But if this is so, this creates two enormous problems for Christianity. First, Christianity's God appears to be just playing games with our lives, with the stakes being heaven or hell, and he's enjoying watching the game from up above, a game that he created and has ill-equipped us to play. If this is true, what type of God is this? Second, and perhaps even worse, although James 1:13 tells us that "God never tempts us to do wrong," if God chooses to allow the devil to continue to exist, knowing he's going to tempt us into sin, isn't God thereby making the devil his agent?

I say this to Christian theologians: These questions are worthy of answers. And if you insist on preaching your nonsense, you have a moral duty to address yourself to them.

16

Praying to
a Tree Trunk

I BELIEVE I'VE ALREADY INDICATED how worthless I believe praying is. That in my opinion, two working hands can achieve far more than one hundred million coupled ones. Indeed, if we're to believe 1 John 5:14, the bible itself seems to say that prayers may be useless words. When it is written that "we can be confident that God will listen to us whenever we ask him for anything *in line with his will*," does that mean that if what we pray for is not in line with God's will, he will turn our prayer down, and if it is in line with his will, our prayer is superfluous since, being his will, it would have happened anyway? Just asking.

For the life of me, I still don't understand why humans pray. If people pray and get what they prayed for, causing them to believe that "God answered my prayers," they should then say to themselves, "If I conclude that this means God has the power to answer prayers, how can I possibly say he is a good God when I know, absolutely know, not think, but know with a 100 percent certainty he *nearly always* turns down the praying party when that party needs him the most?" Like the millions of Jews who prayed to him during the Holocaust, his name probably being the last word on many of their lips before they died. Like the millions out of the incredible 25 million people who have already died worldwide from AIDS. And like the millions who have died from starvation in the poorest nations of the globe. The fact we know that if there is a God up there who has the power to answer prayers he turned these millions of people down should tell us that God doesn't answer prayers, and if we happen to get what we prayed for, *it had nothing to do with God.*

The only other conclusion would be based on the arrogant belief that God answered your prayers because he liked you more than the people whom he turned down. For instance, whenever someone says God answered his prayers (such as for a promotion at work, or that your loved one not die from his or her cancer) by having his football or baseball team win an important game, by definition he is saying that God likes him more than those who prayed for the other team. But isn't it curious, as they say, how God almost always seems to be on the side of those who have the better team? (The point I am making goes beyond prayers. When people, in saying grace before a bountiful Thanksgiving or Christmas dinner, thank God for giving them the wonderful food on their plate, don't they realize they are necessarily saying that God decided not to give millions of starving people around the world no food at all to eat? And that means that either he isn't very nice or that he had nothing to do with the food on their plate. I know that most humans love to rest their minds, but isn't this a thought that should be inevitable for any thinking person?)

Is God merely "not very nice," not a "good" God for not answering the prayers of those in need? Well, it's a little stronger than that. Although what I am about to say is undeniably true, it will change no one's thinking and will have as much impact as my saying, "I saw a bird in a tree." It is that if people say, and believe (as billions have and will), that "God answered my prayers," thereby stipulating that they believe God has the power to answer our prayers, *they are necessarily and incontrovertibly saying that God is bad.* I mean, major, big-time bad. I mean, badder than bad can be. I mean, it can't get any worse than having the power to easily stop, for instance, the deaths of millions of people dying from genocide or AIDS or starvation who are praying desperately for your help, and telling them no, take a walk.

This proposition, if we are to be governed by logic, is not open to debate. It is an Aristotelian conclusion about as easy to avoid as stopping rain from falling, and therefore everyone should accept it as true. But we know that so often in life the truth is the one thing no one will believe.

℮᷎

ONE OF THE MAIN THINGS PEOPLE PRAY FOR is peace. But there have already been trillions upon trillions of prayers for peace through the years, yet peace remains as elusive as mercury, as groups and factions and nations persist in warring viciously with each other, the violence continuing unabated. Wouldn't one think that people would finally come to the realization that either there's no one up there listening to their prayers for peace, or if there is, he doesn't have the power to stop the violence, or if he does, he has no desire to do so? That they may just as well be praying to a tree trunk? I've been told there is some religious sect in the Himalayan Mountains that has been praying for peace, twenty-four hours a day in shifts, for close to five hundred years. Nuns of the Franciscan Sisters in La Crosse, Wisconsin, have been praying for world peace in thirty-minute rotating shifts twenty-four hours a day in an unbroken chain of perpetual prayers dating back to 1878. Even a fire that reached the chapel doors in 1923 never stopped the nuns from praying inside.

When will the poor nuns and millions of others give up? How many more centuries are people going to have to pray and how many more trillions of prayers are they going to have to say before they wake up to the fact that no one is listening to their prayers?* (I mean, if whoever

---

*In a similar vein, twenty-four hours a day, nonstop since 1999, an evangelical church in Kansas City, the International House of Prayer, has been drawing people from around the world who, to the pulsating beat of a Christian rock band, have been supplicating God with upwardly outstretched arms to turn back the forces of Satan and evil throughout the world. How is it possible that these people (as well as tens of millions like them) would not say to themselves—if God is all-good and all-powerful, as we all believe him to be, why should we be begging him to do something he should already want to do? And since we've been praying to him since 1999, why hasn't he been answering our prayers?

is up there ignores even the pope when he prays for peace, and the pope is the spiritual leader of more than 1 billion Catholics and, per Catholicism, God's chief representative on this earth, why would people think that God would listen to common folk like them? Indeed, in a different context, God even turned down the prayers of his own son, Jesus!! [John 18:21].) Not only do they seem incapable of waking up to this fact, but they compound the idiocy of it all by always talking about "the power" of prayer.

How is it that in their daily lives, if these people who pray for peace ask someone to do something for them and they are turned down, they'd probably never ask again. And rarely would they ask a third time. But in praying to God for peace, these same people never give up, and they do this even with the realization and knowledge that there have been millions just like them saying prayers for peace to the same God for centuries. Why isn't this type of behavior considered to be clinically psychotic? But far from being consigned to a diagnosis of psychosis, I have no doubt that these prayers will continue to be considered completely normal, even healthy, and will go on, as an old Indian treaty provided, "as long as the water flows and the wind blows and the grass grows."

What could possibly be on the minds of the countless who never stop praying for peace in the world? Is this surreal praying without end a grand extrapolation of Jacob Riis' Stonecutter Credo of the mason who hammers away at his rock, perhaps one hundred times without as much as a crack showing in it, but at the one hundred and first blow it splits in two, and he knows that it was not that blow that did it, but all that had gone before?

In other words, do these many millions of people praying for peace think that their prayer for peace, which they remarkably say in all earnestness, will be the one out of the trillions already said down through the years that will finally be the one that breaks the camel's back with God, that will cause him to say, "Okay, okay, I don't *need* any more prayers. I'll give you your peace"? Or could they actually believe that God might respond solely and simply because *they* asked him and he might answer *their* prayer? Whichever of the two it is, you have to know this is not insanity. It's beyond insanity. And this is why, although I'd love to approach these people and ask them why they are praying for peace, I don't because I'm afraid to go near them.

It's hard to know which is a bigger mystery—people saying prayers for peace, or, whenever there's a terrible tragedy like 9/11 or Hurricane Katrina, immediately running to their churches, synagogues, or other places of worship to pray for the victims and their loved ones to, believe it or not, the very entity, God, who caused or allowed the tragedy to happen. But hasn't God already shown by what he did or allowed to happen to the victims that he couldn't possibly care less about them? So why are people praying to him?

Frank Geer, a rector at St. Philip's Church-in-the-Highlands in Garrison, New York, has tried, unsuccessfully, to make sense out of prayers in times like 9/11. Geer worked at St. Lukes–Roosevelt Hospital in New York City counseling and comforting survivors of 9/11. During a break in his work, he said he went to St. Paul's chapel, a 250-year old Episcopal church that was a block from the World Trade Center devastation. In the book *Where Was God on September 11?* he says he prayed to God "first and foremost for all the people who had died. I prayed for their families, and I prayed for the workers who were risking their lives every day at the site that God would keep them safe." Speaking of the churches, synagogues, and mosques that were overflowing with people after 9/11, he remarks, "People wanted to be together with other human beings and with God. Going to church was a way to activate and amplify their sense of God. . . . They wanted to be together with a force that cares about them, that cares for them. Religion was an incredible source of comfort for people" after 9/11.

But of course I already knew that religion was a source of comfort for those praying to their God. My question again is, how could they possibly get comfort from praying to the very entity who caused or allowed to happen the horror that killed the victims?* Is this not a form of dementia? How can such numbing, staggering stupidity continue without end? Einstein once said that there are only two things that are infinite: the universe and the stupidity of man. And he added that he was only unsure of the former.

With respect to people praying after a tragedy to a God who caused or allowed it, are we dealing here with an indelible, ineradicable, inerasable, inexpungible psychosis that can no more be removed than can the pigmentation of one's skin? A psychosis that will stop only when the sun rises in the west? When Frenchmen stop drinking wine? Cervantes tells us that every dog has his day, but my God, when is this day ever going to end?

In recognizing the futility of prayer,[1] people could learn from the destitute. They don't pray. They beg. And if believers—who can be first to say that if you believe in Jesus and pray to him, Jesus will answer your prayers—can't learn from the destitute, they might want to look at themselves. When these believers get cancer or diabetes or have a stroke or heart attack, why do they all run to a doctor? They don't they just stay home and pray to Jesus?

❧

LET'S LOOK AT A FEW OTHER explicit examples of how people treat prayer and their relationship to God that completely mystify me. In January of 2006 when thirteen West Virginia coal miners were trapped underground, their families and friends gathered at the little Sago Baptist Church in Tallmansville, West Virginia, and conducted long prayer vigils, begging the Lord to save their loved ones. Since their husbands, sons, and brothers were still alive, if ever prayers made sense, this would be such a time. But when God decided not to answer these

---

*If he didn't cause or allow to happen the tragedy that had occurred, then he's not the omnipotent God they believe him to be who can answer their prayers, and hence, why are they praying to him?

prayers and twelve miners died, the relatives and friends, some two hundred of them, went back to the same Baptist church to conduct a candlelight vigil of prayer to God at the end of which, it was reported, "the mourners raised their candles above their heads and shouted three times in unison, 'Praise the Lord.'"

I am not trying to be cute or sarcastic or anything but serious when I say that I just don't understand things like this, and other than blinding stupidity, if there is something I am missing here, I would hope someone would explain things like this to me. That is a sincere request on my part.[2]

On September 14, 2001, three days after the catastrophe in which close to 3,000 Americans died, some choosing to jump to their deaths out of windows eighty or more stories high, most dying in the raging inferno inside the Twin Towers (a scene of horror and death that Hollywood would not even attempt to capture on celluloid), President George W. Bush, presiding over an ecumenical prayer service at the National Cathedral in Washington, DC, said, "God's signs *are not always the ones we look for*. [You can say that again.] We learn in tragedy that his purposes are not always our own. [*That's* for sure. But who cares? If the horror pleases God, we have no complaints.] Neither death nor life, nor things to come can separate us from God's love. May he bless the souls of the departed, may he comfort our own, and may he always guide our country." Amazing. Absolutely amazing.

By the way, if I may go off on a brief tributary about the president saying that God guides our country, I thought that by the framers of our Constitution omitting the word "God" from the Constitution; indeed, by stating in the very first words of the preamble to the Constitution, "We the people," they were memorializing the precept that the United States of America is a secular nation, guided and governed by the will of the people, not by God's will. (I'm using "secular" here as meaning not under the control of any religious body, not, as religious fundamentalists believe, as a euphemism for atheist or "secular humanism," which they define as the belief that man, not God, is the center of the universe, a belief they believe leads its adherents to advocate situational ethics rather than absolute moral values.) Author Susan Jacoby, in her book *Freethinkers*, notes, "It is one of the greatest unresolved paradoxes of American history that religion has come to occupy such an important place in the . . . public life of a nation founded on the separation of church and state."

After thirteen people, twelve of whom were members of the military, were killed and thirty others wounded on November 5, 2009, by Major Nidal Malik Hasan, a U.S. Army psychiatrist, at the Fort Hood Army base in central Texas, President Barack Obama, that same day, urged all Americans to pray for those who had been killed or wounded.

Now, by virtually all accounts President Obama is a very intelligent man (although my personal view is that the jury is still out on the degree of his *functional* intelligence, for which there is no recognized test), and he says he is also a very religious Christian man. He therefore has to know that his God either caused the murderous rampage in Texas or allowed it to happen. For the omnipotent Christian God to exist, there is no third option. Therefore, as Obama was uttering the words he did, wouldn't he have had to know the innate absurdity of praying for the victims to the very entity responsible for the terrible fate that had befallen them?

Even in those few cases where people openly proclaim that God caused the tragedy, they *still* don't turn on him. One example: On April 19, 1995, a bomb exploded outside the Alfred P. Murrah Federal Building in Oklahoma City, and 168 people, including 19 children, were killed. The consensus in highly religious Oklahoma City, where the citizenry flocked to their churches to pray right after the bombing, was that there had to be a reason God chose one of the most religious areas in the nation, where nearly 75 percent of the population are regular churchgoers, for the blast. The answer was that God had put the city to the test, and it passed. "It's like it had to happen in Oklahoma, in the Bible Belt, where people are neighbors and we do give," a parishioner voiced the sentiment. But although the tragedy was "God's will," said a minister, God, unbelievably, still got credit. "It was one of God's miracles," the minister added, "that so many people were saved."

But if people can believe it's "God's will" that a building is blown up, killing 168 people, and still praise him for saving the lives of others in the building, I have a question. What's God secret? Who's his PR agent?

How does one awaken the great masses of people from their idiotic slumbers? It is not an easy task because it is human nature for people to resist being told that fervent, long-standing beliefs of theirs are simply wrong. The majority of people respond by personally attacking the messenger. Plato quotes Socrates, whose life's purpose was his quest for the truth, as beseeching one, "Please don't be angry with me if I tell you the truth." There is much to be learned from proverbs since they are born of human experience. An old Turkish proverb says that "whoever tells the truth is chased out of nine villages." And a Yugoslavian proverb echoes, "Tell the truth and run."

Is there any possible way, then, for the irrationality of prayers to the Christian God, which are anchored on the whole notion of Christianity, to ever end? Yes, but mostly theoretically. Only if the day comes that a cardinal reports to the pope, "Father, I've got bad news for you. We have to cancel Easter. They found the body," will all of this institutionalized insanity (an insanity that cannot be called such a name for the simple reason that it afflicts the majority of mankind) end, and I'm not sure even then.

We all know Abraham Lincoln's famous dictum that you can fool all of the people some of the time and some of the people all of the time, but you can't fool all of the people all of the time. But there should be an addendum to this: Not just in religion but in all areas of life you can fool most of the people most of the time.

17

Between Morality and Religion, Who Needs Whom?

Throughout history there have always been people killing others over religion, including the early Christians being fed to the lions in Rome's Coliseum, their remains then set on fire "so that when darkness came they burned like torches in the night." Christian theologian Tertullian (AD 160–220), who was in Rome at the time, wrote that "the cry to set the lions upon us is raised every day. 'Toss the Christians to the lions.'" As Somerset Maugham said, "What cruel things men do to each other for the love of God."

Although religious wars continue to this very day, most notably in the Israeli-Palestinian conflict, which began in 1948, the most famous religious wars were the Crusades. From the eleventh to the thirteen centuries, it was usually a Catholic pope who stirred the Christian masses to march on the Mediterranean world and slaughter hundreds of thousands of infidels in the name of God. "*Dieu li volt*" (God wills it), the French pope, Urban II, declared in Latin as he launched the first Crusade (there were eight) to recapture Jerusalem and the holy land from the Muslims. During one of the battles, a Catholic priest who was there wrote excitedly, "Wonderful things were to be seen. Numbers of the Saracens [Arab Muslims] were beheaded or forced to jump from the towers. Others were tortured and then burned to death. One rode about everywhere amid the corpses of men and horses." The Jews were not spared. Forced into their synagogues, they were consumed by fire. Even before the First Crusade in 1096–1099, Pope Gregory (1073–1085) said, "Damned be he who protects his sword from blood."

In the late fifteenth century, the Catholic church demonstrated its commitment to compassion and tolerance by establishing the Spanish Inquisition, a tribunal whose main function was to suppress heresy—that is, punish those who did not accept the teachings of the church. This religious persecution resulted in all kinds of punishment, ranging from incarceration and torture to murder and the expulsion from Spain, in 1492, not only of all Spanish Jews (Sephardics) but those practicing any religion other than Catholicsm. The Inquisition's first inquisitor-general was a gentle soul, Dominican monk Tomas de Torquemada, who was notorious for his cruelty, his specialty being torture. Although some Catholic apologists have attempted to deflect guilt away from the church by pointing out that it was the Spanish monarchy that ran the Inquisition, this is an effort to distort history. It was Pope Sixtus IV who established the church's Court of Inquisition on November 1, 1478. His decree empowered Ferdinand V, king of Castile (most of Spain) and his wife, Queen Isabella I, with jurisdiction to administer it. The consensus is that the Inquisition was "a mixed but primarily an ecclesiastical institution." (See Pastor, *History of the Popes*, [London: J. Hodges Publishing Co., 1891], Vol. 4: 402.)

In the sixteenth century the very wonderful and very religious ("the one true church of Jesus Christ") Catholic church turned the bayonets of its troops on the French Protestants (Huguenots), and in one week alone, commencing on August 24, 1572, St. Bartholomew's Day (known as the St. Bartholomew's Day Massacre), more than 70,000 Huguenots were murdered, the rivers of France so filled with corpses that for months no fish were eaten. Reportedly, when news of the massacre reached the Vatican, there was jubilation and celebration. The pope even commissioned an Italian artist to paint a mural of the slaughter, which hangs in the Vatican to this day.

There are, of course, innumerable other examples of religious intolerance leading to great violence and war. One could almost say that war and religion, if not synonymous, are soulmates. Indeed, the Qur'an, the bible of Islam, expressly says, "Believers, wage war against such of the infidels as are your neighbors. Know that God is with the righteous" (Sura 9:125).

Voltaire, in his book *God and Human Beings*, estimated the number of nonbelievers slain by Christians in various wars and conflicts he chronicled. He concluded that as of 1769 (the date his book was published), an incredible ten million humans were killed "in the name of Jesus." And he says this figure was conservative, "far below the truth," e.g., he believed two million were murdered in the Crusades, but included only one million in his calculation. When we go forward to the present time and add those slain in the name of God by non-Christian religions such as Islam, the number is simply too horrific to think about or get a sense of. ("If we believe absurdities," Voltaire said, "we shall commit atrocities.")

Arguably, the greatest fraud (or at least deception) of the last two millenniums has been organized religion's preemption of morality. Indeed, much of mankind (including great minds such as Fyodor Dostoevsky, who said through one of his characters in *The Brothers Karamazov*, "If God doesn't exist, everything is permissible") has been hoodwinked into believing that religion and morality have a necessary nexus.

Over and over again we hear the fallacy that "morality *needs* religion." But morality, thank you, can stand very well on its own two feet. It is autonomous and self-sufficient and never needs religion[1] or anything else to prop it up. No example has to be given for this obvious proposition, but, for instance, in Scandinavia organized religion and churchgoing are marginalized, almost ridiculed. A Danish pastor told American researcher Phil Zuckerman, "In Denmark, the word 'God' is one of the most embarrassing words you can say. You would rather go naked through the city than talk of God." Yet are we to believe that the people of countries like Denmark and Sweden are less moral than we are here in the United States? Please. Just please. After spending 14 months in Scandinavia in 2008–2009, Zuckerman, a professor of sociology at Pitzer College in Claremont, California, found Scandinavia to be "a society— a markedly irreligious society—that was, above all, moral, stable, humane and deeply good."*

On the other hand, we absolutely know from corrupt popes of the past to the many corrupt Evangelical preachers of today, and mostly from the horrible, devastating wars in the name of God and religion in which being vicious and evil toward one's opponent is a virtue, that *religion needs morality*, religious history being awash in blood. That, we *know*, is an imperishable fact, one that cannot be contested. We also know that the more religious a group of people gets, the more fanatical and vicious it becomes to unbelievers (infidels) who do not share its beliefs. So we absolutely know that religion needs morality. What evidence is there that morality needs religion?

Before I cite an in-depth study that indicates morality not only doesn't need religion, but, from a social and economic standpoint, is apparently actually harmed by it, we should pause to remember the so-called Enlightenment in Europe in the seventeenth and eighteenth centuries, an intellectual, revolutionary movement headed by the likes of Voltaire, Jean-Jacques Rousseau, Baron de Montesquieu, and David Hume that celebrated the power of reason and science over faith and religion. Whereas today Europe seems to be expanding on the Enlightenment, becoming more and more secular, America, almost alone in the Western world, is retreating from it, experiencing increased religiosity. As

---

*Is there any reason why a nonbeliever who doesn't have the rewards or punishment of heaven and hell to serve as a deterrent to immoral conduct can still act morally, indeed even if in some instances it's against his immediate self-interest? Since we know such a reality exists, the reason is really immaterial. But for starters, how about the motivation to be free from the pangs of moral guilt? Or the motivation of affection or love for the object of our good conduct?

Alexis de Tocqueville noted in his 1835 book *Democracy in America*, "It must never be forgotten that religion gave birth to Anglo-American society." So the religious stem goes very deep in American soil and produces an abundant harvest of religiosity in America to this very day. What has the result been?

One of the most searing indictments of religion in the overall moral, social, and economic health of a nation was published in the online journal *Evolutionary Psychology* in July of 2009 (Vol. 7[3], 399–434). Titled "The Chronic Dependence of Popular Religiosity upon Dysfunctional Psychosociological Conditions," and with a reference bibliography of 155 sources ranging from the American Academy of Pediatrics, *American Sociological Review*, and the World Health Organization, to the *Journal of Religion and Society*, the International Social Survey Program, and the *United Nations Human Development Report*, the study by researcher Gregory Paul sought to answer the accuracy of two competing hypotheses: one, that religion is a necessary component of societal health and prosperity, and two, that higher degrees of nonreligiosity are more apt to be associated with better socioeconomic conditions in a nation. Seventeen first world nations (average per capita income of at least $23,000) were studied.

Using criteria such as beliefs in God, biblical literalism, prayer, evolution, and heaven and hell, as well as attendance at religious services and the number of atheists and agnostics, the research showed that overall the United States was the most religious of all seventeen nations. Numbers two, three, and four were Ireland, Italy, and Austria, respectively. The least religious nation was Sweden, followed by Japan, Denmark, and France.

Testing the dysfunction of a nation by, among other things, the per capita number of homicides, incarcerations, suicides, abortions, infant mortality, life expectancy, marriage duration, divorce, alcohol consumption, corruption, income, income disparity, poverty, and employment levels, the study found that the United States, the number one religious nation, also ranked number one as the most dysfunctional of all the nations. Australia was number two (ranked ninth out of seventeen in the most religious of nations), followed by New Zealand and Spain tied for third (ranked tenth and twelfth in the most religious of nations) and Ireland at number four (ranked second in the most religious of nations). The nation that was ranked number one as the least dysfunctional was Norway (ranked seventh out of seventeen in the least religious of nations), followed by Denmark at number two (ranked third in the least religious of nations), Sweden at number three (ranked number one as the least religious nation), and Holland at number four (ranked eighth in the least religious of nations).

This study clearly shows a correlation between religiosity and the dysfunction of a nation. And the lowest rates of dysfunction are found among the most irreligious of countries. I know that Benjamin Disraeli said there were three types of lies—lies, damned lies, and statistics—but I don't believe that. Statistics don't lie, although the interpretation put on them may. Moreover, with the terrible history we all know that ardent religiosity has given rise to, we really shouldn't be too surprised by the results of the study.

Many Christian theologians make the argument—and they do it as if they were certain—that the only reason that man intuitively knows the difference between right and wrong is that God instilled this moral law into the DNA and protoplasm of all humans. If not, they say, it would be impossible for man to have known this on his own.

So we get our morality from God? Really? Apart from the incongruity that the source of our morality would be a being, who, by his own "word" in the bible, is extremely vindictive, vain, and jealous, who commanded the Israelites to plunder the property of their enemies and despoil their virgin women, and who was the most prolific murderer in history (such a being is a good source for our morals?), what evidence could possibly be adduced for the proposition that conscience, our inner sense of what is right or wrong, could not have emanated from any source other than God? As was first popularized by nineteenth-century thinkers like Herbert Spencer, E. B. Taylor, and William

Sumner, man's sense of right and wrong may have developed through our instinct for social survival. Called "Social Darwinism," this concept posits that the morality and culture of humans are subject to the same laws of adaptation and survival as species are. Early man learned that certain behavior, such as being selfish and thinking only of oneself (like newborn babies, who demonstrate no sense of right and wrong), was met with harsh disapproval by those with whom they interacted, since such behavior automatically inured to the detriment of others. And the instinct for social survival was so strong that eventually right or good or decent behavior, at least to a certain depth of social intercourse, was engaged in by man not just because it aided survival but also because man genuinely felt it was, well, right and good and decent, "the way humans should act." Charles Darwin himself, in *The Descent of Man*, flirts with this theory.

℮〜

C. S. LEWIS SAID THAT "I cannot love my neighbor as myself till I learn to love God." So according to Lewis, someone cannot be kind and considerate to his fellow man unless he first learns to love God. Without first doing that, he's going to treat his fellow man terribly. Who could possibly believe such nonsense? I guess all atheists, having no invisible means of support like Christians do, are just terrible human beings who treat everyone they come into contact with terribly. Indeed, in making their case against atheism, Christian theologians are fond of quoting Psalm 14:1, which informs us that "those who say there is no God are corrupt, they do abominable deeds, and there is not one who does good." But isn't it interesting to note that one never hears of atheists killing and torturing people and blowing up buildings? It's usually religious fanatics (the ones who believe in, and know all about, God) who seem to be doing these things. We all know that through the centuries organized religion has bred the evils of intolerance and, often, persecution. This is not nearly as likely to exist in atheism or agnosticism because in both there is an absence of idolatry, and without idolatry, there is little inclination to make others share its abuses. I just can't imagine wars and torture and persecution by atheists trying to get other nations or people not to believe in God.

Is there any evidence at all, anywhere, that morality needs religion, that atheists[3] are simply bad human beings who treat their fellow man worse than religious people do? If so, where is that evidence?

The almost invariable answer to this question one receives from religious stalwarts is a specious one, so specious that those Christian writers who peddle it are either very misinformed or deliberately lying. They cite the horrors of Hitler and Stalin, claiming both were atheists. But where is the evidence that Hitler, an altar boy as a Catholic youth, later became an atheist? The definite weight of the evidence is that he did not. In his book, *Mein Kampf*, Hitler wrote, "I am convinced that I am acting as the agent of our creator," and even spoke of "the greatness of Christianity." In a speech to the Reichstag, the lower house of the German parliament, on March 23, 1933, less than two months after being elected chancellor of Germany, he said that "the Christian faith" possessed the "essential elements for safeguarding the soul of the German people," and "we hope to improve our relations to the Holy See." Although, as it turned out, the Nazi Party did not have an especially good relationship with the Catholic hierarchy, this, per se, is not strong circumstantial evidence that Hitler renounced Catholicism. And there is no evidence that he left the Catholic church during his life. Indeed, we know from German general Gerhard Engel (Engel's 1974 book *At the Heart of the Reich: The Secret Diary of Hitler's Army Adjutant*) that as late as the fall of 1941, less than four years before his death, and *after* his Final Solution decision to exterminate the Jews of Europe, Hitler said, "I am now as before a Catholic and will always remain so."

But even if he did, at some point thereafter, leave the church, this would not necessarily mean he became an atheist. There were multiple attempted assassinations of Hitler starting in 1939. And he came to believe that he survived because he was "under the protection of God." The last and most famous assassination attempt was on July 20, 1944, when a bomb was placed and exploded close to him at a conference with his generals. The following day, less than nine months before he killed himself in his Berlin bunker, he proclaimed that his miraculous survival from the previous day's attempt on his life "only confirmed my conviction that Almighty God has called me to lead the German people to victory." In this regard, it is noteworthy that in the Second World War, the soldiers of Hitler's army, the Wehrmacht, had the words *Gott mit uns* (God is with us) inscribed on their belt buckles. In any event, who would be absurd enough to say that Hitler wanted to conquer the world so that he could stamp out religion and theism?

The anti-atheists feel they have their strongest case against atheism in Stalin, an avowed atheist. Being a Marxist and communist, of course he was an atheist. But everyone knows that in the movement toward communism led by Lenin and a young Stalin in Russia and resulting in the Russian Revolution of 1917, atheism was but an ancillary tenet to the main engine behind the movement—the redistribution of wealth through a class struggle that would bring about the collapse of capitalism. And Stalin was simply a brutal dictator who wanted total control over the physical and economic lives of all Russians, their religious belief being way, way down the list.

To illustrate just how peripheral atheism was to Stalin and the horrors he authored, major biographies on Stalin—e.g., Adam Ulam's 760-page *Stalin: the Man and His Era*; Simon Sebag Montefiore's 786-page *Stalin: The Court of the Red Tsar*—don't even have the word "atheism" in their entire books. Robert Service's 715-page *Stalin: A Biography* has one five-word sentence mentioning atheism. Does anyone believe that the tens of thousands of Soviet citizens who died in Stalin's gulags or were murdered in his purges suffered their fate because of their religion? Or Stalin's atheism? Most of the anti-atheism policy of the Soviet state was confined to means like propaganda, and much more rarely, physical destruction of Russian Orthodox churches or confiscation of church property. Indeed, during the war years Stalin even "made a truce with the hierarchy [of the Russian Orthodox Church] in the interests of wartime unity." (Robert M. Hemstreet, "Religious Humanism Meets Scientific Atheism," *The Humanist,* January/February 1986, 6). For instance, Stalin closed down all anti-religious periodicals in 1941.

To argue that atheism leads to as much or more oppression and tyranny than Christianity is sophistic. The tyranny of Christianity and Islam throughout the ages was *all* about religion, whereas the tyranny of Hitler and Stalin, as well as Mao Zedong, had nothing to do with religion. To say that Stalin was evil *because* he was an atheist is to say that people who are atheists are likely to be evil, a preposterous suggestion. I would imagine some atheists might have a chip on their shoulder, but I doubt one would find too many of them with horns on their head. I reject out of hand Benjamin Franklin's rhetorical question, "If men are so wicked with religion, what would they be without it?" 'Tis a raindrop to an ocean when comparing the atrocities of man caused by atheism to those caused by religion.

Although the public face of religion has always been peace, tolerance, and compassion, it is difficult to think of anything throughout the centuries that has been linked more with the absence of these things than religion. Someone once said that with or without religion, good people do good things and evil people evil things. But for good people to do evil things, that takes religion.

Many atheists will tell you that they were driven to atheism because they felt that Christianity and the culture it espouses are incompatible with what they perceive to be conventional standards of morality. And they find the Christian God who consigns to everlasting punishment in hell those who do not accept him as their savior to be, naturally, incredibly cruel and the antithesis of a "merciful" God. So the Christian religion, ironically, has actually spawned the embracing of atheism by some who see only immorality and cruelty in Christianity, feeling that Christians, particularly the religious right, are anything but "Christian" or Christ-like in their actual conduct. In a similar vein, Gandhi once said that if Christians lived according to their true faith, there would be no Hindus remaining in India.

With respect to the issue of morality needing religion, perhaps this observation should be made: When someone is deterred from a theft, rape, or murder he wants very badly to commit, do we really believe that the main reason he is deterred is not that if he gets caught he will be severely punished by the law, but that even if he somehow is never caught, he fears what God will do to him in the hereafter? Really? We know this is not generally true. Indeed, isn't the need for laws throughout the land an implied admission that God and religion are only marginally effective in deterring bad and immoral human conduct? Or do Christian theologians actually believe that when legislators enacted these laws, they mostly had in mind the irreligious in our society?

VOLTAIRE, while in exile in England, complained that there were only two sauces in the country but 42 religions. As of 2001, according to the *World Christian Encyclopedia*, there were 19 major religions in the world and 270 denominations of these religions. And an incredible 34,000 separate Christian groups were identified, more than half of them independent churches not linked to any big denomination. All of the major religions of the world have two common denominators: They all contradict each other in some important way, and almost all are convinced that their religious belief is the only true and correct one. For instance, three of the world's great religions, Judaism, Christianity, and Islam, feel they are the only true religion because God dealt exclusively and only with them. Judaism claims that God gave his revelations to the prophet Moses in the first five books of the Old Testament. Christianity claims that God inspired every book of their bible. Islam claims that the Qu'ran was written in heaven and brought to the prophet Muhammad by the angel Gabriel. So each religion believes it is the sole custodian of God's word to man.[4]

Just as the patriarchs of the great religions of the world believe their religion is the one true religion of God, they have successfully inculcated into the minds of most of their members this same egocentric thought. How many realize the absurdity of the notion? And how can something like this happen so easily? I once told a Los Angeles Dodgers fan that with more than a 95 percent accuracy I could tell him why, in just five words, sports fans in the major league cities around the country have a lifelong, fanatical devotion to their team. (They may be disloyal to their job, to their friends, even to their wives, but never to their team. And the tremendous irony of it all is that the vast, overwhelming majority of the players themselves, for whom the fans scream their heads off at games, typically have virtually no loyalty at all to them or the team, routinely going to whatever team pays them the most money.) "I live [or was born] in this city." In other words, if a rabid Philadelphia Phillies fan—or a Detroit Tigers, Chicago Bulls, Los Angeles Lakers, New York Jets, or Oakland Raiders fan—lived or was born in Boston, he'd be a Red Sox fan. It's really as simple as that.

Likewise, does any Christian reading this book really doubt that if he were a Jew born in Jerusalem that he would most likely be a member of the Jewish religion? And that if he were an Arab born somewhere in Saudi Arabia he would most likely be a Muslim? Or if he were an Indian born in India that he would most likely be a member of the Hindu faith? Isn't it comforting for people to know that their very firmly held religious beliefs have nothing to do with the quality and merit of the beliefs, and everything to do with geography?

Our sense of superiority over all other religions is a form of prejudice, which can be defined as being down on something you're not up on, and together with the analogous patriotism for the country of one's birth, may be the cause of more conflict in the world than anything else.

18

Hey, Look at Us, We're Just as Silly as They Are

I'VE BEEN TALKING AT LENGTH in this book about the folly of Christianity. But the other great religions of the world want us to know that Christianity does not have a monopoly on silliness, that they have their own patented brand with which they have inebriated the minds of their faithful. Because we're nearing the end of this book, let's very briefly look at those four religions that are considered to be, in addition to Christianity, the greatest religions of the world. Other important but much smaller religions, such as Confucianism, Taoism, and Shinto, are not discussed. Let me start by looking at the least silly major religion of all.

Judaism

Judaism, the religion of the Jews, is by far the smallest of all the major religions of the world, with less than 15 million adherents worldwide. Though small, it has been enormously influential historically, giving substantial birth to the two largest religions, Christianity (at 2.2 billion members, the largest) and Islam. And because of the state of Israel and the national and international importance of many prominent Jews, particularly in American society, the Jewish community is disproportionately influential to this very day.

Before Judaism, the peoples of the world worshipped many gods (e.g., the Greek gods Zeus, Aphrodite, and Ares, and the Roman gods Mars, Jupiter, and Venus). Judaism introduced the concept of only one true god, and this monotheism was adopted by Christianity, and later, Islam.

The first Christians, including Jesus, were Jews. The origin of the Jewish people is believed to be between the Tigris and Euphrates rivers in southern Mesopotamia, modern-day Iraq (Genesis 11:28, 31; Acts 7:2; Judith 5:7 and 8:26). But by the twelfth century BC, after centuries of peregrination, including their exodus from Egypt, they had settled in Canaan (ancient Palestine). A major unsettling of the Jewish people followed the end of their fifty-year Babylonian Captivity in 538 BC, during which many Jews did not return to Canaan but instead dispersed (Diaspora) to the various nations of the world.

Although Judaism fully accepts the Old Testament of the bible and its God, unlike Christianity, it rejects the New Testament completely, viewing Jesus as only a prophet. Interestingly, one of the Old Testament's greatest prophets, Isaiah, in Isaiah 53:1–12 speaks of a servant of the Lord who "grew up in the Lord's presence" and who after a trial was led "as a lamb to the slaughter," the people not realizing that "he was dying for their sins," that he was "suffering their punishment." This and other verses in Isaiah (e.g., "he was put in a rich man's grave" [see Matthew 27:57–60]; "he never said a word" to his accusers [see Matthew 27:12–14]) describe someone who bears a stunning, eerie resemblance to Jesus of Nazareth, and though overwhelmed by virtually everything to the contrary that makes any sense, Isaiah 53 has always been, to me, the single most powerful chapter (merely four paragraphs) in the entire bible that supports Jesus as being the Son of God.*

---

*The immense importance of prophesies in Jewish as well as Christian theology is not limited to the belief that a mere mortal, by himself, could not predict the future, that only by divine inspiration in a vision of the prophet or in his conversation with God could he have done so (2 Peter 1:20–21). Additionally, it's the fact that the God of the bible, in several biblical passages, based the proof of his claim that he was the only true God on his unique power to foretell the future. "I am the First and Last. There is no

Indeed, these few paragraphs in Isaiah are so powerful that the great American patriot, writer, and intellectual Thomas Paine, in his 1807 *The Age of Reason—Part III* (in which he sets forth contradictions in prophesies between the Old and the New Testaments in his defense of deism—the irreligious belief in a disengaged God that had some currency among intellectuals in seventeenth- and eighteenth-century Europe and in America during the late eighteenth and early nineteenth centuries), apparently felt compelled to misrepresent their contents to his readers. He said that Isaiah "employed the whole of this chapter, the 53rd, in lamenting the sufferings of some deceased person, of whom he speaks very pathetically. It is a monody [a poem lamenting someone's death] on the death of a friend." The fact that someone of the reputation for high principles and morality of Paine felt the need to deceive attests to the power of Isaiah 53. The man who had the courage to stand up to the British in the successful American Revolution he largely inspired did not, it appears, have the courage to stand up to four paragraphs in the bible, choosing to put a dent in his reputation, at least by my lights, instead.

When I asked a Los Angeles rabbi how Judaism squares Isaiah 53 with its rejection of Jesus as the messiah, he responded, "Isaiah didn't say the servant [the subject in Isaiah is known by the misnomer "Suffering Servant"] was born of a virgin." "Yes, Rabbi," I replied, "but that's like if I, as a prosecutor, present a very strong case against the defendant, with much evidence, and his only defense is that there's one piece of evidence that points towards his innocence, which, by the way, is

---

other God. Who else can tell you what is going to happen in the days ahead? Let them tell you if they can and thus prove their power. Let them do as I have done since ancient times (Isaiah 44:6–7; see also Isaiah 41:26, 46:10; as to Jesus, see John 13:19). The dispersion of the Jews to the many nations of the world (following their Babylonian Captivity in the 6th century BC) and the gathering of them later in their own land (the creation of the state of Israel by the United Nations in 1948) are frequently cited as prominent examples of prophesies by God (Deuteronomy 28:64, Ezekiel 20:34, and 36:24) that have come true.

the rule rather than the exception in a criminal trial. I mean, he can make that argument, but he's not going to win with it. The jury looks at the totality, the weight of the evidence." (The *reductio ad absurdum* of the position that Isaiah did not say the servant was born of a virgin is that even if Isaiah had said he was, I guess one could say, "Yes, but Isaiah didn't say the servant was a carpenter" [Mark 6:3].)

The rabbi paused, with no response to what I had said. He then said something that I had already thought about as the only possible argument to rebut Isaiah 53: "Isaiah used the past tense." I responded, "Yes, Rabbi, but it is not uncommon, when being literary, to use the past tense in talking of the future, and it couldn't possibly be any clearer that Isaiah was talking about the future. But Rabbi, with respect to your past tense argument, do you know of any historical or biblical event *before* Isaiah that Isaiah could possibly have been referring to that would even remotely fit Isaiah 53?" The rabbi, as he had to, conceded there was nothing, whereupon he retreated to the argument that "Isaiah may have only been sending out a message to the Jewish people in 53." "What conceivable message," I asked, "could Isaiah have been sending out to Jewish people by what he says in 53, one that could possibly be of any benefit to them?" The rabbi had no answer to this, and we went on to other points of discussion.

The Hebrew faith is thought to have originated with Abraham, whom Jews believe God entered into a covenant with to give the promised land of Canaan to his seed and make Abraham the father of the Jewish people. "I will give all this land of Canaan to you and your offspring *forever*" (Genesis 17:2–8). Thus, the Jewish claim to this very day that Palestine was intended by God to be their homeland.

The Jewish religion's rejection of Jesus, and the Jews at the time of Jesus insisting, against the wishes of Pontius Pilate, who believed Jesus to be innocent, that he order Jesus' death (Matthew 27:22–26, Mark 15:6–15, John 19:4,7), are perhaps the most important reasons that, throughout the centuries, non-Jews, particularly Christians, have persecuted Jews.* But why the conflict and hatred between Arabs and Jews? For one thing, both claim ancestral descent from Abraham—the Jews through Abraham's son Isaac, with his wife Sarah, the Arabs through Abraham's son Ishmael, by an Egyptian (Arab) maidservant, Hagar, after Abraham had moved with his family to Canaan (Genesis 16:3–15). This caused much dissension and turmoil among Sarah, Hagar, and Abraham and, most importantly, sowed the seeds for the claim by Arabs that Palestine was theirs by ancestral rights. (See also the "great nation" promise by God to Ishmael's descendants in Genesis 17:20–21, 21:18.) It's hard to believe that so much of the hostility and oftentimes war between the Jews and the Arabs had its genesis (sorry) in an act of coitus between a randy eighty-six-year-old man (Abraham) and a young woman.

We've seen that Jews believe that the first five books of the Old Testament (Torah) are the word of God that God gave to their leader, Moses. It has never been clear to me how Jews reconcile the stark incongruity of the Torah's word that they are God's chosen people (Exodus 19:5–6 and 3:7, Leviticus 26:11, Deuteronomy 7:6–7 and 14:2; see also Jeremiah 31:33, Isaiah 44:1, 1 Peter 1, and Romans 11:28) with the fact that they have been persecuted throughout history more than any other group of people.

---

*When Pilate, after symbolically washing his hands from a bowl of water, said to the crowd of Jews, "I am innocent of the blood of this man. The responsibility is yours," the crowd yelled back, "We will take responsibility for his death. We and our children" (Matthew 27:24–25). Pope Innocent III wrote in 1208, "The Jews, against whom the blood of Jesus calls out, must remain vagabonds upon the earth until their faces be covered with shame and they seek the name of Jesus Christ the Lord."

But it seems that whether the interchange between the Jews and Pilate even took place is, like so many other things in the bible, at least open to question. How would the Jews, completely subservient to the Roman governor, have sufficient influence on Pilate to get him to order the death of a man he believed was innocent, and free Barabbas, a convicted murderer the Jews asked him to spare? True, it was Pilate's custom to release one prisoner each year during Passover whose freedom the people requested (Matthew 27:15). But where was it part of the custom to go along with the request of the people to execute a man Pilate believed to be innocent?

When Palestine, at the time controlled by Arabs, was partitioned in 1948 into independent Jewish and Arab states as a result of a United Nations resolution the previous year, the Jewish people received their own state of Israel. But many people don't realize that Israel is but a tiny sliver of land, just 30 to 60 miles wide through most of it and only 250 miles long, not even large enough for the six letters of its name on a map of the world.

Not believing in Jesus as the messiah has enabled followers of Judaism to avoid the paralyzing idiocies of Christianity, such as original sin, Jesus dying on the cross for our sins, the trinity, and the born-again doctrine. The Torah, along with the Talmud (63 commentaries—in two sections, the Mishnah and the Gemara—written in Aramaic by rabbis and Jewish scholars on biblical texts and early oral Mosaic law and lore containing endless pages of often arcane argumentation, not infrequently on hair-splitting trivialities), are the main repositories of Hebrew doctrine, law, religion, and morals. In them, Judaism gets even further away than Catholicism from the Protestant doctrine that faith alone will ensure final salvation. Amidst the tangle of Jewish ritualism and religious observances is the notion that high morality and fair treatment of one's fellow man is the most important element of their faith. Hillel, the famous Jewish teacher and scholar of the late first century BC whose wisdom and teachings remain to this very day a powerful influence in Judaism, was once asked to sum up Judaism while the questioner was standing on only one foot. "Certainly," Hillel said. "What is hateful to you, do not do to your neighbor. That is all there is in the Torah. All the rest is mere commentary."

Admirably, then, the emphasis in Judaism, as opposed to Christianity, is on how one behaves in life, not on what one says or believes. Whether or not Jews have lived out this elevated life more than non-Jews is beyond the scope of this book. But if they haven't, no one can blame their religion for it. I *have* noticed that, unlike Christian funerals, where, apart from the eulogy, they are celebrations of God and Jesus, Jewish funerals properly focus on a celebration of the decedent's life.

Judaism also has the common sense to largely reject heaven and particularly hell. Judaism mostly accepts the immortality of the soul, but the place where it presumably lives on, *Sheol* (Genesis 37:35, Psalm 139:8, Hosea 13:14), remains shadowy and ill-defined in Hebrew theology.

But like all organized religions, Judaism is brimming over with absurdities. It wouldn't be a religion if it did not. I mean, the Old Testament is a document much of which all rational men should run away from as fast as they can. If you believe, as most traditional Jews do (not as allegories, but as reality), in the Garden of Eden, God's having a tête-à-tête with Moses and Abraham, Noah's ark, etc., and that the monstrously heinous and murderous God of the Old Testament is worthy of your great love and reverence (even Christians aren't that zany, since the main focus of their love, by far, is Jesus), then there's nothing I can really tell you. It's like the fellow who once asked Louis Armstrong, "Louie, tell me what jazz is." "Man," Armstrong answered, "if you don't know, I could never tell you."

Most of today's observant Jews, while still clinging to the Old Testament, particularly the Torah, embrace notions like God creating man in God's image; that Jews are partners with God in uprooting evil in the world; and that God will "redeem us all at the end of time."

Orthodox Jews, the smallest and most traditional and undeviating of the three main branches of Judaism in the literal interpretation of the Torah, and the only branch officially recognized by the state of Israel, also believe, as Reform Jews (the largest and most liberal in their interpretation of the Torah) and Conservative Jews (middle of the road) did for centuries before the Holocaust (and many still do), that the messiah, a descendant of the house of David anointed by God, will be born some day (many Jews believe that any circumcised Jewish baby born, if he receives the proper rearing and inculcation of values, could be the messiah) and will bring a mystical peace and decency to all of mankind, including animals, with lions and lambs lying down next to each other. (See Isaiah 11:6–7.) Italian dictator Benito Mussolini once said, "I'd rather live one day like a lion than a thousand days like a lamb." After the Jewish messiah graces the earth, there apparently won't be much difference between these two mammals.

Islam

Islam, whose adherents are called Muslims, was founded in Mecca, a commercial and religious center in the kingdom of Hejas (present-day Saudi Arabia) in the early seventh century AD by Muhammad, who was born there in AD 570. His father died before he was born, and he was raised by an uncle after the death of his mother five years later. Muhammad was very spiritual and was known as a man of considerable personal virtue who was offended by what he perceived to be the decadence and immorality of Arab life. However, before the age of forty, he contented himself with a life as a married man with six children and being a merchant in the bustling caravan commerce of the city of Mecca.

Starting at age forty, each year during Ramadan—the holy month of fasting from sunrise to sunset in the Arab world—Muhammad would begin days and nights of contemplation in a cave on Mount Hira, the Mountain of Light, near Mecca. During these periods of meditation he started to question his sanity when he had very vivid dreams of angels, and experienced light and sound that appeared to have no source. His wife's cousin assured him, however, that what he was experiencing was revelations from the heavens and that he was "the new prophet of the one God." Whether real or imagined, these experiences would end up materially affecting the lives of billions of people, Islamic and others, the world over.

The "revelations" continued for several years until Muhammad's so-called Night Journey around AD 620. Legend has it that, as author Rodney Stark writes in his 2007 book, *Discovering God,*

> While sleeping at the home of his cousin in Mecca, he was awakened by the angel Gabriel who led him by the hand to a winged horse, whereupon the two were quickly transported to Jerusalem. There he was

introduced to Adam, Abraham, Moses, and Jesus, after which he was taken through each of the seven heavens, and then beyond, where he was allowed to see Allah [the Arabic name for God] who appeared as divine light. On his way back down through the seven heavens, Mohammed had a series of interactions with Moses concerning the number of times that Muslims would be required to pray each day, the number gradually being reduced from fifty down to five times.

By early morning, we are told, Muhammad, after a very busy night, was tucked back in his bed.

Islam (in Arabic "to surrender" to the will of God), which came to replace the polytheism of the Arab world, believes that until Muhammad's death in AD 632 he continued to receive revelations from Allah through the angel Gabriel, who had Muhammad repeat these revelations after him. These revelations were put into the Qur'an (the spelling favored by Muslim writers for Koran). The Qur'an is the holy scripture of Islam, believed by Muslims to be the literal, verbatim "word of God" revealed to Mohammed. Islam believes that the original bound text of the Qur'an is in heaven with God. More than 1 billion Muslims, one in six of the world's population, treat its 114 chapters (called suras, whose verses within are almost poetic in nature) as infallible and as governing their daily life and worship.

Ibn Warraq writes that to Muslims, the Qur'an "is the holy of holies. It must never rest beneath other books but always on top of them; one must never drink or smoke when it is being read aloud; and it must be listened to in silence." Many Christians are unaware that biblical figures such as Moses, Abraham, Noah, and Jesus appear many times in the Qur'an, with their essential biblical acts and roles remaining, for the most part, intact (even Jesus' virgin birth is embraced by the Qur'an, though Islam, like Judaism, rejects the divinity of Jesus, believing him to be only a prophet), although the language to describe the acts and roles differs appreciably from the language of the bible.

One problem with the Qur'an is that there are actually seven versions of it, and although only two of the seven are in popular use today, the differences in the versions, unlike corresponding books in the Catholic and Protestant bibles, are often substantial. Each sura in the Qur'an is preceded by a reference to the place where Mohammed received a revelation, always Mecca or Medina, the latter being where he is buried and to which he and his followers fled (the Hegira) in 622 when they were being persecuted in Mecca for condemning the Arab world's pagan worship of many gods. Islam, being monotheistic, does not tolerate polytheists who worship Allah with other gods. Sura 9:5 says, "Kill those who join other Gods with Allah wherever ye shall find them." It is equally harsh on those who abandon Islam. "If they turn back [to nonbelief or idolatry of gods other than Allah], then seize them and slay them wherever ye find them" (Sura 4:90).

Almost immediately after Muhammad's death in 632, Islamic armies inspired by his word set out to enlighten the world about his teachings. Their method of choice, of course, was the sword and the bloodshed of tens of thousands of people who were slaughtered. Within two years of his death, all of Arabia had fallen to armies of Muslims. In 636, Syria was conquered, followed by Mesopotamia in 637 and Palestine in 638. Egypt and Persia were conquered in 642 and 643, respectively. Further conquests by the sword took place in the ensuing centuries, all in the name of Allah.

The Qur'an is supplemented in Muslim life and culture by the Hadith, an account of the things said or done by Muhammed during his life as well as that of his "Companions," and the Shariah, Islamic law that is derived mostly from the Qur'an but also from the Sunna, the customs and traditions of the Muslim people.

The "Five Pillars of Belief" in Islam, all set forth in suras, are as follows: (1) belief in one God, Allah (Sura 23:116 and 117). (2) Belief in angels (Sura 2:177). (3) Belief in many prophets but one message. Adam was the first prophet. Others include Abraham, Moses, Jesus, and "the seal of the prophets," Muhammad (Sura 4:136 and 33:40), who Muslims believe was the final prophet who completed the prophecies of Moses and Jesus. (4) Belief in a judgment day (Sura 15:35 and 36). (5) Belief in God's omniscience, prior knowledge, and determination of all events (Sura 9:51).

There are also five pillars of observance in Islam followed without variation by all devout Muslims. (1) To repeat every day the confession of faith: "God is great. There is no God but Allah. Muhammad is the messenger of Allah." (2) To pray facing Mecca five times a day. (3) To give a percentage of one's income to charity. (4) To fast during Ramadan. (5) And for every male Muslim, to make a pilgrimage (hajj) to Mecca at least once in his lifetime. Only illness or poverty is a valid excuse for not undertaking the journey.

The principal place in Mecca for the pilgrimage is the Kaaba, the holiest of Islamic shrines. In his *History of the Arabs*, Philip Hitti writes that Islam believes the Kaaba "was originally built by Adam according to a celestial prototype, and after the Deluge [flood] rebuilt by Abraham and [his son] Ishmael." The Kaaba houses the Black Stone, the most sacred object of Islam. It is believed by Islam to be a meteorite sent from heaven that dates back to the days of Adam and Eve, and to have once been kissed by Muhammad.

The Qur'an allows a Muslim man to marry up to four women at a time as long as he treats each one well. However, beating a wife who misbehaves is not considered to be bad treatment. In fact, beatings in such cases are suggested (Sura 4:34). A Muslim woman can be married to only one man at a time.

Islam believes that one's soul goes to heaven or hell at the time of death.

The late social commentator Eric Hoffer once observed that "there is a tendency to judge a race, a nation, or any distinct group by its least worthy members." Too many unenlightened Americans believe that if one is an Arab Muslim (millions of Arabs are actually Christians; indeed, more than one-half of Arab Americans are Christian, and millions of Muslims are not Arab, e.g., Turks), he's probably a terrorist or at least a terrorist sympathizer. It didn't take a research project to expose the fallacy of this benighted view, but a 2003 study published in the book *At the Heart of Terror: Islam, Jihadists, and America's War on Terrorism* by Monte and Princess Palmer found that approximately 4 percent of Muslims worldwide are fanatical Islamic fundamentalists. But only 0.1 percent are militant jihadists (mujahideen) whose goal is to make the world an Islamic state by means that include terrorism.

Hinduism

One of my strengths, if I have any, is that I know my limitations. And I can tell you I am no match for Hinduism. Hindus, who embrace anything spiritual they can get their hands on, are not people to criticize, extol, or ignore. They should be observed and appreciated, even enjoyed in the sense of bemusement.

Writer C. Tara observes about them:

> In Hindu society, it is the religious custom, first thing in the morning, to bathe in a nearby river they believe makes them holy. Then, still without having eaten, they go to the local temple and make offerings of flowers and food to the local Gods. Some will wash the idol and decorate it with red and yellow powder. Nearly every home has a corner or even a room for worship of the family's favorite God. A popular God in some localities is Ganesha, the elephant God. People will especially pray to him for good fortune, as he is known as the remover of obstacles. In other places, [the gods] Krishna, Rama, Shiva, Durga, or some other deity might take first place in devotion.

Hinduism, the third largest religion behind Christianity and Islam, has more than 800 million adherents in the world, most in India. That we know. What no one knows is when Hinduism began or who, if anyone, even founded it, although some say it was by Aryan tribes who migrated to India, circa 2000 BC, and who brought with them their religions based on Persian and Babylonian mythologies and teachings. The so-called Indus Valley Civilization site in Sind, India, in the third century BC is thought by some to be the oldest discoverable link to Hindu culture. Hindu's most sacred scriptures, the Vedas (Sanskrit for "knowledge"), were written around 1500 BC Today, the most popular text of Hinduism is the Bhagavad Gita, written somewhere between 200 BC and AD 200 and containing, it is believed, the ultimate word on ethics and morality from Krishna, one of the ten incarnations of a Hindu god. The Gita became the bible of the Hare Krishna movement that started in America in 1965 and continues to this day around the world. Its focus is on the renunciation of material desires to prepare for a more perfect reincarnation.

Remarkably, no one can even satisfactorily define Hinduism except to say it is a loosely connected amalgam of sects, traditions, rituals, beliefs, and mythologies that go back thousands of years into the mists of time. The *New Larousse Encyclopedia of Mythology* (New York: G. P. Putnam, 1968), states, "Indian [Hindu] mythology is an inextricable jungle of luxuriant growths. When you enter it you lose the light of day and all clear sense of direction."

Though Hinduism has no clearly defined religious creed or governing body, it does have its spiritual teachers or advisers (gurus, swamis). Although it is true that Hinduism is polytheistic, the argument has been made that it is really monotheistic in that some Hindus consider the god Brahma (seen as an old man with four heads and four arms who rides on a swan or goose) as being the creator of the universe, and the hundreds of other gods (e.g., Agni, the god of fire; Ganga, the goddess of the River Ganges; Indra, the thunder god; Soma, the god of delight; Hanuman, the monkey god; Lakshmi, the goddess of beauty, wealth, and good fortune; Manasa, the goddess of snakes; Mitra, the god of light; Nandi, the bull god; Aditi, the mother of the gods; Varuna, the god of forgiveness) as being manifestations of him. However, even many of these Hindus concede that Brahma has lost his preeminence in the pantheon of Hindu gods and in recent years has been merely one of three members of the *trimurti*, or "trinity of gods" that is so prominent in Hinduism, the other two being Vishnu, the preserver of life, and Shiva, the god of fertility and destruction. Indeed, the most current delineation has marginalized Brahma even further by the substitution of the Goddess in one of her various manifestations (such as Durga, the warrior goddess, and Shakti, the goddess of energy) for him.

Certain beliefs govern the conduct of most Hindus, near the top of which is that of nonviolence toward any living organism. It is viewed as a fundamental moral value and exemplified by Hinduism's greatest and most revered modern leader, Mahatma Gandhi, who led India's successful drive for independence from Britain and was assassinated in 1948 just after India had secured its independence in 1947. Gandhi once said, "Nonviolence is the first article of my faith. It is also the last article of my creed." The outer extremity of this belief is seen in the followers of Jainism, a small, ascetic offshoot of Hinduism, whose members wear a mask over their mouths so that they won't kill any insect by accidentally swallowing it. Freedom from the pernicious influence of the material world, and the caste system (which most Indians quietly accept as their karma—Brahmins being the highest of the four major castes of Hinduism, the lowest formerly known and treated as "untouchables") are also at the top of Hindu culture and belief.

The ultimate goal of Hindu philosophy is enlightenment and sublimation of the self to achieve a liberation (*moksha*) of the soul, one or more of several yogas (physical and mental exercises) being the traditional way to achieve this goal. Although Henry David Thoreau, for one, practiced yoga in the mid-nineteenth century, it wasn't until 1893 that an Indian guru introduced yoga to America.

Yoga has had more than its share of charlatan gurus, including one Pierre Bernard, who exploited his followers in every way, including sexually, in the early 1900s. The most famous of all gurus and the one who popularized yoga in the Western world in the 1960s with his Transcendental Meditation (TM) was the late Maharishi Mahesh Yogi (the

Maharishi). He became the spiritual guru to the Beatles and other celebrities like actress Mia Farrow and folk singer Donovan. Actually, TM was a very watered-down version of traditional yoga that some even said was not yoga, which may involve out-of-the-ordinary postures and rhythmic movements that can be a rigorous physical workout, and ancillary regimens such as abstention from meat and alcohol. The Maharishi's technique only required closing one's eyes twice a day for twenty minutes while repeating a mantra to relax the body, eliminate stress, and bring about improved physical, mental, and emotional health.

Many gurus like Maharishi are viewed by their followers as human incarnations of one of the Hindu gods who have come to earth to guide them in their spiritual quest. *Yoga Journal*, the discipline's main magazine in America, claimed in 2008 that 16 million Americans were practicing yoga.

As indicated, though there is no definite religious creed in Hinduism, most Hindus do believe in karma (reward and punishment for past conduct), reincarnation, man as the creator of his own fate, and heaven and hell—but only as temporary lodging places before the soul gets its next reincarnation.

Buddhism

If we define religion in its conventional way as including a belief in God, the supreme being, then Buddhism, one of the world's great "religions," is not really a religion at all. This is so because its founder, Siddhartha Gautama (an original thinker who was born the son of royalty in 566 BC in the small village of Lumbini close to what is now the Nepalese border in northern India), though not expressly saying, "I do not believe in God," said, "If there is a God, it is inconceivable that he would be concerned about my day to day affairs," and "there are no Gods who can or will help man. Look not for assistance to anyone other than yourself." Indeed, a book published by the Buddhist Lodge in London, *What Is Buddhism?* (1929), says, "If by atheist you mean one who rejects the concept of a personal God, we are."

Just as Protestantism arose as a protest against the practices of Catholicism, Gautama, an Indian who wanted to liberate Hindus from the senseless polytheism of Hinduism—as well as practices like undue asceticism, animal sacrifice, the caste system, and the corruption and greed of its highest caste, Hindu Brahmins—gave birth to Buddhism. Shaken by the sight of the real world outside his sheltered palace life, with its sickness, poverty, and death, Gautama left his wife, son, and worldly possessions behind and set out at the age of around thirty on a personal mission to find spiritual peace. He sensed that the answer was somewhere between ascetic self-denial and its counterpart, self-indulgence. Buddhist legend—meaning a fable whose age has given it a certain dignity—has it that after meditating under a fig tree in his native land for four weeks, during which time the daughters of an evil god, Mara, tried to seduce him, and Mara's sons tried to scare him away, Buddha found the dharma ("truth") of human existence and reached nirvana, a state of inner peace, defined as being free from desire, and hence, he reasoned, suffering. In Buddhist theology he had become "the Buddha," meaning the "awakened" or "enlightened one," and for over four decades, until his death at eighty, he journeyed with his increasing band of followers throughout the Ganges Valley in India, preaching his message of enlightenment.

Eventually his disciples would take this message to the four corners of the world, Buddhism today having more than 400 million adherents. Many intellectuals in the Western world have been taken by Buddhism or essential aspects of it, Friedrich Nietzsche saying that it "was a hundred times more realistic than Christianity."

The earliest and, it is thought, most authentic of all Buddhist sacred texts is the Tripitaka, old Indian (Pali) for "Three Baskets" (because the scriptures were originally stored in baskets) or "Three Collections"—the Vinaya, Sutta, and Abhidhamma Pitakas, thirty-one books dealing, respectively, with Buddhist monastic discipline, the Buddha's sermons and sayings, and writings by Buddhist scholars on Buddhist doctrines and philosophy. The Tripitaka was compiled after the death of Buddha by over one hundred Buddhist monks who personally knew the Buddha and were his disciples.

The Buddha's teachings are set forth in his "Four Noble Truths," which can be summarized thusly: (1) All human existence is suffering, including the pain of birth, disease, and death. (2) Suffering is a natural consequence of desire and craving for things like success and gratification of the senses. (3) With the end of desire and craving comes the end of suffering.[1] (4) Cessation of desire and craving can be achieved by adhering to a "Noble Eightfold Path" of virtuous conduct and thinking.

The Eightfold Path is the heart of Buddhist ethics, which optimally will result in good for others and nirvana for the practicing Buddhist. The eight components of the path are "right" understanding, thought, speech, action, livelihood, effort, mindfulness, and concentration. Each of these broad categories is a springboard for other virtues. For instance, the 2005 book *Eastern Religions* (edited by Michael D. Coogan, New York: Oxford University Press) points out that in the Buddhist tradition, "mindfulness" is often viewed as a prerequisite for compassion. "As the mind becomes focused and calm, it is more possible to be attentive to the suffering of others."

The Buddha did not claim any divine inspiration for his philosophy of life and living, and emerging from a culture of childlike gods and mindless philosophy, Buddha, by postmodern standards, would have to be viewed as an impressively sensible, yes "cool," yet holy man.

Although Buddhism shed Hindu rituals and beliefs, some footprints of Hinduism remain on the Buddhist landscape. Though the Buddha himself rejected the notion of the immortality of the soul, Buddhism embraces the notion of karma and the never-ending reincarnation or rebirth (*samsara*) of man from one life to another.

Among several schools of Buddhism is Japanese Zen Buddhism, whose focus is sitting in meditation to achieve a spiritual awakening in which there is no consciousness of self. But meditation on what?

Metaphysical questions such as "What does one find where there is nothing?" and "What is the sound of one hand clapping?" to underline the limitations of one's intellect. (This shows limitations? In what way?)

Another school, perhaps the most prominent, is lamaism, or Tibetan Buddhism. The emphasis in lamaism is on prayer throughout the day, meditation, compassion for others, and rituals so mystical and complex that they can be learned only by way of oral instruction from a Buddhist monk (lama), the leader of all Tibetan monks being the Dalai Lama, the main living symbol and spiritual leader of Buddhism in the world. Forced out of his native Tibet by the Chinese in 1959, the Fourteenth Dalai Lama, who won the Nobel Peace Prize in 1989, now lives in exile in India. Whenever a Dalai Lama dies, a worldwide search is conducted to find the next lama in a child through whom it is believed the last Dalai Lama has been reincarnated.

Siddhartha Gautama, the Buddha, must be spinning in his grave over the mystical silliness to which his teachings and legacy have descended. As indicated, his words and conduct seem to suggest he may have been an atheist or an agnostic. At a minimum, he certainly did not believe, like Christianity, in a personal God, or promote the notion of worshipping a supreme being. But he himself has become so revered in Buddhist thought that, as Bhikkhu Subhadra points out in his book *The Message of Buddhism*, "images and relics of Buddha have become objects of prayers, offerings, and devotion by devout Buddhists. Buddha, who never claimed to be God, has become a God in every sense of the word." Indeed, if one were to go to the holiest of holy Buddhist places like the ancient temple of Borobudur in Yogyakarta, Indonesia, Buddha is referred to as "the Lord Buddha."

∾

I SAID I WOULD NOT BE DISCUSSING any of the other important religions of the world. But I do want to just touch on one of my favorites, the Mormons (or the Church of Jesus Christ of Latter-day Saints) good people by the way, who practice what they preach.

How did the Mormon church (13 million members worldwide) come up with its Book of Mormon, the church's main book of scripture? (Their secondary book is the King James version of the bible.) The church's founder, a poor, uneducated ne'er-do-well named Joseph Smith who turned to religion, claimed that in 1823, at the age of eighteen, he was visited in a vision at his home in Palmyra, New York by the angel "Moroni." The angel told him there was "a book of golden plates" buried on the side of a hill near Manchester, New York, that contained the gospel of Jesus Christ as revealed by Christ, after his resurrection, to ancient settlers in America from the Mid-East, but they were not supposed to be unearthed until four years later. (Mormon church doctrine is that these plates were buried in AD 421, around 1,400 years earlier, by the same Moroni, the son of the military leader and prophet Mormon, before Moroni died and became an angel.) In 1827 (precisely, September 22, 1827, per Smith's "testimony" at the beginning of the Book of Mormon), Moroni returned and led Smith to the hillside where, Smith said, Moroni "delivered the plates up to me." With the plates were two sacred stones, "Urim" and "Thummim," that gave Smith the power to translate the unknown ancient language (called "Reformed Egyptian" by Mormons) engraved on the plates into English and into the Book of Mormon, which was first published in 1830. (Smith, after taking on many wives, was murdered by his followers in 1843 for his tyrannical behavior.)

You should know that a letter, allegedly written by one Martin Harris, one of Smith's original disciples, first publicly surfaced in 1992, but its authenticity has been seriously questioned, and it is believed by most to be a forgery. The letter, dated October 23, 1830, says that it wasn't the angel Moroni who delivered the golden plates to Smith, but a magical white salamander. In any event, God bless these people.

19

The Sense and Morality of Agnosticism

I CAN SAY WITH RELATIVE CONFIDENCE (because what I'm saying, at least it would seem, *has* to be true) that there is only one *necessary* religion that has any merit to the people who inhabit this earth, and that's the Golden Rule: "Do unto others what you would want them to do unto you" (from the Beatitudes of the Sermon on the Mount [Matthew 7:12]). To treat others as you would want them to treat you is the highest, most noble form of human behavior and the basis of all morality. No matter what some papal encyclical says; no matter what some bishops' conference says; no matter how many sacraments of the Catholic church there are, or chapters and verses in the bible, or thick and complex books by theologians, or Sunday school classes and sermons by pastors; no matter how many heated arguments there are about God, Jesus, and religion; no matter how many pilgrimages there are to Mecca, Jerusalem, and other holy places; no matter how many thousands of hours Jewish scholars struggle over the meaning of the Torah; no matter how many multimillion-dollar churches and synagogues and grand cathedrals to Christ are constructed, nothing can ever change that simple reality.

"When I do good, I feel good," Abraham Lincoln said. "When I do bad, I feel bad. That's my religion."

What can any church, religion, priest, minister, rabbi, theologian, seminary, religious book, or college course teach you beyond the Golden Rule that has any value? Anything else has to be man-made piffle.

If we must have religion, the seminal test as to the value and merit of any religion worth its salt has to be not what you *believe*, but what you *do*—that is, how you treat your fellow man. Yet in the thousands upon thousands of books, and billions upon billions of words that have been written, particularly about Christianity and the bible, what percentage of the pages of these books do you think are devoted to the only thing that counts—the Golden Rule?

A second reality is that if there is a God and a heaven after our life on earth, no God who demands of those whom he created that to get to heaven they do something here on earth different from leading a life of the Golden Rule is worth spending one second in heaven with, much less eternity. If his main requirement for getting to heaven is not that we treat our fellow man fairly and decently, but we be born-again Christians who accept Jesus as our savior *and that we love him more than anyone else with all of our being*, then, as indicated earlier, who in the hell would want to spend eternity or even one second with someone who is so unbelievably self-centered and vainglorious? That type of God is not worth a tinker's damn.

The word *faith* is a euphemism for hope and speculation. Indeed, the definition of faith is belief in the unknown, belief in that for which there is no proof. And if I may borrow a clichéd term, I, for one, have never had much faith in faith. Since faith is an acknowledgment that the truth is unknown, it is nothing more than wishful thinking, and the wish is no evidence of anything beyond itself. Yet so many religious people take their wishes for reality. If patriotism is the last refuge of a scoundrel, faith is the first refuge of an idle or apprehensive mind, and though it may perhaps be mentally and emotionally nutritious, it is not intellectually sustainable.

When devout Christians feel inadequate, in conversation or debate, in justifying their belief in God, they very frequently retreat by saying,

"You *have* to have faith," saying this in the sense that faith is something that one *should* have, as if it's the proper and right thing to do. But I wonder if they have ever stopped to ask themselves why. If they are truthful with themselves, is it because they need there to be a God to give purpose to their life and mitigate their fear of death? But if so, is that really an intelligent justification for believing there is a God— merely wanting or needing him to exist to make them feel better?

I certainly do not mean to denigrate the value of faith. Faith has lit candles of warmth and softened pangs of fear and despair throughout human history. As nineteenth-century German Romantic poet Heinrich Heine said, "Human misery is too great for man to do without faith." Tolstoy went so far as to proclaim that "faith is the force of life." It's just that the comfort and solace, even strength, of faith should never be confused with the existence or nonexistence of the object of that faith. Faith and its object bear no relation to each other, though if one were to believe the great religions of the world, faith in God and God should be listed as synonyms in the dictionary. Religion even goes so far as to say that faith is itself virtuous. But under what conceivable theory?

Christianity, since its origins, has tried to infuse faith with a substance it does not have, calling it something it is not in a transparent attempt to change its nature. But as Lincoln pointed out, calling, for instance, the tail of a dog a leg doesn't change the number of legs a dog has from four to five. This is why the apostle Paul only succeeded in revealing that he knew faith is as substanceless as the froth of a vapor when he felt the need to come up with this embarrassing articulation in his letter to the Hebrews: "Faith is the *substance* of things hoped for, the *evidence* of things unseen" (Hebrews 11:1). But we know that faith is only the *dream* of things hoped for, the *imagining* of things unseen.

How or why should someone have faith in something for which there is no proof? But if we must have faith, shouldn't we only have faith in that which does not do violence to our common sense and reason? Why should we want to see, by faith, what the eye of reason rejects?

Being as helpless and impotent as we are in understanding the meaning of our existence, the majority of mankind turns to organized religion for answers, while a much smaller number of humans turn to learned religious writers and theologians. But all we ever get from any of these sources is unintelligible and/or absurd answers to insoluble mysteries. God, if there is a God, would have all the answers. But he is waiting for us, if at all, outside the reach of our minds. Our finite minds cannot comprehend that which is infinite (or as Einstein put it, "The problem is too vast for our limited minds"), and that is why the effort of religion and theology to find and explain God is inherently futile. Thus, my agnosticism; a doctrine that I suppose could be defined as the realization it is just as likely as not that the only place one can expect to find God is inside one's head.

Is the conclusion of agnosticism no more than an intellectual exercise? Can it have any value to the human condition? Perhaps. I believe there is an ethical dimension to agnosticism that has the potential, to the degree it is embraced, to make man more honest. We know that untruthfulness, dishonesty, deceit, hypocrisy, and pretense are so much a part of life that we almost expect these things in our daily living and find it refreshing when we see their absence. And it's not too likely this will ever change. But if man can ever at least hope to reduce the level of dishonesty in his existence, there perhaps is no better place to start than in his relationship with God.

Thomas Huxley, who gave the doctrine of agnosticism its name, wrote in his *Essays upon Some Controverted Questions* (1889) that "a foundation for morality" away from the affliction of "lying" would be "to give up pretending to believe that for which there is no evidence, and repeating unintelligible propositions about things beyond the possibilities of knowledge." And once you deceive yourself, all deceit is easy after that.

But, you might say, even if agnosticism will make a person more honest, if there is a God, how will this agnosticism help me with God, a God who demands that I worship him?[1]

The great religions of the world believe that God created man. In creating us, he gave us, among other things, a mind. And since he gave us our mind, we can assume he wanted us to reason with it. (Can any Christian, Jew, or Muslim be heard to say, "No, God did not want us to use the mind he gave us"?) Indeed, in Matthew 22:37, Jesus said, "You should love the Lord your God with all your heart and with all your soul and *with all your mind*." And in Isaiah 1:18, God said to the people of Judea, "Come now, let us *reason* together." Therefore, if in using the mind he gave us to reason with, we come to the erroneous conclusion that he does not exist, why would he forever punish us for our innocent lack of belief? If he would, then he is not reasonable, and we should not have any desire to spend eternity with him. In other words, if God demands that we sacrifice our reason, which has been described as the highest attribute of man, to be with him, shouldn't our reason tell us he is not worth our time? Moreover, if God is worth anything, shouldn't he want us to reach him through our reason rather than unthinkingly through blind faith? Wouldn't that mean more to him?

But if our reason leads us away from him, is it a situation where, as referred to, God denies us his eternal presence but we don't care since we have no use for him? Not necessarily. Although the bulk of the New Testament makes it very clear that if we don't accept Jesus as our savior we're toast, surprisingly, though rarely cited—understandably, because Christianity would have every reason not to do so, and atheists don't believe in God in the first place, so the issue would be moot—there is some authority in the bible for the proposition that we'll be just fine with God. In the first epistle of Paul to Timothy, he writes that "I used to scoff at the name of Christ. I hunted down his people, harming them in every way I could. But God had mercy on me because I did it in ignorance and unbelief" (1 Timothy 1:13). More powerfully, in a discussion of "spiritual blindness" in John 9:35–41, Jesus said, "I have come to judge the world. I have come to give sight to the blind and to show those who think they see that they are blind." When the Pharisees, who always challenged Jesus' divinity, said to Jesus, "Are you saying we are blind?" Jesus responded, "*If you were blind, there would be no sin in that*. 'But we see,' you say, and your sin remains." And didn't Jesus say on the cross, "Father, forgive them, for they know not what they are doing" (Luke 23:34; see also Romans 11:25, 32, and Luke 12:48).

If I could draw a parallel in the criminal law, two elements must be present to constitute a serious crime: actus reus (the criminal act) and mens rea (the criminal state of mind). An example of the latter is an intent to steal, a necessary element of the crime of theft. If a person takes the personal property of another erroneously thinking it is his property, he is not guilty of theft.

Agnosticism, per some thinkers, is based on empiricism, that all knowledge is derived from experience; that is, sense observation, and because no one has actually experienced God, we should be agnostic on the matter. I reject this notion because it neuters and emasculates the mind as a needless appendage to our cognitive senses of sight, hearing, smell, taste, and touch. If agnosticism acquired its intellectual virility from empiricism, then of course we'd have to be agnostic since no one has experienced or seen God, though some may believe they have. I'm an agnostic because my mental faculties tell me the existence of God is beyond human comprehension, not just beyond human cognition, which of course it also is and which is too simplistic. Because God and the meaning of our existence seem to be unknowable and impenetrable mysteries, I will go so far as to say that agnosticism is the *only* intelligent, *strong* position one can take on the question of God's existence.

Even if we were to hypothesize that whether God exists is not unknowable, doubt is divine in that it impels a search for the truth. It opens the door to knowledge. Faith puts a lock on the door. Indeed, while one is under its spell, faith anesthetizes the desire to seek knowledge and truth. And as knowledge increases, faith recedes.

Even though I don't feel that a belief in God (theism) or disbelief in him (atheism) is unintelligent, I do feel that a certitude about either of these two positions, even a strong belief in them, which is so extremely common, is, perforce, unintelligent. Since the depth of a belief should be in proportion to the evidence, and there is no conclusive evidence on the issue of God, no sensible person should be dogmatic about whether there is or is not a God. Put another way, when it comes to God the only thing one should be certain about is that doubt is the correct position.

The whole matter of God can perhaps be distilled down to this: Is there a God who created the world? Or is God merely a word we use to explain the world? In either event, God should only be a question.

Bookends

Most of us have fanciful thoughts (giving "wings to our imagination") from time to time that we take only half-seriously, if that. With that in mind, and with your forbearance, let me briefly set forth two of mine as bookends to this book.

Flushing God Out

We've been talking about God and whether or not he exists. If he does, we know he has refused to show himself to mankind to settle the question of his existence. But if God does exist, is there any way to flush him out? We all have our own idiosyncrasies and, as indicated, our own unusual thoughts, and with the knowledge on my part that my suggestion, if pursued, may very well turn out to be lacking in merit, let me tell you about something that has popped into my mind more than once through the years. The thought is that the known percentages of mathematical probability simply do not seem to apply, *as they should*, to our daily lives, making life more difficult and exasperating than it already is. The relevance is that if God can be flushed out in the experiment I hereinafter propose, he would be a monster completely in keeping with the one I have written about on the pages of this book.

You're looking for a paper in a box full of papers. There is no valid reason for the paper you're looking for to be at the bottom of the pile more than at the top. Wouldn't the law of percentages require that the likelihood of it being in the top half be 50 percent? But you and I know that's not the way it normally is. Certainly more than 50 percent of the time the paper is either at the bottom, near the bottom, or at least beyond the halfway point. The question is, Why?

I can tell you that when I travel by air, far, far, far more than 50 percent of the time my gate at the airport is at the end or very near the end of the gates, and this is so all over the country. At the small Burbank airport I frequently take out of Los Angeles, there are eight gates. And I can tell you, on my children's lives, that whether I'm flying south to San Diego or north to San Francisco or back East or in the direction of the east, such as to places like Phoenix or Dallas, out of at least one hundred times I have flown out of that airport, not once have I left on a gate below number five. Not once. In fact, 80 to 90 percent of the time I'm at gates 7 or 8. And I'm not the only one who feels this way. I've heard other travelers say the same thing. I got a kick out of the late, legendary sports writer of the *Los Angeles Times*, Jim Murray, asking in one of his columns, "Who are the people who are at the early gates?"

While we're on airports, as my good friend Gardnar Mulloy, one of the all-time tennis greats, said after traveling in thousands of planes throughout the world in his many years of tennis travels, "Why do airplanes never leave on time, unless you are late?"

When I used to do my banking (my wife handles this now) years ago, the branch I went to had six or seven windows with tellers. At one of the windows was a man who always wore a red, white, and blue tie and an American flag pin on his lapel. He was a very pleasant, middle-aged man, but very definitely seemed slightly mentally retarded. Apart from the words he used, his delivery was distinctly abnormal, yet he apparently was able to do his job, which was fortunate. Neither the way he dressed nor his mental retardation bothered me at all. The big problem was that this man was, he told me, "a big fan" of mine, and whenever I got his window, he would talk me to death with a big, simple smile on his face, asking me many questions and never stopping until I finally broke away. He would do this even though he was holding up the line, a sign of his mental retardation. You've probably guessed where I'm going in this discussion. Because I was always in a rush when I came into the bank (I've been rushed for time my whole adult life), I tried to avoid this teller like the plague. But if you think I got him only one out of every six or seven times, which would be mathematically expected, you'd be very wrong. Try one out of two times. It got so bad that, while in line when my turn to approach a window was next, I'd start looking at all the windows and try to calculate the likelihood of my getting him next, sometimes even letting someone in back of me take my place. Why did I get his window more than the law of probabilities would seem to dictate?

You go to a five-tier parking structure at a hospital or shopping mall, and with hundreds upon hundreds of cars parked, you frequently have to drive to the top tier, or the one below it, before you find a place, or you find no parking space and have to turn around and come all the way back. And you say to yourself, "How is this possible? When I go in here, I'm here for an hour or so, and then I come out, leave. You know, I go somewhere else. Are all these people here for the duration? Have they moved in?" Theoretically, since nearly everyone who goes to the mall or hospital or what have you spends only a limited amount of time in the place, then leaves, with sometimes close to a thousand parking spaces, there should *constantly* be many cars leaving their parking places for you to pull in. Constantly. Yet we all know that isn't the case. Why?

If you have call waiting, why is it that in the sixteen or so hours a day you're up, the phone rings far more times than it should (under the law of probability) while you are on the phone, causing an interruption?

Try this experiment. Go into your kitchen, grab a vitamin pill or some tablet, and drop it to the ground fifty, or if you want, one hundred times, *watching it all the way*. Chances are that every single time you drop the pill, it will end up at or reasonably close to your feet, certainly close enough that you can easily see it and pick it up. Now ask yourself the great number of times a small tablet or pill will drop out of your hand when you weren't watching it, and after two or three minutes on your hands and knees cursing and searching for the little s.o.b., either you never find it (not just that day, but ever) or you finally find it in some place across the kitchen floor, and wonder how it was physically possible it could have traveled that far or, sometimes, could have gotten into the unbelievable place you find it.

You have a rattle in your car that's driving you crazy or, for instance, a dragging sound every time you apply the brakes. When you take your car in to the car dealership and the service manager or assistant gets in the car with you to drive around the block so that he can hear the sound, suddenly, for the first time in weeks, your car oftentimes doesn't make the sound for him to hear. You are very irritated and you say, "This is unbelievable. On the way here this morning it was making this sound," and he says, "I know what you mean. People tell me this all the time."

In this same regard, there is a copy machine at the federal Ninth Circuit law library in Los Angeles that I rarely am able to get three or four copies out of before it jams. A sweet assistant librarian lady then comes over with her key to open up the machine and remove the jammed paper, always apologizing to me, with my always responding that it's not her fault. When I asked her recently why the library couldn't get the maintenance man for the firm that owns the machine to fix it, she said, "We've tried, but when he comes, the machine doesn't jam. Then when he leaves, it starts jamming again. I get so angry."

❧

WHY DO THINGS LIKE THIS (and there of course hundreds of other examples) happen all the time?

Obviously, I don't know why, but at some early point in my life the thought became engraved in my mind that the reason for these things happening against the law of probabilities may be that there is some perverse force at play in the universe, and *that* s.o.b. is responsible. I of course realize that I am probably all wet, but in the absence of a logical explanation, I instinctively get angry and I sometimes curse to myself.

Am I all alone in feeling this way? Not really. Although others may not use the words "perverse force at play" that I do, or think the thought I have, the vast majority of mankind *has* always expressed its exasperation with this strange phenomenon. When things go wrong for them against the odds, they say, "That's life." They're in a terrible rush, and the freeway is busier than usual. "That's life," they'll say. In a sense, there's even biblical support for these maddening experiences of life that we have all encountered that add irritation and aggravation to our lives. You know, Adam and Eve ate the apple, and God was determined to give us the toothache. In fact, there's even a so-called rule that addresses itself to one aspect of the phenomenon. I'm talking about where the operation of something physical is involved. It's called Murphy's Law, an expression that started among engineers that "if something can go wrong, it will." There's an addendum to the law that says, "And usually at the worst time."

I've always felt that expressions like these have weight and are usually accurate because, like proverbs, they come down through the ages as a result of man's experience.

One thing that I think I can dismiss out of hand is the argument of those who would scoff at my perverse force-at-play theory by saying it would be impossible, with well over 7 billion people on this earth, for any being to be arranging for a perversion of the law of probabilities for each and every one of the 7 billion people to increase our daily problems. Remember? God is all-powerful and has no limitations. If he could create the universe out of nothing when you and I couldn't create a piece of dust out of nothing, surely he would not be incapable of such villainy in our lives.

What's the bottom line? What has been tantalizing to me is the thought that perhaps tests could be conducted by mathematicians to see if, indeed, the occurrences I've just mentioned, and so many, many more, do, in fact, violate the law of probabilities, or will tests show that they don't, that it's just our imagination that these things seem to happen more often than they should. It certainly would be a fascinating experiment, and if Congress can allot hundreds of thousands of dollars to study a certain species of fish in the Antarctic, or dinosaur eggs in China, why can't Congress or a private research organization conduct this very doable experiment?

For instance, follow a frequent air traveler and see if the gates he gets are, more than 50 percent of the time, farther than the halfway point from where he started. If the tests show that everything is proceeding according to the supposedly immutable and well-known law of averages and probabilities, then I guess we can stop saying, "That's life." But if, per chance, the basis for the expression "That's life" is validated, and the law of probabilities is mysteriously being defied and violated, and no one can figure out why, is it not a possibility that there is a perverse force at play in the universe, a sick creator who delights in playing games with the lives of humans, whom he has, as I've previously indicated, so deliberately ill-equipped to play his game?

Note that the preceding effort to flush God out would apply only to finding out if he is bad, and could not flush him out on the issue of whether he is good.

Embarrassing God

Billions of people throughout history have asked themselves and wondered about whether God exists. Thousands of books have been written about whether he does. Because there's this quenchless thirst to know whether he does, and because if there is a God he would be aware, being all-knowing, that there is this desire on the part of mankind, what conceivable valid reason could he possibly have for not showing us that he exists? He could do this in whatever way he chose, such as appearing in the sky above. Unbelievably, the supposedly great Christian thinker (he is anything but) C. S. Lewis says that God is incapable of showing himself to us mortals. Lewis writes, "If there was a controlling power *outside* the universe [which Lewis says is God], it could not show itself to us who are *inside* the universe, no more than the architect of a house could actually be a wall or staircase or fireplace in that house." But this is pure moonshine. It is no parallel at all since the architect *could* walk into the house.

Moreover, even if his architect story were a good parallel, Lewis apparently is unaware that his argument about God's incapacity to show himself to us directly contradicts what he says in his book *Mere Christianity* that God is all-powerful, and nothing is beyond his capacity. According to Lewis, God is powerful enough to create the universe, but he just can't figure out a way to appear to us *in* that universe. I see. By the way, has Lewis forgotten about God talking to Moses "face to face" (Exodus 33:11) on Mount Sinai, which is here on earth, and that God, in the person of his son, Jesus Christ, died on the cross for our sins here on earth, in Palestine, 2,000 years ago? And since Lewis also believes that God is omnipresent, doesn't that include *everywhere* in the world, including the atmosphere above us?

Christian true believers are fond of telling us that God has already shown his existence to us by the miracles that Jesus, his son, performed. But how is Jesus performing miracles 2,000 years ago before a small number of followers (even with the 5,000 people he fed with only five loaves of bread and two fish, there is no indication they themselves were aware he did this) an adequate way of telling the over 7 billion people of this planet today that he exists? Or they'll tell you that God speaks to us through scripture. They are his words, they say. But as stated earlier, that is circular reasoning. You can't use the bible to prove that God speaks to us in the bible. Moreover, billions of people on earth do not believe that the bible is the word of God.

Or Christians will tell you, "Look around you. God reveals his existence to us every day by the stars in the sky, the songs of birds, the luscious fruit on trees, the beauty of a flower, the cry of a newborn baby."* But this is not a good argument at all because even if what they

---

*Romans 1:20 says, "From the time the world was created, people have seen the earth and sky, and all that God made. They can clearly see his invisible qualities—his eternal power and divine nature. So they have no excuse whatever for not knowing God." (See also Psalm 19:1–4.) But my position is that the brightest person on earth can spend his entire life studying "God" and not know him. Moreover, Romans 1:20 directly conflicts with what Jesus himself said about knowing God. In Luke 10:22, Jesus said, "No one really knows the Father [God] except the Son [Jesus] and those to whom the Son *chooses* to reveal him."

say is, indeed, proof of God's existence, *it's not being accepted* as proof by hundreds of millions of people. So why not give these millions proof that they *will* accept and cannot deny, such as appearing to us in the sky? Since it would be so easy for him to do, why not? They have no answer to this because there is no answer. All they can say is "We can't question God's ways." But as I said about Christians being bound by *their* sense of reason and logic, they don't have the right to give that answer. Since they use their logic and reason to conclude there is a God, when their logic and reason would dictate that with the world wanting and needing to know of God's existence, he should simply make that existence known, they cannot decide not to use their logic and reason anymore. They are only allowed to say, which they never do, "Yes, God's failure to simply make himself known to humanity is circumstantial evidence he does not exist, or if he does, he doesn't care about me. However, I still believe he exists and is all-loving for other reasons. But obviously, you have a good point."

THOUGH TRYING TO FLUSH OUT a perverse force in the universe is probably whistling in the dark, I do believe that we can embarrass God. Before calling for the people in the white jackets to take me away, let me explain. Obviously, it is ludicrous to think of embarrassing the creator of the universe, if there is such a creator. But embarrassing the *Christian* God is quite another story. Remember now, we are inside the sandbox and playpen of the Christian true believer. And if we accept their beliefs, then we, yes we—poor, sorry, pitiful, and impotent mortals who take and take and take the misery and pain and torment that the Christian God, we are told, either causes or allows to happen— can probably strike back at him, thereby bringing about at least a modicum of justice.

As with the perverse force in the universe discussion, what I am about to discuss is another (the last one, some may be pleased to hear) idiosyncratic reverie of mine for which I again ask your forbearance.

How can we possibly embarrass the Christian God? Only because Christians continuously tell us that the God of Christianity is a "personal God" and that they have, as Billy Graham says, a "*personal* relationship" with him. Graham also tells us that God listens to each and every one of our prayers and that "our prayers should be specific. God is interested in everything you do and nothing is too great or too insignificant to share with him." Many Christians, as we know, even claim to have actual conversations with God.

So the Christian God is not some indescribably remote, unreachable figure. He gets right inside the Christian's playpen with him. Most importantly, *he cares how we feel about him*, and loves to be loved, probably as much or more than any other figure in history or fiction. Remember, he said we "must love" him with "all our heart, all our soul, and all our mind." And he admits to being "jealous," saying, "I will not share my glory with anyone else." He wants us to think that he is so great and wonderful that we should love him even more than every member of our family. So he clearly and unequivocally *cares how we feel about him*. Doesn't it follow, then, that someone who is extremely jealous of our feelings for him, desperately needs our love, and has a personal relationship with us can very obviously be embarrassed *by* us? And if we could do so, shouldn't we? We all know from our own experience in life that there are consequences for our misconduct. God should have to pay, too. Should there not be *any* consequences to someone for causing or allowing untold misery and suffering and millions upon millions of people to die horrible deaths through history? If one has any sense of justice, I would certainly think so.

My suggestion is a simple one, and I wouldn't be surprised if an enterprising entrepreneur someday does something similar to what I'm now about to suggest, if for no other reason than that the biggest television audience in history would be guaranteed and, with it, hundreds of millions of dollars in advertising revenue. The first step for anyone implementing my proposal would be to quietly commission a worldwide Gallup Poll (if Gallup is only in the United States, other pollsters would have to be commissioned) to ask people a variation of this question: "If you knew, not just *believed*, but was 100 percent certain that there is a God, and that if you didn't treat your fellow man the way you would want him to treat you, you would burn forevermore in hell, would this cause you to lead a more compassionate, moral life?" We can safely assume that the percentage of people who would answer yes to this question would easily be in the 90 percent range, and they would mean it. The result of this knowledge (not belief) would cause, for instance, a terrorist about to blow up a building to think twice if he knew that instead of ending up in heaven surrounded by adoring young virgins, as we are told the September 11, 2001, terrorists thought, they would be screaming in agony while burning in hell till the end of time.

The next step would be to find some healthy inmate on death row in America who is an atheist or agnostic and has an execution date a month or so away to be used in the event I'm contemplating. This is where a hitch may develop. We all know about the bloodless, robotic bureaucracy, and the cooperation of state officials may be withheld here if for no other reason than that what I am proposing would be against prison rules, even though to go beyond the rules would cause no harm to anyone. The only reason that I'm suggesting a death row inmate here, who is going to be executed anyway, is to foreclose the automatic defense of God by Christians if God failed the test I'm proposing—that he didn't fail it at all, that it just would not have been right for God to do what I am suggesting. But any atheist or agnostic, not just a death row inmate, who is healthy will suffice here for any fair and rational person.

With the world picking up almost overnight by way of television, radio, and the print media what was going to happen, at the scheduled time and place the death row inmate, from the top of a prominent hill and with worldwide television watching, would look up to the heavens and address the Christian God in these or similar words:

Lord, assuming you're up there, which I do not believe for a moment, you know that the world is aflame with war, killing, murder, genocide, where even children and babies are dying horrible deaths, and this has been going on for centuries with no end in sight. Since they say you are all-knowing, you're aware that a worldwide poll of humans shows very clearly that much of the terrible carnage and suffering in the world would probably end if all humans actually knew you existed and there was such a place as a fiery hell for serious sinners. Christianity believes you are all-good. If you are, certainly you should be very willing to do the very small thing I'm going to now ask you to do. And certainly it is something that will be so easy for you. After all, if you could create the entire universe by a wave of a hand, this will be too easy for you to even think about.

I have often wondered why you have always chosen to be absent from your own world. Since you are supposedly all-perfect, it would seem there could be nothing you would not want us mortals to see. I ask now that you—or any apparition of you that you want—appear in the sky above so as to be captured for history by worldwide television. And at a distance I would ask you to show the world what hell looks like. It's not as if what I'm asking you to do is something completely new to you. After all, if you chose to let a mere campfull of Israelites at the bottom of Mount Sinai know of your presence atop the mountain as you spoke to Moses so that, you said, they would have confidence in him and follow the ten commandments you gave him to give them,[*] for the very same reason of causing humans to treat their fellow man better here on earth, you should all the more so be willing to do this for the *billions* of people who inhabit the earth.

If, for whatever reason, you feel that what I have asked you to do is beneath you—even though it would save millions of lives in all the years ahead—I have an alternative for you. Not as explicit, but I think it will make the same point. I'm only thirty-eight and in excellent health. My heart is in perfect condition according to my last prison

---

*Exodus 19:9–12, 16–19.

physical, so if you do what I'm going to ask you to do now, no one can say that it wasn't you, that it was the great excitement of the moment that toppled me. You know, of course, what I'm going to suggest. I ask you now to strike me dead. Since I'm scheduled to die next month anyway for murdering a husband and wife and their two small children, why would anyone care? I don't believe for a moment that you're up there since I don't believe you exist. But if you are, I dare you to strike me dead. Again, if you could create the universe, certainly you should be able to simply still the heart of a wretched little ant like me. Okay, let's go. Either the appearance in the sky or strike me dead. The whole world is watching.

I'm not going to ask and then try to answer the question—what do you think would happen? I'll leave that up to the readers of this book. I will say, however, that the jealous, vain, and personal God of Christian mythology would almost, by definition, be very embarrassed before the eyes of the world if he did nothing (embarrassed, that is, if he exists). And if he did do what the death row inmate asked, the ramifications from this point on in history would not lend themselves to human measurement.

Notes

CHAPTER 1

1. If we look at the etymology of the word "agnostic," the word derives from *gnosis,* the Greek word for "knowledge." And the prefix "a" in English means "not" or "without." For example, the word "asexual" means "not sexual."

2. In modern times, the word "prophet" refers exclusively to those who prophesize; that is, foretell, foresee the future. But in biblical times, there was also a second meaning. It referred to a person, such as Moses, who received a revelation from God to pass on (being the messenger) to God's people, the Israelites, as God's will. The first meaning referred to biblical figures who did, in fact, predict or prophesize the future. Some figures were both, e.g., Isaiah was a messenger of God's will (Isaiah 1:1–20) who foretold the future (Isaiah 2:1–4).

3. I wish to avoid a gender imbroglio as to whether God, if there is a God, is a man or a woman. If there is a God, I would think he'd be a spirit rather than a corporeal entity, and I would assume that spirits would not have a gender. When speaking of God as a pronoun in this book, I will not be appending the words "or she" every time I say "he." I will be using the masculine gender not only because it's the gender that's been used since the beginning of recorded time, which by itself is not a sufficient reason, but also because the word "man," as much a word of masculine gender as "he," has always been a synonym for mankind, which includes the female gender. For instance, in Genesis 1:27, God said, "God created *man* in his image; male and female he created them." Perhaps the best reason to refer to God as "he" rather than "he or she" is that the bible is the principal book used in any discussion of God. And throughout the bible, over and over again without exception, God is referred to as "he"—for example, the aforementioned "male and female *he* created them." In Exodus 18:10–11, Jethro says, "Praise be to the Lord, for *he* has saved you from the Egyptians." Jesus himself said God is male: "Anyone who has seen me has seen the *Father.* So why are you asking to see *him*?" (John 14:9).

4. Many Christians claim that God, in fact, does perform miracles today, such as in cases where, they say, through prayer someone was supposedly cured

of an incurable cancer. But this, of course, is not persuasive because what allegedly happened may be attributable to physiological causes about which we are unaware. Or the person never really had cancer. Or the cancer was in remission. Or there is something else we don't know, such as something about our physical system that the current state of medical science has yet to learn. As has been said, when God, through prayer, starts regrowing amputated limbs, *that* will be something to take notice of.

Is it just a prodigious coincidence, one that has no anomalies in its pattern, that the supposed spectacular miracles of the Old and New Testaments occurred to people who, *before* the miracle happened to which they attested, already believed in miracles, and were living in an ancient time when people were immersed in mythology, mysticism, the supernatural, and grinding (through no fault of their own) ignorance? And that these so-called miracles declined through the years in direct proportion to the enlightenment of man? To the point where today, most people—I'm excepting the Catholic church, which continues to declare from time to time that a miracle took place by the act of a saint—dismiss professed miracles out of hand as being either nonexistent (from innocent imagination or from deception by charlatans such as "faith healers"), or traceable to natural phenomena? That we have learned that no one can pull a rabbit out of the hat when there is no rabbit in the hat?

The alleged miracles of Jesus would add a tad more weight to the matter of his divinity if only he, in history, was reported to have performed any miracles. But miracles before, during, and after the time of Jesus (see Acts 5:12–16 for miracles by Jesus' disciples, to whom he gave the power to perform them; see also Mark 16:17–18) were a dime a dozen. I mean, even the miracle of miracles, Jesus' resurrection, is nothing to talk about. Indeed, as pointed out in the main text, in Matthew 27:52–53, when Jesus "gave up his spirit" (i.e., died) on the cross, "at that moment . . . the earth shook, rocks split apart, and tombs opened. The bodies of many godly men and women who had died were raised from the dead *after* Jesus' resurrection. [As indicated, Matthew first has them rising from the dead. . . .] They left the cemetery, went into the holy city of Jerusalem and appeared to many people."

What diminishes the weight of the miracles of Jesus even more is that most of them were rooted in ancient mythology long preceding the time of Jesus. For example, Jesus' resurrection reportedly occurred on the third day (Sunday) following his crucifixion on Friday (Mark 16:9), and Jesus himself played into an already common mythology of a third-day resurrection. In Matthew 12:40, Jesus says, "For as Jonah was in the belly of the great fish for three days and three nights [Jonah 1:15–17 and 2:10], so I, the Son of Man, will be in the heart of the earth for three days and three nights." But as if this were not bad enough, we learn that the whale and the three days fable goes all the way back before Jonah to ancient Greek mythology. It seems that a whale had his devouring eye on Hesione, the daughter of Laomedon, king of Troy, when Hercules, the son of the Greek god Zeus, rescued her. Recalling the fable, Bernard de Montfaucon, an eighteenth-century French Benedictine monk and scholar, writes, "Hercules was also swallowed by the whale that was watching Hesione, where he remained three days in his belly before he came out bald-pated after his sojourn there."

What I'm saying is that if Christianity must have its miracles, which end up deceiving man, it should have the common decency to show some originality.

In Voltaire's *Miracles and Idolatry,* he writes that the daughters of Anius (the son of the Greek and Roman god Apollo) could change whatever they wanted into wheat, wine, or oil. Aesculapius, the ancient Roman god of medicine and healing, brought Hippolytus, son of the mythical Athenian hero Theus, back to life from death. (In the Old Testament, the prophet Elisha beat Jesus' act with Lazarus to the punch by raising the son of a wealthy woman from the dead [2 Kings 4:8, 17–20, and 32–35].) Indeed, to presage the virgin birth of Jesus, in Roman mythology Romulus and his twin brother, Remus, were born of a virgin and Mars, the god of war.

Even the involvement of deities in the impregnation of women (the Holy Ghost with Mary) is not new. Alcmene, the mother of Hercules, is believed to have been impregnated by the Greek god Zeus, the supreme god of the ancient Greeks.

One observation about the position of atheists concerning miracles should be made. They like to argue that there cannot be miracles for the simple reason that there cannot be deviations from or exceptions to the immutable laws of nature. But one should be careful not to extend principles beyond the limits of their logic. Atheists, by this argument, are thereby assuming the nonexistence of God. If there is a God, and if he created not only the universe but also the laws of nature that guide it, then it is not unreasonable to believe that humans could pray to him, asking him for something that would necessitate the suspension, in a given case, of the law of nature he created, and that he would possess the power to answer their prayer. However, this argument still doesn't account for the reality that miracles all happened millenniums ago. Did God like the prayers of earlier peoples more than those of today?

A coda to this discussion is that even if we were to assume the existence of miracles, that would only allow us to say they are unexplained by science. The next step up would be for us to infer the existence of something supernatural as being the cause. We could do this without too loud a complaint from the voices of reason. But is it not an unwarranted inference to take the next step and say that this "something supernatural" *has* to be a God who created the universe? That is, anything that cannot be explained by science can *only* be explained by the existence of God? Although this conclusion may, perchance, be true, is this not an enormous leap? For instance, if someone were to tell you that at the same time a twin experienced great pain when he was beaten up by a young bunch of thugs, his identical twin, thousands of miles away, felt a sudden severe pain in his body, would it be intelligent for you to say, "that proves there is a God who created the universe"? I think not.

CHAPTER 2

1. Indeed, the entire New Testament was written in Greek, the main literary language of the educated elite in the Mediterranean world at that time, reflecting the Hellenistic influence, extending into the era of the Roman Empire, following Alexander the Great's conquest of the entire region in the fourth century BC In addition, the educated man and the common man spoke their native tongue, in the case of Jews this being Hebrew or Aramaic, the latter the language of Jesus.

As opposed to the New Testament, which was translated from Greek into many languages, the books of the Old Testament, the Hebrew bible, were written in Hebrew. The first translation, among many, was into Greek in the third century BC and is called the Septuagint. Another early translation, in AD 405, was into Latin, called the Vulgate. The first English translation of the bible from the Vulgate was by the English religious reformer John Wycliff in 1382. The most important English translations of the bible from the Vulgate are the King James Version (Protestant) published in England in 1611, and the Rheims Douai Bible (Catholic), the Old Testament of which was first published in Rheims, France, in 1582, the New Testament in Douai, France, in 1609–1610.

2. However, the first known writing about Jesus may have been as early as eighteen to nineteen years after his death in AD 33 by the first Christian writer, Paul. Scholars agree that the epistles (letters) of Paul (all became books of the New Testament, e.g., his letter to the Romans, his two letters to the Corinthians) were written starting around AD 51–52, with his first letter being to the Thessalonians and continuing during the 50s and into the early 60s of the first century.

Although Paul was not one of the original twelve apostles and never saw Jesus (except, he maintained, the risen Jesus after Jesus' crucifixion when Paul had his epiphany on the way to Damascus [Acts 9:3–8]; and indeed, before his epiphany he was a dedicated persecutor of Christians), he became, by almost all accounts, the most important apostle of all, eventually being executed in Rome for his impassioned advocacy of the divinity of Jesus and his teaching. Even though Paul wrote none of the gospels, with his thirteen epistles (his authorship has been questioned on a few) he wrote more of the New Testament's twenty-seven books than any other follower of Jesus (i.e., any other person), and he is considered by most to be, next to Jesus, the second most important (and to some, most controversial, because they believe he was a power-seeking opportunist who wrote too much about himself and rarely actually spoke in his epistles about Jesus' life) figure in the history of Christianity, some going so far as to maintain that it was he, not Jesus, who was the founder of Christianity.

3. Because of John's advanced age, some have suggested that the story about John and John the Elder may have been about one and the same person, though second-century theologian Papias clearly distinguished between the two. And Papias is almost surely correct. In the three epistles of John in the New Testament (1, 2, and 3 John), 2 John and 3 John, both of which are very brief, clearly say, unlike 1 John, that they are from John the Elder. Moreover, in 3 John 1:9, John the Elder writes that he was "ignored" by one of the leaders of the church. If John the Elder were the apostle John, this would have been inconceivable, as the twelve apostles in the early church were widely venerated as the very foundation of the church. (See Revelation 21:14.)

4. The authorship and authenticity of the gospels have been the subject of debate for centuries, and unfortunately no one is in a position to speak with authority on the matter. Perhaps the closest to authority we'll ever be able to have is Eusebius (AD 265–340), the bishop of Caesarea (315–340) in Palestine. There were earlier Christian writers (most of whom elders or "fathers" of the early church) who wrote about the primitive church before Eusebius: Papias, the first major one, around AD 135, whose work, except for fragments, is lost, and who, along with Polycarp, a later martyr, was believed to be a disciple of the apostle John; Origen, an intellectual giant of the early church who was more a philosopher and theologian than a historian, whose extremely prolific work, for the most part, has not survived; Irenaeus, whose celebrated *Adversus Haereses* is mostly a refutation of the Gnostics;[*] Clement of Rome, only two of whose letters survive; and Tertullian, much more of a theologian than a historian, who eventually broke with the early church and joined a heretical Christian sect called the Montanists.

---

[*]The Gnostics were a Christian sect of heretics in the late first and the second centuries who claimed spiritual knowledge of the essence and purpose of life and of true Christianity, and it was this knowledge, gained from a secret understanding of Jesus' words, not faith or holy scripture, that allowed them to find salvation by being liberated from the material and evil world that the true God had not created.

However, it is generally acknowledged that Eusebius, a Christian theologian and historian, in around AD 320 wrote the first scholarly work on the early church—his seminal *History of the Church* (modern title, *The Ecclesiastical History of Eusebius Pamphilus*)—and he is often referred to as the "father of ecclesiastical history." Reading Eusebius, one sees his scholarship in the cautious, very spare words he employs, always acknowledging, where applicable, the absence of sufficient evidence to form a firm conclusion.

Eusebius says that "the whole time of our Savior's ministry is proved not to embrace four entire years," that Jesus, "not very long after the commencement of his public ministry, elected the twelve, whom he called Apostles by way of eminence over the rest of his disciples." Eusebius says that Jesus appointed "seventy others beside these, whom he sent, two and two, before him into every place and city whither he himself was about to go." (Eusebius, *The Ecclesiastical History of Eusebius Pamphilus*, [Grand Rapids, Michigan: Baker Book House, 1977], 40).

On the gospels, Eusebius wrote that Mark was "the companion of Peter." He notes that Peter, in his epistle from Rome, indicates that Mark, whom he affectionately referred to as "my son," was in Rome with him (1 Peter 5:13). Eusebius said that after Peter was executed in Rome, those who had heard "the power and splendor" of his orations in churches and elsewhere "persevered in every variety of entreaties to solicit Mark to leave them a monument in writing of the doctrine orally communicated" to them by Peter, adding that they did this "until they had prevailed with the man." Eusebius says that "this account is given by Clement, whose testimony is corroborated by Papias, bishop of Hierapolis" (Eusebius, 64–65).

If this account is true, this would seem to weaken the accuracy, though not necessarily the essence, of Mark's gospel in that unless divinely inspired, Mark was only *recalling* Peter's words, as opposed to Peter working with Mark on the gospel, as John, some say, did with his scribe, John the Elder. And when you weaken Mark, you weaken Matthew and Luke because it is clear that a good part of their gospels, which *followed* Mark's,* were based on the gospel of Mark, many of their passages being virtually identical to his. The three gospels are referred to as the synoptic (Greek for "seen together") gospels because they are very similar in their outline and content. The gospel of John is not laid out in the same structure as the synoptic gospels and contains events and parables not in the other three. It is also the only gospel in which Jesus sometimes calls himself the "Son of God."

---

*Scholars point to many things supporting Marcan priority in the chronology of the gospels of Matthew, Mark, and Luke, just two of which are that the gospel of Mark is the shortest gospel (not as likely if it were the second or the third in chronology), and that it omits the Sermon on the Mount, considered by most to be the most important part of Jesus' ministry. (Matthew and Luke both include it.) If Mark had the gospels of Matthew and Luke to inform him, why would he omit the heart of Jesus' ethics and teaching?

Eusebius refers to Luke, the only Gentile among all the New Testament authors, as being "born at Antioch [in Syria] and by profession a physician, being for the most part connected with Paul, and familiarly acquainted with the rest of the apostles." Luke was with Paul in Rome (2 Timothy 4:11), and Eusebius seems to be satisfied with the authority of the gospel of Luke, Luke himself referring in Luke 1:1–2 to the "events transmitted to *us* by the original eyewitnesses and ministers of the word" (Eusebius, 84–85).

Eusebius notes that of the twelve apostles and seventy disciples as well as "many others" who had seen and heard Jesus, "Matthew and John are the only ones who have left us recorded comments, and even they, tradition says, undertook it *from necessity*." He explains that Matthew first proclaimed his gospel orally to the people of Palestine, and only "on the point of going to other nations, committed it to writing" so that the Palestinians would have it in his absence (Eusebius, 108).*

Eusebius said John wrote his gospel (he doesn't mention any John the Elder) only because when the three previously written gospels, "having been distributed among all," were "handed to him, they say he admitted them, giving his testimony to their truth," but said they were "wanting in the narrative account of the things done by Christ, [including] the first of his deeds, and at the commencement of the gospel," so he felt the necessity to fill in the gaps with his gospel (Eusebius, 108).†

---

*Jack Dean Kingsbury, professor of biblical theology at Union Theological Seminary in Richmond, Virginia, does not believe that the apostle Matthew himself wrote the gospel of Matthew. He writes that the author of that gospel "exhibits a theological outlook, command of Greek, and rabbinic training that suggest he was a Jewish Christian of the second rather than first generation [as Matthew was]" (*The Oxford Companion to the Bible*, edited by Bruce M. Metzger and Michael D. Coogan, [New York: Oxford University Press, 1993], 502–503).

---

†One wonders how Eusebius squared his conclusion that John wrote the fourth gospel, with John 21:24, which seems to suggest a third party wrote John's gospel. The probable answer is that in ancient times more than today, one was considered an author of a work if he was the authority behind it. And the consensus of most biblical scholars is that a disciple of John, at John's direction and with his guidance, wrote the gospel of John.

Additionally, since the gospel of John, like all twenty-seven books of the New Testament, was written in Greek, and Greek was the literary language only of the educated elite among the Jews, this strongly militates against John being the actual, quill-in-hand writer of his gospel. Acts 4:13 speaks of John, as well as Peter, being "uneducated men of no standing." In the language of the time, the word "uneducated" meant illiterate, being unable to read or write, which the vast majority of people during this period were. In view of this, it can be said, almost by definition, that all twenty-seven books of the New Testament *had* to have been written by writers who not only spoke Greek but also, because of the quality of their prose, were very literate.

If Eusebius is correct in these accounts, is there not a real problem with the whole theory of the words of the gospels being inspired by God? Peter made no effort to write a gospel, and per Eusebius, Mark had to be pressured into telling Peter's story in Mark's gospel. And Matthew and John wrote theirs out of necessity. If Jesus was divine, wouldn't he have wanted his ministry and message to be delivered to the people of the world? Yet, per Eusebius, he apparently didn't make his desire known to at least three out of the four (we don't know about Luke) authors of the gospels. It should be noted, however, that Jesus told his followers that he was coming back soon, within the lifetime of those he was speaking to (Matthew 16:27–28). And his followers believed him (e.g., James 5:8). So the argument could be made that his disciples didn't feel a pressing need to record his life for posterity.

Another point that militates against the conclusion that the four gospels, as well as the entire bible, were divinely inspired is that nowhere is it inferable from the chapters and verses of the gospels that Matthew, Mark, Luke, and John had any feeling or sense that what they were writing was inspired. If they did (as, for instance, their suddenly remembering something they were sure they had forgotten), wouldn't they probably have made a point of saying this, somewhere, in their gospels? Christianity asks Christians to believe that the gospels were divinely inspired when the very authors of these gospels indicate no such thing.*

On the other hand, although the four gospels all are well written, the prose doesn't sparkle with silver-tongued oratory and forever memorable phrases until it changes from the third person (Matthew, Mark, Luke, and John) to Jesus speaking with a towering eloquence and power. One wonders if the writers of the gospels, whoever they were, could turn the magic off and on like a light switch if something wasn't special here.

---

*The great early Christian philosopher and writer Origen (AD 185–254) wrote in Book 4 of his treatise *On First Principles* that strong evidence that books of the New Testament were "inspired by the spirit of God" is the fact that, although the apostles and disciples of Jesus who preached the word of Jesus after his death were "neither very skillful nor very numerous," and the further fact that there was "intense hatred" against them that sometimes led to their torture and death, "this word is preached in all the world, so that Greeks and barbarians, wise and foolish, now adopt the Christian religion." From this, Origen infers that "there can be no doubt that it is not by *human* strength or resources that the word of Christ comes to prevail with all authority and convincing power in the minds and hearts of all men." Although it may be one and the same, and not capable of dichotomy, Origen's thinking goes more in the direction of there being divine support for the promulgation of the gospel of Jesus than that the words of the gospels were themselves divinely inspired.

5. However, it may not be justified to automatically assume that the scribes through the years who made copies of copies of the original gospels did not recognize the historical importance of their work and irresponsibly embellished or deleted scriptural language to fit their fancy or predilection before passing the gospels on to others. If we can use the Old Testament as a possible indicator of the accuracy of the New Testament gospels, we all know about the Dead Sea Scrolls, the first of which was found in 1947 by a Bedouin shepherd boy in a cave on a hillside by the western shores of the Dead Sea near the ruins of what was once the village of Qumran in Jordan. Through 1956, archaeologists discovered in eleven Qumran caves some 900 biblical scrolls, commentaries, prayers, rituals, and codes of conduct, as well as many more manuscript fragments, stored in pottery jars, much of which were copies or fragments of every book of the Old Testament except the book of Esther. Breaking a silence of more than nineteen centuries, the discovered scrolls were part of a library placed there by a small, highly ascetic, and moral Jewish religious sect known as the Essenes (not mentioned, as were their larger rivals the Pharisees and Sadducees, in the New Testament; Jewish historian Josephus calls the Essenes "the most virtuous men on earth"), who are believed to have flourished between around 170 BC to AD 68. It is notable that the scrolls do not differ materially at all from later copies of Old Testament books.

Perhaps the most famous scroll found near Qumran is the complete book of Isaiah, after Moses the Old Testament's most famous prophet. Dated around 100 BC, it is one of the oldest copies of a bible book in existence. Prior to it, the oldest copy of Isaiah known to be in existence was dated around AD 900, which was a thousand years later. Yet biblical scholar Dave Hunt, in his book *Defense of Faith*, writes that a comparison of the two scrolls reveals only "a few spelling variations, some stylistic changes, and a rare word here and there that had either been left out or added but did not change the meaning of the text." This, of course, is quite impressive on the issue of how much Jewish scribes through the centuries preserved the accuracy of the bible.

As if the historical record is not cloudy enough, biblical scholars speak of *The Sayings Gospel Q*. The Q was taken from a German word, *Quelle*, which means "source." The hypothesis of Q originated with nineteenth-century German biblical scholar C. H. Weisse in his *Die Evangelische Geschichte und Philosophisch Bearbeitet* in 1838. The Q gospel is believed to have been lost in the second century, with no surviving copies. Hence, no one has ever seen it, and no one knows who might have authored it. John Shelby Spong, in his book *Jesus for the Non-Religious*, says that Q's "presumed existence results from an inference born out of the study of both [the gospels of] Matthew and Luke. Scholars universally assert that Mark was the primary source underlying both these gospels. Matthew used about 90 percent of Mark in his work; Luke, a little bit less, perhaps 50 percent. . . . However, it is obvious that in addition to that dependence on Mark, Matthew and Luke have a second source in common, for there are non-Marcan passages in the two gospels that are identical (or nearly so) in content." This occurs in the sayings (aphorisms) of Jesus, such as love your enemies; judge not and you won't be judged; everyone who asks, receives; if struck on one cheek, offer the other; give to everyone who begs. Biblical scholars, Spong says, believe that this collection of Jesus' sayings is the Q gospel that was written after Mark (since Mark did not rely on them) but sometime before Matthew and Luke.

That there actually was a Q gospel of Jesus' sayings (Q is believed to have contained nothing more about Jesus) is lent credibility by the Coptic (an ancient Egyptian language) gospel of Thomas. This gospel, unlike Q, *is* in existence. Believed by some to be the gospel of the apostle Thomas, others believe it to be the gospel of Jesus' twin brother (though there is no scriptural evidence to support a twin brother of Jesus) because the author identified himself as "Didymus [twin in Greek] Judas [Jesus had a brother named Judas] Thomas [twin in Aramaic]." Many others believe the true author was neither.

The gospel was discovered in 1945 among thirteen leather-bound volumes written on papyrus (called by some a "Gnostic library" because most of the fifty-two writings in the volumes were by Gnostic Christians, though there isn't too much about the very temperate gospel of Thomas that bears resemblance to the harsh and heretical Gnostics of early Christianity) inside a large earthenware jar found by a peasant digging for fertilizer near Naj (usually spelled Nag) Hammadi, an Egyptian village on the Nile. The gospel is a collection of 114 of the purported "sayings" of Jesus, affirmation that there actually were such collections, as Q is believed to have been, of the sayings of Jesus circulating in the first century.

At least half of the sayings in the gospel of Thomas sound just like Jesus and, in fact, are in the synoptic gospels, though not in the gospel of John. But there are too many sayings that the early Christian church did not feel were in harmony with the known Jesus, and this is one of the main reasons that the gospel was not included among the *canonical* gospels of the New Testament. (The term "canon of Christian scripture" refers to the books of the Old and New Testament, all of which were included there because the councils of bishops of the Catholic church in the fourth century [Councils of Rome in 382, Hippo in 393, and Carthage in 397] determined they met their ecclesiastical standards of being genuine—with respect to the New Testament, authored by a direct disciple of Jesus or someone who was very close to a disciple, and being in general consonance with already established Christian orthodoxy.)

But in one sense, the gospel of Thomas is much more like the Jesus we would expect, not the Jesus of the four canonical gospels. In the 114 sayings in Thomas (actually, with 42 separate sayings in subdivisions, 156), nowhere is there the Jesus who said that those who did not believe in him would be condemned to hell (e.g., Mark 16:16), the antithesis of a benevolent, merciful God. And a major emphasis in Thomas is on self-awareness, and with it, a kingdom of heaven right here on earth, not "in the sky" after our death (e.g., see sayings 3a, 18a, and 113), which, though far-out, is not quite as unrealistic and unbelievable as the heaven (up above in the sky) and hell of traditional Christianity.

The gospel of Thomas, by the way, is one (though the most important one) of more than twenty-five so-called apocryphal books of the bible: certain books written during the period of the Old Testament (e.g., 3 and 4 Maccabees, 1 Esdras, Psalm 151) and New Testament (e.g., gospels of Thomas, Mary, Philip) that are considered books of uncertain authenticity, or merely legendary, and hence not canonical. However, some of these books are considered canonical (called deuterocanonical) by the Catholic church and are in the Catholic bible but are considered apocryphal by Protestants and are not in their bible. They are the seven Old Testament books of Tobit, Baruch, Judith, Sirach, Wisdom, and 1 and 2 Maccabees.

Pushing the gospel of Thomas in apocryphal fame is the Gnostic gospel of Judas, portions of a fourth-century copy of which surfaced sometime in 1983 near Beni Masah in Egypt. It has received a lot of media attention primarily because of its main allegation that Judas did not betray Jesus, as the New Testament and history have him doing. The gospel of Judas depicts Judas as only "betraying" Jesus because Jesus asked him to, so that he, Jesus, could die on the cross for our sins and fulfill prophecy (Isaiah 53:8). (The gospel of Judas suggests that Jesus taught the true gospel, the Gnostic one, only to Judas, not the other apostles.)

Because we have much evidence that Jesus consciously sought to fulfill Old Testament prophecies (see discussion in main text), this is not an improbable story on its face. Moreover, at the Last Supper (Passover meal), Jesus told his apostles that "one of you will betray me" (John 13:21, Luke 22:21). In John 13:24–27, when Peter asked Jesus, "Lord, who is it?" Jesus replied, "It is the one to whom I give the bread dipped in the sauce." When Jesus dipped the bread, he gave it to Judas. As soon as Judas had eaten the bread, "Satan entered into him. Then Jesus told Judas, 'Hurry. Do it now.'" If Jesus weren't Jesus, this would tend to confirm the allegation in the gospel of Judas. But under Christian theology, being Jesus (God), he was omniscient. So he would already know what Judas was going to do without Jesus' having told Judas to do it. In any event, virtually conclusive evidence that Jesus was truly betrayed and Judas was not simply following his command is when Jesus said at the Last Supper, "How terrible it will be for my betrayer. Far better for him if he had never been born" (Mark 14:21). Nonetheless, John 13:24 is at least some evidence that the allegation in the gospel of Judas is true.

However, one doesn't have to go too far beneath the epidermis to see that nothing else about the gospel of Judas and its allegation hold up well at all. For one thing, Judas committed suicide the morning after he "betrayed" Jesus (Matthew 27:1–5). So we know it would have been physically impossible for Judas to have written "his" gospel within that period or even to have conveyed its thirty-one pages of contents (in dialogue, not narrated form, between Jesus and Judas and the other apostles) to a third-party scribe. Indeed, the gospel of Judas doesn't even claim to have been written by Judas, but supposedly by Gnostic followers of Jesus in the first or second century. Irenaeus (AD 130–202), in his *Adversus Haereses* in the second century, refers to a "Gospel of Judas" as being "fictional history." The conclusion of fiction makes sense since how in the world would these Gnostics have the faintest idea of what went on between Jesus and Judas?

Much more importantly, the allegation itself makes little sense. Quite apart from the fact that, if true, Judas would thereby be making Jesus out to be a liar (as indicated, Jesus told his apostles at the Last Supper that one of them would betray him), if Judas didn't, in fact, betray Jesus and merely carried out Jesus' wish or instruction, what reason would he have had to commit suicide? Suicide fits betrayal. It does not wear well with following the wish or instruction of the leader you had followed and thought was divine.

Actually, the whole story, it seems to me, stretches credulity. For three years Jesus practiced his ministry *openly* in Galilee and Judea. He appeared before thousands of people and was already on the radar screens of the Pharisees and Sadducees, who personally confronted him. At the time of the "betrayal," Jesus, in broad daylight, was seen with his followers in Jerusalem, a city with a population believed to be around only 25 to 30,000 people at the time, and he publicly entered Jerusalem astride a donkey. Jesus himself told the mob who arrested him, "Why didn't you arrest me in the [Jerusalem] temple? I was there every day" (Luke 22:53). Indeed, on one visit to the temple, Jesus created a very big scene when he saw money changers there. He chased them all out of the temple after scattering their coins on the floor and turning over their tables. "Don't turn my Father's house into a marketplace," he said (John 2:14–16; Mark 11:15–17). Since Jesus' enemies knew exactly who he was and he wasn't in hiding, why would they have needed Judas to kiss Jesus to identify him (Luke 22:47, Matthew 26:48)? The tale, from the get-go, simply does not have the ring of truth to it.

CHAPTER 3

1. Although Protestant minister and theologian Reinhold Niebuhr, in one of his sermons, used an obvious non sequitur to state this reality, and weakened it further by being only half-right (unless he believed that God deliberately caused the Holocaust and all the horrors of history), he said, "If God is all-powerful he must be the creator of evil as well as of good."

2. The Christian belief that God is everywhere is not quite the same as pantheism. Pantheism, the most famous proponents of which were the Roman stoics and 17th century Dutch philosopher Baruch Spinoza, is a form of theism in the sense that it believes in God. But not that God *created* mankind and the universe. God is *everything*—the entire universe and everything in it. But does pantheistic thinking then lead to the conclusion that God is also Satan? And he was Hitler and Stalin too? This mystical belief has few modern-day adherents. I, for one, prefer to believe that the stop lights I pass while driving are nothing but stoplights.

3. The great irony is that if the notion of people being automatons is a negative one, Evangelicals and Fundamentalists appear to be automatons much more than nonbelievers do. Though I have found many Evangelicals to be decent people, it is not uncommon for them to be almost completely one-dimensional characters who connect God, as the transcendent figure, to every event in their lives, be it birth, death, and everything in between, including everyday living. Christ, if you listen to them, infuses everything they do. For instance, when they get married they say that God brought them together and the two will spend their lives together "serving the Lord."

The further automaton feature about them is the look of tranquility on their faces. They found the truth, and the truth is Jesus. It's the very *uniform* look of the true believer, one I noticed for the first time way back in 1969 when I first met two members of Charles Manson's family in Death Valley, Lynette "Squeaky" Fromme and Sandra Good. I wrote about them in *Helter Skelter*, the book I coauthored with Curt Gentry on the Manson murder case. "I was immediately struck by their expression," I wrote. "They seemed to radiate inner contentment. Nothing seemed to faze them. They smiled almost continuously, no matter what was said. For them all the questions had been answered. There was no need to search anymore, because they had found the truth. And their truth was 'Charlie [Manson] is love.' . . . There was a sameness about them that was much stronger than their individuality. . . . They reminded me less of human beings than Barbie dolls."

I'm not suggesting that all Evangelicals have this look about them, and I'm certainly not suggesting that Evangelicals are bad people, like Manson's followers were, but there very definitely is a common denominator between them—they're both true believers, only worshipping different gods. I'll say this: Evangelicals should find a better word than "automatons" to use when they are trumpeting the value of having evil as well as good in the world. Many of them remind me of an automaton far more than atheists do, whom I would never think to characterize that way. Autonomous? Yes. Automatons? No.

4. Some Jewish scholars (e.g., Steven A. Fisdel), knowing there is no scriptural support for free will in the Hebrew bible, argue that the Israelites agreeing to live up to their end of covenants with God, such as those with Noah and Abraham and the one with Moses at Mount Sinai (where, in return for God's promise to lead them safely to Canaan and destroy their enemies, they promised to follow all of his commandments [Exodus 23:20–23; 24:3, 7]), proves free will in that the Israelites had a choice to agree or disagree with the terms of the covenants, and they chose to agree. But how does this prove free will any more than one deciding to go to a movie or not, cross the street or not, speak or remain silent, vote for one person rather than another, buy a car or not? It doesn't. The aforementioned argument of Jewish scholars presupposes free will. The issue is not the fact that with knowledge of the options, one chose to do B over A, but whether one's choice of B *resulted from free will,* or was foreordained by God ("Whatever good or evil people may practice, their efforts result in the execution of God's judgments," John Calvin said; see also Ephesians 1–11), or, as most prominently argued by famed defense attorney Clarence Darrow, man's acts result from "two things only, his heredity and his environment, not free will."

We can know that Darrow, though perhaps in part right, is not right in the certainty in which he spoke since children with the same heredity and background end up having wildly divergent personalities and character. Indeed, to a lesser extent, twins coming out of the same womb at the same time and growing up in the same environment often have different personalities and emotional makeups. So there has to be something that each human is born with that distinguishes one person from another. Is it the psyche, the mind? Or is it, as Christianity believes, the soul? (But are the psyche and the soul one and the same? My old *Random House* dictionary—my *Webster's* dictionary agrees—defines the word psyche as "the human soul or mind.") You might just as well talk to your local grocer as to a learned scholar or philosopher for a definitive answer as to what this "something" is because no one knows. My daughter Wendy, a registered nurse and a very fine poet, has a subtle mind. She believes that whether we call this unknown thing a soul or something else, it exists and it is not the mind. She asked me once what colors I disliked the most. I said probably purple, with pink second. She then asked me if someone paid me $2 million, could I get my mind to change the way I feel about these two colors? The obvious answer, at least for me, is no. Things like our tastes, desires, personality, she said, as others have, are who we are as human beings, and our mind cannot change these realities. And this fact, she argues, militates against the existence of free will.

It has to be noted that although it is a subject rarely discussed, there is an irreconcilable contradiction between the doctrine of free will, which is embraced by Protestantism, and the Protestant doctrine that one can only achieve salvation through faith in Jesus. This is so because the former implies that man has some say, by his conduct and decisions, in whether he is saved, whereas the latter suggests that *only* through man's faith in Jesus and God's grace can we achieve salvation.

The great irony is that when modern-day Protestants proclaim free will, as they always do, how many of them realize that they are preaching against the position of the founder of Protestantism, Martin Luther? My guess is less than 10 percent, if that. Luther, in his magnum opus, *De Servo Arbitrio* (Latin for "On the Enslaved Will"), which he wrote in 1525 in response to the position of his theological opponent, Desiderius Erasmus, in the latter's short book, *Diatribe*, made it very clear that he did not believe in free will. He says that "God foreknows and wills all things . . . He foresees, purposes [intends], and does all things according to His own eternal and infallible will." This, Luther says, "knocks 'free-will' flat, and utterly shatters it." By that, Luther says, he means that man's "free will" is free only to the extent of doing "the will of God;" that man himself "can do no good" except through "God's grace." That "free will without God's grace is not free." Luther speaks of "the immutable will of God on the one hand, and the impotence of our corrupt will on the other" (Martin Luther, *The Bondage of the Will* [modern edition of *De Servo Arbitrio*. Revell Publishing Company, Grand Rapids, Michigan, 1952], 80–81, 83, 104–105, 107).

Taken to its logical conclusion, when Luther says that God "wills *all* things," this would seem to include saying that even one's faith in Jesus, which Luther says is necessary for salvation, has to be bestowed on us by God through his grace. (Admittedly, this is precisely what Paul says in his letter to the Ephesians, 2:8.) And the logical extension of this is to say that whether we go to heaven or not has absolutely nothing to do with us, and everything to do with *God's whim*. No wonder modern-day Protestantism (or at least the small percent who know) deliberately ignores Luther in this matter, and most Protestants embrace something akin to Arminianism, the doctrine (similar to that of Erasmus) of the Dutch Protestant theologian Jacobus Arminius, who believed man is saved by God's grace and man's free will in accepting it by faith. Thus, the Protestant term "justification by faith." In Pauline theology, justification means "made right in God's eyes." (See Romans 3:21–26.)

5. But if an omniscient God, from the dawn of time, already had foreknowledge of everything to come, does that not make free will an illusion? Not necessarily. It would in the sense that, by definition, foreknowledge of an event means that the event *will* happen, *has* to happen. If it didn't happen, then one could not have had foreknowledge of it. But foreknowledge is not necessarily synonymous with predestination. Predestination suggests, as the sixteenth-century French Protestant reformer and theologian John Calvin (who, along with Zwingli in Switzerland and Henry VIII in England, was influenced by Luther) maintained, that God has *willed* all future events (shades of Martin Luther—see previous endnote), Calvin even saying that God "elected" who would be saved and who, regardless of the life he led, would not. (This so-called doctrine of evolution has ample scriptural support, for example, John 15:16, Acts 13:48.) Although, being omnipotent, God would surely have such power to will all future events, it does not follow that he chose to do so. It is not paradoxical to say that being all-powerful includes the power to limit one's power, which, if there is an omnipotent God, he may have done. God's foreknowledge, then, can mean nothing more than God permitting us to make choices but knowing what choices we're going to make. (Obviously, his permitting us to make choices in no way exonerates God of putting people on earth who he knows, because of their choices, are going to end up in hell.) In any event, society has no choice but to operate on the postulate of free will. If it did not, and believed instead that everything we do is willed by a higher being, no one would be responsible for his criminal conduct since he had no choice but to do what he did, and hence, lacked mens rea (criminal intent), a necessary element of the corpus delicti of every true crime. The result would be a completely lawless society, with no punishment as a deterrent to crime.

However, this reasoning hasn't stopped the Shariah, Islamic law, from severely punishing all criminal offenders even though the Qur'an, upon which, along with tradition, the Shariah is largely based, seems to go in the direction of saying that Allah not only had foreknowledge of everything but predestined it. Sura 87:2 says, "The Lord has created and balanced all things and has *fixed their destinies* and guided them." Sura 9:51 reads, "By no means can anything befall us but what God has destined for us."

CHAPTER 4

1. Dawkins was parroting what one frequently hears that "it is impossible to prove a negative." But this, of course, is pure myth. In many situations in life it

is very easy. For instance, in a criminal case where a defendant says he did not and could not have committed the crime, say a robbery or burglary, because he was somewhere else at the time, the prosecutor routinely proves the negative (that he was not somewhere else) by establishing through witnesses, fingerprints, DNA, or sometimes even film that he did commit the crime and was not where he said he was at the time it happened.

2. How close to certainty is Dawkins in his disbelief in God? In an April 11, 2008, appearance on comedian Bill Maher's television show, Dawkins said that out of seven, he was a six on the atheism scale. Somewhat surprised, Maher asked "Why are you only a six? Why aren't you a seven?" "As a scientist," Dawkins replied, "I can't definitely commit to anything, including that there are no fairies." To laughter from Maher and the audience, Dawkins added, "I can't say I know there are no pink unicorns either, so maybe I'm a six point nine"— that is, Dawkins *knows* there's no God.

It should be noted that in atheist literature, two types of atheism are frequently explored, positive and negative atheism. The former can be exemplified by statements like "God does not exist" or "There is no God." It is the least common of the two atheisms. Annie Besant, in her 1887 book, *Why I Do Not Believe in God*, defined negative atheism, the most common type, as "without God," and exemplified by the statement "I do not believe in God." Dawkins comes very close to saying that God does not exist and therefore would have to be characterized more as a positive atheist.

3. Not only doesn't Dawkins tell his readers that Darwin was not an atheist; he actually goes out of his way to strongly suggest the opposite, that he *was* an atheist. In responding to the argument of Christian apologists that many great scientists like Sir Isaac Newton and Galileo were theists, Dawkins writes that some theistic apologists "even add the name of Darwin, about whom persistent, but demonstrably false rumors of a deathbed conversion [obviously, from atheism to theism] continually come around like a bad smell." He goes on to write that "even before Darwin, not everybody was a believer [i.e., Darwin wasn't the first great scientific mind to be a nonbeliever or atheist. There were great minds who were atheists before him]. And some distinguished scientists went on believing [in God] after Darwin." Dawkins is nothing if not amazing.

4. Remarkably, the central argument of Dawkins' book, one that made him renowned as the world's preeminent atheist, *isn't even his argument*, although the unmistakable thrust of his book is that it is, and he makes no clear effort to disabuse his readers of this notion. Although there was a poorly articulated allusion to the argument in Scottish philosopher David Hume's *Dialogues Concerning Natural Religion* (1779), this cockamamie argument was first unambiguously

set forth not by Dawkins but by Percy Bysshe Shelley. The celebrated English poet and thinker wrote in an 1814 essay, *A Refutation of Deism: In a Dialogue*, that "from the fitness of the Universe . . . you infer the necessity of an intelligent Creator. But if the fitness of the Universe, to produce certain effects, be conspicuous and evident, how much more exquisite fitness . . . must exist in the author of this Universe?" Shelley goes on to say that the likelihood of such a being "is absurd." Dawkins makes no reference to Shelley in his book, and the nature of his two very weak and short offhand references to Hume (one quoting someone else referring to Hume) could in no way inform his readers that the main argument of his book was not his own.

With respect to Shelley, it's not as if Dawkins also doesn't quote others for the source of arguments he used, because he does do this generously throughout his book. But not on *the* central argument of his book, the one, above all, he should have. And it would be difficult to argue that Dawkins may not have been aware of Shelley's writing on this issue. Virtually all highly literate Brits, as Dawkins is, have read all of Shelley, particularly since, dying very young (1792–1822), his output was small. I mean, if I've read the essay by Shelley, a writer who is not really part of my indigenous literary culture, then surely Dawkins has.

It should be noted that unless the matter is too insignificant for attribution, or many have said the same or similar thing, authors routinely acknowledge the source of even less important arguments than the "central" argument of their book.

CHAPTER 5

1. Though we know that the earth is billions of years old, in fairness to the creationists it should be noted that the obviously erroneous position of theirs that the earth (and universe) is only 6,000 years old did not result from their pulling the number 6,000 out of a hat. One James Ussher, the Church of England archbishop of Armagh (Northern Ireland today), proposed in 1650 that God created the world and mankind about 4,000 years before the birth of Jesus. (With the 2,000 and some years since, modern creationists have their 6,000 years.) Ussher reached his 4,000 years by adding up the so-called begats from genealogical lists in the bible (Adam beget Seth, Seth beget Enosh, and so on; see, for example, Genesis 5, 10, and 36) and from events (e.g., the reigns of the various kings of Israel).

Creationists also note the symmetry between the six days that Genesis says God took to create the universe and 6,000 years, and also that six days in the bible is not the same as we know six days to be, citing the New Testament verse "A day is like a thousand years to the Lord, and a thousand years is like a day" (2 Peter 3:8). And here I was so impressed that God created everything in just six days. If it took him 6,000 years, I'm not that impressed anymore.

2. While we're talking about evolving from monkeys instead of God creating us, Christians can't possibly be thinking when they repeat over and over again the inanity that "God created man in his own image." (Genesis 1:27 adds, "God patterned man after himself.") If God, in fact, did create man in his own image, given that we know how pathetic and morally defective man is, as indicated in the main text, *what does that say about who God is?*

3. Tests in mirrors have shown that apes, elephants, and dolphins are the only known mammals other than man who are capable of physical self-awareness.

4. None of this should cause one to overlook the incredible similarities these precious little creatures bear to human beings, having virtually all of the same emotions. We know they love deeply, and many are capable of great loyalty. They experience fear, happiness, insecurity, anger; in some, even jealousy. They enjoy eating, having sex, and playing, even having toys. They bleed like us when they are cut, they procreate (the female becoming pregnant and even nurturing her babies), and, unbelievably, just like humans, they all have different personalities. My God, they even sneeze and yawn like us and dream and snore in their sleep. This is why the terrible cruelty toward these wonderful creatures that exists far too much in our society is so unforgiveable.

I'm probably off base here, but even though I know that murder, in its legal definition, is the "unlawful killing of a human being" with malice aforethought, and animals aren't human beings, because they are so very similar to human beings in their feelings and emotions, and because they are alive and have beating hearts like we do, and because they, like us, desperately want to live, isn't shooting and killing an animal like a sweet and innocent deer just for sport something *akin* to murder?

CHAPTER 6

1. As indicated in the main text discussion of atheist author Richard Dawkins, the argument of intelligent design is also prominently used when the universe is not being discussed, but as a refutation of Charles Darwin's theory of evolution—that human biological structures such as DNA, and living organs like the eye, are so extremely complex that they must have been the work of an intelligent designer, the chance mutations of evolution being incapable of producing something of such startling complexity. The scientific community has

for the most part been disdainfully dismissive of this argument, a representative observation being that the theory of intelligent design is nothing but "creationism in a cheap tuxedo."

After *Daniel v. Waters*, 515 F.2d 485 (1975), held that a law in Tennessee—the state that first dealt with the issue in the famous Scopes trial in 1925—providing for the teaching of creationism in public schools was violative of the establishment clause (separation of church and state) of the First Amendment to the U.S. Constitution and was not entitled to "equal time" with the teaching of evolution, creationists went beyond Genesis with some scientific arguments and came back with what they called "creation *science*." But the U.S. Supreme Court, dealing with a Louisiana statute that mandated that creation science be taught in public schools if evolution was, ruled in *Edwards v. Aguillard*, 482 U.S. 578 (1987) that it, too, violated the First Amendment. The creationists next removed all references to Genesis and the word "creation" in a proposed public school textbook in Dover, Pennsylvania, and came up with "intelligent design," but in *Kitzmiller v. Dover Area School District*, 400 F. Supp. 707 (2005), the court ruled that intelligent design was just another way of saying creationism, that it was not science, and hence that it would violate the establishment clause if it were taught along with evolution in public schools. The federal judge, an appointee of President George W. Bush, also made a finding that Dover school board members had lied under oath to conceal their religious agenda. (But they lied for God. So I, for one, am not troubled by this. I trust you know I am being facetious.)

2. Another argument for God, the ontological argument, is one whose faulty carpentry will soon be evident to you. It is believed to have first been postulated in the eleventh century by St. Anselm, the archbishop of Canterbury. Anselm writes in his short treatise *Proslogium* (following his first treatise, *Monologium*) that God is "omnipotent, compassionate, just, wise, good, eternal, everywhere. [He] lacks nothing." In other words, God is perfect; or as Anselm put it in awkward syntax, "a being than which nothing greater can be conceived." Anselm went on to say that if "that, than which nothing greater can be conceived, exists in the understanding *alone,* the very being, than which nothing greater can be conceived, is one than which a greater being *can* be conceived. But obviously, this is impossible. Hence, there is no doubt that there exists a being than which nothing greater can be conceived, and it exists both in the understanding *and* the reality."

In addition to the obvious straw man Anselm sets up ("if that, than which nothing . . .") and the just as obvious non sequitur of his conclusion (If I conceive of a perfect basketball player, one that no one can be better than, does that mean that such a player exists?), there is a more serious defect to Anselm's reasoning that makes it remarkable it survived beyond the time it took for the ink to dry on his words. The courtroom handles inanities like this that are stated in the form of a question by the well-recognized objection, "The question assumes a fact in issue (or assumes a fact not in evidence)." In other words, here, the question to be resolved is whether or not there is a God. You can't start your discussion of this issue by asserting "God is perfect" because to do so assumes the very fact (that God exists) that is in issue.

3. Where do we end up if we assert the probability that there is no intelligent life on any body other than earth in the universe? Since it makes no sense that out of the trillions of heavenly bodies in space, the laws of nature were such that only earth was hospitable to life, this is one piece of circumstantial evidence that goes in the direction of there being a supernatural being (God) who created us for some reason unknown to us, perhaps as a laboratory in which to conduct an experiment. (But being omniscient, wouldn't he already know the result of the experiment?)

If not that, a problem with the Christian belief that God created the universe is that does it not presuppose—in fact, require—that of the billions of planets in the universe, either ours is the *only* one that God, for no apparent reason, decided to put intelligent life on, or the only one of other hospitable planets whose inhabitants had a sinful nature that required God to have his son die for their sins?

4. The argument of intelligent design, though generally not thought to be of ancient origin, goes at least back to Aristotle (384–322 BC), who said, "The world functions according to some deliberate design." It was also articulated in the 45 BC book *De Natura Deorum* (On the Nature of the Gods) by Roman statesman and orator Marcus Tullius Cicero, one of the three books of theological dialogue by Cicero. "The constellations are so accurately spaced out that their vast and ordered array clearly displays the skill of a divine creator" (*De Natura Deorum*, 2:110). "On seeing the regular motions of the heaven and the fixed order of the stars and the accurate interconnection and interrelating of all things, who would deny that these things possess any rational design, and maintain that [this] phenomena takes place by chance?" (2:97). The great Voltaire, calling *De Natura Deorum* "perhaps the best book of all antiquity," thought enough of the argument to say, "The universe impresses me. I cannot help but balk to think that there should be no clockmaker for such a clock."

5. Although if God created the universe, I do wonder what he did with his time before he did it. Doodle? Just like I wonder what scientists mean when they say the "universe is finite" and "expanding" because of the big bang. The words "finite" and "expanding" necessarily mean that at any given point in time there's an end to the universe. But if so, what's at the end of the universe? Cer-

tainly not a fence or wall. An invisible line? But if so, what's on the other side?

6. Whatever the answer to this conundrum is, it certainly is not that given by German philosopher Immanuel Kant in his 1788 treatise *Critique of Pure Reason*. Kant writes, "This [question] is incorrect because the causal principle concerns only what *begins* to exist, and God never began to exist, but is eternal." But how could a supposedly great mind like Kant's utter something so off base? The whole argument of first cause is to prove the logic of the conclusion that there is a God. You don't do this by assuming the existence of God, the very thing sought to be proved. Because this is so obvious, was there something wrong with Kant?

The first time I began to wonder if Kant was not, shall we say, quite right was when he insisted that all lies were morally wrong and never permissible, *even in situations of imminent peril*. But not only are lies absolutely necessary in some circumstances (During wartime, Churchill said, "the truth has to be protected by a bodyguard of lies"), but also sometimes lying is the only moral thing to do. Imagine German SS agents knocking on the door of a residence in Berlin in the late 1930s and asking a young Jew the whereabouts of his parents, who are in hiding. Kantian ethics would apparently dictate that the only moral thing for the lad to do was tell the SS the truth. Perhaps the very pejorative word "lie" should be reserved only for deliberately telling a falsehood to someone who is *entitled* to the truth.

7. Indeed, if God created the universe, would not the law of cause and effect, among all other laws, have also been created by him? And if so, would it not follow that he would have the concomitant power to void or render inapplicable what he created as it applied to himself?

CHAPTER 7

1. Although traditional, rabbinic Judaism still clings tenaciously to the belief that Moses is the author of Genesis as well as the other four books of the Torah, it is holding both ends of the rope in the water on this matter, with most biblical scholars recognizing the reality that the authorship of all five books of the Torah (called Pentateuch in Greek) is unknown and most likely forever will be. David J. A. Clines, professor of biblical studies at the University of Sheffield, England, writes, "The overwhelming tendency in biblical scholarship has been to explain the origin of the Pentateuch as the outcome of a process of compilation of various documents from different periods [and hence, different authors] in Israelite history" (*The Oxford Companion to the Bible*, 580).

Although there were several earlier scholars and theologians who, starting in the seventeenth century, began to enunciate and expand upon this belief in their writings (e.g., Thomas Hobbes, Jean Astruc, Baruch Spinoza, Richard Simon, and Wilhelm Martin Leberecht de Wette), the first one to publish a comprehensive study of the theory was German theologian Julius Wellhausen. In his 1876 book, *Die Komposition des Hexateuch* (The Composition of the Hexateuch, which is the Pentateuch plus the Book of Joshua), a book that has not been translated into English, he set forth his theory of four sources for the Torah, none of whom was Moses.*

Called the "Documentary Hypothesis," the four "documents" (actually believed to be texts in narrative form) are called J (Jehovist), E (Elohist), D (Deuteronomy), and P (Priestly), dating from the ninth, eighth, sixth, and fifth centuries BC, respectively. Believed to come from different eras of Jewish history and, as indicated, with different, multiple authors, the documents were in many cases contrasting accounts of events in that history, and hence, had to be edited by redactors who put the Pentateuch into the present form before the canon of the Torah was formalized in the fifth century BC (The canon of the Prophets followed in the third century BC, and the remaining books of the Hebrew bible, the Hagiographa, in around AD 90.) The letters J, E, D, and P are scholarly shorthand for the unknown authors of the documents, named because of signature references in their writing. For example, in the E, or Elohist, document, the author used the more personal Hebrew name for Yahweh, Elohim, and Elohist is derived from Elohim. The P, or Priestly, source came by its name because the document stressed Jewish ritual and religious observance, from which the inference was drawn that the authors of the document were probably Jewish priests. (The term "rabbi" didn't come into use until the first century AD)

But these biblical scholars, though they deserve to be commended for their work, which has resulted in conclusions more likely to be true then those of Judeo tradition (e.g., does it make sense that Moses would write two contradictory stories of creation? See Genesis 1 and 2. On the other hand, where was the editing by redactors here?), and though they sensibly never claimed divine authorship for their unknown Torah authors, in the last analysis are merely clothing the same almost assuredly apocryphal story of God and his personal relationship with the Jewish people in more academically respectable garb.

The biggest weakness in the Documentary Hypothesis by far is that its entire foundation is inference. The proponents of this theory speak about the four

---

*Wellhausen's 1878 book, *History of Israel*, and its second edition in 1883, *Prolegomena to the History of Israel*, have been translated into English, and they incorporate a discussion of the four sources into their narrative on the history of Israel and the Judeo religion, particularly their discussion on the parallels and differences, mostly parallels, of the Priestly and Jehovist writings in the narrative of the Hexateuch.

documents as if they exist and they have seen them. But they exist only by way of scholarly analysis and inference. The proponents thus far have failed to produce one page (original or copy) or even one snippet of a page of any of the so-called J, E, D, or P documents. So we cannot be 100 percent sure that they ever existed.

CHAPTER 8

1. Per the publisher of the books, Tyndale, 71 percent of the readers are primarily from the South, followed by those from the Midwest. Only 6 percent are from the Northeast.

2. Now, these faithful believe, as St. Augustine wrote in his treatise *Faith and Works*, that if you accept Christ as your savior, "good works will follow." But notwithstanding what is implied in 1 John 5:18, nowhere do they say that if you accept Jesus into your life you will never sin again, that you will lead the life of a saint. Because of this reality, the common assertion by most Protestants and born-again Christians that "once saved always saved," i.e., once you accept Jesus into your life you are saved (which suggests that it is irrelevant what you do thereafter) is a meaningless statement that cannot be supported even in theory. Or scripturally. 2 Peter 2:20–22 says that "when people escape from the wicked ways of the world by learning about our Lord and Savoir Jesus Christ, and *then* get tangled up with sin *again*, they are worse off than before." (See also, Hebrews 6:4–6; Luke 8:13–14.)

3. Actually, a smaller percentage of more moderate Evangelicals, including Billy Graham, has in recent years at least allowed the possibility that those who don't accept Jesus as their savior (because they have never read or heard the gospel of Jesus and do not know of him) might still reach heaven. But these moderates are still so harsh and restrictive that those who do not know of Jesus aren't too much better off. A nonbeliever in Jesus can reach heaven, they say, only if he recognizes the existence of God—for instance, through nature—*and* submits to him (not Jesus, whom he does not know) as his only salvation. Christian apologists Norman Geisler and Frank Turek, unbelievably, say, "*Everyone* knows of God because of the starry heavens above and the moral law within. Those who reject that natural revelation will reject Jesus, too." Graham says that since God has "spoken through his universe, men and women are *without excuse* for not believing in him."

CHAPTER 9

1. For those who think that maybe only Jesus' spirit, not his body, was resurrected, and that all his disciples and others saw was an apparition or ghost of

Jesus, they are unfamiliar with the bible. Jesus himself, confronting his originally skeptical disciples, said to them, "See my hands and my feet, that it is I myself; handle me, and see, for a spirit has not flesh and bones as you see that I have" (Luke 24:39). Jesus talked to his disciples, let them touch his wounds, ate with them. (See Luke 24:35–43; Matthew 28:9; Mark 16:14–19; John 20:19–29 and 21:4–12; Acts 1:3–4; and John 1:1.)

2. As is obvious, the main value of Josephus' paragraph in determining the historicity of Jesus is that he was not a Christian. But as has been pointed out by several anti-Christian scholars, one of the biggest problems with his account is that although Christian writers of the second and third centuries wrote prolifically about Jesus, none that we know of mentioned the all-important reference to Jesus by Josephus until Eusebius, around AD 320, wrote his *History of the Church*. So even though Josephus' work, *Antiquities*, was the most important secular book about the Jewish people written up to that point, and obviously was read by religious scholars of that era, almost three centuries went by (around 287 years) before any Christian writer, all of whom were seeking to promote the health and advancement of Christianity, saw fit to quote Josephus' celebrated reference to Jesus, a reference, again, so consequential because it came from a non-Christian writer.* This naturally raises questions about whether the original *Antiquities* (only copies have survived) even contained the reference, and has caused these anti-Christian authors to allege that Josephus' reference to Jesus was a fraudulent invention by Christianity.

This is not an automatically invalid argument on its face. However, it could be argued in rebuttal that because the early Christian writers treated the existence of Jesus as a fait accompli (as opposed to what some writers today maintain), they may have felt no need to mention Josephus' reference to Jesus, Jesus' existence not being an issue at the time. In reading, just for an example, Tertullian's (AD 160–220) essay *Prayer*, I have to say I would have found it odd to see a reference to Josephus and his paragraph. To these early Christian writers it would

---

*Josephus mentions Jesus one more time in his book. He writes that "the brother of Jesus, who was called Christ, whose name was James," and some others were brought before the Sanhedrin (judges), who, after finding they had broken the law (no indication of the violations of law), "delivered them to be stoned" (Flavius Josephus, "Antiquities," in *The Life and Works of Flavius Josephus*, [New York: Holt, Rinehart, and Winston, 1977], 598). However, Eusebius, who is more of an authority on the early Church than Josephus, wrote that when the Jewish leadership asked James to "renounce the faith of Christ," he refused, "declaring that Jesus Christ was the son of God, our Savior and Lord," and they "slew him." Citing Clement as his source, Eusebius said James "was thrown from a wing of the temple, and beaten to death with a club" (Eusebius, *Ecclesiastical History*, 75–76).

have seemed as uncalled for and inappropriate as quoting authority for the existence of the sun.

There is one thing, however, that stands out in Josephus' paragraph like a sore thumb: the "ten thousand" other wonderful things about Jesus. The number is so wrong, extravagantly so (even if one believes everything in the bible, such as all the fulfillments of prophecies (44) and miracles (37) of Jesus, the number would probably not be in excess of one hundred), that it sounds more like it came from the equivalent of a modern-day hack who was just getting started as a press agent and was enthusiastically trying to promote his client, than from a very careful, scholarly historian, as we know Josephus was.

To me, this problem with the paragraph is also exacerbated by the fact that in the extant *Antiquities*, the one paragraph reference to Jesus (*Antiquities*, 535) does not seem to fit the context, giving further support for the contention that it was inserted by early Christians after Josephus died in AD 100. The paragraph that precedes the reference to Jesus concerns Pilate killing "a great number" of Jews who had protested against his use of "sacred money" (presumably Jewish religious money) to bring a "current of water to Jerusalem." The next paragraph is the Jesus paragraph. Then the following paragraph reads, "About the same time, also, *another* sad calamity put the Jews into disorder." This paragraph flows much better from the paragraph before the Jesus paragraph than it does from the Jesus paragraph. I did not read Josephus' entire 578-page *Antiquities of the Jews* (pages 29–603 of the 1,055-page *The Life and Works of Flavius Josephus*), a book of small print. But in spending around three hours reading portions of it of interest to me here and there, I did not see any similar examples of such a glaringly disjointed flow in his writing.

Another question has to be asked about the lone Jesus paragraph in Josephus' *Antiquities*. Since Josephus, who was Jewish ("The only Jew who was considered by the Romans as having some common sense," Voltaire wrote) and a Pharisee, started his meticulous and thorough history of the Jews with Genesis and proceeded up to the date of his book's publication in AD 93 (thereby covering the entire period of the life of Jesus), and since the life of Jesus was so important to Christianity that it takes up the entire New Testament, and since Josephus, although being born four years after Jesus' crucifixion, was, per his brief autobiography, *The Life of Flavius Josephus*, born, raised, and lived the first thirty years of his life in Jerusalem,* why would the spectacular and mo-

---

*He spent most of the remainder of his life in Rome following his service as a Jewish general in Galilee during the unsuccessful Jewish revolt against the Roman empire in the late 60s through 70 AD (70 AD was when the all-important temple in Jerusalem was destroyed by the Romans.)

mentous nature of Jesus' life not cause him to write far more than one solitary paragraph in his long history of the Jews?

It wasn't as if Jesus was merely an itinerant preacher who drew the attention only of those small groups he spoke to. To the contrary, per the New Testament Jesus was a phenomenon whose message suggested he was the messiah and whose miracles of healing attracted the intense notice and scrutiny of all of Palestine. In Mark 3:7–8 it is written, "Jesus and his disciples went out to the lake, followed by a huge crowd from all over Galilee, Judea, Jerusalem, Idumea, from east of the Jordan River, and even from as far away as Tyre and Sidon. The news about his miracles had spread far and wide, and vast numbers of people came to see him for themselves." (See also Luke 5:15.) How many? Well, for instance, we're told there was one crowd of 5,000 (Matthew 14:21), another of 4,000 (Matthew 15:38). As a percentage of the population back then, wouldn't that be the equivalent of several hundred thousand people today? Mark 6:56 says that "wherever Jesus went—in villages and cities and out on the farms—they laid the sick in the market plazas and streets" for Jesus to heal them.

And it wasn't just the masses who came from everywhere to see Jesus. Jesus' suggestion that he was the messiah drew the attention and ire of almost the entire Jewish religious establishment. Speaking of a day that "Jesus was teaching" in Galilee, Luke (5:17) wrote that "Pharisees and teachers of religious law showed up, it seemed, from every village in all of Galilee and Judea as well as Jerusalem." Mark 6:14 says, "Herod Antipas, the king, soon heard about Jesus, because people everywhere were talking about him."

The question is, How is it that Josephus, particularly back then when the oral tradition of communication was a hundred times more prevalent than today and the area of Jesus' ministry involved was so small (from Nazareth in Galilee to Jerusalem in Judea is only around seventy-five miles by the way the crow flies), would not know all about Jesus and his enormous impact on the Jews of his time? And if he did, why in the world would he devote only one paragraph in his 578-page history of the Jews to Jesus? I mean, in Josephus' companion volume on Jewish history, *War of the Jews*, he wrote much more about another Jesus who idiotically walked around the city of Jerusalem day and night for several years crying out, "Woe, woe, to Jerusalem, and to its people and to the holy house," until a stone thrown at him struck and killed him, finally silencing his cry. Are we to believe that this Jesus was worth more than four times the space as the story of Jesus of Nazareth, upon which the entire New Testament is based? It just doesn't make sense.

Another Jesus, identified by Josephus as the "eldest of the high priests next to Ananus," got up on a tower and spoke to the Idumeans (Edomites) who had come to Jerusalem at the request for assistance of a radical Jewish sect called the Zealots, who claimed the Jewish leadership in the city was about to betray the city into the hands of the Romans, and Jesus told the Idumeans that this was a lie. Josephus set forth, word for word, Jesus' entire speech, almost fifteen times as many words as Josephus' paragraph on the life of Jesus, the founder of Christianity.

And these are just references to two other men named Jesus in Josephus' history of the Jews. Throughout *Antiquities*, he spends much more time on very obscure figures than on Jesus of Nazareth. For instance, he spends pages talking about Helena, the queen of Adiabene, a small Assyrian kingdom in Mesopotamia, and her son Izates, who became its king.

In leaving this issue, I can only say that although the Jesus paragraph in Josephus may be as clean as a hound's tooth, in my opinion there is something strange about it. And if, indeed, the Jesus paragraph was inserted at a later time, the considerable implications are too obvious to state.

3. In AD 112, a Roman writer and administrator, Pliny the Younger, nephew of Pliny the Elder (author of the thirty-seven-volume *Natural History*), referred, in a letter to Roman emperor Trajan that was included in his book of letters titled *Letters*, to followers of a "Christ, whom they worship as a God."

4. On the other hand, the bible says that God created man "in his own image," and we all know that Christians believe that God is "all-perfect," which theoretically should make all of us, as many have pointed out, perfect, too. Yet we are also told that God sees us all as sinners. And Christians agree. "God is pure and perfect," they say, so perfect that "no greater being can be conceived by our thoughts," but "we are all sinners." I don't get it. What am I missing here?

5. Easily one of the biggest misconceptions among Christian laypeople is what the term "immaculate conception" means. Many believe it refers to the virgin birth of Jesus, but I remember from way back in my catechism classes that it instead refers to the Catholic belief that the Virgin Mary was the only human ever born without original sin on her soul. Her soul was sanctified by grace from the beginning and never stained. Although nothing in the scriptures expressly says this, in 1854 Pope Pius IX declared it to be so and cited two bible passages, perhaps the strongest of which is in the gospel of Luke that he said helped him infer this. The angel Gabriel said to Mary, "Hail, favored woman, *full of grace*, the Lord is with thee; blessed art thou among women" (Luke 1:28, 30). It is believed that Pius was also influenced by the principal Catholic (and Christian) belief that Mary gave birth to Jesus, and hence, God would have likely spared her original sin.

6. In an article in *Mensa Magazine* in 2002 (Mensa is the international organization of very bright people whose members have to have an IQ at or above the ninety-eighth percentile in standardized IQ tests), Paul Bell writes, "Of 43 studies carried out since 1927 on the relationship between religious belief and one's intelligence and/or educational level, all but four found an inverse connection. That is, the higher one's intelligence or education level, the less one is likely to be religious."

7. The notion of Jesus' descent into hell has little biblical support. Of several references, including Jesus saying, "I will be in the heart of the earth for three days" (Matthew 12:40), which is virtually no support at all, the only two that seem to have any substance at all are 1 Peter 3:19, where it is written that after Jesus suffered physical death, "he went and preached to the spirits in prison," and Revelation 1:18, where Jesus said, "I am the living one who died. . . . And I hold the keys to death and the grave," the grave in the Greek translation of the bible being Hades, or hell.

Despite the tenuousness of the notion, the words "descended into hell" (after he was crucified and buried and before he rose from the dead) actually appear in the Apostles Creed, one of the very most important prayers in the Catholic church, a prayer that dates back to around AD 500, yet traditionally is attributed to the twelve apostles.

8. C. S. Lewis, in a homespun way that has seduced millions of people into buying his books and recommending them to others, has a modus operandi of comparing apples to oranges throughout his entire book *Mere Christianity*, and the gullible reader thinks he's comparing apples to other apples. His style is to take a nonsensical Christian belief that no one understands, including himself; use fuzzy reasoning to try to explain it; and then close his sale with his Christian buyers by speaking to them in a language they all understand, which is supposed to explain the ludicrous Christian belief. For instance, as previously indicated, Christianity believes that God is divided into three persons, the Father, the Son (Jesus), and the Holy Ghost. Yet these three persons are only one. Say what? Lewis says he understands how this can be. He proceeds to write two and a half full paragraphs trying poorly to explain the notion in *mere* Christianity, then says, "In God's dimension, you find a being who is three persons while remaining one being [now for the language everyone understands], just as a cube is six squares while remaining one cube." Brilliant sounding, but pure drivel. Lewis speaks of the Son and the Holy Spirit being God. But a side of a cube is not a cube. It's a side that could just as well be a side of a piece of wood, box, loaf of bread, or book. He gets by with this terribly defective reasoning throughout much of his book.

9. How soon did Jesus mean? *Very* soon. Indeed, in Matthew 16:27–28 he said, concerning his returning to "judge all people" (Judgment Day), "I assure you that some of you standing here right now will not die before you see me, the Son of Man, coming in my Kingdom." (See also Mark 9:1, Mark 13:30 ["this generation"], and Luke 9:27.) James 5:8 proclaims, "The coming of the Lord is at hand." (This clearly made Jesus, for whatever else he may or may not have been, a failed prophet, at least with respect to this one very important prophecy.) This poses what would seem to be an insurmountable problem for bible Fundamentalists (creationists). To get around the fact that science has proved that the world is billions of years old when they say it is only 6,000 (some say 10,000) years old, as previously indicated, they argue that 6,000 years in biblical time is not the same as we know 6,000 years to be, or that the earth was created in such a way that it erroneously gives the appearance of being much, much older than it actually is. But how can they get around Jesus saying he was going to return *during the lives of many of those living during his time?*

Not to worry. At least one of those living at the time of Jesus (but not "many"), per legend, is still alive. In John 21:19–22 Jesus told Peter to follow him. When Peter turned around and saw John lagging behind, he asked Jesus, "What about him?" whereupon Jesus replied, "If I want him to tarry until I return, what is that to thee?" For centuries, the belief among some was that John must not have died and was wandering the earth waiting for the second coming of Christ. But it was the consensus of too many that John had, in fact, died in Epheseus, after living into his nineties. In the thirteenth century, after several other candidates for the Wandering Jew had failed to catch on, the enduring story of a Jewish shopkeeper—who, legend (not the New Testament) has it, pushed Jesus and told him to walk faster as he carried his cross in agony past his shop, causing Jesus to level a curse at him, "I will go, but you will tarry till I return"—emerged in Europe, where it became very popular.

Eventually, the legend spread throughout the globe, being memorialized in many plays, poems, novels, and even movies, up to and including the twentieth century (e.g., Wilson Tucker's 1959 novel *The Planet Earth*, in which the Wandering Jew is the last man on earth alive, and the 1948 Italian movie *L'Ebreo Errante*, starring Vittorio Gassman). Indeed, and as can be expected, several men through the centuries have steadfastly claimed to be the Wandering Jew. Although the story has slight variations, the basic theme is that the Wandering Jew is very tired of living and desperately wants to die, but he either keeps getting older or remains the same age. Even his many attempts to kill himself, including walking into raging fires, have proved unsuccessful. It seems only the Lord, when he returns, can end his hell on earth.

CHAPTER 10

1. In a similar vein, the Jewish elders in Jerusalem claimed after Jesus' purported resurrection that the tomb in which Jesus had been buried was now empty because Jesus' disciples came in the middle of the night while the Roman guards were sleeping and stole his body (Matthew 28:11–15), presumably so they could deceive people into believing that Jesus had risen from the dead. But if this were true, as indicated in the main text, why would Jesus' followers, knowing the fraud they had perpetrated, and now knowing that Jesus was not divine, have been willing to continue to preach his gospel, gladly accepting persecution and severe physical punishment,* even death, over something they knew to be a lie?

2. Saul of Tarsus (Paul) cannot be considered to be an exception to his not appearing to his nonbelievers since Jesus only appeared to him as a "brilliant light from heaven" and a voice, not in his body (Acts 9:3–6). And even if Paul, in 1 Corinthians 15:7, was not referring to the apostle James but to Jesus' own brother James, who at one time was an unbeliever, Jesus appearing to his brother would hardly qualify as a good exception.

3. Jesus had four brothers—James, Joseph, Judas, and Simon (Matthew 13:55; Mark 6:3). He also had sisters (Mark 6:3), although nowhere in the New Testament are their names or number given. The brother of Jesus who is mentioned the most in Christianity is James (not one of the twelve apostles [Matthew 4:21 and 10:2–3]). James is believed to be the author of the epistle of James in the New Testament. He became the first bishop of the early Christian church in Jerusalem (Eusebius, *The Ecclesiastical History*, 75, 470), and as indicated earlier, ultimately died a martyr's death. Many Christian scholars deduce from this that James, once skeptical of his brother's divinity, must have been won over by his awareness of Jesus' resurrection for him to have become a church leader and die for his belief. See also, Acts 1:14, 15:13, 21:18; Josephus, *Antiquities*, 598; and 1 Corinthians 15:7, although from the context in his letter to the Corinthians, Paul may have been referring to the apostle James, not Jesus' brother, when he says that Jesus "was seen by James and later by all the apostles," which could be read to mean James being one of the twelve, and "all" referring

---

*It should be noted that the persecution of Christians continued up to the reign of Constantine 1, the first Roman emperor who was Christian. After his conversion to Christianity in AD 312, Constantine mandated tolerance of Christianity throughout the Roman Empire by his Edict of Milan in 313.

to the rest of the apostles. But this is not clear here, as it is in Galatians 1:19, where Paul refers to the James in that case as the brother of Jesus.

With respect to the brothers and sisters of Jesus, it is Catholic dogma that Jesus' mother, Mary, was a virgin not only when she gave birth to Jesus, but always. As early as the fourth century, "ever-virgin" was a popular name for Jesus' mother, and at the Council of Trent in 1555 Pope Paul IV reaffirmed the church's long-standing belief in the dogma by declaring that Mary was a virgin "before [the] birth [of Jesus], during birth, and forever after birth." But this is not a certainty at all under the bible. Matthew 1:25 states, "[Mary] remained a virgin *until* her son was born," which could suggest she did not remain a virgin, as Pope Paul IV declared, "forever after." And Luke 2:7 says that Jesus was Mary's "*first child,*" the strongest (though not only) implication being that Mary had subsequent children with Joseph.

If we accept that Catholic dogma is correct, how can we account for the "brothers and sisters" of Jesus? One way is to assume that Joseph, Jesus' foster father, fathered them before he married Mary. Hence, they would be Jesus' half-brothers and sisters. Indeed, at the time of Jesus, Greek-speaking Jews used the Greek words *adelphos* and *adelphi* (the words that appeared in the New Testament) not only for a blood brother and sister, but also for a half-brother and half-sister as well as a nephew, niece, and cousin. This latter possibility is least likely for James, however, who is referred to several times in the New Testament as Jesus' "brother" and in the writings of early Christian scholars like Eusebius as "the brother of our Lord."

A footnote to all of this is the reference in the gospel of Mark to a "Mary," who, along with Mary Magdalene (about whom, by the way, there is no suggestion in the New Testament that she was a prostitute), was present at the crucifixion and burial of Jesus on Friday and came to the tomb of Jesus on Sunday morning and found it to be empty, an angel telling them that Jesus had risen from the dead (Matthew 27:56, 61; 28:1, 5–6). Some have speculated that she was Jesus' mother, Mary, but this is very unlikely. Although she is identified as the "mother of James and Joseph" (Matthew 27:56, Mark 15:40), and we know from the bible that Jesus had two brothers with the same names, this would appear to only be a coincidence, as everything else indicates she was not Jesus' mother, and therefore James and Joseph referred to a different James and Joseph, two very common names at that time in Palestine. Jesus also had two brothers in addition to James and Joseph—Judas and Simon (Matthew 13:55, Mark 6:3). So why would they say that "Mary" was only the mother of James and Joseph? Additionally, if Mark and Matthew were referring to Jesus' mother, it is highly improbable that they would mention Mary Magdalene's name before Mary, who was the mother, they believed, of Jesus (Mark 15:40, Matthew 27:56). Most importantly by far, if the Mary whom Matthew and Mark referred to was Jesus' mother, it is almost inconceivable that they would not refer to her as such, referring to her instead as the mother of James and Joseph. Moreover, Mark also identifies this Mary along with Mary Magdalene and Salome (who was also present at the crucifixion) as "followers of Jesus" (Mark 15:40–41). It is extremely unlikely he would refer to Mary, the mother of Jesus, as just a "follower" of Jesus. See also Matthew 27:61, where Matthew refers to Mary as "the other Mary" (i.e., other than Mary Magdalene), a characterization he would not be expected to use if he were referring to Jesus' mother.

Who was this "other Mary"? The only reference to the identity of the third Mary (i.e., in addition to Mary, the mother of Jesus, and Mary Magdalene) at the crucifixion or the tomb is in John 19:25 where it is written: "Standing near the cross were Jesus' mother, and his mother's sister, Mary (the wife of Clopas), and Mary Magdalene." But unless the word sister was, as indicated earlier, being used here to include half-sisters as well as nieces and cousins, it seems very unlikely that the parents of Jesus' mother, Mary, would name two of their children Mary.

4. Christian scholars have argued that some of the prophecies were beyond the control of Jesus. But most of the ones they cite are not exact, indisputable parallels on all fours with the purported fulfillment, for example, Zechariah 11:12, Matthew 26:15; Isaiah 50.6, Matthew 26:67; Psalm 22:7–8, Matthew 27:39–43, Zechariah 12:10, John 19:33–37. Arguably the closest in circumstances is Psalm 22:16,18 and Matthew 27:35 dealing in circumstances is Psalm 22:16,18 and Matthew 27:35 dealing with those who put Jesus on the cross throwing dice for his clothing.

5. On the subject of who Jesus was, although Jesus left no ambiguity that he came from God, his father in heaven (e.g., "my Father in heaven" [Matthew 16:17]), he repeatedly referred to himself (eighty-one times), particularly in the gospels of Matthew, Mark, and Luke, as the "Son of Man." The term "Son of Man" appears several times in the Hebrew bible, mostly in the Book of Ezekiel (e.g., Ezekiel 2:1), where the prophet says God, in a vision Ezekiel had, called him the son of man. (See also Psalm 8:4 and Acts 7:56.) However, from the context, Jewish scholars believe that God clearly was not referring to the divinity of Ezekiel, but merely "a man within the created order" of man whom he was using to convey messages to the people of Israel. But nowhere in the New Testament are we told what Jesus meant by this term, and most biblical scholars see it, do a double take, then move on, although there is a body of literature on the meaning and derivation of the term, none of which is satisfying (e.g., see C. C. Caragounis, *The Son of Man* [Tubingen, Germany: J. C. B. Mohr, 1979]; J. Fitzmyer, "The

NT Title 'Son of Man' Philologically Considered," in *A Wandering Aramaean: Collected Aramaic Essays* [Missoula, Missouri: Scholars Press, 1979]).

Let's take a look at a recent take on the issue by the chairman of the Department of Religion at a major eastern university (whose name, to avoid embarrassing him, I will not mention). Remarkably, he says that in some bible passages when Jesus used the words "Son of Man," he "does not appear to be speaking about himself" but about a "cosmic judge" whom "God" will send down "from heaven" on Judgment Day and "who will overthrow the forces of evil . . . and judge all the living and the dead" here on earth. But the professor is obviously wrong and this is a nonissue since in the synoptic gospels, Jesus, over and over and over again says, "I, the Son of Man" (e.g., Matthew 9:6, 16:27, and 19:28; Mark 8:38, 10:33, and 14:21; Luke 6:5, 9:22, and 18:8; John 3:13, etc.). On those few occasions when he doesn't say the word "I" before "the Son of Man," it is nearly always obvious from the context he is speaking about himself (e.g., Luke 17:22 and 18:31–33). So there is nothing to even discuss since Jesus couldn't have made it any clearer that he, not someone else, was the Son of Man, that there were not two sons of man.

The professor has more to say. Even though the scriptural verses explicitly say that "God" or "the Lord" will judge us on Judgment Day (e.g., Ecclesiastes 3:17, 1 Corinthians 4:5, 2 Peter 3:10, Revelation 20:11–15), this biblical scholar came up with a verse in Daniel that he says, without any evidence to support his claim, refers to a son of man other than Jesus, a biblical passage that, in effect, overrules all that everything else in the bible says about this matter. In Daniel 7:13, the Hebrew prophet writes that he had a vision of "someone who looked like a *son of man* coming with the clouds of heaven" down to earth; apparently, per the professor, not to rule the world, as Daniel says in 7:14, but to destroy God's enemies and pass judgment on man. So if we're to believe this professor, this vision was not of the Lord Jesus Christ. But not only, as indicated, did Jesus routinely refer to himself as the Son of Man, at Jesus' trial before the Sanhedrin in the high priest's home after his arrest in the Garden of Gethsemane, Jesus specifically said it was he who would be "coming with the clouds of heaven" (Matthew 26:64), a clear reference, by Jesus, to Daniel's vision, the cherished vision in Daniel upon which the professor based his whole bizarre theory. So the learned professor apparently feels that either Jesus was lying in Matthew 26:64, or he was simply wrong.

If, per the professor, Daniel wasn't referring to Jesus, and he certainly wasn't speaking of Jesus' father, God, since it is God, per the professor, who will send this son of man to earth, and the professor never suggests that this son of man was the Holy Ghost, then whom was Daniel referring to? If we're to believe the professor, by definition he had to be referring to a *fourth*, yes, a fourth entity. Someone who, in the entire bible, we can find only in Daniel's vision. And *he* is the one who is going to destroy all of God's enemies and judge all of us on Judgment Day. And I repeat. This professor is the head of the Department of Religion at his university.

I've never read any adequate explanation for this curious phrase, Son of Man, one of which was that "the absence of a definition or explanation in the Gospels may imply that the term was so well known to Jesus' contemporaries that any such explanation would be superfluous." Whatever the explanation, it should be noted that, although the literal meaning of the words is that Jesus came from the loins of man, not from God, the context in which he used these words makes it clear that he did not believe he came from a mere mortal, but from God (e.g., "If a person is ashamed of me and my message in these adulterous and sinful days, I, the Son of Man, will be ashamed of that person when I *return* in the glory of *my Father* with the holy angels" [Mark 8:38]. "In the future, you will see me, the Son of Man, sitting at God's right hand" [Matthew 26:64]).

Although we cannot say with any degree of assurance why Jesus used the puzzling words "Son of Man," one possibility to consider is that he deliberately used this term as a nonincriminating substitute for Son of God. Although he would not lie and deny his divinity if he was asked (John 18:33 and 36–37), perhaps he did not want to advertise who he was to the hostile Pharisees and Sadducees of Judea and Galilee, not wanting to provoke them into killing him before he felt he had completed his public ministry of preaching the word of God. When he asked Peter, "Who do you say I am?" Peter answered, "You are the Messiah, the Son of the living God." Jesus then said, "You are blessed, Simon [Peter], because my Father in heaven has revealed this to you." But then he sternly warned Peter and his other disciples not to tell anyone that he was the messiah (Matthew 16:15–17, 20; see also Mark 3:11–12).

But this is indeed peculiar since Jesus' entire ministry could only convey the message that he was the messiah. If he was the Son of God (which, in addition to the Son of Man, he also proclaimed he was ["I am the Son of God" he told the Jewish leaders in the temple in John 10:36; see also Mark 14:61–62 and Luke 1:35]), performed miracles, and fulfilled Old Testament prophecies, who else could he have been but the messiah? Yet for the most part he was evasive. When the Jews in the temple said to him, "If you are the messiah, tell us plainly," he answered, "I have already told you, and you don't believe me. The proof is what I do in the name of my Father" (John 10:24–25). However, Jesus explicitly told the Samaritan woman, "I am the Messiah" (John 4:26). When Pilate asked him, "Are you the King of the Jews?" Jesus replied, "Yes, it is as you say"

(Matthew 27:11). "I was born for that purpose. And I came to bring the truth to the world" (John 18:33, 37). There is no confusion or ambiguity in the words of the New Testament that Jesus was the messiah. It remains a mystery, however, why he called himself the Son of Man, calling himself this much more than he called himself the Son of God.

CHAPTER 11

1. Atheists consistently attack the four gospels, the historical foundation of Christianity, citing some contradictions among the gospels as proof to them that, as Richard Dawkins says, "the gospels are not reliable accounts of what happened." Christopher Hitchens says it is an error to believe that the gospels are "in any sense a historical record" because their authors "cannot agree on anything of importance." (As indicated in the main text, this is flat-out wrong.) Although these inconsistencies and contradictions are good circumstantial evidence that the bible is not divinely inspired (Why would God have any reason to inspire a biblical author to contradict another biblical author? Moreover, two contradictory accounts cannot both be correct. At least one has to be wrong, and how could an all-perfect God even be capable of inspiring anything that is wrong?), they are not good evidence, in my view, that the gospels are not authentic. Indeed, as I will point out, they are circumstantial evidence of the precise opposite—their authenticity.

But first, these are just a few of many other gospel contradictions. Right off the bat, the ancestors from that part of the genealogy of Jesus starting with David down to Joseph (How is Joseph, only Jesus' foster father, listed as an ancestor— one from whom one is descended—of Jesus and a part of Jesus' genealogy, which deals with genes and heredity?) are dramatically different between Matthew 1:6–16 and Luke 3:23–32. Matthew lists twenty-eight generations, whereas Luke has forty-three. Perhaps worse yet, other than David and Joseph, I could find only six ancestors (Eliakim, Shealtiel, Amos, Zerubbabel, Elieser, and Judah) who appear in both genealogies (although the spellings on a few others were close and could have been referring to the same person). None of the other ancestors do.

The gospels of Matthew (2:1) and Luke (2:4–7) say that Jesus was born in Bethlehem, but the gospel of John (7:41–42) suggests that he was not. Mark is silent on this matter. With respect to the Sermon on the Mount, Matthew (5:1) says that Jesus went up the mountainside with his disciples to teach them by way of the Beatitudes, but Luke (6:12, 17) says that Jesus gave the Beatitudes on level ground after he had come down from the mountain. In the synoptic gospels, Jesus drives out the merchants from the Jerusalem temple near the end of his ministry (Luke 19:45), but in John this occurs near the very beginning (2:13–16). After the resurrection, Matthew 28:16–17, says that Jesus met his disciples in Galilee, but in Luke 24:33, 36, he met them in Jerusalem.

There are many more such contradictions. But the reality is that on the main points and essential story of Jesus' life, the gospels are remarkably consistent. And the contradictions, almost all in the details, not only are normal but they very definitely give the gospels strength and credibility, showing they weren't written by one person or edited to fit an agenda, which, by my lights, actually makes them more supportive than subversive of each other. If all of the gospels agreed with each other on everything, this would affect their credibility inasmuch as such conformity, we know from human experience, would be abnormal. For instance, we know that eyewitnesses to the same event will very often differ, sometimes markedly, in their recollections. Five people witness an automobile accident. From their respective reports, it's startling to see the differences in what they think they saw. And that's when their report is prepared within days thereafter, not several decades later.

I wouldn't have had whatever success I've had in the courtroom if juries wouldn't convict defendants unless every prosecution witness I called to the stand to testify to an event described it in the same way, right down to all the details.

About details, in an 1846 book (*The Testimony of the Evangelists: The Gospels Examined by the Rules of Evidence Administered in Courts of Justice*) by Simon Greenleaf, a prominent professor of law, the author quotes a Dr. Chalmers as writing, "Had the evangelists been false historians, they would not have committed themselves upon so many particulars. They would not have furnished the vigilant inquirers of that period, on every page of their narrative, so many materials for a cross-examination, which would infallibly have disgraced them." Greenleaf adds, "There are other internal marks of truth in the narratives of the evangelists. . . . Among these may be mentioned the nakedness of the narratives; the absence of all parade by the writers about their own integrity, or to impress others with a good opinion of themselves or their cause. . . . [And] there is apparently the most perfect indifference on their part whether they are believed or not."

There is something else pointing to the credibility of the gospels. Several things in the gospels clearly are not favorable to the authors' belief that Jesus was the Son of God—that is, the authors weren't just trying to sell a product. Perhaps the best example is the inclusion in the gospels of Jesus crying out on the cross, "My God, my God, why hast thou forsaken me?" (Mark 15:34), as well as Jesus's family saying he was "out of his mind" (Mark 3:20–21).

Where I disagree with Greenleaf, who believes the authors of the gospels to be wholly credible, is in his conclusion that Jesus was divine. There are two aspects to credibility. One is whether the declarant is honest. I am satisfied beyond a reasonable doubt, though not beyond all doubt, that the gospels are an honest, though not necessarily accurate, record. Does that satisfy the second part of credibility, that what the authors of the gospels say in their writings (Jesus was born of a virgin, the miracles, the resurrection, etc.) is true? No. For that you have to look beyond an author's honesty and sincerity to whether what he is saying makes sense or is corroborated by other witnesses or evidence. I have had personal contact with true believers, as the disciples of Jesus certainly were, who were sincere but spoke inanities. Charles Manson's followers, who believed he was the second coming of Christ and the devil all wrapped up into one, believed he could read their minds and was watching them (literally), though he was hundreds of miles away. They also reported that they saw him do things like bring dead birds back to life.

On the issue of sincerity and honesty, many atheists go beyond merely saying that the gospels are not reliable because the four evangelists couldn't agree on so many things. They suggest that in many places the gospel authors actually fabricated what they wrote. They particularly make this argument with respect to the position of Christianity that the life of Jesus fulfilled Old Testament prophecies, strong evidence for Christians that Jesus was divine.

For example, Micah 5:2 says that the messiah would be born in Bethlehem. Because Mary and Joseph lived in Nazareth before Jesus was born, what to do? Richard Dawkins writes, "So how to get [Mary and Joseph] to Bethlehem at the crucial moment [of Jesus' birth] to fulfill the prophecy?" He goes on to say that Luke fabricated a tale about a census for taxation purposes that took Mary and Joseph to Bethlehem, a story that was historically inaccurate and "complete nonsense."

Sam Harris writes about "the numerous strands of Hebrew prophecy that were *made* to coincide with Jesus' ministry. The writers of Luke and Matthew, for instance, *in seeking* to make the life of Jesus conform to Old Testament prophecy, insist . . ." Elsewhere he refers to "the *attempts* to make the life of Jesus conform to Old Testament prophecy."

It's difficult to know where the truth lies here. I say that because, even though I believe, as indicated, that the authors of the gospels were honest, it is also a fact of life that sometimes people who are telling the truth will fudge here and there to make what they are saying more believable. This may or may not have happened in the gospels.

There are more than forty Old Testament prophecies that, according to Christianity, are fulfilled in the New Testament, Isaiah 53 being, to me, the most important and prominent. (See discussion in main text.) Some are too general in nature to be of any real significance (e.g., Genesis 49:10 and Matthew 1:2–16). And some, like Zachariah 11:12 and Matthew 26:15, are in too much of a different context to be meaningful. Even many of the ones that are right on deal with only narrow points (e.g., Zachariah 9:9 and Matthew 21:5).

For some other prophecy fulfillments, see Psalm 41:9 and Matthew 26:47–50; Psalm 22:1 and Mark 15:34; Micah 5:2 and Luke 2:4–7; Isaiah 61:1–2 and Luke 4:18–21; Psalm 69:21 and Matthew 27:34; Psalm 22:16 and Luke 24:39; Psalm 22:18 and Matthew 27:35; Psalm 16:10 and Matthew 28:5–6; Isaiah 53:5 and John 19:34, 37; Jonah 1:17 and Mark 15:42–47 and 16:9; Isaiah 53:9; and Matthew 27:57–60.

2. For those who would add that we don't even know Jesus' surname (Christ is the English translation of the word *Christos*, Greek for messiah or anointed one), the reason is that from the time of Genesis in the bible through and several centuries beyond the time of Jesus, Jews had no family name, only a first name, and to distinguish those with the same first name from each other, they were known by their first name followed by "son [or daughter, father, mother] of ____." For instance, Seth, son of Adam, Mary, mother of Jesus.

3. When we say the years start with Jesus' birth, if we're going to use the English language that necessarily means Jesus was born in the year AD 1, the first day of the first year being the day of Jesus' birth. Yet Matthew 2:7 says that Herod, the king of Judea, was alive at the time of Jesus' birth, and the year for Herod's death is always given as 4 BC Remarkably, it is frequently said this means Jesus must have been born in 4 BC or earlier. (Indeed, since Matthew 2:16 suggests that Herod was still alive at least two years after Jesus' birth, that means Jesus could have been born as early as 6 BC) But this is ridiculous on its face. Since BC means *before* Christ, how could Jesus be born four years before he was born? Likewise, how could Herod die four years before Jesus was born when he was alive when Jesus was born? Because this is an impossibility, I would think the most reasonable inference is that whoever first said Herod died in 4 BC made a mistake (or Matthew was mistaken [but see Luke 1:5, 26–31]; or Dionysius Exigius, the Russian monk who in the sixth century calculated the year that Jesus was most likely born, made a mistake), and everyone thereafter just repeated it. I mean, even today, with the best of technology, errors much more significant than the date of death of a Judean king who died 2,000 years ago are routinely made, yet repeated by millions. In any event, this matter is purely academic and is of little importance.

4. Although the God of the Old Testament told Moses, in general terms, that one shouldn't "seek revenge" (Leviticus 19:18), the specific, at least in law, always takes precedence over the general, and God later tells Moses, "Anyone who injures another person must be dealt with according to the injury inflicted—fracture for fracture, eye for eye, tooth for tooth. Whatever anyone does to hurt another person must be paid back in kind" (Leviticus 24:19–20).

5. Poor Tolstoy. He unfortunately didn't know where to look for an answer to the riddle. Just as fortunately, I did: St. Thomas Aquinas, by virtually all accounts the greatest theologian the Catholic church (and, many say, Christianity) has ever produced. Here is his explanation of the church's holy trinity—the Father, Son, and Holy Ghost—though three, being one:

> Number is twofold, namely, simple or absolute, as two and three and four, and number as existing in things numbered, as two men and two horses. So, if number in God is taken absolutely or abstractly, there is nothing to prevent whole and part from being in Him, and thus number in Him is only in our way of understanding, because number regarded apart from things numbered exists only in the intellect. But if number be taken as it is in the things numbered, in that sense, as existing in creatures, one is part of two, and two of three as one man is part of two men and two of three; but in this way it does not apply to God, because the Father is of the same magnitude as the whole Trinity. (*Summa Theologica*, First Part, Question 30, Reply to Objection 4, 167–168)

It all makes perfect sense to me now. I had to go all the way to the top of the intellectual hill to get it, but my journey was worth it. (I assume the reader knows I'm being facetious here.)

One common assault on the Christian notion of the trinity, that it has no scriptural foundation and was manufactured by the Catholic church, is correct, but with an asterisk. Although the word "trinity" is not used in the bible, the three members of the trinity are mentioned many times in close proximity to each other, though the bible does not say they are all one (e.g., Matthew 28:19, John 14:15–17, Jude 20–21, and Luke 1:32, 35). However, we do know that Jesus said, "The Father and I are one" (John 10:30). The first formal statement of the doctrine of the Catholic church was by the General Council (of Catholic bishops) of Constantinople in AD 381 in its revised version of the Nicene Creed of 325 AD, the principal liturgical profession of faith of Catholicism and most of Christianity.

Where there clearly seems to be a problem is in the position of the church that, although the Father, the Son, and the Holy Ghost are distinct (though one), they are, per St. Augustine in The Creed, "co-equal." (See also *The Teachings of Christ: A Catholic Catechism for Adults*, edited by Ronald Lawler, Donald W. Wuerl, and Thomas Lawler, Our Sunday Visitor, [Huntington, Indiana, 1976], 181; also, Athanasian Creed, H. Denzinger and A. Schonmetzer, 75.) But although, as indicated, Jesus, the son, said, "The Father and I are one," for the most part he didn't seem to think so. He said, "The Father is greater than I am" (John 14:28); that the father is "the only true God" (John 17:3); and he is "My God" (John 20:17). Jesus also said, "No one knows the day or hour when these things [heaven and earth will disappear] will happen, not even the angels in heaven or the Son himself. Only the Father knows" (Mark 13:31–32).

CHAPTER 12

1. One of the very biggest differences between Protestantism and Catholicism is that, as alluded to in the main text, the former believes that only Jesus Christ is infallible, and the bible is the sole source and authority for all teachings and belief, whereas Catholicism does not believe the bible alone is a sufficient guide for salvation, giving equal weight to Catholic tradition, like the seven sacraments and the pronouncements of general councils of the church (twenty-one so far, starting with the Council of Nicea in AD 325). These councils are congregations of all the Catholic bishops of the world, convened by the pope, who meet when it is deemed necessary to establish doctrine, interpret scripture, and resolve disputes on matters of faith or morals. These pronouncements by the bishops and the pope are also considered to be infallible.

2. Interestingly, there are bible references that seem to suggest that good works alone will bring salvation. For instance, Romans 2:6–8, perhaps the most sensible verse in the New Testament on salvation, says that on Judgment Day, "God will judge all people according to what they have done. He will give eternal life to those who persist in doing what is good . . . and will pour out his anger and wrath on those who . . . practice evil deeds." Indeed, Jesus himself said several times, mostly in the gospel of Matthew but also in Luke, that on Judgment Day salvation will depend (by implication) on our deeds (Matthew 16:27). Those who performed good deeds during their life will "inherit the kingdom of heaven"* and those who did not will receive "eternal punishment" (Matthew

---

*There are other references in the bible to being rewarded for good deeds that don't necessarily refer to salvation, e.g., Jesus said "Sell all you have and give to those in need. This will store up treasure for you in heaven" (Luke 12:33). "You know that your work is not in vain when it is done in the Lord" (1 Corinthians 15:58). These verses seem to address themselves more to being rewarded in heaven than in how to get to heaven in the first place.

25:31–46; Luke 3:24–28). Although this arguably contradicts what Jesus says in Matthew 10:32–33, it clearly contradicts what John has Jesus saying in John 6:47 that "I assure you, anyone who believes in me already has eternal life." (See also John 3:16 and 11:25–26; Mark 16:16). If the bible is the word of God, his utterances in these other gospels are still his word, not those of the authors of these other gospels, and hence, cannot be ignored.

It should be noted that references in the bible to salvation being based only on good works are not mentioned by either Protestantism or Catholicism for the simple reason that both, even Catholicism, maintain that faith in Jesus is also necessary for salvation.

3. The exact quote in Matthew 2:23 from Isaiah 7:14 that Matthew cited was "Look! The virgin [actually, young woman] will conceive a child. She will give birth to a son and will call him Immanuel—God is with us," the word "Immanuel" meaning "God is with us" in Hebrew. Note that Mary did not name her son Immanuel, but Jesus. And whatever Isaiah meant by the words "God is with us," it would not change the fact that Isaiah was not saying the child would be born of a virgin.

Could Immanuel ("God is with us") be construed to be the equivalent of saying the child was born of a virgin? Or, if not, could the words "God is with us" mean that the son of the young woman was God (Jesus, the son of God, being God under the holy trinity)? When I asked Rabbi Dershowitz about this, he said, "I have never heard that question come up in Jewish or Christian literature. There is no way that one can connect the name Immanuel with the son being born of a virgin, or with the son being God in the form of Jesus. 'God is with us' is simply a Jewish expression of faith in God, a belief in God." He said the expression is routinely prompted by "hundreds of situations," giving an example of a woman who had great difficulty conceiving and finally having a child. She could say, "God is with us." In fact, in Isaiah 8:10, the very next chapter of Isaiah, the precise words "God is with us" are used to mean that God will be on our side in an upcoming battle. The rabbi said that Immanuel is not an uncommon Jewish name, and Jewish parents who name their son Immanuel don't believe they've given birth to God or his son. (But see Emil M. Kraeling,"The Immanuel Prophecy," *Journal of Biblical Literature*, 50, number 4, 1931, 277–295, for virgin birth interpretation of Immanuel.)

4. Prior to the year 1414 (Council of Constance), parishioners used to receive wine with the wafer at Holy Communion.

5. To show just how serious these members of the Catholic church are, Catholics, like others, divorce all the time. But under Catholicism, once a Catholic remarries, he is forbidden from receiving Holy Communion because

he is believed to be "living in sin." What do these Catholics do? Thousands of them through the years have appealed to their archbishop, some even to the Vatican, many even hiring lawyers, asking for some special dispensation that would allow them to once again receive Holy Communion. The church, to my knowledge, has always turned them down, allowing them to receive Holy Communion again only if they have their first marriage annulled, an act that frequently engages in the fiction that the marriage (many times for twenty to thirty years with children) never actually took place. Typical grounds for annulment are that one party deceived the other into marriage in some material way, or was unable to consummate the marriage. But it is well known that the church, like a high-heeled lady of the night, will grant an annulment for enough money, or where the party seeking it has enough influence, making a travesty of its sacred sacrament of matrimony, a spiritual contract it maintains is "indissoluble by man" (*Catechism*, numbers 1611 and 1614).

For instance, it granted one to Frank Sinatra in return, reportedly, for his paying for the construction of a Catholic church in Palm Springs, California. Nancy Sinatra is widely considered by biographers of Sinatra to have been a devoted wife, and she bore Frank three children. But according to the Catholic church, Frank and Nancy, who had been married for twelve years, never had a valid marriage, and hence their three children were born out of wedlock. All to get that new church in Palm Springs.

6. Though Catholicism is quite adept at creating rituals and religious icons out of nothing (e.g., several of their sacraments), it is not 100 percent clear, as Protestants believe, that Catholicism invented purgatory. In 2 Maccabees 12:43–46 (considered to be an apocryphal book by Jews and Protestants but not by Catholics), there is a reference to "praying for the dead, that they may be loosed from their sins." Such a place, of course, could neither be heaven or hell. And Matthew 12:32 speaks of the forgiveness of sins "in the world to come," a reference that implies purgatory, per St. Augustine (*De Civitas Dei*, xxi, 24).

7. We know that Martin Luther, a Roman Catholic priest, started the Protestant Reformation in 1517 by denouncing the church's selling of "indulgences," including by Pope Julius II and Pope Leo X, to Catholics. The indulgence would shorten their stay, whereas a plenary indulgence would end their stay in purgatory. Rather than reform the church, Luther left it and started the Lutheran church, the first Protestant church. Although the Catholic church formally acknowledged at the time the impropriety of selling indulgences, it continued to believe it had the power, from its spiritual treasury, to dispense them, but the practice fell into sporadic use for centuries. Remarkably, although money is no longer required, many dioceses around the world today are now starting to offer,

in exchange for certain prayers or pilgrimages, indulgences to Catholics, which will reduce the time they have to stay at the halfway house. Can you imagine that? The whole notion of purgatory is already glorified madness. And now the church, unbelievably, is popularizing indulgences once again, necessarily saying that it can determine how long you have to spend there before you get to see God in heaven.

8. Although it is not yet a part of church doctrine, in an interview with a German journalist in July of 2010, Pope Benedict said that to counter the transmission of AIDS, "there may be" an exception to the rigid condom rule "perhaps when a male prostitute [infected with the HIV virus] uses a condom." Though not made clear by the pope, the belief was that he was only referring to sex between males. If so, since sex between males can never result in procreation, Benedict's tentative relaxing of the no-condom rule is no exception at all to the Catholic church's position on condoms—that their use is prohibited because they prevent procreation, the only authorized purpose for sexual relations between men and women. However, the pope's unofficial statement has been widely interpreted as a signal that in the future the Vatican may relax further the church's prohibition on condom use. In fact, Vatican spokesman Reverend Frederico Lombardi told the media on November 23, 2010, that when he asked the pontiff in a private conversation "if there was a serious, important problem in the choice of masculine over the feminine" with respect to prostitutes infected with the HIV virus, "he said no." The latter, if formalized into official church doctrine, would be an important change.

9. In partial mitigation, if that's even possible, of the Catholic church's conduct in this case, its prosecution, conviction, and sentence of Galileo resulting from the publication of his book was based just as much on Galileo's violating a written injunction given to him by a church emissary, Cardinal Robert Bellarmine, on February 25, 1616, seventeen years earlier, to cease and desist promulgating his view that the earth revolved around the sun. In other words, no prosecution of him was contemplated back then. Galileo had written letters (the most famous of which was his letter to the Grand Duchess Christina in 1615) to several people that became public in which he stated his emerging view. In its June 22, 1633, sentence of Galileo, the Inquisition court told Galileo that in February of 1616 "we wanted to treat you with benignity," but by his later book he had "violated explicitly the injunction given you."

10. Which is, admittedly, virtually never. The First General Council of the Vatican declared (some say, affirmed) on July 18, 1870, that it was a "dogma divinely revealed" that when a pope "speaks ex cathedra, that is, when acting in

the office of shepherd and teacher of all Christians he defines doctrine concerning faith or morals," he "is possessed of infallibility." Since that time over 140 years ago, no pope has spoken ex cathedra except Pope Pius XII on November 1, 1950, saying on that day, "We proclaim, declare, and define it to be a dogma revealed by God that the immaculate Mother of God, Mary ever Virgin, when the course of her earthly life was finished, was taken up *body and soul* into the glory of heaven." This is called the "Assumption of Mary." It should be noted that there is no reference in the New Testament to such bodily ascension by Mary.

CHAPTER 13

1. As to the latter only, fear of death, I thought something in my late teens or early twenties—I'm sure others must have had a similar thought—that, at least if we limit ourselves to logic, should eliminate fear of death. I must also add that this thought of mine hasn't helped me personally at all. Logically, death is nothing to be feared because if there is life after death and death is merely a door to another conscious existence, then there is no real death. And if there is no life after death, since the dead have no consciousness and cannot suffer, there is no cause for fear.

2. If anyone would be unable to describe the glory of life, certainly it would be I, whose passion for life is very, very rarely expressed and played out as it is with millions of people, and whose sense of aesthetics is so underdeveloped that I prefer the sight of buildings in a warehouse district, a train coming down the track, a few very old sunlit adobes on a New Mexico hillside, to the finest of paintings and sculpture and, except for the first half minute or so, the most breathtaking of panoramic views. Not only don't I like things like art, sculpture, and ballet, or even poetry, they actually depress me. I once told an interviewer that if I were given a choice between a day at the Louvre (when there one day with my family, I stared at the *Mona Lisa* in wonderment, unable to figure out what all the fuss was about) and reading a newspaper in a small, windowless room, it wouldn't even be a close call. I'd choose the latter.

My only aesthetic interests are music, perhaps the one harmonious thing in an essentially disharmonious world, and reading. And even with reading, unless I'm giving a quote for a book, I am virtually allergic to the most artistic and literary kind, fiction, being constitutionally unable to get past the first paragraph since I know it never happened. I am someone whose main pursuit of happiness throughout my life has been peace of mind, a condition I've never achieved, the few moments I thought I possessed it being dissolved by the realization that thousands, at that very moment throughout the world, were enduring great suffering and tragedy. Oh, as it is said, if I could just steal one day in my life to live.

3. If I were to hazard a guess as to one component *of the whole* about life that makes it so indescribably precious that it simply cannot be captured in words, I would say it's the feeling of hope. Not just hope that you win the lottery, or become heavyweight champion of the world, or get elected president of the company by the board of directors, but a woman's hope she will be able to get the recipe to the great dish she had at a friend's home, that you'll be able to get a ticket to tomorrow's play, that it will stop raining so that you can play golf today, that you can get home in time to watch the game on TV, that your daughter gets a good grade on her test, that your new medication lowers your blood pressure—in broader terms, that things will turn out for the best or improve. This hope, we know, springs eternal in human beings and keeps people going, there being no medicine like hope. There is a Mexican saying, "*La esperanza muere al ultimo*," meaning "Hope dies last."

The wonder of hope is probably why not only America but, with the notable exception of China, which ridiculed his memory, the whole world mourned the death of President John F. Kennedy in 1963 more than any other public figure in history. Historian Stephen Ambrose said that the unprecedented outpouring of grief over Kennedy's death was mostly because of "his promise, the hope he held out." Political commentator James Reston wrote, "What was killed in Dallas was not only the President but the promise. The heart of the Kennedy legend was what might have been. All of this is apparent in the faces of the people who come daily to the grave on the Arlington Hill." White House correspondent Helen Thomas said that Kennedy's death "was a transforming moment for America because we lost hope. Every president who succeeded Kennedy—they all had good points and bad points—but the legacy of hope died with him. We never had that sense again that we were moving forward, that we could do things."

4. Very few things in the bible leapt off the page at me like Genesis 6:3. No one, even those who view the bible as a fable, or at least with a jaundiced eye, can blithely ignore it. Here's something allegedly from God way back in the first book of the Old Testament whose quaint edict hasn't changed one whit since then. Although the *life expectancy* of man has inexorably continued to increase through the centuries with the advances of medical science, man's maximum *life span* has remained constant, 120 years. The longest life, *on record*, that any human has ever lived belonged to Jeanne Calment, a woman from Arles, France, who died at the age of 122, the only known human since the bible to have lived beyond 120 years. (A Japanese man who died in 1986 may have lived to be 120, but during his life his claim of age was disputed.) For two years and 164 days,

Calment, who was born on February 21, 1875, snubbed God and his edict, finally succumbing on August 4, 1997, after 44,724 days of life.

When a seemingly random number (120) that could just as well have been 77 or 245 has proved to be the rooftop of our existence, does not this fact at least add a speck (not more) of credibility to the existence of the purported source of the number?

But as you can see, every single one of these biblical passages deal, in one way or another, with man being punished more severely for his improper treatment of God or Jesus, not one's fellow man. Where does the bible clearly suggest that, for instance, those who commit petty theft rather than grand larceny, burglary rather than murder, an unwanted sexual touching rather than rape, and so forth, will not be punished as severely in hell?

CHAPTER 15

1. The bible does say that anyone who defiles Jesus or the Holy Spirit will suffer in hell more than those who reject the law of Moses (Hebrews 10:26–29); and those who "devour widows' houses, and then, like hypocrites, say long prayers to God, will receive greater condemnation (Matthew 23:14); and those who reject the apostles who preach Jesus' ministry will suffer more on judgment day than the citizens of Sodom and Gomorrah (Matthew 10:14–15); and those in cities where Jesus had performed miracles who did not turn from their sins and turn to God will be worse off on judgment day than the citizens of Tyre and Sidon (Matthew 11:20–22); that those who have known Jesus and returned to a life of sin will be worse off than those who never knew him (2 Peter 2:20–21); and in a parable of Jesus' about masters and servants, those who knew the Son of Man was coming but did not prepare will be punished more than those who did not know (Luke 12:35–48).

When I went looking for proportionality of punishment outside of the bible in Christian literature, the only serious reference to this issue I could find was in Thomas Aquinas' thirteenth-century *Summa Theologica*. Aquinas, referred to by Catholics as "the greatest intellect the Catholic Church has ever known," buys into proportionality, but only halfway. He says "the degree of intensity in the [afterlife] punishment corresponds to the degree of gravity in the sin; therefore, mortal sins unequal in gravity will receive a punishment unequal in intensity" but, he then adds, "equal in duration." It is noteworthy that Aquinas does not cite any biblical or church authority for this assertion because there is none. In an earlier discussion on the issue, Aquinas cites perhaps the only vague, arguable allusion to proportionality in the bible, one in the least authoritative and least read (by biblical scholars) book of the bible, the Book of Revelation: "As much as she [the ancient city of Babylon, which had fallen] hath glorified herself and lived in luxury and pleasure, so much torment and sorrow give ye to her" (Revelation 18:7). This seems to be less an enunciation of a doctrine of proportionality than an assertion that the people of Babylon would pay dearly for their many sins. The two words "as much" in the Book of Revelation, of all books, cannot even begin to override the many explicit references to eternal damnation in the four gospels, several by Jesus himself, which, with every opportunity, make no reference or even vague allusion to proportionality.

In any event, it seems clear that this was just Aquinas' common sense speaking to him and what he said is not Catholic or Christian dogma. However, it was at least the voice of reason. But then, as indicated, Aquinas slipped intellectually when he bought completely into disproportionality with this non sequitur: "The punishment of mortal sin is eternal, because one thereby offends God who is infinite" (Thomas Aquinas, *Summa Theologica*, vol. 2, Supplement to Third Part, Question 99, Article 1 [of 5], Answer, then Reply to Objection 2, [Chicago: Encyclopedia Britannica Inc., Great Books of the Western World, 1952], 1079–1080). So according to Aquinas, no matter what the mortal sin is, even if it's not a harmful act against a fellow human, such as consensual sex between adults, because the sin offends God and God is infinite, the sinner will have to suffer infinite torment in hell. Only the intensity of his suffering will be taken into consideration.

Thomas, you're head and shoulders above your peers on this matter, which isn't saying much, but you still ended up by being ludicrous.

2. There are several references to the soul in the bible, but none speaks of the immortality of the soul in heaven or hell.* For instance, after saying that a fellow human cannot kill your soul, Matthew 10:28 says that "God can *destroy* both soul and body in hell," which is the opposite of the immortality of the soul in hell with Satan. Indeed, Ezekiel 18:4 suggests that a sinner's soul "dies."

Luke 16:22–24 may be the only place in the bible that clearly refers to the soul going to hell, but the notion of suffering without end (i.e., immortality) is not mentioned. Moreover, nowhere does it say that the rich man's soul is in hell because of his sins. We only are told he was rich. But although Jesus said it

---

*Wisdom 3:1 could be viewed as an exception, at least for heaven, when it says, "The souls of the just are in the hand of God and no torment shall touch them." But Wisdom 3:1 has several problems. Certainly, Christianity can't embrace it because it bases salvation not on a belief in Jesus, who wasn't even born at the time it was believed to have been written (about 100 B.C.), but on being just. Secondly, the Book of Wisdom is viewed as an apocryphal book by Jews and Protestants and not in their bibles. Most importantly, Wisdom 3:1–8 is widely viewed as only speaking about the souls of martyrs. For instance, 3:4 refers to the souls of men who were "punished before [i.e., by, in front of] men." And 3:6 says these were the souls of men who were "sacrificial offerings."

would be extremely difficult for a rich man to get into heaven ("It is easier for a camel to go through the eye of a needle than for a rich man to enter the kingdom of heaven" [Matthew 19:24]), Jesus never said that a rich man is precluded from reaching heaven. So Luke 16:22–24 doesn't even make too much sense. Further, in Luke 16:23–25, the rich man's counterpart, the beggar Lazarus, is not in heaven, but down where the rich man is, except he's being protected from the flames of hell.

Ecclesiastes 12:7 says, but not even in the context of salvation, that "the *spirit* will return to God who gave it." (Note that the word "soul" isn't even used. Indeed, 1 Thessalonians 5:23 ["your whole spirit and soul"] and Hebrews 4:12 ["divides soul and spirit"] speak of the spirit and soul being different.) And again, the notion of immortality is not referred to.

And then there is 1 Corinthians 15:52–53, where it is written that on Judgment Day the "Perishable earthly bodies" of those Christians raised from the dead will be "transformed into heavenly bodies that will never die." (See also 2 Corinthians 5:2–8.) But "heavenly bodies" doesn't sound too much like a soul. (Remarkably, in *The City of God*, Saint Augustine maintains that the *earthly* bodies of those who are saved will return to life and ascend to heaven at the end of time.)

Some say that John 11:25–26, 1 Thessalonians 4:15–17, and Daniel 12:2 suggest that the soul of Christians will be reunited with the body at the end of time, and will ascend to heaven to be with God forevermore. (See also Fifth Lateran Council, AD 1513; Danzinger and Shonmetzer, 1440). But none of these citations say this. Either expressly (Daniel) or by implication (John and 1 Thessalonians), they only talk about the *body* of man, not the *soul*.

Indeed, either through willful deception or very sloppy scholarship, those Christian writers who maintain that the immortality of the soul is found in holy scripture consistently cite verses that speak of, or imply, the body, not the soul. Their favorite bible reference, in fact, is the resurrection of Jesus, which they claim proves that death is not the end and the soul is immortal. But the bible only says that Jesus' body was no longer in his tomb (Matthew 28:6, Luke 24:3–6). His body had been resurrected. See also citations they give such as Isaiah 26:19 ("Their bodies will rise again"); Job 19:26 ("In my body I will see God"); and Wisdom 2:23 ("God formed man to be imperishable"). Or, without justification, they infer the soul from language that does not expressly say it, e.g., John 20:36: "By believing in him you will have life," etc. Although the whole notion of bodily resurrection* before Judgment Day at the end of time, with the body

---

*Christianity has never said *what* body. Is it the body that has burned to a crisp (see main text) that will present itself to God in heaven? Or does God not wanting to share heaven with termites, give us back the old bodies we died with?

living on forever in heaven or hell thereafter, has some biblical support (e.g., see the chapters and verses above; also, Revelation 20:11–15, 1 Thessalonians 4:15–17), it is largely rejected and ignored today by virtually all religious scholars. The sole emphasis is on the soul.

It is very noteworthy that in their recitation of bible references to prove their point, the Christian proponents of immortality of the soul conveniently neglect to mention 1 Timothy 6:16, which, as is pointed out in the main text, says: "God *alone* has immortality." Whether body and/or soul, that's pretty explicit, isn't it?

3. Catholicism, of course, knowing it needs to come up with something to deliver on its threat to make souls in hell suffer if it can somehow get these souls there for eternity, has to resort to its chief theological heavyweight, Aquinas, to extricate it from the stranglehold of common sense. But Aquinas can't deliver, coming up with just terrible tripe. Aquinas says that once a soul is separated from the body at death, although it has no "external" senses, "the senses which the soul takes away with it are not the external senses, but the internal, those, namely, which pertain to the intellectual part, for the intellect is sometimes called sense. . . . [And this] soul suffers from a corporeal fire" because (listen to this) "the fire of its nature is able to have an incorporeal spirit united to it as a thing placed is united to a place; that as the instrument of Divine Justice it is enabled to detain it unchained as it were, and in this respect this fire is really hurtful to the spirit, and thus the soul, seeing the fire as something hurtful to it, is tormented by the fire" (*Summa Theologica*, Supplement to Third Part, Question 70, Article 1, Reply to Objection 2; and Article 3, Answer, 895, 900). Can you believe this absolutely incredible nonsense?

CHAPTER 16

1. Not that any study was necessary to establish what common sense and history proclaim so loudly, but a March 2006 clinical trial of 1,802 patients from six hospitals conducted by the Harvard Medical School titled "The Therapeutic Effects of Intercessory Prayer" found that those who received third-party (family and friends) prayer for complication-free recovery from coronary artery bypass surgery fared no better than those who did not. The report of the study said that "intercessory prayer had no effect" on the presence or absence of complications, including death. The medical school said the clinical trial was the largest ever conducted on the effect of intercessory prayer. For an example of intercessory prayer working, at least in the bible, see Deuteronomy 9:19–20.

2. Let me make a quick stab at trying to explain what, from all appearances, would seem to be seriously demented behavior. When you place your faith, and fate, in God, whom you believe is all-good, all-powerful, and loves you, who

could possibly be more reliable and trustworthy to look after your interests? So therefore, no matter what happens, even the murder of your infant child, *must* be okay since it's God's will.

I have two contradictory thoughts about such people. One, I envy them. Two, they need a good brain transplant.

CHAPTER 17

1. Not only doesn't morality need religion, but it also doesn't need the two main texts, the bible and the Qur'an, that are the principal foundation of the world's three great monotheistic religions, Christianity and Judaism (bible) and Islam (Qur'an), to tell us about it. As atheist Sam Harris points out as an example, "If a person doesn't already understand that cruelty is wrong, he won't discover this by reading the Bible or the Qur'an, as these books are bursting with celebrations of cruelty, both human and divine."

2. Although perhaps less secular than Denmark and Sweden, most of the rest of the European continent is sufficiently secular that it is common for commentators and sociologists to speak of the "secularization of Europe" and to frequently refer to Europe as "post-Christian," a continent, as one writer puts it, that "has lost its ear for the spiritual." A *Los Angeles Times* article not too long ago referred to Europe today as being "as close to a Godless society as there has ever been," with churches closing in a great number of places because of very low attendance.

3. The word "atheist," to this very day, has a pejorative ring to it in America. But atheists have come a long way in their acceptance by the American public from the days of the founding of this country when the political ideas of British philosopher John Locke were embraced by several of our Founding Fathers and are particularly apparent in our Declaration of Independence. In his 1689 "Letter Concerning Tolerance," Locke advocated an open-minded tolerance of people of all faiths. But atheism, he felt, was just going too far, writing, "Lastly, those are not all to be tolerated who deny the being of God. Promises, covenants and oaths, which are the bonds of human society, can have no hold upon an atheist. The taking away of God, though only in thought, dissolves all."

4. We all know that the three monotheistic (one God, as opposed to polytheistic, which, for instance, the Arab world was before Muhammad) religions of the world are Judaism, Christianity, and Islam. Loose language is used when you often hear that these three religions, being monotheistic, have "the same God." Indeed, in a chapter of his book *The God Delusion* titled "Monotheism," Richard Dawkins writes that for the purposes of his book on the subject of God, "all three Abrahamic religions can be treated as indistinguishable." But, of

course, among the three major monotheistic religions there are at least two separate and distinct Gods. The God of Christianity has a son, so he cannot be the same God as the God of Judaism and Islam, neither of which views Jesus as the son of God. Indeed, in the Qur'an, Sura 19:35 says, "It beseemeth not the majesty of Allah that he should beget a son." And the son of the Christian God died for our sins, a notion, we know, rejected by Judaism and Islam.

CHAPTER 18

1. Gautama's third noble truth caused me to recall something different but vaguely analogous I thought about in my youth. I ruminated then on whether there was such a thing as happiness. My undeveloped thought was that at our moment of birth, or at some point of nothingness or physical, mental, and emotional numbness, we are, let's say, at zero. Anything below is unhappiness; anything above, happiness. What we erroneously construe as happiness (going above zero) is nothing more than rising back to zero, a state of neither happiness nor unhappiness. We're below zero when we have a desire or need, the unfulfillment of which makes us unhappy. When we eliminate the need or desire, we're not going above zero, merely rising back to zero. For instance, if we are very thirsty, and hence "unhappy," while we are satisfying that thirst with a cold drink, are we going above zero or merely back to zero where we have no thirst? Though we enjoyed the drink, we couldn't have enjoyed it if we hadn't *first* been suffering from thirst. And once that thirst (or feeling of cold, pain, loss, etc.) is satisfied or eliminated, we've reached a ceiling, and continuing to drink the beverage will give us no pleasure at all, i.e., continuing to drink will not take us above zero. What we call happiness, then, is nothing more than the elimination of a need or a desire.

CHAPTER 19

1. It is obvious that if there is a God, and he is sick enough to have such views, this discussion is a very serious one. Therefore, for someone like Blaise Pascal, the French mathematician, scientist, and supposedly great thinker of the seventeenth century, to reduce the discussion to almost the equivalent of a bet at the racetrack is more than remarkable. You see, Pascal had it all figured out with his now-celebrated "Pascal's wager." It is prudent, he said, to "choose that God is," because if he exists, "you gain all," and "if you lose, you lose nothing," meaning you're no worse off than you would have been if you hadn't bet on the horse named God. In other words, even if your profession of belief in God is as phony as the words of a Bourbon Street hawker, you can still get past St. Peter

at the gate. But wait. Since God is supposed to be omniscient, couldn't he spot the phony coming a mile away?

The closest I can come to Pascal's wager is the only prayer I'd ever see fit (and I wouldn't) to say: "Dear God, if there is a God, please let me go to heaven, if there is a heaven."

About the Author

VINCENT BUGLIOSI received his law degree in 1964. In his career at the Los Angeles County District Attorney's office, he successfully prosecuted 105 out of 106 felony jury trials, including 21 murder convictions without a single loss. His most famous trial, the Charles Manson case, became the basis of his classic, *Helter Skelter*, the biggest selling true-crime book in publishing history. Two of Bugliosi's other books—*And the Sea Will Tell* and *Outrage*—also reached #1 on the *New York Times* hardcover best-seller list. No other American true-crime writer has ever had more than one book that achieved this ranking. His *Reclaiming History: The Assassination of President John F. Kennedy* has been heralded as "epic" and "a book for the ages." HBO, in association with Tom Hanks's PlayTone Productions, will be producing this as an eight-hour mini-series in 2013, the 50th anniversary of the Kennedy assassination.

Bugliosi has uncommonly attained success in two separate and distinct fields, as an author and a lawyer. His excellence as a trial lawyer is best captured in the judgment of his peers. "Bugliosi is as good a prosecutor as there ever was," Alan Dershowitz says. "If you created a prosecutorial Hall of Fame, Vince would be in the entranceway." F. Lee Bailey calls Bugliosi "the quintessential prosecutor." "There is only one Vince Bugliosi. He's the best," says Robert Tanenbaum, for years the top homicide prosecutor in the Manhattan D.A.'s office. Most telling is the comment by Gerry Spence, who squared off against Bugliosi in a twenty-one-hour televised, scriptless "docu-trial" of Lee Harvey Oswald, in which the original key witnesses in the Kennedy assassination testified and were cross-examined. After the Dallas jury returned a guilty verdict in Bugliosi's favor, Spence said, "No other lawyer in America could have done what Vince did in this case."

Bugliosi lives with his wife, Gail, in Los Angeles.

Index